new inspiration

Judy Garton-Sprenger and Philip Prowse
with Amanda Bailey, Sheila Dignen
and Susannah McKee

MACMILLAN

Teacher's Book

4

Macmillan Education
Between Towns Road, Oxford OX4 3PP
A division of Macmillan Publishers Limited
Companies and representatives throughout the world

ISBN 978-0-230-41021-3

Text © Judy Garton-Sprenger and Philip Prowse 2012
Additional text by Amanda Bailey, Sheila Dignen and Susannah McKee
Original photocopiable material by Hannah Fish, Nilgun Demirkaya, Bernadette Harvengt, Michael Kedward, Nick McIver, Susannah McKee, Agnieszka Mulak, Wayne Rimmer, Adam Trim
Design and illustration © Macmillan Publishers Limited 2012

This edition published 2012
First edition published 2007

Original design by Giles Davies Design Ltd and eMC Design Ltd
Page make-up by Expo Holdings and eMC Design Ltd
Illustrated by Kathy Baxendale p173; Mark Duffin pp169, 172; Gillian Martin pp170, 179, 180; Julian Mosedale pp174, 178, 184; Julia Pearson p182; and Harry Venning p185.
Cover design by Designers Collective

The authors and publishers would like to thank the following for permission to reproduce the following copyright material:
Page 187 *Spooky* – Lyrics by Mike Shapiro, J R Cobb, Buddy Buie and Harry Middlebrooks. Copyright © 1968 Sony//ATV Lowery Songs LLC, All rights administered by Sony/ATV Music Publishing. All Rights Reserved. Used by Permission;
Page 188 *Every Breath You Take* – Words and Music by Gordon Sumner. Copyright © 1983. Reproduced by permission of G M Sumner/EMI Music Publishing Ltd, London, W8 5SW;
Page 189 *Hanging on the Telephone* – Words & Music by Jack Lee. Copyright © 1978 Rare Blue Music Incorporated, USA. Chrysalis Music Limited. All Rights Reserved. International Copyright Secured. Used by permission of Music Sales Limited;
Page 190 *True Colours* – Lyrics by Billy Steinberg & Tom Kelly. Copyright © Sony/ATV Music Publishing. All Rights Reserved. Used by Permission.

The authors and publishers are grateful for permission to reprint the following copyright material:
Extract from '2020 Vision: Live to 120' taken from www.smh.com.au copyright © Australian Associated Press 2004 reprinted by permission of the publisher;
Extract from 'The School We'd Like' by Dea Birkett, copyright © Dea Birkett 2001, first published in the *Guardian* 05.06.01, reprinted by permission of the author;
Extract from 'How mobile phones are transforming Africa' by Fred Bridgland, copyright © Fred Bridgland 2005, first published in *Sunday Herald* 13.03.05, reprinted by permission of the author;
Extract from 'This man is worth £100,000 a year' by David Crystal, copyright © David Crystal 2000, first published in High Life Magazine June 2000, reprinted by permission of the author;
Extracts from 'The Professor and the Ferryman' and 'The Two Painters' both taken from *Stories For Thinking* by Robert Fisher (Nash Pollock, 1996), copyright © Robert Fisher 1996, reprinted by permission of the author;
Extract from 'Fun is my Business' by Laura Barton, Susie Steiner, Dominic Murphy, Simon Hattenstone, Kirsty Scott, Caroline Roux and Gareth McClean, copyright © Guardian News and Media Limited 2003, first published in the *Guardian* 09.08.03, reprinted by permission of the publisher;
'Confessions of a Runner' from *Wicked World* by Benjamin Zephaniah (Puffin, 2000), text copyright © Benjamin Zephaniah 2000, reprinted by permission of the publisher;
Extract from *The Lost Continent* by Bill Bryson (Black Swan, a division of Transworld, 1989) copyright © Bill Bryson 1989, reprinted by permission of Random House Group Ltd. and Greene & Heaton. All rights reserved;
Extract from 'It's a Man's Game' by Jo Tuckman copyright © Jo Tuckman 2005, first published in the *Guardian* 05.01.05, reprinted by permission of the author;
Extract from interview with Piers Vitebsky 'Day in the Life' by Sarah Woodward, taken from *CAM* magazine no. 47, reprinted by permission of Piers Vitebsky.

For full photographic acknowledgements please refer to the Student's Book.

New Inspiration Test CD 4
ISBN 978-0-230-41252-1
Text by Barbara Mackay
© Macmillan Publishers Limited 2012
This product is copyright and unauthorised copying is illegal
Audio produced and recorded by James Richardson Productions Limited.

Printed and bound in Thailand

2016 2015 2014 2013 2012
10 9 8 7 6 5 4 3

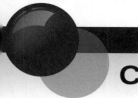

Contents

NEW INSPIRATION

New Inspiration is a four-level course designed to take teenagers from beginner to intermediate level (CEF A1–B1+). The course aims to appeal to the modern teenager through imaginative and exciting topics, introduces up-to-date language and expressions, increases confidence through learner independence activities, provides regular opportunities for revision and self-assessment, and caters for different learning styles. For the teacher it offers everything needed for successful lessons with full support at every stage.

KEY IDEAS

A fundamental concept in the organisation of *New Inspiration* is that of *difference*.

Different ages

Teenagers are passing through a challenging period of their lives with great physical, social and psychological changes. A 13-year-old lives in a different world from a 16-year-old. In designing *New Inspiration* our aim has been to create a course which grows with its students.

Different abilities

Every class is a mixed-ability class. We see mixed ability not as a problem, but as a fact of life to which we need to respond in our teaching. Our response in creating *New Inspiration* has been to develop *flexible* materials which offer a variety of learning paths to success.

Different interests

One of the most striking findings of the research phase in preparing this course was the wide variety of different interests among students. We have therefore provided a broad range of materials to engage students in challenging but achievable tasks. The topic syllabus gives the opportunity for cross-curricular and cross-cultural work so that students learn about life and the world at the same time as learning English. Language learning also needs to be fun to be effective, so we have included lots of games, poems and puzzles, as well as a story in the Workbook and songs in the Teacher's Book.

Different backgrounds

Teenagers come to the language classroom with a wide range of backgrounds – not only in social and educational terms, but also because of different learning histories. Students in the same class may have had positive, negative or no language learning experiences at primary level; they may have started learning another language, or had private lessons or extra classes in English. Students who started learning English at primary level may have been exposed to predominantly oral activities, games and songs, and be surprised at the different demands of the class they are now in.

New Inspiration aims to provide a safe transition to the new level, and to revise and recycle language in fresh contexts.

Different learning styles

We believe that it is important for students to 'learn how to learn'. We have provided opportunities for students to experiment with different learning styles and develop language learning strategies which suit them. We have tried to make students aware that, while they may have a preferred learning style, they could benefit from experimenting with others.

Different aspirations

Within each teenager there is a young adult in the making, and all have differing goals and aspirations for the future. We have aimed to provide students with practical language skills and a positive attitude to learning. This will lead them to success in examinations and prepare them for using English in the real world.

Different class sizes and numbers of hours a week

The Teacher's Book provides lesson plans full of extra optional activities which can be given to less confident learners or to fast-finishers, and the Workbook exercises can all be used for self-study. Teachers with more hours at their disposal will find that they have material for considerably more than the 90–120 hours of the core course if they use the optional activities.

KEY FEATURES OF *NEW INSPIRATION*

Multi-syllabus

The course has a topic-led syllabus which integrates separate communicative, lexical, grammatical, pronunciation, skills and learner independence syllabi. This provides a principled approach to vocabulary acquisition and to the development of the four skills. The Contents pages of the Student's Book list the topics, lesson titles, communicative aims, language areas, pronunciation points, skills and learner independence training.

Reading

At Level 4, students encounter new language in the first three lessons of each unit through dialogues and prose texts. The dialogues feature various different teenage characters with whom the students can identify, while the prose texts focus on topics of interest and relevance to the students' lives and studies. Dialogues and texts are preceded by pre-reading/listening tasks to develop predictive skills.

Vocabulary and grammar

The topic-led syllabus provides a firm basis for systematic coverage and development of vocabulary. Lessons contain Word Banks and activities to revise and extend lexical fields, and students are encouraged to maintain their own vocabulary notebooks. At the back of the Student's Book there is a unit-by-unit Word List with phonemic transcriptions.

There is a clearly structured approach to grammar, leading to fluency activities where students apply the target language in communicative situations. Language Workout boxes at the end of each lesson are cross-referenced to a comprehensive Language File at the back of the Student's Book, which provides full paradigms and explanations of grammatical points with controlled practice exercises.

Pronunciation

The first three lessons of each unit provide explicit work on pronunciation, stress and intonation arising from the lesson language. Phonemic symbols are given as support where relevant; these are intended for recognition only. There is a Pronunciation Guide at the back of the Student's Book.

Skills development

Careful attention is paid to the development of the four language skills in each unit, both in the first three lessons and in the fourth Integrated Skills lesson. Guided writing, a carefully staged programme of tasks, helps the growth of students' writing skills. There is further work on reading and writing skills in the Workbook, together with suggestions for extensive reading.

Learner independence

The Integrated Skills lessons in each unit offer work on the development of learner independence, and this is supported by parallel sections in the Workbook and advice in the Teacher's Book lesson notes.

Cognitive development, and language awareness and enjoyment

New Inspiration contains a range of activities, such as quizzes and questionnaires, which encourage students to think in English. 'Your response' activities after a text or dialogue also encourage the development of critical thinking and personal responses to reading.

Inspiration EXTRA! sections at the end of each Student's Book unit contain either a full project, or a Language Links activity focusing on plurilingualism and a sketch for students to act out. There are also word games and puzzles. Games can also be found in the Student's Book lessons, and the Workbook contains more puzzles, crosswords and brainteasers.

Mixed ability

The first three lessons of each unit contain Extension activities for fast-finishers. Inspiration EXTRA! also includes both a Revision and Extension section which caters for two different ability levels – revising and extending language from the preceding four lessons – and a Your Choice! section where students can choose between activities reflecting different learning styles. There are further Revision and Extension sections in the Workbook.

Recycling and reviewing

The syllabus regularly recycles new language. As well as the Revision and Extension sections, there are four Review sections at each level, providing further revision and learner independence self-assessment sections. There are further Review sections in the Workbook.

Culture and CLIL

Each level also features four Culture sections which build cross-cultural awareness, encourage discussion, develop vocabulary, and lead up to Mini-projects. The Workbook contains further Culture sections with reading, writing and vocabulary exercises. There is a wealth of CLIL material appropriate to the students' age and level throughout the course, including a dedicated section in each Workbook.

COURSE COMPONENTS

Student's Book

The Student's Book provides 90–120 hours of teaching material within eight units. Each unit has four lessons – each on two pages for ease of use – and an Inspiration EXTRA! section. The first three lessons in each unit present and practise new language, and the fourth is an Integrated Skills lesson. Each pair of units is preceded by a Preview, which gives the learner a taste of what is to come, and followed by a Review. At the back of the book there is a Language File, a Word List, a Pronunciation Guide and a list of Irregular Verbs.

Workbook

The Workbook offers exercises which can be done in class or as self-study. It mirrors the Student's Book in its organisation, providing a wealth of extra language practice material, integrated skills and learner independence work, mixed-ability Revision and Extension exercises, Culture pages and Review sections. It includes pronunciation exercises, brainteasers, crosswords and suggestions for follow-up work on the Internet. The Workbook also contains CLIL materials linked to other subjects studied at this level, and a unit-by-unit story for extensive reading with associated language practice activities.

Teacher's Book

The Teacher's Book features a practical approach to methodology with step-by-step lesson notes. There are stimulating ideas for warmers to start each lesson as well as optional activities throughout the lesson notes. There are follow-up activities at the end of each lesson and suggestions for homework. Useful cultural information is provided to help answer student queries, and downloadable songs with activities are also included. Full audioscripts are integrated within the notes, as are answers to all the Student's Book exercises. There is also a complete Workbook Answer Key.

Tests CD

The editable Tests are designed to cater for mixed-ability classes by providing Basic, Standard and Higher Tests for each Student's Book unit. Teachers can use the test that best suits their students and adapt it as necessary. There is also a placement test, three term tests and a final test. Tests include grammar, vocabulary, reading, listening and writing.

Class Audio CD

All the Student's Book dialogues, texts and pronunciation exercises are recorded. Recorded items are indicated by the symbol ⊙ 1.04 in the Student's Book and Teacher's Book.

New Inspiration Digital

Interactive Whiteboard Software is available for the course. Macmillan Practice Online – New Inspiration provides self-marking support materials which mirror the structure of the course. The *New Inspiration* Resource Site provides the teacher with extra language practice materials and CLIL cross-curricular or culture lessons. The *New Inspiration* Student's Website offers interactive activities, webquests and a social networking section.

www.macmillanpracticeonline.com
www.macmillanenglish.com/inspiration

New Inspiration and the Common European Framework

The Common European Framework (CEF) is a widely used standard created by the Council of Europe. In the classroom, familiarity with the CEF can be of great help to any teacher in identifying students' actual progress and helping them to set their learning priorities.

New Inspiration offers a wide range of teaching materials in various components which give teachers the opportunity to develop all aspects of their students' language ability. The CEF can be used to follow their progress.

Below are the B1–B2 descriptors (description of competencies) covered in *New Inspiration* 4 which students are aiming to reach. A1–A2 descriptors are available in the *New Inspiration* 1 and 2 Teacher's Books and B1–B2 descriptors in the *New Inspiration* 3 Teacher's Book. They are also on the *New Inspiration* teacher's website. A high level of confidence with the A2–B1 descriptors is expected as students start using *New Inspiration* 4. By the end of the course students should be able to accomplish all the B1 level and some of the B2 level descriptors. Many of the B2 descriptors talk of greater confidence with the same kinds of ability already described at B1: others only emerge for the first time at B2.

On the teacher's website you will also find a list of unit-by-unit descriptors with suggested targets which you can print out and copy for your students to assess themselves. Students can use these at any point to get a detailed picture of their own individual progress.

What is a CEF Portfolio?

If you are using portfolios as a way of evaluating your students' coursework over the year, you will find a wide variety of opportunities within each *New Inspiration* unit to provide material for the dossier.

A portfolio is a means to document a person's achievements. Artists, architects or designers collect samples of their work in portfolios. The basic idea is that students collect samples of their work in their portfolio. Most of the time, these samples will be texts created by the students, but they could also include photos of classroom scenes, wall displays, audio recordings and DVDs. All these documents provide evidence of a student's performance, e.g. during a discussion, an oral presentation or a role play.

The portfolio consists of three parts: the **Language Passport** with information about a student's proficiency in one or more languages i.e. qualifications; the **Language Biography** where students reflect their learning process and progress and say what they can do in their foreign language(s); and the **Dossier**, a collection of materials and data put together by students to document and illustrate their learning experiences.

Although it may be a demanding task to set up in the beginning, the overall aim is for students to be involved in planning, collecting and evaluating their own work – taking responsibility for their own learning. This in turn may lead to increased participation and autonomy on the learner's part.

	New Inspiration 4 TB descriptors	Unit 1	Unit 2	Unit 3	Unit 4	Unit 5	Unit 6	Unit 7	Unit 8
Listening B1	I can follow clearly articulated speech directed at me in everyday conversation, though I sometimes have to ask for repetition of particular words and phrases.						77	93	
	I can generally follow the main points of extended discussion around me, provided speech is clearly articulated in standard dialect.	17, 19, 20		44	49, 55	63, 71	74, 77	89, 93, 95	107
	I can listen to a short narrative and form hypotheses about what will happen next.		29						
	I can understand the main points of radio news bulletins and simpler recorded material on topics of personal interest delivered relatively slowly and clearly.	12, 13, 17	23, 27	37, 41, 42, 43	50, 53, 54	63, 65, 69	77, 81	89, 93, 94, 95, 99	103, 104, 107
	I can catch the main points in TV programmes on familiar topics when the delivery is relatively slow and clear.								
	I can understand simple technical information, such as operating instructions for everyday equipment.								

Listening B2	I can understand in detail what is said to me in standard spoken language even in a noisy environment.	18	29	41	50, 53	63, 65, 69, 70	77, 80	93	107
	I can follow a lecture or talk within my own field, provided the subject matter is familiar and the presentation straightforward and clearly structured.	13	23, 26, 27, 28	37, 41	55	65		94, 95, 99	105
	I can understand most radio documentaries delivered in standard language and can identify the speaker's mood, tone etc. by using contextual clues.							99	103
	I can understand TV documentaries, live interviews, talk shows, plays and the majority of films in standard dialect.							89	104
	I can understand the main ideas of complex speech on both concrete and abstract topics delivered in a standard dialect, including technical discussions in my field of specialisation.	17			55	69		93, 95	
	I can use a variety of strategies to achieve comprehension, including listening for main points; checking comprehension.		27, 28	37, 43	50, 53, 54	62, 69	77, 80	93	103, 104, 105, 107
Reading B1	I can understand the main points in short newspaper articles about current and familiar topics.								
	I can read columns or interviews in newspapers and magazines in which someone takes a stand on a current topic or event and understand the overall meaning of the text.	16				68		90	
	I can guess the meaning of single unknown words from the context thus deducing the meaning of expressions if the topic is familiar.	18		39, 40, 42	47, 51	65		91, 92	100, 101
	I can skim short texts (for example news summaries) and find relevant facts and information (for example who has done what and where).	10, 11, 14	26	47	50	65, 66, 69	78, 79, 80	88	100, 104
	I can understand the most important information in short simple everyday information brochures.								
	I can understand simple messages and standard letters (for example from businesses, clubs or authorities).								
	In private letters I can understand those parts dealing with events, feelings and wishes well enough to correspond regularly with a pen friend.					74			
	I can understand the plot of a clearly structured story and recognise what the most important episodes and events are and what is significant about them.							94	

Reading B2	I can rapidly grasp the content and the significance of news, articles and reports on topics connected with my interests or my job, and decide if a closer reading is worthwhile.	12		40	52	68	80	88	104
	I can read and understand articles and reports on current problems in which the writers express specific attitudes and points of view.	16, 20	26	46	48, 54	64, 66, 67	76, 78, 80	92, 94	100, 104
	I can understand in detail texts within my field of interest or the area of my academic or professional speciality.	12, 14, 16, 18		36, 38, 42, 46	48, 54	62, 64, 65, 70	76, 80	88, 90, 96, 98	102
	I can understand specialised articles outside my own field if I can occasionally check with a dictionary.	18	24, 28	42	54	69	81	98	
	I can read reviews dealing with the content and criticism of cultural topics (films, theatre, books, concerts) and summarise the main points.	20	22, 26					94	
	I can read letters on topics within my areas of academic or professional speciality or interest and grasp the most important points.								106
	I can quickly look through a manual (for example for a computer program) and find and understand the relevant explanations and help for a specific problem.								
	I can understand in a narrative or play the motives for the characters' actions and their consequences for the development of the plot.		29						102
Spoken Interaction B1	I can start, maintain and close simple face-to-face conversation on topics that are familiar or of personal interest.	11	23	37, 47	51				
	I can maintain a conversation or discussion but may sometimes be difficult to follow when trying to say exactly what I would like to.	11, 21	25	43		67	75, 81	89, 93	
	I can deal with most situations likely to arise when making travel arrangements through an agent or when actually travelling.					73			
	I can ask for and follow detailed directions.								
	I can express and respond to feelings such as surprise, happiness, sadness, interest and indifference.								
	I can give or seek personal views and opinions in an informal discussion with friends.	11, 15, 21	29	37			78	89, 99	101
	I can agree and disagree politely.								

Spoken Interaction B2	I can initiate, maintain and end discourse naturally with effective turn-taking.	11	23, 30	49	51	73, 75	78, 81, 82	96, 99	105
	I can exchange considerable quantities of detailed factual information on matters within my fields of interest.	15	25, 29	37, 43	53	67		89, 95, 97, 99	105, 107
	I can convey degrees of emotion and highlight the personal significance of events and experiences.							97	
	I can engage in extended conversation in a clearly participatory fashion on most general topics.	21		37	55	69	75, 81	91, 93, 95	105, 108
	I can account for and sustain my opinions in discussion by providing relevant explanations, arguments and comments.	14, 21	29	43, 47	55	67, 69		95	101
	I can help a discussion along on familiar ground confirming comprehension, inviting others in, etc.				51			97	
	I can carry out a prepared interview, checking and confirming information, following up interesting replies.	15	30	37	53		77, 81, 82	89	103, 105
Spoken Production B1	I can narrate a story.								
	I can give detailed accounts of experiences, describing feelings and reactions.			39					
	I can describe dreams, hopes and ambitions.								
	I can explain and give reasons for my plans, intentions and actions.								
	I can relate the plot of a book or film and describe my reactions.								
	I can paraphrase short written passages orally in a simple fashion, using the original text wording and ordering.	13		49		66	81		
Spoken Production B2	I can give clear, detailed descriptions on a wide range of subjects related to my fields of interest.	10, 13	27	36, 39	49, 57	66	76, 80	89, 94	104
	I can understand and summarise orally short extracts from news items, interviews or documentaries containing opinions, argument and discussion.	17			53	62, 65, 66	80		105
	I can understand and summarise orally the plot and sequence of events in an extract from a film or play.								
	I can construct a chain of reasoned argument, linking my ideas logically.		25, 30	39, 40	51, 55	62, 65	76	91, 95	104
	I can explain a viewpoint on a topical issue giving the advantages and disadvantages of various options.	12		41, 47	53, 54				102, 104
	I can speculate about causes, consequences, hypothetical situations.	15, 19	25, 27, 30	39, 40, 41	48, 49, 53	63, 65, 67, 69	74, 76	99	100, 102, 104

Strategies B1	I can repeat back part of what someone has said to confirm that we understand each other.								
	I can ask someone to clarify or elaborate what they have just said.								
	When I can't think of the word I want, I can use a simple word meaning something similar and invite "correction".								
Strategies B2	I can use standard phrases like "That's a difficult question to answer" to gain time and keep the turn while formulating what to say.	17	29	43	55	69	81	95	
	I can make a note of "favourite mistakes" and consciously monitor speech for them.								
	I can generally correct slips and errors if I become aware of them or if they have led to misunderstandings.	17				69		95, 99	108
Language Quality B1	I can keep a conversation going comprehensibly, but have to pause to plan and correct what I am saying – especially when I talk freely for longer periods.								
	I can convey simple information of immediate relevance, getting across which point I feel is most important.								
	I have a sufficient vocabulary to express myself with some circumlocutions on most topics pertinent to my everyday life such as family, hobbies and interests, work, travel, and current events.	11, 13							
	I can express myself reasonably accurately in familiar, predictable situations.	11, 14, 15							
Language Quality B2	I can produce stretches of language with a fairly even tempo; although I can be hesitant as I search for expressions, there are few noticeably long pauses.		29	39, 43	49, 51	67	79	89, 95	101
	I can pass on detailed information reliably.	13, 17				63		91	107
	I have sufficient vocabulary to express myself on matters connected to my field and on most general topics.	11, 13, 14, 15, 17, 19, 21	23, 25, 26, 29, 31	39, 40, 41, 43, 45, 47	49, 51, 52, 55, 57	62, 69, 73	76, 79, 81	91, 92, 93, 95, 96	100, 101, 102, 105, 104, 109
	I can communicate with reasonable accuracy and can correct mistakes if they have led to misunderstandings.	11, 13, 15, 19, 21	23, 25, 27, 30, 31	37, 39, 41, 45	49, 51, 53, 55, 57	63, 65, 67, 71, 73	75, 77, 78, 82, 83	89, 91, 93, 96, 97	101, 103, 105, 107, 108, 109

Writing B1	I can write simple connected texts on a range of topics within my field of interest and can express personal views and opinions.	11, 13, 15, 19	25	37, 39		63			91	
	I can write simple texts about experiences or events, for example about a trip, for a school newspaper or a club newsletter.		30						93	
	I can write personal letters to friends or acquaintances asking for or giving them news and narrating events.									
	I can describe in a personal letter the plot of a film or a book or give an account of a concert.									
	In a letter I can express feelings such as grief, happiness, interest, regret and sympathy.									
	I can reply in written form to advertisements and ask for more complete or more specific information about products (for example a car or an academic course).									
	I can convey – via fax, e-mail or a circular – short simple factual information to friends or colleagues or ask for information in such a way.									107
	I can write my CV in summary form.									
Writing B2	I can write clear and detailed texts (compositions, reports or texts of presentations) on various topics related to my field of interest.	11, 13	29, 30	41, 43, 45	49, 56	65, 71, 73	75, 77, 81	89, 91, 99	101	
	I can write summaries of articles on topics of general interest.	17	23, 25			67	75, 77			
	I can summarise information from different sources and media.	13	27, 30		56		77, 82	99	108	
	I can discuss a topic in a composition or "letter to the editor", giving reasons for or against a specific point of view.				51, 55	69			108	
	I can develop an argument systematically in a composition or report, emphasising decisive points and including supporting details.	11		47		67, 69	81	91, 95	107, 108	
	I can write about events and real or fictional experiences in a detailed and easily readable way.			41, 43		67	79	89	103, 109	
	I can write a short review of a film or a book.									
	I can express in a personal letter different feelings and attitudes and can report the news of the day making clear what – in my opinion – are the important aspects of an event.									

Using *New Inspiration*

There are four **Preview** sections at each level of *New Inspiration* giving students a brief introduction to the communicative aims and topic/vocabulary areas they will cover in the following two units.

PREVIEW

UNITS 5-6

COMMUNICATIVE AIMS
LEARNING HOW TO ...

1 Talk about unreal or imaginary past events

2 Express regret about the past

3 Express obligation and lack of obligation

4 Make deductions and speculate about the past

5 Report what people said

6 Report what people asked

7 Describe problems

8 Suggest solutions

TOPICS AND VOCABULARY

Historical events

Routines

Qualifications

Aviation

Phrasal verbs with *up*

Sport

Travel

Restaurant

Food

Shops and services

Phrasal verbs with *in/into*

Holidays

Communicative Aims

Students match photographs with contextualising sentences or questions to the correct communicative aim from the box. This activity helps prepare students for the context in which they will learn each communicative aim.

Topics and Vocabulary

Categorisation activities introduce students to some of the key vocabulary of the following two units, and they are also encouraged through brainstorming to identify other words that they already know for some of the topics.

The team needs to clean the inside of the tank wall* regularly so that visitors can see the fish clearly.

If your bicycle had a puncture, would you mend it yourself?

1 Match six of the communicative aims (1–8) with the pictures (A–F).

2 Complete the words on the right and put them into categories.

Aviation   Restaurant   Sport

a_rcraft cl_b fl_ght fo_k g_me gl_ss g_al l_nding m_tch m_nu p_ssenger p_lot pl_ne pl_te pl_yer s_up t_am w_itress

60

12

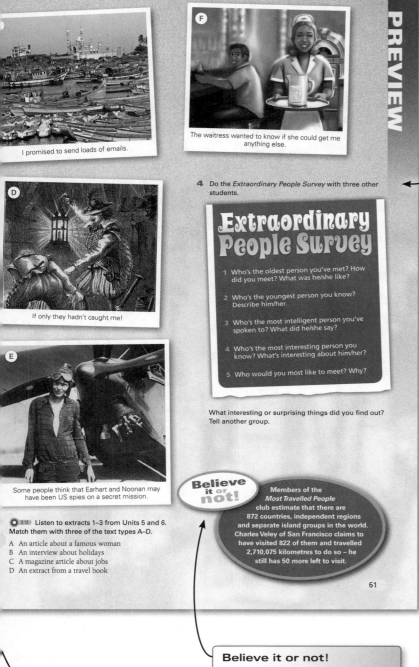

I promised to send loads of emails.

The waitress wanted to know if she could get me anything else.

PREVIEW

If only they hadn't caught me!

4 Do the *Extraordinary People Survey* with three other students.

Extraordinary People Survey

1 Who's the oldest person you've met? How did you meet? What was he/she like?

2 Who's the youngest person you know? Describe him/her.

3 Who's the most intelligent person you've spoken to? What did he/she say?

4 Who's the most interesting person you know? What's interesting about him/her?

5 Who would you most like to meet? Why?

What interesting or surprising things did you find out? Tell another group.

Some people think that Earhart and Noonan may have been US spies on a secret mission.

2.12 Listen to extracts 1–3 from Units 5 and 6. Match them with three of the text types A–D.

A An article about a famous woman
B An interview about holidays
C A magazine article about jobs
D An extract from a travel book

Believe it or not!

Members of the *Most Travelled People* club estimate that there are 872 countries, independent regions and separate island groups in the world. Charles Veley of San Francisco claims to have visited 822 of them and travelled 2,710,075 kilometres to do so – he still has 50 more left to visit.

61

Survey

In groups, students complete a survey related to one of the topics of the following two units, to encourage them to personalise their knowledge of the topic. The Teacher's Book provides suggestions for students to use the results of the survey to complete a project.

Believe it or not!

Interesting facts related to one of the topics of the following units.

Listening Preview

Students listen to short extracts from the following units and identify what kind of passage the extracts are taken from or what topic they discuss.

The first three lessons in each unit present **new language**. While these lessons follow a similar pattern up to the After Reading exercise, the subsequent practice activities vary from lesson to lesson but always include pronunciation and end with writing and Language Workout. Lessons may also include

Word Banks and vocabulary exercises, games and role plays as appropriate for the lesson aims. There are usually one or two Extension activities for fast-finishers. In every case there is a progression from controlled presentation and practice of new language to freer, more communicative activities.

Lesson heading

The heading shows the lesson topic – in this case *What could have happened to them?* – and the communicative aim(s) and target language of the lesson.

Warmers

The Teacher's Book suggests one–three warmers for each lesson. These may revise previously learnt language or prepare students for the lesson topic.

1 Opener

The aim of the Opener is to set the scene for the reading text or listening passage or to pre-teach vocabulary, or both.

2 Reading/Listening

The new language is presented in a text or listening passage which is preceded by pre-reading/listening tasks or prediction activities. Students then read the text or listen to the passage. Teachers may then wish to play the recording, pausing to answer queries about language or content, or to ask students to close their books and listen without reading.

3 After Reading/Listening

These exercises use a variety of different formats including true/false, open questions, matching questions and answers, and completion. The aim is intensive reading/listening. After Reading/Listening ends with Your response: an activity which invites the student to respond personally to the text or dialogue.

5 3 EXTRAORDINARY PEOPLE

What could have happened to them?

Making deductions and speculating about the past
must have and *can't have*
could/may/might have

Amelia Earhart
Pioneer in the Sky

Born in 1897, Amelia Earhart was a record-breaking American pilot, who in 1932 became the first woman to make a solo flight across the Atlantic. The flight was difficult and dangerous. She flew through strong winds and a lightning storm, and once almost crashed into the ocean. It took her 13½ hours to make the trip from Newfoundland to Ireland, where she had to make an emergency landing in a field. But she had completed the crossing – and set a new world record. Earhart was also the first person to fly solo across the Pacific Ocean, when she flew from Hawaii to California in 1935. Every previous attempt had failed, not least because the distance is greater than a transatlantic crossing.

Her most daring journey was in 1937, when she attempted to fly round the world with navigator Frederick Noonan. But after they had completed three-quarters of the trip, their plane disappeared during the flight from New Guinea to tiny Howland Island in the Pacific. No trace of the aircraft or Earhart and Noonan was ever found.

What could have happened to them? There has been a great deal of speculation. Many believe the plane must have run out of fuel and crashed into the Pacific Ocean – Earhart had reported over the radio that they were short of fuel. But there was a massive search operation, so why wasn't the plane found? It can't have blown up in mid-air because it had used up most of its fuel. Some people think that Earhart and Noonan may have been US spies on a secret mission, and the Japanese might have shot down their plane. Others think that they could have ended up on a desert island, or even that aliens might have abducted them. Or did Earhart and Noonan simply get lost? Neither of them knew much about using the radio equipment on the aircraft.

Whatever happened, Earhart may have died as she had wished. 'When I go,' she often said, 'I'd like best to go in my plane.'

1 OPENER

Look at the photo and the map. You are going to read about a brave woman pilot. What do you think she did?

2 READING

2.19 Read the text. Why didn't Earhart and Noonan complete the flight round the world?

3 AFTER READING

True, false or no information? Correct the false sentences.

1 Amelia Earhart was the first person to fly solo across the Atlantic.
2 She flew from Newfoundland to Ireland in under 14 hours.
3 She beat the previous transatlantic record by three hours.
4 Her flight from Hawaii to California took longer than her transatlantic flight.
5 Earhart and Noonan disappeared over the Atlantic Ocean.
6 Earhart had reported over the radio that they were short of fuel.
7 Although there was a major search for their plane, it was never found.
8 The plane could have blown up in mid-air.
9 Earhart and Noonan were probably US spies.
10 Earhart wanted to die in her plane.

Your response What were the difficulties and dangers in long solo flights in the 1930s? In what ways is flying a different experience today?

66

5 Pronunciation

Each of the first three lessons in every unit contains a pronunciation exercise focusing on particular sounds or stress and intonation. The Teacher's Book provides more information about the phonological area being treated and suggests further activities.

Extension

Lessons have one or more Extension activities offering more challenging practice for fast-finishers.

Follow-up activities and homework

The Teacher's Book offers optional follow-up activities, usually including a game, to help with mixed-ability teaching and to cope with variable aptitude and amounts of time available. Homework suggestions (usually writing) are also provided for each lesson.

Weblink

The Teacher's Book provides at least one URL relevant to each lesson (in this case a website where students can read about other unexplained mysteries). Teachers are advised to check these links before sharing them with the students as web addresses frequently change.

Language Workout

The Language Workout boxes highlight the target language with sentences from the reading text or paradigms for the students to complete. The bottom of the box refers students to the Language File at the back of the book where they can check their answers, find a fuller treatment of the grammatical point and do a practice exercise focusing on the form of the target language. The Teacher's Book provides suggestions for further practice activities and additional information about the target language.

Teachers may decide when to draw students' attention to the Language Workout, and the Teacher's Book gives suggestions for when it can be used. For example, it may be appropriate to refer to it before learners are expected to produce the target language, and/or for consolidation at the end of the lesson.

WRITING

Rewrite the sentences about Earhart and Noonan using the verb in brackets and *have*.

1 She must have been very brave.

1 She was certainly very brave. (must)
2 I'm sure she didn't sleep during her solo flight. (can't)
3 It's possible that they survived. (might)
4 Perhaps they landed on a desert island. (could)
5 I'm sure aliens didn't abduct them. (can't)
6 Maybe the plane came down in the sea. (could)
7 It's possible that they got lost. (may)
8 I'm sure she loved flying. (must)

Extension What do you think happened to Earhart and Noonan? Write at least two possible explanations.

PRONUNCIATION

🔊 2.20 Listen and check your answers to exercise 4. Repeat the sentences and mark the stressed words in each sentence. What happens to *have* in these sentences?

VOCABULARY

Complete with the correct form of these verbs.

Word Bank Phrasal verbs with *up*

blow end grow look make
sum take use wake

1 We've run out of milk – we've _____ it all up.
2 My little sister wants to be a pilot when she _____ up.
3 Guy Fawkes failed to _____ up parliament.
4 I don't believe his story – I think he _____ it up.
5 After travelling round the world, he _____ up in Brazil.
6 Now I'd like to _____ up what I've just said.
7 A loud noise _____ me up in the middle of the night.
8 Earhart _____ up flying when she was a young woman.
9 I didn't understand the word, so I _____ it up in the dictionary.

Which of these phrasal verbs with *up* can you find in the text in exercise 2?

SPEAKING

Discuss the stories in *Unexplained Mysteries* and say what you think happened in each case.

Carolyn must/can't have …
She could/may/might have …

WRITING

Write about another unexplained mystery that interests you – or make one up!

Describe the event and say what you think happened, giving your reasons.

UNIT **5**

Unexplained Mysteries

Mystery island
In June 1974, pilot Carolyn Cascio was flying to Grand Turk Island in the Bahamas. When she flew over Grand Turk, people on the island could see her plane, but she sent a radio message: 'There is nothing down there!' Then Cascio's plane suddenly disappeared and she was never seen again.

Tunnel vision
In the winter of 1975, Mr and Mrs Wright were driving to New York City in a snowstorm. When they reached the Lincoln Tunnel, they stopped to clean snow off the car windows. Mrs Wright went to clean the back window – and she disappeared for ever.

Foreign visitor
In 1905, a man was arrested in Paris because he was a pickpocket. He spoke a completely unknown language, but finally he found a way to communicate with people. He said he came from a city called Lisbian – which doesn't exist.

Time travel
A National Airlines 727 plane was flying to Miami in 1969 when it suddenly lost contact with air traffic control. Ten minutes later, it reappeared on the radar screen. No one on the plane had noticed anything unusual, but when the plane landed on time, the watches of all the passengers and crew were ten minutes slow.

LANGUAGE WORKOUT

Complete.

Deduction
must have and *can't have* + past participle
The plane _____ _____ run out of fuel.
It _____ _____ blown up in mid-air.

Speculation
could/may/might have + past participle
What could _____ happened to them?
They could _____ _____ up on a desert island.
Earhart and Noonan may _____ _____ US spies.
Aliens _____ _____ abducted them.

We use _____ _____ when we are sure something happened.
We use _____ _____ when we are sure something didn't happen.
We use *could/may/might have* to talk about what possibly happened.

▶ **Answers and Practice**
Language File page 117

67

---

8 Writing

Each of the first three lessons in each unit ends with a writing activity. These typically have the dual function of writing skills development and reinforcement of the target language. In this lesson students write about another unexplained mystery.

7 Speaking

In the Speaking activity, students *use* the target language to communicate, in this case saying what they think happened. This activity often also *personalises* the target language and students use it to talk about their own lives and opinions.

6 Vocabulary

Lessons may also offer explicit lexical development through Word Banks of lexical sets and vocabulary exercises.

The fourth lesson in each unit is an **Integrated Skills** lesson. In these lessons the four skills support each other, usually moving from a reading text to a listening activity, then a speaking activity based on the listening or reading and concluding with a writing activity for which the reading, listening and speaking have prepared the students. The lesson ends with a Learner Independence section.

Lesson heading

The lesson heading identifies the text type, in this lesson, facts and ideas.

1 Opener

The aim of the Opener is to introduce the topic or to revise and pre-teach vocabulary, or both.

Warmers

The Teacher's Book suggests one or two warmers. These may revise vocabulary or prepare students for the lesson topic.

Weblink

The Teacher's Book provides at least one URL relevant to each lesson (in this case a website giving information about British football). Teachers are advised to check these links before sharing them with the students as web addresses frequently change.

---

5 **4**

EXTRAORDINARY PEOPLE

Integrated Skills

Contrasting facts and ideas

1 OPENER

Look at the photo. How popular is women's football in your country? Are there other sports which more men than women play? Are there sports which more women than men play?

'IS IT A MAN'S GAME?'

ASKS MARIGOL

1. Mexico's star woman footballer, Maribel Dominguez, is known as 'Marigol' because she scores so often – 46 goals in 49 international matches. But life isn't, and hasn't been, easy for her in a man's world – football.

2. Maribel started to play when she was nine years old on wasteland near her new home in Mexico City. But she played with boys. The short-haired new arrival was soon accepted into the group of boys. They called her Mario.

3. 'I tricked them for years,' Maribel confesses. 'They only found out I wasn't a boy when they saw my picture in the paper. I'd got into a junior national team. They went to my house and asked if I was a girl. They were pretty shocked.'

4. Maribel was 20 when she joined the Mexican national team and played in the Women's World Cup in the USA in 1999. The team lost all their matches, but Maribel was soon playing for a professional women's team in Atlanta in the USA. Then came the 2004 Athens Olympics and the Mexican women's team reached the quarter-finals, while the men's team were knocked out in the first round. By now Maribel was famous and also lucky that she had escaped serious injuries.

5. 'Maribel really is very, very good,' says Nora Herrera, one of a few women football journalists in Mexico. 'She has an incredible nose for a goal, she can smell it, and she's fast and courageous, and surprisingly strong too.'

6. In 2005 Maribel shocked the Mexican football world by joining a second-division club called Celaya, which was looking for a centre forward. It was a men's club. The Mexican Football Association said it had no problem with her playing in a male team, but they had to ask FIFA, the world football organisation. Just before Christmas 2005 FIFA announced its decision: 'There must be a clear separation between men's and women's football.' In other words, no!

7. 'I just wanted to be given the chance to try,' said Maribel. 'If I had failed, I would have been the first to say that I couldn't do it. But at least I would have tried.' So Maribel moved to Europe to play professional women's football for Barcelona.

8. Maribel scored the goal which qualified Mexico for the 2011 World Cup and she hopes to continue playing. When she retires, she wants to start a football school for girls. She is saving money for it, but women footballers are paid much much less than men. In Mexico Maribel got £600 a month, whereas a top male player got £60,000. 'To play in international competitions feels fabulous. It is the best thing for a woman. The very best. Well, for a female footballer it's the best thing that can happen. For a man, maybe earning a million dollars a month is better. I don't know.'

68

6 Speaking

Students now work in groups to discuss the questions arising from the topic, and then report back to the class. The Teacher's Book offers further optional activities, including a class discussion.

2, 3 and 4 Reading

There are usually one or two reading activities encouraging detailed reading. Detailed comprehension questions have the dual function of encouraging intensive reading and highlighting the structure of the text in preparation for the subsequent skills activities.

5 Listening

These activities develop intensive listening skills. Here students listen for information about Maribel Dominguez and Hanna Ljungberg, two well-known international female footballers.

UNIT 5

READING

🔊 2.21 Read 'Is it a man's game?' asks Marigol and match these topics with the paragraphs.

A discovery   A review   The future   A surprise decision   Her career
Introducing Marigol   A new continent   Early days

Find the highlighted words in the text which mean:

1 woman *adj*
2 says that he/she has done something wrong *v*
3 series of games in a competition *n*
4 man *adj*
5 unused open ground *n*
6 last four games between eight players or teams in a competition *n*
7 put out of a competition after losing a game *v*
8 brave *adj*
9 group of teams who play against each other *n*

Linking words: *whereas* and *while*

We can use *whereas* or *while* to contrast two facts or ideas. Find an example of each in the text.

LISTENING

🔊 2.22 Read and complete as much of the text as you can for Maribel. Then listen and take notes so you can complete the text for Hanna as well.

Both Maribel Dominguez and Hanna Ljungberg are well-known international ___1___. Maribel has scored ___2___ goals in ___3___ international matches, whereas Hanna has scored ___4___ goals in ___5___ internationals. Maribel started playing when she was ___6___, while Hanna started when she was ___7___. Maribel joined the Mexican team when she was ___8___, whereas Hanna joined the Swedish team when she was ___9___. Maribel played in the ___10___ World Cup in the USA but Hanna ___11___. Both women are ___12___ footballers and both were asked to play for ___13___ teams. Neither did. Hanna retired in ___14___, whereas Maribel continues to play in Spain.

Hanna Ljungberg, Sweden.

Now listen and check your answers.

SPEAKING

FIFA say that boys and girls can play football together until they are 13, but after that there must be separate male and female teams. Do you agree? And why are men footballers paid so much more than women?

In what other areas of life do men and women have different opportunities and pay? Think about sport, education and jobs. Discuss your ideas with other students.

GUIDED WRITING

Write three paragraphs contrasting the situations of men and women in your country. Is it easier to be a man or a woman – what are the advantages and disadvantages?

LEARNER INDEPENDENCE

8 Thinking skills: Revising groups of words or phrases

● Make a word map on a big piece of paper of a group of words and phrases you want to review, for example, words to do with sport.
● Stick the piece of paper on your door and look at it every time you leave your room.
● After a week take the paper down, and make a new word map for another topic.
● You can save the papers for last-minute revision.

9 Word creation: Make adjectives ending in *-ous* from these nouns and complete the sentences.

courage   danger   infection
luxury   nerve   poison
space   superstition

1 She's very _____ – she's not afraid of anything.
2 The hotel was really _____ – I've never stayed anywhere as nice.
3 It's not safe – in fact it's quite _____
4 People who believe in magic are often _____.
5 My cold's getting better – I don't think I'm _____ now.
6 All footballers get _____ before a match.
7 The room is very _____ – it can hold up to fifty people.
8 Those mushrooms are _____, so you mustn't eat them.

10 🔊 2.23 Phrasebook: Find these useful expressions in Unit 5. Then listen and repeat.

I don't know why.
Which isn't a good thing, really.
You needn't worry.
What could have happened?
In other words …
I just wanted to be given the chance.

Now write a six-line dialogue using at least three of these expressions.

69

Learner Independence

Learner Independence sections typically include three activities, focusing on learning to learn, vocabulary development, and idiomatic expressions.

8

In this lesson students look at revising groups of words or phrases. Discussion may take place in English or the mother tongue, as appropriate to the learner's level. The emphasis here is on learning *how* to learn. The Teacher's Book offers optional activities to further explore this area.

9

The aim here is to make adjectives ending in *-ous* from nouns.

10 Phrasebook

This section occurs in every unit and helps students learn idiomatic expressions in context. Students find the expressions from within the unit, practise pronunciation and then complete a small follow-up activity, in this case writing a six-line dialogue using three of the expressions.

Follow-up activities and homework

The Teacher's Book offers optional follow-up activities, usually including a game, to help with mixed-ability teaching and to cope with variable aptitude and amounts of time available. Homework suggestions (usually writing) are also provided for each lesson.

7 Writing

Here students write three paragraphs for the class magazine based on their discussions. The Teacher's Book suggests ways to monitor and check their work.

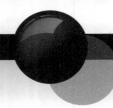
Inspiration EXTRA! follows the Integrated Skills lesson in each unit and always includes, on the left-hand page, a Game/Puzzle, plus either a Project, or Language Links and a Sketch.

On the right-hand page there are mixed-ability activities giving opportunities for both revision and extension, and Your Choice!, which allows students to choose from four different activities.

Language Links

The aim of the Language Links section is to raise plurilingual awareness. Here, students are encouraged to see how the brain is used for producing language.

Game/Puzzle

Here, students play a word game in teams. There is often a game on this page, and there are also games throughout the book in the lessons and in the Teacher's Book optional activities.

---

5 EXTRAORDINARY PEOPLE
Inspiration EXTRA!

LANGUAGE LINKS

Read *Language and the mind.* Which part of the brain is normally used to produce speech? Which part is used to understand what we hear?

Language and the mind

Humans are cousins of the apes and modern humans evolved around 200,000 years ago. We probably started to develop language 100,000 years ago and the first humans walked out of Africa into Asia about 75,000 years ago. As humans spread around the world (arriving on the American continent possibly as late as 30,000 years ago), different languages developed.

Humans have extra-large brains and in most cases it is the left hemisphere of the brain which deals with language. The front part of the left hemisphere produces what we say, while the back part understands what we hear. When we learn a new language, the brain operates in the same way.

Children are born with the ability to speak, and start to say their first words by the age of one. But reading and writing are not natural abilities – they are skills that children have to learn and they involve making new connections in the brain. So learning to read is literally a mind-changing experience.

We write and read English from left to right. Do you know of any languages which are written and read from right to left?

SKETCH *The Break-In*

🔊 224 Read and listen.

A couple have just walked into their apartment after a holiday.

WOMAN Oh, no – what a terrible mess!
MAN There must have been a break-in! Burglars!
WOMAN They could have got in through the window – look, it's broken.
MAN They can't have come in through the window. We're on the 15th floor!
WOMAN Then they must have come through the door.
MAN They can't have – the door was locked.
WOMAN They might have had a key. Perhaps it was someone we know.
MAN I can't believe that. But what's missing? What have they taken?
WOMAN They haven't taken the computer. What about the T
MAN Let's check the sitting room.
WOMAN Oh, heavens – it's total chaos in here.
MAN Look! There's a body under a blanket on the sofa!
WOMAN Is it alive?
MAN I don't know. We'd better call the police.

The person on the sofa throws off the blanket.

SAM Oh, hi, Mum. Hi, Dad.
WOMAN Sam!!! Are you all right?
SAM Yes, of course I'm all right. I'm just a bit tired, that's all.
MAN But there's been a break-in, hasn't there? What on earth happened?
SAM Ah, sorry about the mess. A few friends came round last night. If I'd known you were coming home toda I'd have tidied the place up.

Now act out the sketch in groups of three.

Game *Link-up*

- Form two teams.
- One team chooses a letter square from the game board. The teacher asks a question about a word beginning with the letter. If the team guesses the word, they win the square.
- Then the other team chooses a letter square ...
- The first team to win a line of *linked* squares from top to bottom or from left to right is the winner. You can go in any direction, but all your squares must touch!

C	A	M	R
B	J	Q	F
W	T	P	Y
D	G	S	E

70

Sketch

The aim of the sketches is for students to enjoy using English while also getting valuable stress and intonation practice. The Teacher's Book has suggestions for using the recording and for acting out the sketches.

Revision

The Revision exercises provide further writing practice for less confident students in mixed-ability classes. In this unit, students write sentences in the past perfect, about qualifications needed for a job, and rewrite sentences about a footballer. They are always given sections of the unit to refer back to.

Extension

The Extension exercises provide challenging writing activities for more confident students in mixed-ability classes. In this unit, students write a paragraph about an event that changed their life, then write a conversation, and also write sentences making deductions.

The Revision and Extension exercises are a flexible resource and may be done at the end of the unit or after the relevant lesson. Alternatively the students can do them as homework. The Teacher's Book provides possible answers.

UNIT 5

REVISION

LESSON 1 Write sentences using *wish/if only* and the past perfect.

1 He failed his exams and can't go to university. (If only)
2 She got the message and it was bad news. (wish)
3 There wasn't much food and I wanted more. (wish)
4 I took your advice and everything went wrong. (If only)
5 She didn't back up her computer and it crashed. (wish)
6 He stayed in his job and hated it. (If only)

LESSON 2 Look at exercise 5 on page 65 and write about the qualifications needed for the job you didn't write about in exercise 6.

LESSON 3 The famous footballer Terry Wayne has disappeared. Rewrite the sentences using the verb in brackets.

1 What do you think has happened to him? (can)
2 I'm sure he was tired of the publicity. (must)
3 Perhaps he's gone to stay with friends. (may)
4 It's possible that he's had an accident. (might)
5 Perhaps he wanted a holiday. (could)
6 I'm sure he hasn't decided to give up football. (can't)

EXTENSION

LESSON 1 Look at exercise 7 on page 63. Think of an event that changed your life or the life of someone you know. Write a paragraph saying what would/wouldn't have happened if things had been different.

My mother met my father when she was a nurse. He was brought into hospital after breaking his leg in a football match. If he hadn't ...

LESSON 2 Look at the text on page 64. Write a conversation between Jo Kinsey and Jeanette Ewart in which they compare their jobs.

LESSON 3 Read about the mystery voyage of the *Mary Celeste*. Then write sentences making deductions and speculating about what happened to the people on the ship.

On 7 November 1872, the *Mary Celeste* set out from New York to sail to Italy with a cargo of wine. On 4 December, the *Mary Celeste* was found sailing off the coast of Portugal. There was no one on board and the lifeboat was missing. The captain and crew had apparently left in a hurry, and they were never seen again. But everything on the ship was tidy, and there was plenty of food and water.

YOUR CHOICE!

CONSTRUCTION *needn't* or *don't have to?*
Complete with *needn't* or *don't have to*.

You mustn't miss your train. Let me drive you to the station.
Thanks but you __1__ bother. There's plenty of time and I __2__ to catch this train. Anyway you've got lots to do.
You __3__ worry about me – I can always finish my work tomorrow. I __4__ to finish it today.
I know that I __5__ worry about you – you __6__ to keep reminding me!
I know I __7__ drive you but I thought I'd offer! Never again! You __8__ get angry with me!

ACTION Picture flash
You need a number of magazine pictures on cards. The pictures can be of people, places or objects. Student A holds a picture upside down with its back to the other students. Holding the picture at the sides with both hands, he/she flashes it so that the other students only see it for less than a second. The other students say what they think the picture *must/may/could/might/can't have been*. Student A flashes the picture again until one student guesses correctly. That student flashes the next picture card.

REFLECTION Modal verbs
Match the examples a–i with language functions 1–4.

1 Obligation 2 Lack of obligation 3 Deduction 4 Speculation

a You mustn't take everything I say seriously.
b It might have been your boyfriend on the phone.
c You have to wear a safety belt in the car.
d It can't have been my boyfriend – he's lost his phone!
e She could have got lost – she doesn't know the city well.
f You must turn off your phone in the cinema.
g You don't have to pay to get into the museum.
h I may have been wrong – I don't know.
i You don't have to thank me – I was happy to help.

INTERACTION My favourite English words

● Work in a small group.
● On your own, think of five English words which you like for a special reason – it could be the sound of the word, or something it makes you think of, for example.
● Share your words with the rest of the group, saying why each word is special to you.
● Listen and ask questions as other students tell you about their favourite English words.

71

Project

Projects provide a valuable resource for student creativity, self-expression and language consolidation. They also allow students of varying abilities to contribute. Students are encouraged to save their projects to add to their portfolios. While intended for use with the whole class, the projects could also be used for homework or as supplementary material with more confident students in mixed-ability classes. The group size for projects will vary from class to class, but teachers may prefer to have groups of three to six members.

1 Projects require students to go back through part of the unit which models the writing they will do. Then students brainstorm ideas, choosing a few to write about.
2 There is then a research phase using reference books, libraries or the Internet to gather information for the project. This could involve interviewing people, for example, family members.
3 Finally the group works together to produce their project, reading each other's work, editing and illustrating it. The Teacher's Book offers suggestions for organisation.

Your Choice!

The aim here is for students to choose and do the activity they like best. The activities reflect different learning styles and the aim is to encourage awareness of learning styles and to foster learner independence. Your Choice! activities may involve individual, pair or group work.

Culture

There are four Culture sections at each level of *New Inspiration* providing both factual information and the opportunity for cross-cultural comparisons. The section illustrated here deals with the topic of saying the right thing.

Warmer

The aim of the Warmer is to introduce the topic and stimulate discussion. For this lesson, the Teacher's Book provides useful information about shops and shopping in the UK. There are further Useful information sections throughout the Teacher's Book.

1 Reading

Here, students read and answer a shopping questionnaire.

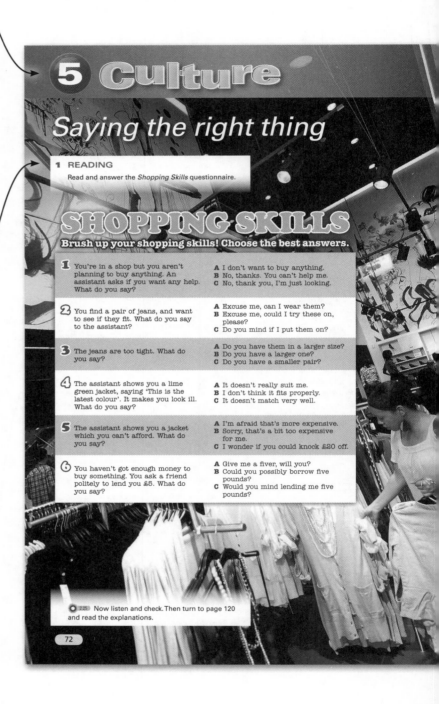

5 Culture

Saying the right thing

1 READING

Read and answer the *Shopping Skills* questionnaire.

SHOPPING SKILLS

Brush up your shopping skills! Choose the best answers.

1 You're in a shop but you aren't planning to buy anything. An assistant asks if you want any help. What do you say?
   A I don't want to buy anything.
   B No, thanks. You can't help me.
   C No, thank you, I'm just looking.

2 You find a pair of jeans, and want to see if they fit. What do you say to the assistant?
   A Excuse me, can I wear them?
   B Excuse me, could I try these on, please?
   C Do you mind if I put them on?

3 The jeans are too tight. What do you say?
   A Do you have them in a larger size?
   B Do you have a larger one?
   C Do you have a smaller pair?

4 The assistant shows you a lime green jacket, saying 'This is the latest colour'. It makes you look ill. What do you say?
   A It doesn't really suit me.
   B I don't think it fits properly.
   C It doesn't match very well.

5 The assistant shows you a jacket which you can't afford. What do you say?
   A I'm afraid that's more expensive.
   B Sorry, that's a bit too expensive for me.
   C I wonder if you could knock £20 off.

6 You haven't got enough money to buy something. You ask a friend politely to lend you £5. What do you say?
   A Give me a fiver, will you?
   B Could you possibly borrow five pounds?
   C Would you mind lending me five pounds?

🔊 2.25 Now listen and check. Then turn to page 120 and read the explanations.

72

2 Vocabulary

The Culture section texts provide a rich source of useful new vocabulary, and there are a variety of activity types here to give practice.

Culture

VOCABULARY

Complete the sentences with verbs from the questionnaire.

1 It's very cold today – _____ on a coat before you go out.
2 It's important to buy shoes that _____ properly.
3 The shirt is a nice colour but it doesn't _____ my trousers.
4 I need some new clothes – I haven't got a thing to _____!
5 Black doesn't really _____ you – it makes you look pale.
6 It's sensible to _____ on clothes before you buy them.

SPEAKING

Make and respond to requests using expressions from the box. Remember: the bigger the request, the more important it is to ask your partner politely!

> Can I borrow a pen, please?

1 Ask to borrow a pen.
2 Ask to borrow his/her MP3 player.
3 Ask him/her to open the window.
4 Ask him/her to help with your homework.
5 Ask to share his/her book.
6 Ask if you can use his/her mobile.
7 Ask if you can use his/her mobile to phone New York.
8 Ask him/her to look after your dog while you're on holiday.
9 Ask him/her to help you paint your room.

aking requests	Responding to requests
ill you …?	Yes, of course. 😊
ould you …?	I'd rather not. 😕
an I/you …?	No problem. 😊
uld I/you …?	I'm afraid not. 😕
ore polite	
ould you mind __ing …?	No, of course not. 😊
o you mind if I …?	Not at all. Go ahead. 😊
wonder if I/you could …	Yes, certainly. 😊
uld I possibly …?	I'd rather you didn't. 😕

4 LISTENING

You are going to hear a tourist in three different situations. First, try to match the sentences below with these places.

A — Bank

B — Railway station

C — Hostel

1 Could I change 100 dollars into euros?
2 I'd like a room for tonight, please.
3 How would you like the money?
4 Single or return?
5 Have you made a reservation?
6 Single or double?
7 Tens and twenties, please.
8 A day return, please.
9 Single, please, with a shower if possible.
10 Here's your change.
11 There's one in five minutes.
12 Here's your receipt for the exchange.
13 Which platform does it leave from?
14 Would you mind filling in this form, please?
15 Do I have to change?

Now decide which sentences the tourist says, and which sentences the tourist hears.

🔘 2.26 Listen and check.

5 ROLE PLAY

Choose one of the situations in this lesson: shopping for clothes, changing money, buying a train ticket or booking a room. Act out a similar conversation between a tourist and a shop assistant, a bank/booking clerk or a receptionist.

Now change roles and situations.

6 MINI-PROJECT *Advertising*

Work with another student and write about how advertising makes us want to buy things. Think about:

- Different kinds of advertising, eg posters, TV commercials, web pop-ups, junk mail
- Your favourite and least favourite adverts
- How adverts get their message across

Collect examples of adverts (in English or your own language). Choose three and write a paragraph about each one, describing how they work and your reaction to them.

73

4 Listening

The students listen to dialogues connected to the cultural topic. These are often followed up by role play activities.

Weblink

The Teacher's Book provides at least one relevant URL (in this case a BBC website for teenagers). Teachers are advised to check these links before sharing them with the students as web addresses frequently change.

6 Mini-Project

The Mini-Projects in the Culture sections typically use the text as a model and invite the students to work in pairs to write about an aspect of culture, e.g. an advert.

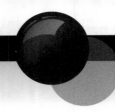

There are four **Reviews** at each level of *New Inspiration*. Each Review covers the new language of the preceding two units. The Teacher's Book contains the answers to all the exercises.

Review exercises are contextualised, often using information from the relevant lesson, so that students are creating meaningful sentences.

Language points reviewed include not only main verb tenses but problem areas such as *must/mustn't* and *need/needn't*.

The Workbook offers a parallel Review with text and multiple-choice questions, examination-type exercises, and a self-assessment Progress Check including 'my learning diary'.

REVIEW

UNITS 5-6

Reindeer man

Researcher Piers Vitebsky spends part of each year with the Eveny people. They live in the Verhoyansk Mountains of north-east Siberia, where winter temperatures fall to −71°C.

'I communicate mostly in Russian, but if I hadn't learnt Eveny, I __1__ have been able to understand everything. The Eveny language has about 1,500 words to describe the appearance and behaviour of reindeer. I learnt Eveny because otherwise I __2__ have misunderstood exactly what people meant.

The Eveny move camp every few days. We're moving camp today, and I wake in a tent full of the smells of reindeer fur and wood smoke. One of us makes sweet tea. Another has already used his dog to help bring the herd of 2,000 reindeer back to the camp. Then we catch the reindeer. We __3__ catch all 2,000, just the ones we'll ride and use to carry our things.

Now it's time we __4__ our tents. I've calculated that the old lady in the family I'm with __5__ have packed and unpacked 1,500 times. When the Eveny leave a camp, they believe they __6__ look back or they will never return to the place. And they always leave wood and stones behind for the next year. Other people can use these, but they __7__ always replace them.

On the first morning in a new camp it's important to tell each other what you dreamt about in the night. These dreams show how successful the new camp will be. Last time we moved I told the herders that I __8__ about mountains, animals and running water. They asked me __9__ I dreamt about these things when I was back home in England. I replied that I only dreamt about reindeer when I was in the Verhoyansk Mountains. I explained that soon I would have to return to Britain. As always I wished that I had had more time with the Eveny. There is never enough time to get everything __10__ .

1 Read and complete. For each number 1–10, choose word or phrase A, B or C.

1 A can't	B won't	C wouldn't
2 A can	B will	C might
3 A mustn't	B needn't	C didn't have to
4 A packed	B to pack	C are packing
5 A had to	B must	C will
6 A don't have to	B mustn't	C needn't
7 A must	B need	C had to
8 A am dreaming	B dream	C had dreamt
9 A if	B when	C where
10 A doing	B do	C done

84

2 Write sentences saying what would and wouldn't have happened if things had been different.

The Gunpowder Plot didn't succeed. The King didn't die.
If the Gunpowder Plot had succeeded, the King would have died.

1 Amelia Earhart was daring. She tried to fly round the w[...]
2 Something strange happened. The plane didn't reach th[...] island.
3 The boys didn't realise Maribel was a girl. They called h[...] 'Mario'.
4 Maribel was a brilliant footballer. She played for Mexic[...]
5 FIFA said Maribel couldn't play for a men's club. She [...] play for Celaya.
6 Nisha invited her. Laura went to India for the holidays.
7 The restaurant looked friendly. Bill Bryson decided to h[...] dinner there.
8 Isabel didn't speak Spanish. She was worried about meeting her relatives.

3 Nick planned to fly to Greece for a holiday, but everythi[...] went wrong. What does he regret? Write sentences beginning *I wish ...* and *If only ....*

He decided to drive to the airport.
'I wish I hadn't decided to drive to the airport.'

1 He didn't take the train.
2 The traffic was heavy.
3 He didn't stop for petrol.
4 The car ran out of petrol.
5 He didn't get to the airport in time.
6 He missed his flight.
7 He didn't have a holiday.

4 Complete with *mustn't*, *need(s) to* or *needn't* and these verbs.

| book forget go have look start stay stop |

1 He _____ his eyes tested because he often gets headac[...]
2 We _____ a table – the restaurant is never full.
3 I _____ up too late – I've got an exam tomorrow.
4 She _____ taking malaria tablets before she goes to In[...]
5 There's plenty of food in the fridge, so you _____ to th[...] supermarket.
6 I _____ at the road map because I know the way.
7 You _____ to lock the door when you leave.
8 We _____ at a garage before we run out of petrol.

5 You're waiting for a friend to join you at a gig, but she's late. Talk about what could/might have happened to he[...]

get the date wrong
A She could have got the date wrong.
B Yes, she might have got the date wrong.

1 lose the address   4 go to another gig
2 forget about it   5 miss the bus
3 feel too tired   6 decide not to come

Exercise 1

Each review begins with a text covering the new language of both units with KET/PET examination-type objective test questions, usually multiple-choice cloze.

Weblink

The Teacher's Book provides at least one relevant URL (in this lesson a website about the Eveny people). Teachers are advised to check these links before sharing them with the students as web addresses frequently change.

REVIEW

9 Write the sentences in reported speech using the correct form of these verbs.

> complain explain invite offer
> refuse remind suggest warn

1 Paul: 'Sue, don't forget to phone me this evening.'
2 Sally: 'Tom, would you like to go to the cinema?'
3 Robert: 'You press the red button to turn on the DVD player.'
4 Marta: 'I'm not going to tidy my room.'
5 Dan: 'Emma, don't drive too fast.'
6 Doctor: 'Why don't you take a holiday, Mr Evans?'
7 Jenny: 'I can't concentrate with all this noise.'
8 Bill: 'I'll carry your suitcase, Mum.'

Marion is a tourist in the UK. Report her questions using the words in brackets.

1 'When does the next train leave?' (want to know)
2 'Do I have to change trains?' (wonder)
3 'How long does the journey take?' (ask)
4 'Is the hotel near the station?' (want to know)
5 'How much does a single room cost?' (wonder)
6 'Can I pay by credit card?' (ask)

Ask and answer questions about what Laura did before going to India.

> have/her clothes/wash ✓
> A Did she have her clothes washed?
> B Yes, she did.

1 get/a new passport photo/take ✓
2 have/eyes/test ✗
3 have/her hair/cut ✗
4 get/her teeth/check ✓
5 have/nails/paint ✗
6 get/shoes/repair ✓

Now write sentences.

She had her clothes washed.

VOCABULARY

Complete with correct form of these verbs.

> collapse install pick point out push off
> spill stick supervise tip warn

1 People shouldn't _____ the flowers in the park.
2 She _____ him that the dog was dangerous but he didn't listen.
3 The waitress was very helpful so we _____ her well.
4 It's not at all polite to tell someone to _____!
5 After the explosion a lot of buildings _____.
6 The instructor _____ us when we made our first dives.
7 Can you help me _____ this new software on my computer?
8 Her father _____ that the air ticket would be quite expensive.
9 My fingers _____ to the wet paint when I touched it.
10 The glass was too full and I _____ a lot of water.

10 Match these words with their definitions 1–8.

> abduct aisle blow up defrost
> massive puncture remote trace n

1 enormous
2 raise the temperature of frozen food to over 0°C
3 kidnap
4 hole in a tyre which lets the air out
5 explode
6 sign
7 where you can walk between lines of seats
8 far away from everything

11 Match the verbs in list A with the words and phrases in list B.

	A	B
1	catch	a tablet
2	fly	a goal
3	give	light to
4	score	solo
5	set	someone a chance
6	take	someone red-handed

LEARNER INDEPENDENCE SELF ASSESSMENT

Look back at Lessons 1–3 in Units 5 and 6.

How good are you at …?	✓Fine	? Not sure
1 Talking about unreal or imaginary past events Workbook pp50–51 exercises 1–3	☐	☐
2 Expressing regret about the past Workbook p50 exercise 4	☐	☐
3 Expressing obligation and lack of obligation Workbook pp52–53 exercises 2–4	☐	☐
4 Making deductions and speculating about the past Workbook pp54–55 exercise 1–4	☐	☐
5 Reporting what people said Workbook pp62–63 exercises 1–4	☐	☐
6 Reporting what people asked Workbook pp64–65 exercises 1–4	☐	☐
7 Describing problems Workbook pp66–67 exercises 2 and 4	☐	☐
8 Suggesting solutions Workbook pp66–67 exercises 2 and 4	☐	☐

Not sure? Have a look at Language File pages 116–118 and do the Workbook exercise(s) again.

Now write an example for 1–8.

1 What would have happened if the gunpowder had exploded?

85

Collocation

All the Review sections include an exercise to raise awareness of the importance of collocation.

Learner Independence: Self Assessment

This Self Assessment section for each two units lists the communicative aims and invites students to rate their confidence in each one. Students who are not sure about their ability in a particular area are referred to the Language File and the relevant Workbook exercises. The Teacher's Book offers guidance on handling this.

Follow-up activities and homework

The Teacher's Book offers optional follow-up activities, usually games. Homework suggestions (usually writing) are also provided.

Vocabulary

Vocabulary exercises include completion, matching words with their definitions, and collocation.

Welcome!
Thinking skills

WARMER 1

Getting to know you. Draw four pictures related to your life on the board, e.g. a swimmer if you like swimming, a motorbike if your favourite possession is a motorbike. Students ask questions to find out the significance of the drawings. Give detailed answers to their questions. Students then draw four pictures related to their lives. They get up and move around, asking different students about their pictures.

WARMER 2

Me too! Each student writes down one thing they did last weekend, one thing they did last year, one thing they have just bought, a job they would like to do, one thing they are going to do in the next year. The aim is then to find other students who have the same answers. Students move around, asking appropriate questions, e.g. *Did you go shopping last weekend?*

MAXIMISE YOUR BRAIN POWER!

Useful information

It is true that people learn differently, and it is true that the same person learns differently in different situations.

For this reason, the approach to learning styles taken in *New Inspiration* involves raising the student's awareness of different ways of learning, rather than saying 'you're this type of learner'. This has two benefits. Firstly, by becoming aware of their preferred learning style, students can be encouraged to experiment with other styles and therefore extend their learning repertoire. Secondly, through talking about learning styles, students gain a 'vocabulary of learning' so that they can discuss the learning process. It is important to stress to students that one learning style is not 'better' than another, and that successful language learners will use a range of styles reflecting their learning aims and circumstances.

LEARNING POWER

- The aim is to get students thinking about different ways to approach and improve their learning ability.
- Introduce the topic by writing the title *Maximise your brain power!* on the board and asking students to suggest ideas for how to do this, e.g. some people recommend doing crosswords, trying to read upside down, eating eggs for breakfast.

- Students work individually to complete the questionnaire by writing U (Usually), S (Sometimes) or R (Rarely) next to each statement.
- Students work in pairs and find out whether they learn in similar ways. Ask some students to report back to the class and pass on any useful tips they have.

MEMORY BUILDING

- Give students one minute to remember the 20 words. Students then close their books and write down all the words they remember.
- Find out who remembered the most and what technique they used. Point out that words are often easiest to remember if you put them into groups (e.g. all the jobs together).

DEVELOPING LOGIC

- Give students one minute to read the puzzle and try to solve it. The answer is at the bottom of page 7.
- Point out that there are brainteasers and crosswords like this one in every unit of the Workbook.

BODY AND MIND

- Ask students to work in pairs and discuss how they study best, e.g. with music playing, while eating snacks.
- Students read the text. Ask students to close their books and summarise it with their partner and to say whether they think they will try this. If possible, allow students to try out the 'walking meditation' technique in class!*

*'Walking meditation' is a technique inspired by *The Language Teacher's Voice* by Alan Maley (Macmillan Heinemann, 2000)

LEARNING STYLES

- The aim is for students to gain awareness of their language learning style(s) in order to help them learn more effectively and enable them to choose the most appropriate style for different tasks.
- Ask students to read the four learning styles and put a tick next to any statements which are true for them. By counting the number of ticks in each learning style, students should be able to see which type of learner they are. It will probably also show them that they have elements of other learning styles and this will encourage them to try different ways of learning.
- Show students *Your Choice!* on page 19 of the Student's Book and tell them that they can choose the preferred learning style, or experiment by choosing another one.

Optional activity

Students scan through the first unit of the book and identify an exercise or activity which they think will particularly suit their learning style.

Units 1–2

Activities		**Project**	**Vocabulary**
Identifying the function of communicative language	Categorising vocabulary Contextualising listening extracts	Healthy living	Food and drink Health and illness Materials

WARMER 1

Game *Vocabulary challenge* Focus on the photos and elicit the topics, *art, health and illness, kitchen equipment, film-making* and *food and drink*. Divide the class into two teams. Within their teams, ask students to work in pairs and brainstorm as much vocabulary as they can for each topic. Set a time limit of three minutes for the activity. Divide the board into five sections and ask students from each team in turn to offer one item of vocabulary and say which topic it belongs to. Write the word on the board in the correct section and explain it if necessary. Award a point to the team. Once a word has been suggested, it cannot be suggested again by the other team. Continue until you have brought together all the words. See which team brainstormed the most vocabulary overall.

WARMER 2

Focus on the photos and ask *Which topic do you find most interesting? Why?* Elicit a few answers, then ask *Which things are most important for a country? Which things should governments spend money on? Why?* Try to generate a class discussion and encourage students to express their opinions and agree and disagree with each other.

1 • The aim is to introduce students to the main areas of communicative language they will cover in Units 1 and 2.
   • Focus on the two boxes on the left and explain that they show the communicative language and topics/vocabulary that students will learn in Units 1 and 2. Students match five of the communicative aims 1–7 with the pictures A–E.

   Answers
   1 E   2 C   3 -   4 B   5 A   6 D   7 -

Optional activity

Students write another example sentence for each of the communicative aims 1–7. Monitor and help where necessary. Ask students to read out some of their sentences, and ask the class to decide which communicative aim they go with.

2 • Check that students understand the meaning of the categories. Check they understand that *materials* refers to anything that things are made of. Give students two minutes to complete the words and write them in the correct categories.
   • Allow students time to check their answers in pairs before you check with the whole class.

   Answers
   Food and drink: biscuit, butter, fruit, juice, onion, vegetable
   Health and illness: drug, headache, operation, pain, patient, surgery
   Materials: bronze, cardboard, concrete, iron, plastic, rubber

Optional activity

Students work in pairs or small groups and add as many words as they can to the *Materials* category. Bring the vocabulary together on the board. Elicit some ideas about what things are made from each material.

3 • The aim of the activity is for students to contextualise short listening extracts by working out what kind of listening text each is from. Remind students that for this type of activity they should listen for the main gist, and should not worry if they don't understand every single word. Remind them that there is one text type they do not need.
   • Play the recording. Students match the extracts 1–3 with A–D.

1.01 Recording

1

There was once an old ferryman who lived in a hut by the River Ganges in India. For as long as anyone could remember his family had rowed people across the river.

2

Do you like making toasted sandwiches? Then this sandwich toaster is the answer. It produces perfect toasted sandwiches and it's small enough to fit in a kitchen drawer. It comes with lots of delicious recipes and you can use it at home, on the barbecue, or when you go camping.

3

I've only had two jobs so far and they were both commercials. There seems to be very little work about. Last year my first job was in February – a football film. Freezing! What's it been like for others?

Answers

1 D   2 A   3 B

Optional activity

Play the recording again and ask students comprehension questions, e.g.

1 *Where does the story take place?* (India)
2 *What can you make with this object?* (toasted sandwiches)
3 *When did the person get their first job?* (last February)

4 • Give students a few minutes to look through the Healthy Living Survey. Deal with any vocabulary issues.

• Students do the survey in groups of four, noting down any interesting or surprising answers.

• Divide each group into pairs, and put pairs together into new groups of four. Students report on anything interesting or surprising that came up in their discussions.

• Point out the 'Believe it or not!' fact at the bottom of the page. Ask students if they know any other strange or surprising facts like this about food and calories.

Healthy living project

• Ask students to work in pairs and decide on the top five tips for healthy living. Brainstorm ideas with the class first if students are struggling, e.g. *eat fruit and vegetables every day, walk or cycle to school, join a sports team*. Ask students to produce a poster promoting healthy living, including their top five tips and illustrations or photos to accompany them. Display the posters in class so that students can look at each others' work.

Follow-up activities

♦ Put students into pairs and ask them to choose three other vocabulary categories in the *Topics and vocabulary* box on page 8 and brainstorm vocabulary for them. Put pairs together to form groups of four, and ask them to compare their lists and add any more words that they can.

♦ Ask students which of the topics in the list they would like to learn more about at school. Students can discuss the question in pairs and choose one or two topics, then compare their answers in small groups and discuss any similarities or differences.

HOMEWORK

Ask students to interview someone else for the Healthy Living Survey and to write down the person's answers. They can give an assessment of how healthy or unhealthy the person is.

BODY AND MIND

It doesn't matter

Communicative aims	Language	Pronunciation	Vocabulary	Optional aids
Talking about food and drink	Verbs not used in continuous forms	Syllable stress	Food and drink	Follow-up activity 2: example food diary Follow-up activity 3: small blank cards

WARMER 1

Game *Food chain* Students stand up. Starting with the student on the far left and then one after the other, each student says the name of a food or a drink. If they can't think of one quickly enough or repeat one that has been said before then they sit down. The winning student is the one left standing. Set a rhythm by asking the students to clap their hands. Each student has five claps to say a word.

WARMER 2

Write the headings *meat, fish, vegetarian food, vegetables, fruit, drink* on the board. Ask students for one example to go under each heading. In pairs, students race to add another three words for each heading. The winning team is the first to finish. Write all the ideas on the board. Check comprehension and pronunciation by giving a translation for a word and asking students to say the word in English.

1 OPENER

- The aim is to set the scene for the reading and review or pre-teach some of the vocabulary.
- Students read the eight statements and tick them if they think they are true and cross them if they think they are false. Be prepared to explain/translate *pure, dried fruit, margarine, a label, a diet drink.* In pairs, students compare their ideas.

2 READING

- Encourage students to read for gist rather than reading every word by setting a short time limit for students to match the statements with the texts. Students then listen and check their answers.

🔘 1.02 Recording and Answers

1 *Bottled water is purer than tap water.*
 H This is a popular myth. Although some people think that bottled water tastes or smells better, there is nothing to prove that it is always purer than tap water. In fact, in the USA it's believed that 25–30% of bottled water comes from tap water. And do you realise that bottled water can cost up to 10,000 times more than tap water?

2 *A vegetarian diet is the healthiest.*
 F It depends. Vegetarian diets can be very healthy. But if your vegetarian diet consists of chips and biscuits, then that's a different matter. Make sure that your diet includes food with the protein, vitamins and minerals you normally get from meat.

3 *Eating cheese gives you nightmares.*
 *E It's not **what** you eat but **when** you eat that matters. Scientists agree that it's not a good idea to eat just before you go to bed. You can't relax properly while you are digesting food.*

4 *Dried fruit is not as healthy as fresh fruit.*
 C As part of a balanced diet we need to eat at least five portions of different fruit and vegetables a day. It doesn't matter whether they are fresh, frozen, tinned or dried (but fruit juice only counts as one portion a day). The only thing which dried fruit lacks, and fresh fruit has, is vitamin C, but both are equally healthy.

5 *Margarine contains less fat than butter.*
 D It often seems from advertising that this is true. However, while butter and margarine contain different kinds of fat, they both contain a similar amount of fat.

6 *A food label which includes the words 'low fat' indicates a healthy choice.*
 G Not at all. 'Low' products must contain 25% less fat than usual so people suppose that they are OK. But these types of food are often very high in fat to start with. So a 'low fat' product can still have quite a high amount of fat.

7 *Neither fruit juice nor diet drinks are bad for your teeth.*
 B In fact, both are. Fruit juice contains sugar, which can damage your teeth. Diet drinks are often acidic, which means that they can cause tooth decay. The best drinks for your teeth are water or milk.

8 *Experts disagree with each other about what healthy eating is.*
 A In fact, the main messages about healthy eating have stayed the same for some time. For example, 20 years ago experts were saying that we should reduce the amount of fat that we eat. And over 50 years ago they were emphasising the importance of fruit and vegetables. They appear to disagree because the media often exaggerate when reporting scientific research.

3 AFTER READING AND LISTENING

- Students read the questions and then read the texts again more carefully to answer the questions. They compare answers in pairs. Encourage them to work

out the meaning of new words from context and ignore words which are not necessary to complete the exercise. Be prepared to explain/translate *myth, exaggerate, digest, taste, smell.*
- Check the answers orally with the whole class.

Answers

1 None are true, seven are false, statement 2 could be true or false.
2 Because the media often exaggerate when reporting scientific research.
3 We should reduce the amount of fat that we eat.
4 It makes us believe that margarine contains less fat than butter.
5 Because you can't relax properly while you are digesting food.
6 Chips and biscuits.
7 They think they are OK because they contain 25% less fat than usual. They are wrong because these types of food are often very high in fat to start with.
8 They think it tastes and smells better.

Optional activity

Ask students to note all the two-word expressions related to food in the text, e.g. *healthy eating, fruit juice, diet drinks, fresh fruit, dried fruit, balanced diet, bottled water.* Ask them to work in pairs and see if they can add any more expressions.

Your response

Ask students to work in pairs to discuss the questions. Ask some pairs to report back to the class and continue a class discussion if students are interested and have plenty of ideas.

4 PRONUNCIATION

- Write *biscuit* on the board and elicit the number of syllables and where the main stress falls. Do the same with *contain.* In pairs, students practise saying the words and decide which column to write them in.
- Play the recording for students to listen and check. Play the recording again, pausing after each word for students to repeat.

🔘 1.03 **Recording and answers**

■ ■ *biscuit bottled fiction label nightmare portion product protein*
■ ■ *contain decay depend digest prefer reduce relax suppose*

Optional activity

Students race to find two more examples of the two patterns in this lesson, e.g. ■ ■ *healthy, sugar, water, message, promise,* ■ ■ *amount, include, appear, consist, discuss*

LANGUAGE WORKOUT OPTION

If you want to pre-teach the language students will use in the following activities, you may like to go to the Language Workout box now.

5 SPEAKING

- Students read the statements. Check they understand *to lose weight* (to get thinner), *to skip a meal* (to not have a meal), *junk food* (food which is unhealthy but quick and easy, e.g. chips, burgers).
- Give students a few minutes to think about their answers and how to use the verbs from exercise 5 in their answers. Allow them to note the verbs they are going to use but not to write complete sentences.
- Give students five minutes to discuss the statements with their partner. Monitor and help/correct as necessary. Ask some pairs to report back to the class and ask other students to respond to their ideas.

Optional activity

Write further statements on the board for fast-finishers to discuss, e.g. *Our national food is healthy. Teenagers aren't worried about healthy eating.* They can report back to the class after the activity, and other students can respond by agreeing or disagreeing with them.

Extension Ask students to work individually or in pairs to find the verbs and write sentences. Monitor and help as students work. Ask some students to read out their sentences and ask other students to say whether they agree or disagree.

6 WRITING

- Read the questions with the class and brainstorm some ideas. Write useful vocabulary and expressions on the board.
- Give students ten minutes to write their paragraphs. Encourage them to use some of the verbs in exercise 5. Monitor and note examples of good language and errors.
- Read out the examples of good language and errors and ask students to identify and correct the errors. Write the corrections on the board for students to copy.
- Ask students to read another student's paragraphs and comment on whether they agree or disagree.

Optional activity

Students will regularly be asked to write a paragraph on a topical issue. Establish the idea of a student magazine which will include the best four or five paragraphs on each topic. Ask students to choose a name for the magazine. Students choose four or five of the paragraphs they have written on junk food for the magazine page 'Our opinions on food today'. They could choose them because they are well-written or easy to read or, together, present a variety of opinions.

LANGUAGE WORKOUT

- Ask students to look at the Language Workout box and to complete the sentences. Confident students can complete first and then check, while others can look back at the text and then complete.
- Students turn to page 112 of the Language File to check their answers.

  Answers
  contains seems doesn't matter suppose think, tastes

- Highlight that these verbs are not usually used in the continuous form. Point out that verbs referring to states, e.g. *contain, matter, suppose, think* or senses, e.g. *taste* are not usually used in the continuous form.

Optional activity

With a confident group, show students that some of these verbs can be used in the continuous form but with a slightly different meaning: Write *I don't think I eat enough vegetables, I'm thinking of changing my diet.* on the board. Ask students to identify the difference in meaning (the first is an opinion, the second is a current plan).

PRACTICE

- Students do Practice exercise 1 on page 112 of the Language File. They complete the sentences with the correct form of the verb. They work individually and then compare their answers in pairs. Check the answers by asking different students to say the completed sentences.

  Answers
  1 believe, contains   2 see, are making   3 realises, doesn't like   4 smells, are ... cooking   5 are ... eating, know 6 am reading, includes

Follow-up activities

- Tell students that they saw 32 verbs in this lesson which are not usually used in the continuous. In teams, students have two minutes to write down as many of the verbs as possible.
- Ask students to keep a food diary for a week, noting down everything that they eat and drink each day. The following week, students can read each others' diaries and comment on how healthy or unhealthy their diets are.
- Students start a Vocabulary box. Encourage students to look back through the lesson for new words and expressions they've learnt. They write these on cards with a definition, translation, illustration or example sentence on the other side.

HOMEWORK

Students write a letter of complaint about the food in a restaurant. They can complain about the selection of food or about the quality of the food. Ask them to include at least five of the verbs in exercise 5.

WEBLINK

Students may like to visit www.bbc.co.uk/health/treatments/healthy_living/nutrition to read about healthy living.

Revision and Extension p19

Language File p112

Workbook Unit 1 Lesson 1 pp2–3

Photocopiable worksheet p163, notes p154

2 What's it for?

Communicative aims	Language	Pronunciation	Vocabulary	Optional aids
Describing objects and saying what they're for Describing a sequence of events	Gerund as subject *by/for* + gerund *after/before* + participle clause	Linking consonant sounds	Kitchen equipment Recipe	Warmer 1: cards with simple words Optional activity: pictures of gadgets, two copies of each

WARMER 1

Write the following verbs from Lesson 1 on the board: *contain, know, like, love, need, prefer, remember, see, seem, smell, sound, taste, think, want*. Tell students they are going to define some words, but they can only say sentences that use one of these verbs. Demonstrate by reading out this definition of *sugar* and asking students to guess the word: *I **like** this, fruit juice and cakes **contain** this, I **know** it is bad for my teeth.* Give each student two words to define and put them into pairs. Say that they should take it in turns to define their words, and their partner must guess the words.

WARMER 2

Game *Guessing game* Students work in teams. Tell students that you are thinking of a thing that you find in the house, e.g. a spoon. They have to guess what it is but each team only has one guess. If their guess is wrong, they are out. They can ask questions about the thing but you can only answer *yes* or *no*. Each team takes it in turn to either ask a question or guess the object.

1 OPENER

- The aim is to set the scene for the reading.
- Check students understand *gadget* (a small useful machine or tool). Students look at the photos and guess what these gadgets are for. Accept all suggestions, and don't confirm or reject students' ideas at this stage.

2 READING

- Students match the photos to the texts. Play the recording. Students listen and check their predictions.

  🔘 **1.04** **Recording**
  See text on page 12 of the Student's Book.

  Answers
  1 C 2 A 3 B 4 E 5 D

3 AFTER READING

- Students read the sentences and then read the texts again and decide if they are true or false.
- Check the answers before students correct the false sentences. Encourage students to work out the meaning

of new words from the context and ignore words which are not necessary to complete the exercise. Be prepared to explain/translate *plug in/into*, *wind something up*.

Answers
1 False. The bottle opener looks like a key.
2 True
3 True
4 False. They recommend wearing it for 30 minutes a day.
5 False. It's for toasting sandwiches.
6 True
7 False. It's for generating electricity.
8 True

Optional activity

Get students to cover the text and practise describing the objects in the pictures to each other. They should say what the object looks like and what it is used for. Their partner guesses the object being described.

Your response

Individually, students choose the two gadgets they would like to have. Students compare answers with their partner and explain their choices.

4 VOCABULARY

- Students match the words with the photos and then listen to check. Play the recording again, pausing for students to repeat the words.

  🔘 **1.05** **Recording and answers**
  1 tin opener
  2 frying pan
  3 corkscrew
  4 coffee maker
  5 toaster
  6 bread knife
  7 kettle
  8 cheese grater

- Check that students understand *boil, fry* and *slice*. Ask two students to read the example question and answer. Students continue in pairs. Monitor and help as necessary.

Optional activity

Say different things you find in a house, e.g. *a newspaper*. Give students the sentence head *It can be used for …* Students work in pairs/small groups and race to think of five different uses, e.g. *for finding out what's on TV, for hitting insects, for putting on the floor when you clean your shoes*, etc. Other suitable household items might be: a hat, a glass, a cushion, a spoon.

LANGUAGE WORKOUT OPTION

If you want to pre-teach the language students will use in the following activities, you may like to go to the Language Workout box now.

Extension Students prepare their sentences individually. Monitor and help as necessary. Students can work in pairs to read their sentences to each other and guess the gadgets. Alternatively, students could do the task as a mingle activity, reading their sentences to different students and guessing the gadgets.

5 PRONUNCIATION

- Students look at the words in the box and predict how they are said. Play the recording. Ask students what happens to the pronunciation when the two words are said together (the final sound of the first word more or less disappears). Play the recording again, pausing for students to repeat.

🔘 1.06 **Recording and answers**

front door
bed time
sand wich
bedside table
great fun
foot ball
bread knife
cork screw

Optional activity

Students try to put three of the expressions in one sentence which makes sense, e.g. *Why are the corkscrew and the bread knife on the bedside table?* They read their sentence to a partner. Ask some students to read their sentences to the class.

6 LISTENING

- Students look at the recipe. Ask *Do you eat/like Spaghetti Carbonara? Do you know how to make it?*
- Students read the instructions and put them in order. Encourage students to work out new vocabulary, e.g. *stir, chop, sprinkle, drain*, from the context.

- Students then listen to check their answers. Don't go through the answers in detail at this stage. Deal with any outstanding vocabulary queries students may have.

🔘 1.07 **Recording**

Spaghetti Carbonara   Serves 4
Ingredients: 350g spaghetti, 175g bacon, 2 medium onions, 50ml olive oil, 50ml white wine, 4 eggs, 100ml cream, 100g grated Parmesan cheese, salt
Chop the onions and bacon into small pieces. Heat the oil in a frying pan and fry the onions and bacon slowly until the onions are almost clear. Add the white wine and turn down the heat.
Meanwhile, boil 3–4 litres of water in a saucepan. Put the spaghetti in the boiling water, add salt and stir for a few seconds. While the pasta is cooking, use a fork to beat the eggs and cream together in a bowl, and then add half the Parmesan cheese.
When the pasta is cooked, drain it and add the onions and bacon. Then stir in the egg, cream and cheese mixture. Sprinkle with the rest of the Parmesan cheese and serve immediately.

Answers
1 C   2 H   3 D   4 A   5 G   6 I   7 F   8 B   9 E

Optional activity

Write these questions on the board for students to discuss in pairs: *Do you like cooking? What dishes can you cook? Who does most of the cooking in your house? Do you think it's important to be able to cook?*

LANGUAGE WORKOUT OPTION

If you have not already gone through the Language Workout box, you may like to go to it now, before moving on to the Speaking exercise.

7 SPEAKING

- Ask two students, A and B, to read the example dialogue aloud. Students continue in pairs, checking their answers to exercise 6. Monitor and help/correct as necessary.

8 WRITING

- Students can look up a dish that they like in class or at home, for homework. Ask students to write down the name of the dish and the ingredients. Be prepared to help with vocabulary. If some students have chosen the same dish, they could work together.
- In pairs, students discuss how to make their dishes and think about the order in which they prepare the ingredients.
- Ask students to identify useful time expressions in the Spaghetti Carbonara recipe and see how they are used: *meanwhile, then, when, while, before/after + -ing*. Elicit that the imperative form of the verb is used for a recipe.

- Give students ten minutes to write the recipe. Monitor and help/correct as necessary.
- Students exchange recipes and decide if they could make them. They could also try to follow them at home and report back on their success!

LANGUAGE WORKOUT

- Ask students to look at the Language Workout box and complete the sentences. Confident students can complete first and then check, while others can look back at exercises 2 and 3 and then complete.
- Students turn to page 112 of the Language File to check their answers.

  Answers
  Going Playing wearing opening struggling turning

- Highlight that:
- the gerund (verb + -*ing*) is used when a verb, e.g. *go, play* is used as a noun, for example as the subject of a sentence or after a preposition, such as *by* and *for*.
- after the words *before* and *after* the present participle, which is the same in form as the gerund, can replace subject plus verb, e.g. *She came up with the idea after she struggled to …* or *after struggling to … .* This is only possible when the subject of the two clauses in the sentence is the same, i.e. it would not be possible in the sentence: *She came up with the idea after her brother struggled to get up in the morning.*

PRACTICE

- Students do Practice exercise 2 on page 112 of the Language File. They complete the sentences. Do the first one together as an example.
- Check the answers by asking different students to say the completed sentences.

Answers
1 for waking   2 Before going   3 Counting   4 by turning
5 Cooking   6 after eating   7 Listening   8 by taking

Optional activity

Give students a picture of a gadget each. Make sure there is an even number of students, and two pictures of each gadget are given out. Students work individually and prepare a description of their gadget. Students then mingle and read their definitions to each other, without showing the pictures. If students think they have the same gadget, they can show each other the picture they have. Once students have found their partner, they can sit down. Continue until all the pairs are matched up.

Follow-up activities

♦ In teams, students invent a gadget. Encourage them to think about things that are difficult to do or take a long time and invent a gadget to solve the problem, e.g. a gadget to find your house keys, a gadget to massage your feet. They draw a picture of the gadget, say what it is for and how to use it. Each team then presents their gadget to the class and the class vote on the best gadget.

♦ Guess the activity. Students think of an activity, e.g. going to bed. Students say what they do before and after the activity, e.g. *Before doing this, I get into my pyjamas. After doing this I sometimes read a book.* Their partner guesses the activity.

HOMEWORK

Students write about one or two gadgets in their own home. They say what they are used for, how they work and when they are used, e.g. *before/after …-ing.* They could also include other information, e.g. who uses it most, who bought it, how much it cost, how old it is.

WEBLINK

Students may like to visit www.kidscom.com/create/gadgetmaker/gadgetmaker to invent their own gadget, say what it's for and then send it to a friend.

Revision and Extension p19

Language File p112

Workbook Unit 1 Lesson 2 pp4–5

Photocopiable worksheet p164, notes p154

3 When people expect to get better ...

Communicative aims	Language	Pronunciation	Vocabulary	Optional aids
Talking about illness and medicine	Verb + gerund or infinitive	Weak forms	Health Illness and treatment	Warmer 2: names of common illnesses on cards Follow-up activity 1: copies of the *Find someone who ...* chart

WARMER 1

Game *Word race*   Tell students the topic of the lesson is health and medicine. Write *medicine* vertically down the board. Ask students to copy it into their books. In pairs/small groups students race to think of one word for each letter. The words must be connected with health and medicine, e.g.

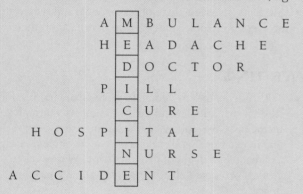

WARMER 2

Game *Mime the illness*   Organise the students into teams. One student from each team comes to the front. Show them a card with a common illness written on it. They mime the illness for their team. The first team to shout the correct word for their illness wins a point.

Useful information

Alternative medicine includes acupuncture, herbal medicine, homeopathy (a system of treating diseases in which ill people are given very small amounts of natural substances), massage, meditation, traditional Chinese medicine, hypnosis and osteopathy (the treatment of injuries to bones and muscles using pressure and movement).

1 OPENER

- The aim is to set the scene for the reading and pre-teach some useful vocabulary.
- Use the photo of acupuncture to pre-teach *acupuncture*, *needles*, *alternative medicine*. Discuss the questions with the whole class.

2 READING

- Students read and listen to the text. Ask individual students what information they found the most surprising.

   Recording
  See text on page 14 of the Student's Book.

3 AFTER READING

- Students read the sentences and then read the text again more carefully and decide if they are true or false. Check the answers before correcting the false sentences. Encourage students to work out the meaning of new words from context and ignore words which are not necessary to complete the exercise. Be prepared to explain/translate *open-heart surgery* and *a general anaesthetic*.
- When checking answers, ask students to underline the part of the text where they found the answer.

  ### Answers
  1 False. They saw the doctor less often.
  2 True   3 True   4 True   5 True   6 True   7 True
  8 False. The effects were the same.

Optional activity

Read out or write on the board these definitions of words from the text and ask students to find the words.
not causing any harm (harmless)
not natural (synthetic)
a drug that stops you feeling pain (anaesthetic)
earning a lot of money for someone (profitable)

Your response

Have students discuss the question in pairs and then as a whole class.

4 PRONUNCIATION

- Write *at, of, for, to* on the board and ask the students how they are pronounced. Students are likely to say the strong form of these words: /æt/ /ɒv/ /fɔː/ /tuː/.
- Students look at the expressions in the box. Play the recording and ask students to listen carefully to the pronunciation of these four words.

- Highlight the weak form of the four words: /ət/ /əv/ /fə/ /tə/. Play the recording again, pausing for students to repeat.

🔘 1.09 Recording

at best … at worst …
at selected points
thousands of years
system of medicine
a group of patients
acupuncture for headaches
operation for knee pain
remember to take it
two sides to the issue
appeared to change

LANGUAGE WORKOUT OPTION

If you want to pre-teach the language students will use in the following activities, you may like to go to the Language Workout box now.

5 SPEAKING

- Students look at the three situations. With a less confident class, do the first situation as a whole class. Be prepared to teach/translate *risk* + gerund.
- Students complete the sentences and compare their ideas with their partner.

Optional activity

Make the activity more competitive by organising the students into teams. Do one situation at a time. For each situation, the students write their ideas individually. They then compare with all the students in their team. For each sentence that is identical to that of someone else in the team they win a point, e.g. if three students have written *I'd try to study at the weekend* they win three points.

Extension Students write three more situations and then ask a partner.

6 VOCABULARY

- The aim is to improve students' vocabulary learning skills by encouraging them to relate new words to one another and to words they already know.
- Students copy the word map and then work in pairs to add as many words as they can. Point out that they can use words from this lesson and any other words they know related to medicine.

- Ask students to compare word maps with other groups and add any new words to their own map. With weaker classes, draw a mind map on the board and ask students to come out and add their ideas to it. Students can then copy the completed word map.

Optional activity

With weaker classes, give students a list of vocabulary to organise and add to the word map, e.g. *herbal medicine, headache, stop smoking, backache, a general anaesthetic, a pill, aspirin, drugs, surgery, pharmacy/ chemist's, a prescription, an injection, homeopathy.*

7 SPEAKING

- Students read the example dialogue. Ask students for possible questions they could ask each other, e.g. *Do you think modern medicine works? Do you think there are any advantages to alternative medicine? Would you try alternative medicine?*
- Students interview three other students and record their answers. Ask some students to report back on their conversations.

8 WRITING

- Tell students they are going to write a paragraph for a student magazine giving their opinion on alternative medicine. Give students a few minutes to re-read the text in exercise 2 and make a note of advantages and disadvantages of alternative medicine. With weaker classes, you could elicit ideas and write them on the board.
- Give students ten minutes to write their paragraph. Monitor and note examples of good language and errors. Write these on the board and ask students to identify and correct the errors. Ask students to check their writing and correct any mistakes.

Optional activity

Students choose four or five paragraphs to make up the magazine page 'Our opinions on alternative medicine'. This page could then be added to the ongoing student magazine.

LANGUAGE WORKOUT

- Ask students to look at the Language Workout box and complete the sentences. Confident students can complete first and then check, while others can look back at the text and then complete.
- Students turn to page 112 of the Language File to check their answers.

  Answers
  having to stop going to take

- Highlight the change in meaning depending on whether the infinitive or the gerund is used.
- Check students understand by asking questions about the examples: He tried to stop smoking: *Did he attempt to stop?* (Yes) *Did he actually stop?* (No) They tried having acupuncture: *Did they have acupuncture to see what would happen?* (Yes) He didn't remember to take it: *Was it a necessary action?* (Yes) *Did he take it?* (No) I remember going to the doctor: *Did I go to the doctor? Did I remember it afterwards?* (Yes)
- Point out that *forget* is rarely used with the gerund except when the sentence starts *I'll never forget/I've never forgotten …*

Optional activity

Write the following sentence heads on the board: *I tried to …, I tried + -ing …, I remembered/didn't remember to …, I remember/don't remember + -ing …* Students write true sentences about themselves. Do an example with the students first, e.g. *I tried to call my friend last night. I tried calling his parents' house but he wasn't there. I remembered to lock my door this morning. I remember arriving at this school for the first time.*

PRACTICE

- Students do Practice exercise 3 on page 113 of the Language File.
- Tell students to read the text once for general meaning, ignoring the gaps. Ask *How did the doctor become interested in alternative medicine?* (He/She visited China and saw a woman having an operation without anaesthetic.)
- Students complete the gaps individually and then compare their answers in pairs. Check answers by asking different students to read the sentences to the class.

  Answers
  1 travelling 2 going 3 to see 4 to be 5 thinking 6 to take 7 to find 8 telling 9 to discuss

Optional activity

Write the answers on the board. Books closed, students try to recreate the story using the verbs.

Follow-up activities

◆ Hand out a copy of the chart below to each student. Students complete the sentences with their own ideas. They then move round the classroom, asking each question until they find someone who says *yes*. They write the student's name next to each sentence.

Find someone who …	Name
remembers meeting ………… for the first time	
loves playing ………	
has pretended to be ………	
chose to watch ……… on TV last night	
promised to do something and then forgot	
forgot to ……… this morning	
has tried to watch a film in English	
wants to ……… tomorrow	

◆ In pairs, students invent a short dialogue between a patient and a doctor. The doctor is recommending some alternative medicine. The patient might be happy with this or confused or not believe in alternative medicine. Students practise the dialogue and act it out for the class. Write the following questions on the board for the listeners to answer after each role play: *What is the matter with the patient? What exactly does the doctor recommend? Is the patient happy with this?*

HOMEWORK

Students write six true sentences about themselves using six of the verbs from the lesson followed by the gerund or infinitive.
Students make a wordsearch of ten words related to medicine. Students can write the words going across or down, forwards or backwards. Students can exchange puzzles as a Warmer to the next lesson.

WEBLINK

Students may like to visit en.wikipedia.org/wiki/List_of_branches_of_alternative_medicine

for a list of branches of alternative medicine.

Revision and Extension p19

Language File pp112–113

Workbook Unit 1 Lesson 3 pp6–7

Photocopiable worksheet p165, notes p154

Integrated Skills Discussing and correcting information

Skills	Speaking Correcting	Learner independence	Vocabulary
Reading Matching statements and paragraphs: *Reality check*	*Speaking* Correcting information	Thinking skills	Popular beliefs
Listening Noting details: beliefs	*Writing* A paragraph discussing the truth of a statement	Word creation: noun and adjective suffixes	Natural events Useful expressions

WARMER 1

If you set the homework suggested in the previous lesson, students exchange wordsearch puzzles and race to find the ten words in their partner's puzzle.

WARMER 2

Game *True or false?* Write the following sentence on the board: *In the USA about half of all bottled water comes from tap water.* Students recall whether this is true or false (according to the article in Lesson 1, it's false – it's about a quarter). Ask students to look back at the first three lessons and write two true sentences and one false one. Students exchange sentences and try to identify and correct the false statement.

1 OPENER

- Students read the statements and match them to the photos. Encourage students to work out the meaning of new words using the photos. Check understanding of *lightning, to strike* and *visible*.
- Ask students whether they think the statements are true or false.

Answers

Lightning never strikes the same place twice.   C
Spinach is a great source of iron.   A
It takes seven years to digest chewing gum.   F
You get less wet by running in the rain rather than walking.   E
Flying is the safest way to travel.   B
The Great Wall of China is the only man-made structure visible from the moon.   D

2 READING

- Encourage students to read for general understanding and to match the statements. You could set a time limit of two or three minutes, to encourage students to read quickly. Students then listen and check their answers.
- Check how many of the statements are true (one). Ask students whether they guessed correctly. Ask what information in the article they find surprising.

🔘 1.10 Recording
See text on page 16 of the Student's Book.

Answers

1 *It takes seven years to digest chewing gum.*   F
2 *The Great Wall of China is the only man-made structure visible from the moon.*   F
3 *Flying is the safest way to travel.*   T
4 *Spinach is a great source of iron.*   F
5 *You get less wet by running in the rain rather than walking.*   F
6 *Lightning never strikes the same place twice.*   F

Optional activities

♦ Students find five new words in the article. They check the meaning in a dictionary, if possible an English-English dictionary and write the definitions for the five words. Students exchange their definitions and identify their partner's words in the text.

♦ Ask students if they know any more popular myths like the ones in the article. Discuss the myths as a class and decide if you believe them.

3

- The aim is to raise students' awareness of the use of general nouns and pronouns to link ideas in a text. Point out that there is one sentence from each paragraph. Do the first one together as an example.

Answers

1 *chewing gum*   2 *the Great Wall of China*   3 *flying*
4 *spinach*   5 *people*   6 *the Empire State Building*

4 LISTENING

- Students discuss the statements in pairs/small groups. Ask some students to report back on their ideas.
- Students listen to check their ideas. The aim here is to develop gist listening skills so tell students they only need to listen to find out whether the statements are true or false.

🔘 1.11 Recording

*1 The number of people alive today is greater than the
number who have ever died.*
*A lot of people say this, but it isn't true. The estimated
number of people who have died in the last 5,000 years
is about six billion, which is quite close to the current
world population. But the truth is that modern humans
appeared around 200,000 years ago. Most experts
believe the number of dead in human history is over
60 billion, around ten times more than the number of
people alive today.*
2 It's essential to drink at least eight glasses of water a day.
*This is a myth. Our bodies lose water daily, and we need
to replace it. But actually a lot of the water we need is
provided by the food we eat. And we don't have to drink
water – we can take in water by drinking milk, tea, fruit
juice and other soft drinks, although tap water is the
cheapest option if it's safe to drink. The sensible thing
is to drink regularly so you don't get thirsty – obviously
you are likely to want to drink more after taking
exercise, or when the weather is hot.*
3 We use only ten percent of our brains.
*This is nonsense. In fact, brain scans and other tests
show that most of the brain is used at one time or
another during a normal day. We use different parts of
our brain for different activities, for example, reading,
taking exercise, watching TV, listening to music, learning
a language – even sleeping. We don't use all our muscles
at the same time, so why should we use all of our brain
at the same time?*

Answers
All three statements are false.

5

- The aim is to develop listening for detail. Give students
time to read through the notes. Point out that more
than one word is needed to complete the sentences.
In pairs, students briefly discuss any answers they
remember.
- Students listen again to complete the notes. Students
compare their answers in pairs. If necessary, play the
recording again, pausing after each answer.

Answers
1
5,000 years is about 6 billion
200,000 years ago
60 billion
2
the food we eat
milk, tea, fruit juice and other soft drinks
drink regularly
3
*that most of the brain is used at one time or another during
a normal day*
*for example, reading, taking exercise, watching TV,
listening to music, learning a language – even sleeping*
why should we use all of our brain at the same time?

Optional activity

This is an alternative approach to the listening. Label
the incomplete notes in exercise 5 A, B and C for each
section. Students work in groups of three. Each student
in the group listens for the information to complete
one of the sentences for each section, e.g. one student
listens and completes all the A sentences, etc. Students
then exchange their information with their group to
form a complete set of notes. Play the recording again
for students to check each other's ideas.
With stronger classes, put students into pairs. Tell
them to take turns to read the sentences in exercise 4
to each other. The other student must reply with the
facts from the listening.

6 SPEAKING

- Students look at the expressions in the box for
correcting information. The expressions are all used
in the *Reality Check* article. Ask students to find these
expressions in the article and see how they are used.
- Give students one minute to look at their notes for
exercise 5. Students then tell each other the facts about
the three statements. They start by saying *Many people
think that …* and include one of the expressions for
correcting information.

7 GUIDED WRITING

- Students choose one of the statements and write a
paragraph about it. Ask students to use some of the
language from the *Reality Check* article, their notes from
exercise 5 and an expression for correcting information
from exercise 6. Encourage more confident students not
to copy their notes but use their own words.

Optional activity

Students write a short paragraph about a 'reality check'
of their own, e.g. Many people think that it would be
wonderful to be rich and famous. The truth is that people
who are rich and famous often have a difficult life.

8 LEARNER INDEPENDENCE

- The aim is to show students one way to help remember
new words and to show them all the aspects of a word.
The exercise also consolidates words from the unit.
- With a less confident class, do the first one together as
an example. Point out that the answers can be organised
as a word map, e.g.

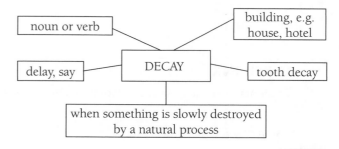

- Students answer all the questions for each of the words. Students then compare their answers with a partner and answer the final two questions.

Optional activities

- ◆ As an alternative, students could work in groups of three and do two words each and then exchange information.
- ◆ Each student finds a different word from the unit and answers the five questions. They then tell their partner the answers to the questions. Their partner listens and guesses the word they are describing.

9 WORD CREATION

- The aim is to build students' vocabulary by looking at noun and adjective forms. The exercise also makes students aware of some typical noun and adjective suffixes and some irregular forms.
- Students can try to complete the chart first and then check by looking back through the unit.

Answers

Noun	Adjective
acid	acidic
danger	dangerous
harm	harmless
health	healthy
herb	herbal
illness	ill
importance	important
reality	real
risk	risky
sense	sensible
strength	strong
thirst	thirsty
truth	true

Optional activities

- ◆ Fast-finishers can mark the stress on words of more than one syllable in the exercise. Ask if they notice anything (the stress sometimes moves when the part of speech changes, e.g. *acid, acidic*.
- ◆ Students race to write down three more nouns ending in *-th* or *-ance* or *-ness* or adjectives ending in *-ous* or *-ant* or *-y*.

EXTRA PRACTICE

If you would like to give your students more practice in nouns with adjective forms, e.g. *danger – dangerous*, please see the Vocabulary EXTRA! Worksheets on the Teacher's Resource Site (www.macmillanenglish.com/inspiration).

10 PHRASEBOOK

- Ask students to look through the unit to find the expressions, and look at how they are used. Be ready to help with translation as necessary.
- Play the recording, pausing after each expression for students to repeat.

  🔘 1.12 Recording and answers

  It's not a good idea to … (Lesson 1, exercise 2)
  That's a different matter. (Lesson 1, exercise 2)
  Not at all. (Lesson 1, exercise 2)
  Do you realise that …? (Lesson 1, exercise 2)
  It didn't work. (Lesson 3, exercise 2)
  It's nonsense. (Lesson 4, exercise 2)
  On the other hand … (Lesson 4, exercise 2)
  The sensible thing is to … (Lesson 4, exercise 5)

- Individually, students write sentences that could come before five of the expressions. They say their sentence to their partner who chooses the correct expression to continue. Monitor and help as necessary.
- Students can add expressions they like to their Personal Phrasebooks.

Follow-up activities

- ◆ In groups, students prepare a news bulletin in which information previously believed to be true is revealed as being false, e.g. *Research now shows that drinking a glass of red wine a day is good for you.* Students can use real information or invent it. There are three roles: a news presenter, a journalist and someone relevant to the story who is interviewed by the journalist. Students act out the news bulletin and take a class vote on the best performance and the most original idea.
- ◆ Students choose ten words from this lesson and previous lessons in the unit and make anagrams. In pairs, they exchange lists and see who can rewrite all the words correctly first.

HOMEWORK

Students ask friends and family whether they think the six statements in exercise 1 are true or false. They then write a report on their results. Suggest expressions students could use, e.g. *Nobody believed …, Most people believed …, My parents knew …*

WEBLINK

Students may like to visit www.thethinkingbusiness.co.uk/brainfacts to read more about the human brain.

Revision and Extension p19

Workbook Unit 1 Lesson 4 pp8–9

Inspiration EXTRA!

LANGUAGE LINKS

- Focus on the words in the box and ask students if any of the words are the same in their language. Elicit or explain that they are all international words that are used in many languages. Elicit that they all refer to food. Students read the descriptions and match them with the words. Allow time for them to compare their answers in pairs before you check with the class.

  Answers

  1 pizza   2 tea   3 curry   4 banana   5 coffee
  6 salad   7 yoghurt   8 chocolate   9 sushi
  10 hamburger

- If students have access to the internet in class, they can do this activity in pairs. Otherwise, they can do it for homework. Check the explanations with the whole class at the beginning of the next lesson.

  Answers

  Chop suey is a Chinese dish. The word comes from a Cantonese word meaning 'mixed bits'.
  Fondue is a Swiss or French dish of melted cheese. The word means 'melted' in French.
  Kebab came into English from the Arabic word kabab.
  An omelette is a dish of egg, which is beaten and then fried in a flat shape. It came into English from French.
  Paella is a Spanish dish of rice and fish.
  Salami is an Italian word for a cured sausage.
  Spaghetti is an Italian dish of long, thin pieces of pasta.
  Sauerkraut is a German dish of preserved cabbage. The name means literally 'sour cabbage' in German.
  A tandoor is a clay oven used for cooking in India, Pakistan and some other countries. Tandoori dishes are traditionally cooked in such an oven. The word came into English from the Urdu or Punjabi word.
  Tortillas are Mexican flat breads. The word is Spanish, and means literally 'a little cake'.

Optional activity

Give students two minutes to study the descriptions again then ask them to close their books. Divide the class into two teams and read out a word from the Language Links box to each team in turn. If they can give the correct origin of the word, they get a point. If not, the other team can offer an answer.

GAME   ACROSSWORDS

- Ask students to read the instructions carefully and look at the example. Check comprehension by asking *Where do you find the word?* (in Unit 1) *Do you choose a long or a short word?* (long) *How many times do you write it on the paper?* (three) Give students three minutes to find a suitable word, copy it onto a piece of paper as shown in the example, and make a second copy for their partner.

- Use the example to show that they need to find words that begin with the letter on the left and finish with the letter on the right. Tell students they win a point for each letter so the student in the example has 25 points (not including the first and last letters). If possible, provide students with dictionaries.

- Divide students into A and B. A gives B a copy of their paper. Students count up their scores. B then gives A a copy of their paper and they compete again. At the end, students total their scores to find out who the winner in their pair is and who the overall class winner is.

Optional activity

Do one as a class competition. Choose a word from the unit, e.g. *unhealthy*, and write it on the board as shown in the example. Students work in teams to find words and win points.

SKETCH   THE EXPERT

- The aim is for students to enjoy using their English while also reviewing language presented in this unit and getting valuable stress and intonation practice.

- Ask the students to look at the title and the cartoon. Ask *Who is the expert? What kind of advice does the woman want? How does the woman feel? Why?*

- With a more confident class, play the recording with books closed. With a less confident class, play the recording while the students follow in their books. Check the answers (the man is the expert, the woman wants advice on dying her clothes, she is getting angry because the man thinks she wants to go on a diet and to change her genes).

  🔘 1.13 Recording
  See text on page 18 of the Student's Book.

- Divide the class into two equal groups and play the recording again, with one group repeating the man's role in chorus and the other group repeating the woman's role. Encourage students to exaggerate stress and intonation.

- Ask the students to close their books and play the recording again. Then ask the students to work in pairs and practise the sketch. Choose several pairs to act out the sketch in front of the class.

Optional activity

Make an audio or video recording of students performing the sketch if possible.

REVISION

Lesson 1
Students' own answers.

Lesson 2

Answers

A bread knife is for slicing bread.
A cheese grater is for grating cheese.
A coffee maker is for making coffee.
A corkscrew is for opening bottles.
A frying pan is for frying food.
A kettle is for boiling water.
A tin opener is for opening tins.
A toaster is for making toast.

Lesson 3
Students' own answers.

EXTENSION

Lessons 1–3
Students' own answers.

YOUR CHOICE!

- The aim is to give students more learner independence and help them to identify their preferred way of learning. Encourage students to choose an activity that they feel less comfortable with if they want a challenge or are aware that they need practice in a particular area.
- Monitor and help groups. Check answers if necessary, or provide written answers for groups to check their own work against.

Language File pp112–113

CONSTRUCTION

Answers

1 going, to understand   2 to help, having
3 to take, to risk having   4 setting   5 to lock   6 meeting
7 to explain   8 taking   9 to give

REFLECTION

Answers

gerund
infinitive
forget, try
remember + infinitive
remember + gerund
either   same

ACTION

- Students work in small groups. Make sure each group has chosen six topics and one letter and that no students are using a dictionary.
- Students could report back on who scored the highest.

INTERACTION

- Students work in small groups. Allow students time to think of their ideas individually before they take turns to talk to their group. Encourage the listeners to ask questions.
- Students could report back to the rest of the class on any interesting points.

Workbook Unit 1 Inspiration EXTRA! pp10–11

Happiness and success

Focus on the title *Happiness and success* and the four captioned photos of the people. *Ask What are their names? Where are they from?* For the two photos at the bottom of the page ask, *Where are they? How are they feeling? Which of these two photos shows happiness? Which shows success?* Elicit a range of answers.

1 READING

- Focus on the four captioned photos of the people, then read the instructions for the task with the class. As a class, read the two questions in the text that were asked. Students read the text, then complete the statements with the correct names. Ask students to underline in the text where they found the answers. Check the answers and where they can be found as a whole group.
- Students could listen to the text and follow it in their books.

1.14 Recording

See text on page 20 of the Student's Book.

Answers

*1 Alex   2 Lucy   3 Takumi and Lucy   4 Alex   5 Natalia
6 Takumi   7 Lucy   8 Takumi and Lucy   9 Natalia
10 Natalia*

Optional activity

Students cover the texts and, in pairs, try to recall the opinions of the four teenagers. With stronger groups, you could give students one of the four roles each, and they could answer the questions again in small groups from memory.

2 VOCABULARY

- Ask students to find the words in the reading. Student use the context in the reading to help match the words to the definitions.

Answers

1 d   2 f   3 j   4 g   5 b   6 i   7 a   8 e   9 c   10 h

Optional activities

- With a confident class, students cover the words and try to find/recall the word in the text for each definition.
- Fast-finishers can mark the stress on the words and think of related words, e.g. *capitalist, essential, generosity.*

3 SPEAKING

- Students read the questions and think about their answers. Organise students into small groups to ask and then discuss their answers to the questions. Encourage students to note each other's answers as these notes will be useful for the following writing exercise.
- Monitor and note examples of good language and errors made. Write these on the board and ask students to identify and correct the errors.
- For each question, ask a different group to report their discussion back to the class. Encourage other students in the class to respond as they speak.

4 MINI-PROJECT
HAPPINESS AND SUCCESS

- Students work in pairs and discuss their answers to the two questions. They then work individually to write two paragraphs answering each question. Make sure they understand that they must give reasons for their points of view.
- Allow students time to read through and correct their work.
- Students then work in groups of three and read their paragraphs. They can discuss in their groups whether they agree or disagree with each other's views.

Optional activity

Choose one of the questions as a class. Allow students a few minutes to formulate their opinions. Tell students they are going to debate the question as a class. Revise expressions for giving opinions and agreeing and disagreeing, and write these on the board. Ask a confident student to start the debate by expressing an opinion. Encourage all students to join in and express their views.

WEBLINK

Students may like to visit news.bbc.co.uk/1/hi/programmes/happiness_formula/4785402.stm to read about happiness and take a quiz.

Workbook Culture pp12–13

 # I don't think it's art!

Communicative aims	Language	Pronunciation	Vocabulary
Talking about activities which continue up to now	Present perfect continuous with *for* and *since*	/b/ bare /p/ pair	Materials Art

WARMER 1

Write *Art* on the board and brainstorm different kinds of art with the whole class, e.g. *painting, sculpture, photographs, fashion designs, pop videos, graffiti, portraits, CD covers, living statues*. Ask students to discuss with a partner which of the things they think are and are not art, which they like best and their favourite examples of each. Ask some pairs to report back to the class.

WARMER 2

Game *Materials race*   Point to something in the room, e.g. the wall, and ask students *What's it made of?* (brick/ plaster). Give students one minute to work with a partner and make a list of materials they can see around them. The pair with the longest list reads their examples to the rest of the class and wins the game. Possible examples are *wood, glass, stone, rubber, plastic, gold, silver, cotton, concrete, brick.*

1 OPENER

- The aim is to introduce the context for the reading in exercise 2.
- Ask students to look at the photos of works of art. Before they discuss the questions, check that the students understand the materials in the box by asking for examples of typical objects made from each. Explain that *bronze* is the metal of the third Olympic medal and that *dung* is waste produced by animals. Students discuss the questions and photos in pairs. Ask some pairs to report back to the rest of the class.

2 READING

- Students read and listen to the text and match each artist with a photo A–D. Encourage students to concentrate on general understanding of the text at this stage and guess unknown words from context.

🔘 **1.15** **Recording**
See page 22 of the Student's Book for the text.

Answers

1 B   2 D   3 A   4 C

3 AFTER READING

- Students answer the questions individually. Check the answers together as a whole class.

Answers

1 Since the 1980s
2 Iron
3 Since the late 1980s
4 Concrete
5 Plastic, plaster, rubber and polystyrene
6 Since 1992
7 Bronze
8 He uses elephant dung.

Optional activities

- ♦ Ask the students to cover the text. Looking at the photos in pairs, have them remember as much as possible about each work of art.
- ♦ Divide the class into four groups according to their favourite work of art (A–D). Each group tries to 'sell' their work of art to the others. In their groups they plan how to explain what it's made of, what it shows, why it's interesting/beautiful/a good buy. Groups then present their artwork to the rest of the class. Students vote on which of the other three works they would buy.

Your response

Ask students to work in pairs to discuss the question. Ask some pairs to report back to the class.

4 LISTENING

Useful information

Living statues are street entertainers who paint their skin and clothes and stand still to look like a statue. They earn money by entertaining passers-by. An area of London which is well-known for living statues and other street entertainers, including jugglers and buskers, is Covent Garden.

- Ask the students *Is there anything unusual about the statue in the photo?* Try to elicit that it is a *living statue* (a person standing very still) and ask students if/where they have seen these before. Try to elicit ideas of what could be good or bad about the job.

- Allow students time to read through the questions. Stronger classes could predict the answers to the questions before they listen.
- Students listen to the recording and answer the questions.

1.16 Recording

GIRL Oh – look! It's a living statue! How long has she been standing there?

MAN I don't know, but I've been taking photos of her for about 10 minutes.

GIRL Has she been standing completely still?

MAN No, she moved once – I got a terrible shock. Until then I thought it was a real statue – you know, made of stone.

GIRL Excuse me – can I ask you some questions?

STATUE OK, I need to sit down for a bit. I've got backache.

GIRL How long have you been standing here?

STATUE For about an hour and a half.

GIRL Really? And you're quite wet.

STATUE Yes, I know, it's been raining.

GIRL How long have you been performing as a living statue?

STATUE Every weekend for about eighteen months.

GIRL And how did you learn to be a statue?

STATUE Well, I'm a drama student – I've been studying drama for two years.

GIRL Do you make much money as a living statue?

STATUE I've been trying to make some money, but it's hard work standing still!

Answers

1 10 minutes
2 No, she moved once
3 For about an hour and a half
4 Because it's been raining
5 Every weekend for about 18 months
6 Drama
7 To make some money

5 PRONUNCIATION

- Highlight the /b/ sound in *bare* and the /p/ sound in *pair*. Tell students that the mouth position with the lips together is the same for both sounds, but that if they place their hand gently on the front of their throat, they should feel vibration for /b/.
- Students listen and repeat the words in the table.

1.17 Recording

/b/ **bear** back bowl bulb cab symbol
/p/ **pair** pack pole pulp cap simple

- Ask students to listen and write down the words they hear in their notebooks.
- Ask students to compare what they have written in pairs.
- To check the answers, nominate different students to say each word and spell it. Write their spelling on the board and ask other students if they agree.

1.17 Recording and answers

pair back bowl pulp cap simple

Optional activity

Ask individual students to say a word from the pronunciation exercise. The other students identify if it is a word from column one or two.

Extension Have students work individually to think of five more words for each sound /b/ and /p/. Then have students work in pairs, tell each other their words and have their partner write them under the correct heading.

LANGUAGE WORKOUT OPTION

If you want to pre-teach the language students will use in the following activities, you may like to go to the Language Workout box now.

6 ROLE PLAY

- Set the context for the role play by asking students if they have seen or read any celebrity interviews recently.
- Divide the class into two groups, journalists and celebrities. Students look at the role play guide and prepare what to say. The journalists prepare their questions and the celebrities think about their identity, work, leisure and relationships. Encourage them to be imaginative and create an interesting interview. With weaker classes, students could work in pairs to prepare their ideas for the interview (with two 'celebrities' working together and two 'journalists' working together).
- Students work in journalist/celebrity pairs to do the role play. Ask some confident students to perform their interview in front of the class.
- Students change roles and repeat the role play with a different celebrity.

7 WRITING

- Ask students to write an article for the class magazine about the celebrity they interviewed in exercise 6. Remind them to use the present perfect continuous where necessary.
- Monitor and note examples of good language and errors. Put these on the board and ask students to identify and correct the errors.

LANGUAGE WORKOUT

- Ask students to look at the Language Workout box and complete the gaps. Confident students can complete first and then check, while others can look back at exercises 2 and 3 and then complete.
- Students turn to page 113 of the Language File to check their answers.

  ### Answers
  been making   has been using
  has ... been creating

- Highlight that:
  - the present perfect continuous is formed *has/have + been* + verb + *-ing*.
  - it is used to talk about a continuous or repeated activity which started in the past and continues now or which has present results.
  - *since* indicates the time the action started and *for* shows how long it has been going on. Both are used with the present perfect continuous (and simple) and answer the question *How long …?*
  - state verbs are not generally used in the present perfect continuous.
- Check students' understanding by asking questions, e.g. *Is she still working on her drawings and prints of birds now? How can we say 'since 1992' using 'for'?*
- Drill the examples for pronunciation, highlighting the *'s/'ve* contraction, the weak pronunciation of *been* /bɪn/ and the stress on the main verb.

Optional activity

Students work with a partner to ask and answer *How long …?* questions about the people in the text, e.g. *How long has Rachel Whitehead been creating unusual sculptures? Since the 1980s.*

PRACTICE

- Students do Practice exercise 4 on page 113 of the Language File. Go through the example with the whole class, eliciting possible answers with *for* and *since*.
- In pairs, students make the questions and answers.
- Ask different pairs to say a question and answer.

Answers

1 How long has Steven Spielberg been directing feature films? He's been directing feature films for … years / since 1971.

2 How long has Robbie Williams been performing pop songs? He's been performing pop songs for … years / since 1990.

3 How long has JK Rowling been writing stories? She's been writing stories for … years / since 1971 / since the age of 6.

4 How long has Orlando Bloom been acting? He's been acting for … years / since 1993.

5 How long has Beyonce been singing? She's been singing for … years / since she was seven / since 1988.

6 How long has Cristiano Ronaldo been playing professional football? He's been playing since he was 17 / since 2002 / for … years.

(Answers with 'for' depend on the current date.)

Optional activity

Students write sentences using present perfect continuous about activities that they have been doing, e.g. *I've been studying English for five years, I've been singing in a choir since I was 10.* Two sentences should be true and one false. They read the sentences to a partner who tries to spot the false statement.

Follow-up activities

- On the board, write a contentious statement about celebrities, e.g. *Celebrities earn too much money, Journalists should not follow celebrities when they are on holiday, There is too much celebrity gossip in magazines and newspapers.* Divide the class into students that agree and disagree with the statement. Groups formulate reasons why they agree/disagree, which they present to the other half of the class. Encourage students to respond to the other group's arguments to create a debate.
- Ask students to work in small groups to plan an art installation they would like to have in the school. They describe each work (type of art, colour, materials, size, meaning) and say where it would stand in the school and why they have chosen it. The rest of the class decides which group has the best plan.

HOMEWORK

Ask students to choose a favourite creative work, e.g. a painting, photograph, music, sculpture, film, CD cover and write a few sentences about it, e.g. why they like it, what it shows, what they know about the creator and how long he/she has been creating.

WEBLINK

Students may like to visit wikipedia.org/wiki/Contemporary_art to find out more about the world of contemporary art.

Revision and Extension p31

Language File p113

Workbook Unit 2 Lesson 1 pp14–15

Photocopiable worksheet p166, notes p155

2 CREATIVITY

2.2 I've been hoping ...

Communicative aims	Language	Pronunciation	Vocabulary
Talking about recent events	Present perfect simple and continuous	Syllable stress	Acting Film-making

WARMER 1

Game *Guess who?* Tell students that you are thinking of a famous actor and that they must ask you yes/no questions to try to guess their identity, e.g. *Is it a man? Is he over 40? Is he American?*

WARMER 2

Brainstorm as a class all the different people involved in making a film, e.g. *actors, director, producer, camera operator, set designer, costume designer, make-up artist, extras, script writer*. In pairs, students discuss what each person does and who has the easiest/best job.

1 OPENER

- The aim is to introduce the context for the reading in exercise 2.
- Establish what an *extra* is and ask students to discuss the questions in pairs. Encourage students to predict the working hours for an extra, and their pay and feelings about the job. Ask a few pairs to report their ideas to the class.

2 READING

- Tell students that they are going to read and listen to more about extras in a web forum (an open website to which visitors are invited to contribute).
- Students read and listen to the text, checking their predictions about the life of an extra. Encourage students to concentrate on general understanding of the text and to guess unknown words from context. Ask what facts they found most interesting.

🔘 1.18 Recording
See text on page 24 of the Student's Book.

3 AFTER READING

- Ask students to complete the questions with the missing words. Check the question forms as a class before students read the text again to answer the questions.

Answers
1 When   2 What   3 Who   4 Who   5 When (or What)
6 Who   7 Where   8 Who   9 Who   10 How   11 Who
12 How
1 6 or 7am   2 Calling the agencies   3 Jon   4 Anastasia
5 February/a football film   6 Nicky   7 On location
8 Nicky   9 Frankie   10 £85 or so a day   11 Nicky
12 Join an agency

Optional activity

Ask Which film would you most like to be an extra in? Why? *Ask students to discuss the question in pairs and then report back to the class. See if one film is popular with a lot of students.*

Your response

Ask students to work in pairs to discuss the questions. After a few minutes, put pairs together into groups of four to compare their answers. Ask a student from each group to report back on their discussions.

4 VOCABULARY

- Before looking at the box, ask students if they can remember any words or phrases connected with films.
- Students find the words and phrases in the box in the lesson and match them with a definition.

Answers
1 take   2 on screen   3 double   4 agency   5 on set
6 commercial   7 on location   8 feature film

Extension Students work individually or in pairs to write five sentences using the words and phrases in exercise 4. Ask some students to read their sentences to the class, and ask other students if they agree or disagree with the opinions.

5 PRONUNCIATION

- Students listen and check their answers to exercise 4. Pause between each word, so students can repeat the word and mark the stress.

🔘 1.19 Recording
1 t̲a̲k̲e̲   2 on sc̲r̲e̲e̲n̲   3 d̲o̲u̲ble   4 a̲gency   5 on s̲e̲t̲
6 comm̲e̲rcial   7 on loc̲a̲tion   8 f̲e̲ature film

LANGUAGE WORKOUT OPTION

If you want to pre-teach the language students will use in the following activities, you may like to go to the Language Workout box now.

6 SPEAKING

- Give an example of something you've always wanted to do and have done this year and of something you've been looking forward to doing, but haven't done yet. Alternatively refer students to the example sentences in the speech bubbles, checking which tenses are being used.
- Students make a list of five examples of each, using the prompts for ideas. Monitor and check correct use of present perfect simple and continuous.
- In pairs, students compare lists and discuss what they have written.

7 WRITING

- Read through the words and phrases in the box. Remind students that we use *but* in the middle of a sentence, but we use *however* at the beginning of a sentence. Check that students understand the meaning of *On the other hand*.
- Students write a paragraph comparing their own list with that of another student. With a less confident class, put model sentences on the board to follow, e.g. *We've both been looking forward to …, Marcus has always wanted to …, but I haven't.*
- Monitor and help with vocabulary and use of tenses. Make a note of good language and errors. With fast-finishers, highlight where they have made mistakes and encourage them to self-correct.
- Students check their own work for spelling, grammar and punctuation, before exchanging writing with a partner to read and check each other's work.
- Go through a few examples of good language or errors with the whole class, writing corrections on the board.

LANGUAGE WORKOUT

- Ask students to look at the Language Workout box and complete the sentences. Confident students can complete first and then check, while others can look back at exercises 2 and 3 and then complete.
- Students turn to page 113 of the Language File to check their answers.

  Answers
  has been   I've (only) had   I've been working
  I've been calling   I've had
  's been ringing

- Highlight:
- the present perfect continuous is formed with *has/have + been +* verb *+ -ing*, while the present perfect is formed *has/have +* past participle.
- the uses of the two tenses are described in the grammar box.
- that state verbs are not generally used in the present perfect continuous.
- Check students' understanding by asking *Which do we use to focus on 'how long'?* (present perfect continuous) and *Which on 'how many'?* (present perfect simple).
- Drill the examples in chorus for pronunciation and point out the pronunciation of *have* in the question form *How long have …?*
- If students ask why the present perfect simple is used, instead of the past simple, to describe a completed action or series of actions, point out that the choice of the present perfect tense still implies some connection to the present, e.g. *I've only had two jobs so far* (but I'm still looking and expecting to get more jobs now), *Some of the work has been quite badly paid* (with reference to work that has been offered this week).

PRACTICE

- Students do Practice exercise 5 on page 113 of the Language File. They read the text quickly, without completing the gaps, to find out what Adrian's job change was and what kind of work he has done (from a teacher to an extra; he's worked on over 40 films and TV shows).
- Students complete the gaps with the present perfect simple or continuous. Encourage students to check their answers with a partner before checking them together as a class. If the students have doubts about the answers, read through the notes in the Language File with the class to establish the reason for each choice of tense.

  Answers
  1 has made   2 has appeared   3 've been working
  4 've never been   5 've been doing   6 've just changed
  7 has been working   8 've shown   9 've had
  10 haven't been sitting

HOMEWORK

Students think of five questions they would like to ask one of the extras, *e.g. Why did you decide to become an extra?* They write out the questions and anticipated answers in the form of a magazine interview.

WEBLINK

Students may like to visit www.actingbiz.com for more information on how to become an extra.

Revision and Extension p31

Language File p113

Workbook Unit 2 Lesson 2 pp16–17

Photocopiable worksheet p167, notes p155

2 CREATIVITY

3 She had been reading a book

Communicative aims	Language	Pronunciation	Vocabulary	Optional aids
Talking about a sequence of past events	Past perfect simple and continuous	Syllable stress	Books Story telling	Follow-up activity: pictures of people and activities

WARMER 1

Write jumbled sentences using present perfect simple or continuous from the previous lesson, e.g. *so jobs I've only far two had.* Students put the words in the right order to reconstruct the sentences.

WARMER 2

Ask *What books do you like reading? Why?* Try to elicit some possible 'ingredients' of a good book from the students. If they have no ideas, you could suggest: *interesting characters, description of places, funny dialogue, romance, suspense.* In pairs, students discuss which of the ingredients are most important for them and what makes them choose a book.

1 OPENER

- The aim is to introduce the context for the reading in exercise 2.
- Ask students to discuss the question in pairs. Ask one or two pairs to report back to the class.

2 READING

- Ask students to look at the pictures and establish whether they know the author or the book. Encourage students to guess the answer to the question before reading and listening to the text. Encourage students to guess unknown words from context.

  🔘 1.20 **Recording**
  See text on page 26 of the Student's Book.

  Answer
  She had a dream about a scientist creating a monster.

3 AFTER READING

- Students read the text again and say if the sentences are true or false or if no information is given. Ask them to underline the words in the text that helped them decide on their answers.
- Check the true/false answers as a class before students correct the false sentences. Monitor and help where necessary.

Answers
1 True.
2 False. The eruption was the previous year.
3 False. She had written stories as a child.
4 True.
5 False. She began writing it in June 1816.
6 False. The book was about chemistry.
7 False. The scientist is called Frankenstein.
8 No information given on use of electricity.
9 False. He was horrified by it.
10 True.

Optional activity

Fast-finishers can find words connected to books and writing in the text, e.g. *best-selling, adventure story, comic, novel, folk tales, ghost stories, Greek myths.* They can list the words on the board for the rest of the class.

Your response

Put students into pairs to discuss the questions. Ask students to report back on their answers.

4 PRONUNCIATION

- Ask students to look at the words in the box, count the syllables and mark the stress. Do *abroad* as an example first, then ask students to do the rest in pairs.
- Play the recording for students to check their answers. Pause between words to confirm the answers and for students to repeat each word.

  🔘 1.21 **Recording and answers**
  ■ ■ ■ ■ ■
  abandon   artificial   author   chemistry   childhood
  ■ ■ ■ ■
  electricity   eruption   horrified   inspire
  ■ ■ ■ ■
  interact   investigate   precious   terrified

  2 syllables: author, childhood, inspire, precious
  3 syllables: abandon, chemistry, eruption, horrified, interact, terrified
  4 syllables: artificial, investigate
  5 syllables: electricity

Optional activity

Divide the students into teams of four or five and ask them to look back through the book and choose 10 words of more than one syllable and write them in a list. Groups swap lists, mark the stress and indicate the number of syllables for each word. They get their original list back and mark the work of the other group, giving them a score out of 20 (1 point for correct stress, 1 for correct number of syllables).

LANGUAGE WORKOUT OPTION

If you want to pre-teach the language students will use in the following activities, you may like to go to the Language Workout box now.

5 SPEAKING

- Ask students to look at the picture. Elicit that it shows a café, a girl, her boyfriend, an artist and a waiter.
- Students make sentences about the people and what had been happening, using the verbs in the box in the past perfect continuous. Elicit an example from the class before the students work in pairs to make more sentences.

Suggested answers

The girl had been doing a crossword, reading a book, drinking coffee, looking at her watch and waiting for her boyfriend.
Her boyfriend had been shopping and running.
The artist had been drawing the girl, drinking juice and eating.
The waiter had been washing his hands.

Optional activity

To review and contrast present and past perfect continuous, stronger students write a dialogue between the girl and her boyfriend, starting with the girl saying *I've been waiting for ages. What have you been doing?* Confident students could act out their dialogue in front of the class.

Extension Students work individually to write three true and two false sentences about the picture. Then have them work in pairs to work out which sentences are false.

6 LISTENING

Useful information

Students may be familiar with Roald Dahl's famous stories, including *Charlie and the Chocolate Factory*, the story of a boy who wins a competition to visit Willy Wonka's chocolate factory. The story was re-made as

a film in 2005, starring Johnny Depp. Other famous Roald Dahl works include *James and the Giant Peach*, made into an animated film by Disney in 1996, *Matilda*, *The Twits*, *Revolting Rhymes* and *The BFG*.

- Ask students if they know of Roald Dahl or any of his books. Ask students to read the biography chart and, with a partner, guess what kind of information is needed for each gap, e.g. *Born in* + place.
- Students listen to the recording and complete the gaps in the chart.

1.22 Recording and answers

*Roald Dahl was born in **Wales** on 13 September, 1916. His parents were Norwegian and he was named after the famous explorer Roald Amundsen. Dahl went to school in the UK but he spent his summer holidays in Norway. After Dahl had left school in **1934**, he started working for the Shell Petroleum Company in **London**. In 1938 he was sent by Shell to **East Africa**, but the second world war started the following year. So, in November **1939**, Dahl joined the Royal Air Force in **Kenya**. In September 1940 he was badly injured when he crash-landed in the Libyan desert. The doctors said he would never fly again. But after he'd spent **five months** in hospital, he took to the air in **1941** as a fighter **pilot** in Greece and Syria.*
*In 1942 Dahl was sent to **Washington**, and there he started to write short stories for **adults**. His first collection of stories, Over to You, was published in **1946**. He married **American actress** Patricia Neal in 1953 and they had **five** children. In **1957** Dahl started writing books for **children** because he'd been making up bedtime stories for his daughters.*
*In 1960 Dahl and his family moved to **England**, where he continued writing until he died on **23 November** 1990. His stories for both children and adults have been translated into dozens of languages and are best-sellers all over the world. Extremely popular books include Charlie and the Chocolate Factory and Tales of the Unexpected.*

- In pairs, students check their answers, linking the events together using the past perfect simple and continuous, where possible, following the example. With weaker classes, do a few examples with the whole class before students work in their pairs.
- Check the answers by asking different students to read out their sentences to the whole class.

7 WRITING

- Brainstorm the names of other popular authors.
- Ask students to choose one and find out information about him/her, using the Internet, books, other students and their own knowledge. They should make notes using the chart in exercise 6 as a basis.
- Students write two or three paragraphs about the author, using the text in exercise 2 as a model.
- Monitor and help with vocabulary and use of tenses.
- When they have checked their own work, students read that of other students and choose the best for the class magazine.

Optional activities

♦ Students work in pairs. They read their paragraphs to their partner and their partner takes notes in chart form, using the chart in exercise 6 as a model.

♦ Students read their paragraphs to each other, leaving out the name of the author. Their partner tries to guess the author.

LANGUAGE WORKOUT

• Ask students to look at the Language Workout box. Focus on the timeline and check that students understand the meaning of the past perfect simple and continuous.

• Students complete the gaps. Confident students can complete first and then check, while others can look back at exercises 2 and 3 and then complete.

• Students turn to page 113 of the Language File to check their answers.

Answers
realised, hadn't made, had produced had been thinking, had started, had been reading

Past perfect continuous
• Highlight that:

– the past perfect continuous is formed *had + been* + verb + *-ing*, while the past perfect is formed *had + past participle*.

– we use these tenses to emphasise that something happened or was happening before another past event. If the earlier action was continuous or repeated, we use the past perfect continuous.

• Check students' understanding by asking questions about the examples and timeline, e.g. *Was Pullman a teacher or a full time writer first? Was his teaching a continuous or a single event?*

• Drill the examples in chorus for pronunciation, reminding students of the *'d* contraction and the weak pronunciation of *been* /bɪn/.

PRACTICE

• Students do Practice exercise 6 on page 114 of the Language File. They complete the gaps with past simple and past perfect tenses, using the past perfect continuous where possible.

Answers
1 was, had been
2 wrote, had (had)
3 had been reading, started
4 had created, abandoned
5 decided, had killed
6 had been writing, was

Optional activity

Ask students to write three sentences similar to sentence 1 about themselves, e.g. *By the time I was 11, I had …* They could also change the age, e.g. *By the time I was 5, I …*. With weaker classes, write the sentence stems on the board for students to use for their own sentences, and elicit which tense should be used for each gap, e.g. *By the time I was …, I …; I … for years before I …; After I …, I started …*

Follow-up activities

♦ Bring a selection of pictures cut out from magazines and newspapers showing people doing activities, similar to the café scene in exercise 7. In pairs, students are given a picture each, which they keep secret from other students. They prepare and write sentences about what they think had happened or had been happening before the picture was taken. Collect in all the pictures and writing, jumble them and stick them randomly on the walls. Students walk around the room, trying to identify which writing goes with which picture.

♦ **Game** *Which author?* Students work in groups of three or four, with one 'writer' per group. Read out information about different authors, e.g. Roald Dahl and Mary Shelley, and ask students to identify and write down the correct author. Possible information could be: *He/She started writing after having a dream. He/She was injured during the war.* Include information about other authors known to the students, e.g. those written about in exercise 7.

HOMEWORK

Ask students to find a book which they have enjoyed and prepare some sentences about the story and the author. They should bring the book to the next lesson and tell other students about it. This could lead to a book exchange if students are happy for other students to borrow the book.

WEBLINK

Students may like to visit www.teenreads.com for information about popular books among English-speaking teenagers.

Revision and Extension p31

Language File pp113–114

Workbook Unit 2 Lesson 3 pp18–19

Photocopiable worksheet p168, notes p155

Integrated Skills Telling a folk tale

Skills

Reading Connecting ideas: *The Professor and the Wise Ferryman*
Listening Checking predictions

Speaking Discussion
Writing A folk tale

Learner independence

Thinking skills
Word creation:
noun suffix -*ment*

Vocabulary

School subjects
Folk tales
Useful expressions

Optional aids

Follow-up activity 2: photos of different people
Exercise 3 Optional activity: word cards

Useful information

The story of William Tell: At one time, the Swiss people were ruled over by an Austrian named Gessler, who insisted that all his people bowed down before a monument to him. One man, William Tell, who was famously good at shooting with a crossbow, refused to obey. As a punishment, he was ordered to shoot an arrow at an apple balanced on top of his son's head. William successfully hit the apple. He proved his own skill, kept his son safe and some time later, shot an arrow at Gessler to kill him and liberate his country.

WARMER

Focus on the picture and the title of the reading. Check that students understand *professor, ferryman, row* and *briefcase*. Ask *What do you think the professor knows about? What do you think the ferryman knows about? Who do you think knows more? Whose knowledge is more valuable/useful?*

1 OPENER

- The aim is to set the context for the reading.
- Ask students if they know the Swiss story of William Tell. If not, tell them the story. Elicit examples of folk stories from your own country. Be ready to give a few examples in case students do not have any ideas.

Optional activity

Dictate a summary of the William Tell story for the students to write down in their notebooks. They compare what they have written with a partner, whilst you write the correct version on the board, so that they can correct their work.

2 READING

- Give students five minutes to read the text and complete with phrases a–i. Encourage students to guess unfamiliar words from context and tell them that the meaning of the highlighted words will be dealt with in exercise 3. Be prepared to translate *wise*.

- Play the recording for students to check their answers. Ask students which words in the phrases helped them complete the gaps, to help less confident students understand the answers.

🔘 1.23 Recording

The Professor and the Wise Ferryman – an Indian folk tale
There was once an old ferryman who lived in a hut by the River Ganges in India. For as long as anyone could remember his family had rowed people across the river. His father had been a ferryman and so had his grandfather before him.

Like all the people from his village the ferryman was poor. The money he made from the ferry was hardly enough to feed his family. He had taken over the job when he was a young boy and had been doing it ever since. Although life was hard, he never grumbled and was pleased to help his passengers.

The ferryman had learnt a lot about life by listening to his passengers. He had heard about life in the city, but couldn't understand why people chose to live there. It seemed to him that city people spent all their lives rushing about with no time to think. The ferryman rowed slowly and was in no hurry. He had time to talk and think about things. People said that he was wise and often asked his advice.

One day a well-dressed professor from the city with a shiny briefcase climbed into his boat. He was wearing a smart suit and well-polished shoes. Slowly the ferryman began to row his passenger across the river. After a while the professor spoke.

'Have you studied any history?' he asked.

'No, sir,' said the ferryman.

'What!' said the professor in surprise. 'You haven't studied history? Aren't you proud of your country? Why don't you know any history?'

'Well, sir,' the ferryman replied, 'I've never been to school. I've been rowing people across the river all my life, so I haven't learnt any history.'

'There's no excuse for not learning,' said the professor. 'And I suppose you haven't studied geography either.'

'No, sir,' the ferryman replied.

'Geography tells us about the world,' the professor said almost angrily. 'Don't you know anything about the world – the countries, mountains and rivers?'

'I haven't been to school, sir,' the ferryman replied. 'I don't know anything about these things.'

After a few minutes, the professor asked if the ferryman had studied science, and got the same answer. 'You've studied neither geography nor history, and you haven't heard about science!' he shouted in amazement. 'Scientists are the most important people in the world today. Look at me. I'm a professor of science. Do you see my briefcase? It's full of important books and papers. If you don't know about science, you don't know about the world. You have learnt nothing! And if you don't know anything, you might as well be dead.'

The ferryman looked sad. No one had ever spoken to him like this before. He felt terrible. There was so much knowledge hidden in books which he had never learnt.

Answers

1 b   2 h   3 e   4 g   5 c   6 d   7 f   8 i   9 a

3

- The aim is to encourage the students to deduce meaning from context. Ask the students to match highlighted words in the text with definitions 1–6.

Answers

1 professor   2 rushing   3 amazement   4 hardly
5 shiny   6 grumbled

Optional activities

♦ Ask students to find examples of the past perfect and past perfect continuous in the text. Look at the verbs as a class and discuss why one tense is used in each case.

♦ Fast-finishers can put the words on cards for the vocabulary box, with a definition or example sentence on the reverse.

4

- Ask the students to find an example of *neither … nor …* in *The Professor and the Wise Ferryman*. Write the example *You've studied neither geography nor history* on the board. Check that students understand by eliciting the equivalent, *You haven't studied geography or history*. Point out that *neither … nor* gives a negative meaning to the sentence, *but* is used with affirmative verbs.
- Students rewrite the sentences using *neither … nor …*
- Nominate students to say their sentences to the class, correcting their pronunciation where necessary.

Answers

1 The ferryman had neither a suit nor a briefcase.
2 The ferryman had neither been to school nor university/ had been to neither school nor university.
3 The ferryman had studied neither history nor science.
4 Neither the ferryman nor the professor knew what was going to happen next.

Optional activity

Ask fast-finishers to write a sentence about themselves and members of their family using *neither … nor*.

5

- Ask the students to discuss the questions about the story with a partner. Elicit a range of ideas for what will happen next in the story.

6 LISTENING

- Play the recording for students to check their predictions from exercise 5.
- Ask students to discuss the questions with a partner. Check their ideas as a class, encouraging them to deduce the meaning of unknown vocabulary, such as *capsize*, from context. Try to elicit different ideas on the message of the story and students' feelings about it.

◯ 1.24 Recording

Suddenly dark clouds moved across the sky and there was a roar of thunder. 'We're going to be caught in the storm,' said the ferryman. 'Can you swim?' The professor was terrified and held on tightly to his briefcase. 'Oh dear!' he cried. 'I can't swim. I've never learnt to.'
Lightning flashed, a strong wind blew and rain poured down. Huge waves crashed over the tiny boat. Then a giant wave hit the boat and it capsized, throwing both men into the water. The old ferryman lost sight of his passenger and swam slowly to the shore. But the professor, still holding on tightly to his briefcase, disappeared in the dark waters of the river.

Answers

1 Their boat capsized. The ferryman swam slowly to shore, but the professor disappeared/drowned.
2 'Education' from real life can be more helpful than formal education. Or students' own answers.

7 SPEAKING

- Divide students into small groups to discuss the questions.
- Ask a student from each group to report back to the whole class on their discussion. Continue with a whole-class discussion if students have a lot of ideas.

Optional activity

Pyramid discussion: Ask students to write down the five subjects/skills they think are most important to learn in life, e.g. *sewing, communication, maths*. They compare lists with a partner and agree on the five most important from their two lists. They then compare with another pair in a group of four, then again in a group of eight, until a whole class consensus can be reached.

8 GUIDED WRITING

- Focus on the time phrases and adverbs in the box, and ask students to find examples of them in the story. Point out that they are used to show the sequence of events.
- Ask students to find examples of different narrative tenses that are used in the story (past simple, past perfect, past perfect continuous). Elicit or point out that the past simple is used for the main events of the story, and the past perfect and past perfect continuous are used for things that happened earlier.

- Brainstorm national folk tales as a class, writing a list on the board. Students discuss the story and possible message of each, with a partner.
- Ask students to choose one of the folk tales from their country, using the text in exercise 2 as a model. Remind them to use narrative past tenses, and time phrases and adverbs. Encourage them to try to use examples of *neither ... nor* to link ideas.
- Monitor and help where necessary. Note down errors or examples of good language.
- When they have checked their own work, students exchange writing with a partner to read and check each other's work.
- Go through a few examples of good language or errors with the whole class, writing corrections on the board for students to copy down.

9 LEARNER INDEPENDENCE

- The aim is to encourage students to think more about their learning.
- Students complete the chart individually at the end of the week, and each week subsequently. With a less confident class, go through each sentence first as a class, eliciting an example to check students can complete them accurately. With a confident class, encourage students to discuss their sentences with a partner rather than checking as a class.
- Point out that where the chart says *A problem for me at the moment is*: students should fill in a date by when they would like to have solved the problem.

10 WORD CREATION

- Ask students if they can remember the noun from the folk tale meaning *great surprise* (Answer: *amazement*). Write the suffix *-ment* on the board and elicit other examples of nouns ending with this suffix, e.g. *excitement, disappointment*.
- Students add the suffix *-ment* to the nouns in the box. Check the correct spelling of *argument* and check the meaning of *treatment* by asking *Where can you get treatment for a broken leg?*
- Students use five of the nouns to complete the sentences. Check the answers as a class.
- Students copy the words into their vocabulary notebooks.

Answers

1 amazement   2 argument   3 payment
4 advertisement   5 movement
(*arrangement, equipment, treatment* are not used)

Optional activity

Students write example sentences for the other three nouns ending in *-ment*.

EXTRA PRACTICE

If you would like to give your students more practice in forming words with the suffix *-ment*, please see the Vocabulary EXTRA! Worksheets on the Teacher's Resource Site (www.macmillanenglish.com/inspiration).

11 PHRASEBOOK

- Students look through Unit 2 to find the expressions, noting how they are used.
- Play the recording and students listen and repeat.
- Students find which expressions match meanings 1–4.

1.25 Recording and answers

Lesson 2, exercise 2
It's a complete waste of money!
Believe it or not
So what's it like?
No luck yet.
That's odd!

Lesson 4, exercise 2
after a while
There's no excuse for ...
You might as well ...

1 That's odd!   3 Believe it or not
2 after a while   4 No luck yet

Optional activity

Students work in pairs and think of a situation in which they might say each expression, e.g. *So what's it like? (A person asking a friend about a new CD.)* Students can add expressions they like to their Personal Phrasebook.

Follow-up activity

♦ **Game** *Subjects quiz*   Ask students to name 8–10 important subjects, e.g. history, music, health. In small groups, students write one quiz question on each subject, e.g. *Geography: What is the capital city of Iceland?* Groups exchange papers and have five minutes to answer the questions, before returning the paper. The group with the most correct answers wins.

HOMEWORK

Ask students to write a paragraph giving their opinion on one of the questions discussed in exercise 7.

WEBLINK

Students may want to visit www.mainlesson.com/display.php?author=baldwin&book=fifty&story=_contents
to read more traditional stories.

Revision and Extension p31

Workbook Unit 2 Lesson 4 pp20–21

Inspiration EXTRA!

Optional aids
Newspapers, magazines and the Internet

PROJECT   GROUP MAGAZINE

1

- Explain to students that the aim of the project is to write a collection of articles for a group magazine. If your class have already started a class magazine (Unit 1, lesson 1, Writing optional activity), this is an opportunity to extend it. If not, it is a chance to start one which can be added to in subsequent writing activities.
- Divide the students into groups.
- Give students three minutes to make a list of creative subjects which they could contribute to the magazine, pointing out the examples given and the ideas shown in the photograph.
- Groups then choose people or topics to write about.

2

- Ask students to find out information for their articles using newspapers, magazines and the Internet. Remind them to take notes, for example based on the questions in the box. Encourage students to find examples of articles, reviews and interviews in the magazines and newspapers to use for ideas on how to structure their own.

3

- Ask students to read the example article about Miss Jones. Ask *Is it written in a formal or informal style?* (informal). Point out that it uses questions, quotes and exclamations to make it interesting.
- Students work together to write the articles. Encourage them to write in an informal style and make the articles interesting.
- Students read their work carefully to correct any mistakes. They then copy the articles out neatly and choose photos from magazines or newspapers to illustrate their work.
- Students show their magazine articles to other groups and put them together in a file to make their own group magazine. Encourage them to think about how best to group together and order their work and make an interesting magazine that people will want to read. If you prefer, students could choose the best articles from each group to put together into a class magazine.

GAME   ALIBI

- Set the context by telling the students about the crime that was committed yesterday evening. Check that they understand *suspect* and *alibi*.
- Choose two confident students to be the suspects and ask them to prepare their alibi together, using the information in the first box. Encourage them to prepare as many details as possible, e.g. times and places, as they must both give exactly the same story to the police to prove that they were together yesterday evening. If possible, the two suspects should go to another room to prepare their alibis.
- The other students are the detectives and prepare as many questions as possible to ask the suspects about yesterday evening, using the ideas in the second box.
- Suspect B stays outside the room while the detectives ask Suspect A their questions and note down the answers.
- Suspect B returns and the detectives ask the same questions.
- The detectives decide whether or not the suspects' stories match and if they are therefore guilty or innocent.

REVISION

Lesson 1
- Remind students to use the phrases in the box and the example to help.
Students' own answers.

Lesson 2
Students' own answers.

Lesson 3
- Remind students to check their work carefully for grammar, correct tenses, spelling and punctuation.
Students' own answers.

EXTENSION

Lesson 1
Students' own answers.

Lesson 2
- Remind students to look at the differences between present perfect simple and continuous.
Students' own answers.

Lesson 3
- Encourage students to be imaginative in their responses as there is more than one possible answer.

Students' own answers.

YOUR CHOICE!

- The aim is to give students more learner independence and help them to identify their preferred way of learning. Encourage students to choose an activity that they feel less comfortable with if they want a challenge or are aware that they need practice in a particular area.
- Monitor and help groups. Check answers if necessary, or provide written answers for groups to check their own work against.

CONSTRUCTION

Answers

*1 had been rescuing   2 had first appeared   3 had arrived
4 had come   5 had taken   6 had not been   7 had met
8 had been living*

Language File pp113–114

Song – photocopiable worksheet p187, notes p162

REFLECTION

Answers

1 b, d, f   2 a   3 c, e

ACTION

- Students work in small groups. Each person thinks of activities to mime to the others.
- They take it in turns to perform their mimes, as if in a film. After 5–10 seconds, someone says *Pause!* and the performer stops, as if in freeze frame. The other students in the group ask *yes/no* questions to guess what the performer has been doing.

INTERACTION

- Students work in small groups. Each person thinks of a favourite possession, using the example questions to prepare what they will say.
- Students take it in turns to ask and answer questions about each other's favourite possessions. Remind students to try to use the correct tenses, e.g. to say how long they have had the possession.

You may now like students to do the song *Spooky*. See p162 for the notes and p187 for the worksheet.

Workbook Unit 2, Inspiration EXTRA! pp22–23

1 Ask students to look at the picture and headline and predict what the boy does. Give students one minute to read the story and check their predictions. Students read the story again and choose the appropriate word for each space. Do the first one together as an example. This can be done in pairs or individually as a short test.

> **Answers**
>
> 1 A   2 A   3 B   4 B   5 C   6 B   7 C   8 B   9 C
> 10 A   11 B   12 C

> **Optional activity**
>
> Confident students can attempt the task before looking at the word options.

2 Students write sentences using the infinitive or gerunds of the verbs. Do the first one together as an example.

> **Answers**
>
> 1 applying, to hope   2 getting, to go   3 to look, to stay
> 4 being, to get   5 arriving   6 to see
> 7 to double, to do, to see   8 being, to say

3 Set the context by asking *What does the photo show? What has happened?* Students read the paragraph quickly to check their prediction, before reading again to complete the gaps with the present perfect continuous of the verbs and *for* or *since*.

> **Answers**
>
> 1 for   2 Since   3 has been collecting   4 have been using
> 5 have been talking   6 've been visiting   7 for
> 8 have been getting   9 since   10 have been walking
> 11 for   12 since   13 have been considering

> **Optional activity**
>
> Ask fast-finishers to cover the text and looking only at the verbs in the box, try to remember how each was used in the paragraph.

4 Students complete the text with the present perfect simple or continuous of the verbs in the box.

> **Answers**
>
> 1 has been showing   2 have started
> 3 have been developing   4 have won   5 have sold
> 6 has given   7 has been getting   8 've been working
> 9 has rung   10 have answered   11 have let

5 Ask students to read the text quickly, to find out what the competition was, who won it and why. Check their ideas as a class (Answers: *A painting competition, the second painter, because his painting was so life-like that it fooled the people*). Be prepared to translate *fooled* if necessary. Students read the text again to complete the gaps with the past perfect simple or continuous.

> **Answers**
>
> 1 had been   2 had finished   3 had invited
> 4 had arrived   5 had been waiting   6 had been flying
> 7 had been waiting   8 had fooled   9 had fooled
> 10 had found

> **Optional activity**
>
> Students discuss with a partner whether or not they think art should be realistic and true to life.

VOCABULARY

6 Students complete the sentences with the correct word from each pair in the box.

> **Answers**
>
> 1 snooze   2 poor   3 myths   4 screens   5 bowl
> 6 needles   7 crowds   8 diet   9 chop   10 lives
> 11 cream   12 toast

> **Optional activities**
>
> ♦ Drill the pairs of words for pronunciation practice, highlighting the sound differences.
> ♦ Students say words from the box to their partner, who identifies if they were saying the first or the second word from any pair.

7 Students match the verbs with the words and phrases. Remind students that it is useful to learn words that go together.

> **Answers**
>
> 1 beat the eggs   2 catch sight of something
> 3 charge a mobile phone   4 come up with an idea
> 5 skip a meal   6 sprinkle with cheese   7 take vitamins

> **Optional activity**
>
> Fast-finishers can write example sentences including these expressions.

8 Students match the words and definitions. Confident students can attempt the task without looking at the words in the box, and then check.

> **Answers**
>
> 1 margarine   2 mineral   3 struggle   4 grater
> 5 heritage   6 tribute   7 domestic

9 Students choose the word which is different from the others in the group. Ask students to explain their choices. Do the first one together as an example.

> **Answers**
>
> *1 fresh (all the others are ways of preserving foods)*
> *2 juice (all the others are contained in different foods)*
> *3 consist (all the others are sense verbs)*
> *4 cook (all the others are specific ways of cooking)*
> *5 natural (all the others are not natural)*
> *6 agency (all the others are things we watch on screen)*
> *7 wood (all the others are metals)*
> *8 comic (all the others are types of story. A comic is the object, not the story itself)*

Optional activity

Fast-finishers can make other odd word groups to test each other.

LEARNER INDEPENDENCE SELF ASSESSMENT

- Explain to students that the aim of the self-assessment is to encourage them to check their own progress and take any necessary action to improve. Point out that the list 1–7 covers areas of functional language from Units 1 and 2. Students tick the 'Fine' box for functional language that they feel confident using, but put a question mark in the 'Not sure' box for functional language that they have difficulties with or still cannot use confidently.
- Encourage students to look at the Language File and re-do exercises from the Workbook in areas where they have problems. They may also like to re-do exercises from the lessons and from the Revision and Extension sections in Units 1 and 2.
- Students write an example sentence for each language area in the list. You may like to elicit the grammar students need for each example before students write their sentences, e.g *Talking about food and drink: verbs not used in continuous forms*. Students can refer back to the lessons and the Language File.
- Ask students to compare their sentences with a partner's and to discuss and correct any mistakes.
- Check their sentences and note down any language areas for further practice.

Follow-up activities

- ♦ **Game** *Outburst* Divide students into groups of three students and give each group a vocabulary area, where possible related to the previous units, e.g. *materials, recipe verbs, health and illness, food and drink, film words*. Groups write a list of six examples in their category, e.g. *materials: stone, plaster*. They do this silently. Groups then take it in turns to say their category name and ask all the other groups to write a list of any items they guess have been included in the prepared list. They may write more than six. After one minute, the original list is read out and other groups score points for how many they correctly guessed.
- ♦ **Game** *Noughts and crosses* Draw the grid below on the board. Divide the class into two teams: Noughts (O) and Crosses (✕). Each team chooses a square and gives an example sentence using the relevant grammar item or structure. If their sentence is correct, they write O or ✕ in the square. The first team to get a line of three noughts or crosses in any direction wins.

neither	past perfect simple	present perfect continuous
since	gerund as a subject	verb + infinitive
past perfect continuous	verb + -ing form	*on the contrary*

HOMEWORK

Ask students to find an interesting story in a newspaper or magazine with an accompanying photo. It can be in their own language or in English. They should write an English headline to accompany the photo and write three or four sentences to summarise the key points of the story.

WEBLINK

Students may want to visit entertainment.howstuffworks.com/stuntmen6 to find out more about the work of stuntmen and women.

Language File pp112–114

Workbook Review Units 1–2 pp24–25

Units 3–4

Activities		Project	Vocabulary
Identifying the function of communicative language	Categorising vocabulary Contextualising listening extracts	Time travel	Space flight Medicine Politics

WARMER 1

Game *Vocabulary challenge* Ask students to focus on the photos on pages 34–35 and, in pairs, brainstorm as much vocabulary as they can to do with each picture. Set a time limit of two minutes for the activity. Bring the vocabulary together as a class and see who managed to write the most words.

WARMER 2

Ask students to look at the photos and captions/speech bubbles on pages 34–35 and to match them with the topics on page 34. Ask *Which topic do you find most interesting? Which one do governments spend most money on? Which do you think they should spend more money on? Why?* Lead a class discussion which could cover areas such as whether more money should be spent on medicine or space exploration, studying the natural world or developing new technologies.

1 • The aim is to introduce students to the main areas of communicative language they will cover in Units 3 and 4.
   • Focus on the two boxes at the top of the page and explain that they show the communicative language and topics/vocabulary that they will learn in Units 3 and 4. Students match the communicative aims 1–8 with the pictures A–E.

Answers

1 B   2 E   3 –   4 D   5 C   6 C   7 A   8 –

Optional activity

Students write another example sentence for each of the communicative aims 1–8. Monitor and help where necessary. Ask students to read out some of their sentences, and ask the class to decide which communicative aim they go with.

2 • Check that students understand the meaning of the categories. Check they understand that *medicine* refers to the whole subject area. Give students two minutes to write the words from the word grid in the correct categories.

• Allow students time to check their answers in pairs before you check with the whole class. Elicit which three words do not fit the categories. Elicit which categories they could belong to, e.g. *bottle opener: gadgets, cupboard: furniture, gold: metal.*

Answers

Space flight: astronaut, planet, orbit, satellite, spacecraft, weightlessness
Medicine: bacteria, disease, germs, infectious, pulse, vaccination
Politics: democracy, demonstration, media, politician, protester, vote

Optional activities

♦ Students work in pairs or small groups and add as many words as they can to each category. Remind them to think about word families, e.g. *infectious – infection* as well as completely new words.

♦ In small groups, students discuss which of the three topics is the most important in the world today and why. Ask groups to report back to the class on whether they agreed or disagreed within their group.

3 • The aim of the activity is for students to contextualise a short listening extract by working out what kind of listening text it is from.
   • Remind students that for this type of activity they should listen for the main gist, and should not worry if they don't understand every single word. Remind them that there is one text type they do not need.
   • Play the recording. Students match the extracts 1–3 with A–D.

🔘 1.26 Recording

1

Supporters of direct action say that their methods get results. For example, they claim that anti-GM food demonstrations have made people aware of the dangers of genetically modified food. And the world knows about the cruelty of whale hunting thanks to direct action against Japanese and Norwegian whaling ships.

2

We're diving in a comfortable, spacious, modern Russian submersible. The three of us – the pilot, myself and another observer – are having such an amazing time as we go deeper and deeper! We're heading towards hydrothermal vents called the Rainbow Vents – they're a kind of underwater volcano.

3

He discovered that there were germs called bacteria in the air which caused liquids to turn sour, so he developed the process called 'pasteurisation'.

Answers

1 B   2 D   3 A

4
- Give students a few minutes to look through the *Time and Age Survey*. Deal with any vocabulary issues.
- Students do the survey in groups of four, noting down any interesting or surprising answers.
- Divide each group into pairs, and put pairs together into new groups of four. Students report on anything interesting or surprising that came up in their discussions.
- Point out the 'Believe it or not!' fact at the bottom of the page. Ask students if they know any other strange or surprising facts like this.

Time travel project

- Ask students to work in pairs and decide on a time and place in the past that they would like to travel to. Ask students to do some research on the Internet on the time and place they have chosen. Students should then imagine they have travelled back and are now in that time and place. Ask them to write a short letter to a friend, telling them what it is like. They can include pictures to illustrate their letter.
- Display the letters in class so that students can look at each others' work.

Follow-up activities

♦ Put students into pairs and ask them to choose three other vocabulary categories in the Topics and vocabulary box on page 34 and brainstorm vocabulary for them. Put pairs together to form groups of four, and ask them to compare their lists and add any more words that they can.
♦ Ask students to prepare a list of the top five things that they would like to do in their life, and at what age. Students can compare their answers in small groups and discuss any similarities or differences.

HOMEWORK

Ask students to interview someone else for the *Time and Age Survey* and to write down the person's answers.

Light travels incredibly fast

Communicative aims	Language	Pronunciation	Vocabulary	Optional aids
Describing and comparing the way things happen	Comparison of adverbs Adverbs of degree Position and order of adverbial phrases	Numbers	Science	Exercise 6: tape measure

WARMER 1

Game *Broken Telephone* Divide the students into two groups. Give one student in each group a sentence which includes a difficult number, e.g. *It's 6,380 kilometres from the surface of the Earth to the centre.* He/She memorises the sentence and then passes it on to the next student by whispering. This student in turn whispers it to the next student and so on, until it gets to the final student who stands up and says the sentence aloud. The game can be played as a race.

WARMER 2

Tell students the topic of the lesson is *science*. Give students one minute to write as many words as they can which are related to science. Ask the student with the most words to read them out. Other students listen and then add different words they wrote.

1 OPENER

- The aim is to set the scene for the reading and listening.
- Ask students to describe what they can see in the photos. Tell students these photos are all related to the Big Bang. Ask students to discuss the question in pairs.
- Ask some pairs to report back to the class on their ideas. Ask other students to comment and add their own ideas.

2 READING

- Focus on the quiz and check that students understand *universe* (all space, including all the stars and planets), *surface*, *rotate*, *Equator* and *North Pole*.
- Give students two minutes to read and answer the quiz questions in pairs.

Optional activity

Find out which answers students have chosen by asking students to raise their hands. Record their answers on the board for comparison with the real answers.

3 AFTER READING

- Students read the text and check their answers. Allow students time to compare their answers in pairs before you check with the class. Ask students to identify the line in the text where they found the answer. Find out who got the most answers right. Ask students what they find most interesting or surprising.
- Students could listen and follow the text in their books.

🔘 1.27 **Recording**
See text on page 36 of the Student's Book.

Answers
1 B   2 A   3 A   4 B   5 A   6 A   7 B

Optional activities

- 🔘 1.27 Play the recording of the text for students to read and listen. Stop at any words you think may cause pronunciation problems, e.g. *universe, oxygen, weighs* and ask students to repeat.
- 🔘 1.27 With a confident class, ask students to cover the text and just listen the first time to check their answers. If necessary, replay the sections which include the answers.
- Ask students to note vocabulary in the text related to science. Remind students that when they note down new vocabulary they should include a definition, translation, example sentence or illustration.

Your response

Ask students to work in pairs to discuss the questions. Ask some pairs to report back to the class.

LANGUAGE WORKOUT OPTION

If you want to pre-teach the language students will use in the following activities, you may like to go to the Language Workout box now.

4 LISTENING

- Ask students to look at the photo. Ask *What do you call this person?* (astronaut) *What is he doing?* (He's walking on the moon.) *Do you know the names of any astronauts? What did they do?*
- Students read the text and predict the missing numbers. They then listen and complete the text. Check answers with the class.

1.28 Recording and answers

*The three astronauts who have been in space longest are all Russian: Sergei Krikalev with a total of **804** days, Sergei Avdeyev, 747 days, and Valeri Polyakov, **678** days.*
*The two astronauts who have flown most often (**seven** flights each) are Franklin Chang-Diaz and Jerry L. Ross, both from the USA.*
*The first two spacewalks took place in 1965. In March Alexei Leonov left his spacecraft for **24** minutes and in June Edward White did the same for **20** minutes.*
*The first moonwalk was from Apollo 11 on 21 July 1969 when Neil Armstrong and Buzz Aldrin walked on the surface of the Moon for **two** hours, 31 minutes and 40 seconds. Soon after, on 19 November 1969, Pete Conrad and Alan Bean left their spacecraft, Apollo 12, for a walk which lasted **three** hours, 56 minutes and three seconds.*

- Students use the prompts in the speech bubbles and the completed information to compare the astronauts.

5 PRONUNCIATION

- The aim is to review and practise the pronunciation of difficult numbers. In pairs, students try pronouncing the numbers in the box. They then listen to the recording to check their pronunciation. Pause after each one for students to repeat.

1.29 Recording

13.7 billion years
four and a half billion years
300,000 kilometres a second
1,675 kilometres an hour
28,000°C
95%
six billion trillion tonnes
two hours, 31 minutes and 40 seconds

Optional activities

- ◆ Ask students to cover the text on page 36 and work in pairs to see if they can remember what the numbers refer to. Elicit answers from the class and make sure that students pronounce the numbers correctly when they give their answers.
- ◆ Students work individually and write down three difficult numbers on a piece of paper. They should not let anyone else see their numbers. They then work in pairs and dictate their numbers to their partner, who must write them down. Students can compare the numbers they have written with the originals. Students can then swap numbers with another pair and repeat the activity.

LANGUAGE WORKOUT OPTION

If you want to pre-teach the language students will use in the following activities, you may like to go to the Language Workout box now.

6 SPEAKING

- Students read the questions. Be prepared to demonstrate *How high can you reach?*
- Students copy the questions into their notebook and leave space for four answers (their own and the three students they interview), e.g.

	Me	1	2	3
How fast can you say the alphabet backwards in English?				
How far can you throw a tennis ball?				

- In pairs, students time each other saying the alphabet backwards in English, and measure how high each other can reach. If you don't have a tape measure, then this could be measured in relation to things in the classroom, e.g. to the top of the board. Students note their own answers to the questions.
- Each student then interviews three other students and notes their answers.
- In pairs, students make comparisons between themselves and the students they interviewed. Do one or two as examples with the whole class. Monitor and help as necessary.

Optional activity

Students might like to find out who is the best in the class at each of the activities. Ask each group: *Who can say the alphabet the fastest in your group? Who can reach the highest?* and ask for their 'scores'. Make sure students use full sentences to answer, and so practise the superlative adverbs.

Extension Ask students to work individually or in pairs to write five similar questions. Be prepared to feed in ideas, e.g. *How long can you hold your breath? How fast can you count to twenty? How far can you swim?* Students interview three different students, then work in pairs to make comparisons.

7 WRITING

- Students use the notes they made in exercise 6 to write a paragraph comparing themselves and other students. Remind students to use both comparatives and superlatives.

Optional activity

With a more confident class, encourage students to use adverbs of degree, e.g. *Stefan gets up extremely early on Saturdays because he has to work. He gets up earlier than …*

LANGUAGE WORKOUT

- Ask students to look at the Language Workout box and complete the sentences. Confident students can complete first and then check, while others can look back at exercises 2 and 3 and then complete.
- Students turn to page 114 of the Language File to check their answers.

  ### Answers
  more later most best extremely really

- Ask students which adverb of degree makes the adverb weaker (*quite*) and which makes it stronger (*really, extremely, incredibly*). Highlight that the adverbs of degree are in order from least (*quite*) to most (*incredibly*).
- Model and drill the pronunciation of the adverbs of degree: *quite* /kwaɪt/, *really* /rɪəli/, *extremely* /ɪkstriːmli/, *incredibly* /ɪnkredəbli/.

Optional activity

With a less confident class, revise adverbs which have the same form as adjectives: *fast, soon, early, late, hard, long, near* (and in informal English *slow, loud, quick*). Give students sentences to complete to elicit these, e.g. *My mother and I are very different – she drives slowly and I drive …, She gets up … and I get up …*

PRACTICE

- Students do Practice exercise 7 on page 114 of the Language File. They complete the sentences with the correct form of the adverb. They work individually and then compare their answers in pairs. Check the answers by asking different students to say the completed sentences.

  ### Answers
  1 incredibly quickly 2 faster 3 most rapidly
  4 more slowly/slower, further 5 completely

Optional activity

Fast-finishers can make other sentences using the adverbs in each sentence, e.g. *My brother can run incredibly quickly.*

- Students do Practice exercise 8 on page 114 of the Language File. They write the sentences in order. Check answers by asking different students to say the completed sentences.

  ### Answers
  1 The Big Bang happened suddenly over 13 million years ago.
  2 Life developed slowly in the sea for billions of years.
  3 Organisms started to breathe oxygen on land 400,000,000 years ago.
  4 Apes walked on two feet over 3,000,000 years ago.
  5 The Earth rotates at roughly the same speed in both London and Paris.

Follow-up activities

- **Game** *The adverb game*   Elicit or give a list of actions, e.g. *eat an orange, put on a pair of jeans, play football, drink a cup of coffee, brush your teeth.* Then elicit a list of adverbs, e.g. *angrily, calmly, carefully, happily, slowly.* Students work in groups. Two students from each group choose an action and an adverb and mime it for the group. The group identify the action and adverb and make a sentence comparing the two acts, e.g. *Sara sat down more slowly than Manuel.*
- Organise students into teams. Give students one minute to look again at all the numbers in the lesson. Read a statement, e.g. *Light travels at 30,000 kilometres a second, the Earth weighs five billion trillion tonnes.* Teams confer and note whether it is true or false. If it is false, they correct the sentence. They win one point for knowing whether it is true or false and two points for an accurate correction.

HOMEWORK

Students write two paragraphs comparing the members of their family. Remind students to use adverbs, not adjectives to compare. Give students some suggestions for actions they can compare, e.g. *walk, run, travel, study, work, eat, talk, get up, go to bed.*

WEBLINK

Students may like to visit www.space.com/54-earth-history-composition-and-atmosphere to find out more interesting facts about Earth.

Revision and Extension p45

Language File p114

Workbook Unit 3 Lesson 1 pp26–27

Photocopiable worksheet p169, notes p156

What a fantastic sight!

Communicative aims	Language	Pronunciation	Vocabulary	Optional aids
Making exclamations Expressing result	*What (a/an)...! so/such (a/an)...* Result clauses: *so/such ... that* Order of adjectives	Exclamations	The world under the sea Adjectives	Warmer 2: photos of people snorkelling and diving Language Workout Optional activity: pictures from magazines or the Internet

WARMER 1

Game *Spelling chain* All the students stand up. One student says a word in English. The student next to him/her says a word that begins with the last letter of the word, e.g. if the first students says *house*, the second student says a word beginning with *e*. Set up a rhythm by getting the students clapping in time and give each student the time for five claps to say their word. If a student can't think of a word in time or says a wrong word, they sit down and are out of the game. The game continues until there is only one student left standing.

WARMER 2

Show photos or draw people snorkelling and diving. Elicit the words *snorkel* and *dive*. Ask *Has anyone ever been snorkelling or diving? When? Where? What did you see? Would you like to go snorkelling or diving? Why / Why not?*

1 OPENER

- The aim is to start students thinking about the topic of the deep sea and pre-teach vocabulary for the reading.
- Ask students to look at the photos. Ask *What do you call a ship like this which can travel under water?* (a submersible) *When do you think the photos of the submersible and the deep sea were taken?*
- Give students two minutes to read the text and find the answers (*1930* and *1960*). Ask students if any of the facts surprised them.

2 READING

- Students look at the reading and identify what type of writing it is (*blog*). Check students understand what this is. (A website which may provide commentary or news and information on a particular subject, or may function as an online diary.)
- Students read the text and answer the question. Tell students to read the text quite quickly at this stage and not to worry if there are words that they don't understand.

Answer
The vents are multi-coloured.

 **Recording**
See text on page 38 of the Student's Book.

3 AFTER READING

- Check that students understand *vent* (a small opening through which air, water or heat can pass), *hydrothermal vent* (a small space through which heat can pass from the seabed into the sea) and *molten rock* (rock that is liquid because it is so hot). Students complete the questions and then match them with the answers. Encourage the students to re-read the text more carefully to confirm their choices. Check answers by asking different students to say the questions and answers aloud.

Answers
1 Where e   2 What j   3 How many a
4 How many f   5 How h   6 What c   7 How i
8 What d   9 When g   10 How many b

Optional activities

- Confident students cover the answers. They complete the questions and find the answers in the text.
- Fast-finishers find the three sea creatures named in the text (*shrimps, crabs, mussels*). If necessary, they can check their meaning in a dictionary. They can note down these words and other new vocabulary related to the sea, including definitions and an illustration.

Your response

Ask students to work in pairs to discuss the questions. After a few minutes, put pairs together into groups of four to compare their answers. Ask a student from each group to report back on their discussions.

4 VOCABULARY

- Students copy the headings into their notebooks. Point out that the columns are in the right order to use the adjectives. Check that students understand *origin* (where something comes from).
- Give students five minutes in pairs to organise the words into the six columns. Check comprehension of *average, enormous, giant, huge, tiny* by asking for examples of things which are that size, e.g. *the classroom, a whale, an ant.*
- Check answers by asking students to read out the words in a category. Check that students understand all the adjectives, and model pronunciation of words that students might find difficult, e.g. *ancient* and *spacious.*

Answers

Opinion	Size	Age	Shape	Colour	Origin
average	enormous	ancient	flat	blue	Brazilian
beautiful	giant	modern	long	green	Chinese
comfortable	huge	new	narrow	grey	French
fantastic	small	old	round	purple	Italian
incredible	spacious	recent	square	red	Russian
unknown	tiny	young	thin	white	Spanish

Note:
Size here refers to how big or small a thing is.
Shape refers to its dimensions in proportion to each other, therefore *long, narrow* and *thin* are shape and not size.
Unknown is difficult to categorise but the opposite, *famous*, is an opinion therefore it also comes under opinion.

Optional activities

♦ Fast-finishers can mark the stress on the words of more than one syllable.
♦ Tell students you are thinking of a particular chair which can be described using three of the adjectives, e.g. *comfortable, old, green chair.* Students guess what type of chair you are thinking of. Tell the students which adjectives are right after each guess, e.g. Student says *a comfortable, new, blue chair*, you say *It is comfortable.* Students continue until they have worked out the complete expression. Students do the activity in pairs with other nouns, e.g. *a flat, a fish, a plate, a dining table, a car.*

Extension Students work individually or in pairs to prepare their definitions. Ask students in turn to read out their definitions and see if the class can guess what is being described. Encourage students to correct any errors in the order of adjectives.

5 PRONUNCIATION

- In pairs, students practise saying the exclamations in the box. They then listen to the recording to check their pronunciation. Pause after each one for students to repeat. Highlight the linking between *What a/an* and *such a/an* and the stress on *so* and *such.*

  🔘 1.31 Recording
  What a fantastic sight!
  What a discovery!
  It's so unexpected!
  We're having such an amazing time!
  It's such a high temperature!
  It's been such an exciting dive!

Optional activity

Students hum the sentences, i.e. they make the sounds of the sentence with the right stress but they don't say the words. Their partner identifies the sentence they have just said.

LANGUAGE WORKOUT OPTION

If you want to pre-teach the language students will use in the following activities, you may like to go to the Language Workout box now.

6 SPEAKING

- Tell students they are going to talk about exciting events in their lives. Students look at the examples in the speech bubbles. Give students time to think of some examples, real or imaginary, of their own and make notes. If necessary, prompt students with ideas, e.g. *winning a competition, going to a concert, seeing a famous person, arriving in a new city, trying a sport for the first time.*
- In pairs, students talk about their exciting events. Encourage confident students to talk more extensively or ask further questions about the event. Monitor and note examples of good language and errors. Write these on the board and ask students to identify and correct the errors.
- Ask some students to report back on one of their partner's exciting events.

Optional activity

Students think of five exciting events in their life. Two are true and three are false. They tell their partner about the five events. At the end, their partner guesses which ones are true and which are false.

7 WRITING

- Students use their notes from exercise 6 to write about five exciting events in their life.

Optional activity

Students imagine they are a celebrity of their choice. They write a paragraph about exciting events in their life as if they were this famous person. They can talk about purchases they have made, meeting their partners, starring in films, going to lunch with other celebrities, and so on.

LANGUAGE WORKOUT

- Ask students to look at the Language Workout box and complete the sentences. Confident students can complete first and then check, while others can look back at exercises 1 and 2 and then complete.
- Students turn to page 114 of the Language File to check their answers.

  Answers
  What   such   so
  so … that   such … that
  beautiful small flat blue
  comfortable, spacious, modern Russian

- Highlight that
  - *What* is used in exclamations with nouns (or adjective + noun, e.g. *What amazing fish!*). With singular countable nouns, *a* or *an* is necessary.
  - *such* and *so* are used for emphasis. Ask students to identify which one is used with a noun or adjective + noun (*such*, e.g. *such fun* or *such an exciting dive*), and which one is used with an adjective (*so*, e.g. *so unexpected*).
  - *so/such … that* is used to show the result or consequence of a situation. Ask students to look at the two examples and identify which part of the sentence is the situation and which part is the result (*It was so deep* – situation, *they didn't expect to see any life* – result, *It's been such an exciting dive* – situation, *I haven't noticed the time* – result).

Optional activity

Show pictures which will provoke a strong positive reaction, e.g. a picture of a mansion and say *This is my house* or a picture of a Caribbean beach and say *This is where I went for my last holiday*. Elicit reactions from the students using *What (a/an)…! It's so …!*

PRACTICE

- Students do Practice exercise 9 on page 114 of the Language File.

  Answers
  1 such a   2 so   3 such an   4 such a   5 so   6 so, such

Follow-up activities

- ◆ **Game** *Telepathy*   Students work in groups of five. Dictate the beginning of a sentence, e.g. *It was so hot that …* Students work individually to complete the sentence. Groups then compare their answers. If two students have the same ending, they win two points, if three students have the same ending, they win three points, and so on. Other possible sentence heads to dictate: *The weather was so terrible that …*, *It was such a boring film that …*, *She was such a good cook that …*, *The lesson was so interesting that …*

- ◆ Remind students that the title of this lesson was *What a fantastic sight!* Give students five minutes in groups to invent a story which includes this phrase. Reinforce that it must be something that they can *see* that is fantastic. Tell students that they will take a vote on the best story at the end. Students make notes but they don't need to write the story out in full. Students tell their stories to the class and then the class vote on the most imaginative, the most descriptive or the most realistic.

HOMEWORK

Students imagine that they were on the trip to the moon with Neil Armstrong in 1969 and write a blog describing the experience.

WEBLINK

Students may like to visit www.thesea.org to read about the sea and sea life.

Revision and Extension p45

Language File p114

Workbook Unit 3 Lesson 2 pp28–29

Photocopiable worksheet p170, notes p156

It won't be cheap

Communicative aims	Language	Pronunciation	Vocabulary	Optional aids
Talking about future events, schedules, arrangements and plans	Future review: future simple, present simple and continuous, *going to*	Exclamations	Space flight and tourism Phrasal verbs with *down*, *on* and *off*	Follow-up activity: small blank cards for Vocabulary box

WARMER 1

Tell students the topic of the lesson is *space*. Write anagrams for things you find in space on the board, e.g. *star, planet, asteroid, comet, meteor, black hole, moon, satellite, alien*. Students race to order the anagrams.

WARMER 2

Elicit the order of the planets from the sun and teach the names of the planets in English: *Mercury, Venus, Earth, Mars, Jupiter, Saturn, Uranus, Neptune*. Students try to think of a sentence in English to remember the order of the planets, e.g. *Many vegetarians eat marmalade (and) jam (and) swim up (the) Nile.*

Useful information

The first space tourist was a billionaire businessman from California who paid $20million (£14 million) for a seven-day trip to the International Space Station in April 2001. The first female space tourist spent ten days on the same space station in September 2006.

1 OPENER

- The aim is to set the scene for the reading and pre-teach some useful vocabulary.
- Ask students to look at the photo of Virgin Galactic spaceship. Ask students what they think the spaceship is for. Elicit that it is designed to take tourists into space.
- Check comprehension of *to orbit* (travel in a circle around a much larger object) and *weightlessness* (when you have no weight, especially in space). Students predict which words will be in the text and say why they think they will be in the text.

2 READING

- Students read, listen and check which words are in the text (all except *helicopter* and *lightning*).
- Ask students to discuss in pairs or small groups what they find most surprising in the text. Ask some students to report back on their discussions and continue the discussion with the whole class if students have plenty to say.

⊙ 1.32 Recording
See text on page 40 of the Student's Book.

3 AFTER READING

- Allow students time to read the questions. Check they understand *highlights* (the most enjoyable parts). Give students five minutes to re-read the text more carefully and note the answers. Encourage students to guess the meaning of unfamiliar words from context.
- Students compare answers in pairs. Check answers orally with the whole class.

Answers

1 *The space tourists will fly at three times the sound of sound, they'll experience six minutes of weightlessness and they'll be able to look down on Earth. They'll have a spectacular view, large windows and luxurious seats.*
2 *Three days of pre-flight training at the new Spaceport America in New Mexico.*
3 *Virgin boss Sir Richard Branson and members of his family. There are also rumours that Angelina Jolie and Brad Pitt have put their names down to fly.*
4 *The cost of space flights will come down in the future.*
5 *Book a spaceship flight because it's too expensive.*

Optional activity

Fast-finishers find words connected to space in the text, e.g. *spaceship, space tourist, spaceport*. They can then use a dictionary to find more words e.g. *spacecraft, space station, spacesuit, spacewalk*.

Your response

Put students into pairs to discuss the question. Ask pairs to report back on their discussion and their reasons for thinking that they will or won't be space tourists one day.

4 LISTENING

- Ask students what the interviewer from exercise 2 was going to do next (*go on a tour of the Kennedy Space Center*). Tell students that he has now arrived at the centre and is listening to the schedule for the day. Ask students to predict what the tour will include.
- Ask students to read the schedule. Play the recording for students to listen and complete the schedule with the times. Check the answers with the whole class.

🔘 1.33 Recording

Good morning, everyone, and welcome to the Kennedy Space Center. We have an exciting programme of events for you today, and we're sure that you'll have a fun time.

So first of all, at 10am, we're going to see a thrilling space movie on an enormous IMAX screen – and you'll experience what it's like to be in space. After that, at 11 o'clock, we'll visit the Astronaut Hall of Fame, where you'll discover the heroes of space history and you will also have the chance to ride a spaceflight simulator. Then we return to the Space Center for lunch at 1.15pm – there's a big variety of menu options, including pasta, pizza, hamburgers, and even sushi – so there's something for everyone. And during lunch you'll meet an astronaut who can tell you about his experiences in space. People always find this extremely interesting. You'll have an hour for lunch, and then we take the NASA bus tour which stops at the International Space Station – you don't want to miss this fascinating tour, there's lots to see and explore, so make sure you're on the bus, which departs at 2.15.

The bus tour lasts two hours, and then at 4.15 we return to the Kennedy Space Center, where you'll have time to see many other attractions, including robots and giant rockets. The tour ends at 5.15pm, when the bus departs from the Space Center to take you back to your hotels. So have a wonderful day – enjoy!

Answers

10:00am	*11:00am*	*1.15pm*
2:15pm	*4.15pm*	*5:15pm*

- Refer students to the example. Elicit one or two more example questions, e.g. *What time does the space movie start? How long does it last?*
- Students ask and answer questions across the class.

Optional activities

- ♦ With a confident class, play the recording twice. The first time, students listen for the times. The second time, ask students to note any extra information about the tour, e.g. *IMAX space movie – experience what it's like to be in space, Astronaut Hall of Fame – discover the heroes of space history.*
- ♦ Students do a role play. One student works at the Kennedy Space Center. They are carrying out a survey to find out how happy their visitors are. They interview their partner (a tourist) at the end of the tour and ask questions about the different parts of the tour, e.g. *Did you enjoy the space movie?*

5 PRONUNCIATION

- Ask students to complete the exclamations.
- Play the recording for students to check their answers, then play the recording again, pausing for students to repeat the expressions.

🔘 1.34 Recording and answers

*It costs over a million dollars. That's extremely **expensive**!*
*It flies at three times the speed of sound. That's incredibly **fast**!*
*The temperature is minus 30 °C. That's terribly **cold**!*
*We're going to meet an astronaut. How **exciting**!*

Optional activity

Students make similar sentences using the opposite adjectives, e.g. *cheap, slow, hot, boring*, e.g. *This souvenir T-shirt is only three dollars. That's extremely cheap!*

LANGUAGE WORKOUT OPTION

If you want to pre-teach the language students will use in the following activities, you may like to go to the Language Workout box now.

6 SPEAKING

- Ask students to read the predictions. Check they understand *mining, elevator, base, aliens*. Give students a few minutes to decide whether they agree or disagree with the predictions.
- Give students five minutes to discuss the predictions in pairs. Monitor and help/correct as necessary.
- Ask some students to report back on the predictions they agreed with/disagreed with. Ask students if they think that all these events would be positive for the world.

> **Extension** Have students make some predictions about changes on Earth. Then have them work in pairs and discuss their predictions.

7 VOCABULARY

- Students find the phrasal verbs in exercise 2. Encourage them to use the context to work out/confirm the meaning of the phrasal verbs.

Answers

1 hang on   2 come down   3 put down   4 take off
5 count down   6 look down

Optional activity

Students choose four of the verbs and include them in a short story or dialogue.

8 WRITING

- Elicit some ideas for plans and changes. Point out if necessary that we use *going to* for plans and *will/won't* for predictions, e.g. *I'm going to eat lunch at my favourite Chinese restaurant* and *I think it will be hotter and drier than when I left.*

- Give students 10 minutes to write their ideas as a diary entry or blog. They start with the line: *Tomorrow we are returning to Earth. We are landing at 9am.* Monitor and note examples of good language and errors. Write them on the board and ask students to identify and correct the errors.
- Students read each other's entries and find out if they have any similar ideas. Ask some students to report back on plans or predictions that they have in common with other students.

LANGUAGE WORKOUT

- Ask students to look at the Language Workout box, read the rules and complete the sentences. Confident students can complete first and then check, while others can look back at exercise 2 first.
- Students turn to page 115 of the Language File to check their answers.

  Answers
  will   will   won't   Will
  starts   'm visiting   's going   'm going

- Highlight that
  - when *will* is used for prediction, it is often used with *I think, I don't think, I'm sure, I doubt.*
  - we tend to use *I don't think + will,* rather than *I think + won't,* e.g. *I don't think it will be expensive.*
  - when the present continuous is used to talk about the future, the sentence almost always includes a future time reference, e.g. *tomorrow, on Saturday.*
  - there is overlap between the present continuous and *going to. Going to* can almost always be used instead of the present continuous, e.g. *I'm going to visit the Kennedy Center tomorrow.* However, the present continuous cannot be used with future meaning where there is just a vague intention, so it would not be possible to say *I'm booking a ticket someday.* To use the present continuous there must be some kind of arrangement.
- Read the notes on the future continuous and future perfect with the class. Highlight the difference between these pairs of sentences: *I think people will work longer in the future.* (a general prediction about the future) *In 2020 people will be working longer.* (an action in progress at a particular time in the future) *In 2020 scientists will invent flying cars.* (2020 is the time of the action) *In 2020 scientists will have invented flying cars.* (the action is completed before 2020)

PRACTICE

- Students do Practice exercise 10 on page 115 of the Language File. Point out that students need to choose between three verb forms. Students complete the sentences individually and then compare in pairs.
- Ask students to say why the answer is in that form as you check the answers.

  Answers
  1 will carry   2 won't be   3 are flying   4 departs
  5 are staying   6 will travel   7 are you going   8 ends

Optional activity

Students write one future fact or prediction about themselves, e.g. *I will be 15 next month* or *I think I'll pass the English exam,* one arrangement they have made and one intention they have. Students tell their partners their sentences. Their partner listens and asks a question about each one, e.g. *When's your birthday? When's the exam?*

Follow-up activities

- ◆ **Game** *Password*   Organise students into teams of at least three. One student from each team sits with their back to the board. Write a word from the lesson on the board. The teams describe the word to the team member who can't see it. They must not say the word. The first student to guess the word wins a point for their team. Students move so a different student has their back to the board and then continue. Students can then write the words on cards for the Vocabulary Box. Possible words include: *astronaut, colony, highlight, fare, orbit, passenger, spaceship, spectacular, weightlessness.*
- ◆ In pairs, students prepare the dialogue for an interview with a famous person of their choice. The interview must be about their future plans and include the future simple, present continuous and *going to.* Set a 10 minute time limit. Students then act out their interviews but don't say the name of the famous person. The rest of the class listens and tries to identify the famous person.

HOMEWORK

Students write their own predictions for life in the next fifty years, using exercise 6 as an example. Suggest topics they could write about, e.g. *school, books, shopping, food, sport, health, relationships.*

WEBLINK

Students may like to visit www.bbc.co.uk/science/space to read about space and life on other planets.

Revision and Extension p45

Language File p115

Workbook Unit 3 Lesson 3 p30–31

Photocopiable worksheet p171, notes p156

Integrated Skills Describing events and consequences

Skills		Learner independence	Vocabulary	Optional aids
Reading Connecting ideas: *People Who Changed The World* *Listening* Correcting mistakes	*Speaking* Giving reasons for an opinion *Writing* Profile of a significant person	Thinking skills Word creation: noun suffixes –*sion* and –*tion*	Medicine Environment Radio Navigation Useful expressions	Exercise 3 Optional activity: small cards for Vocabulary Box Exercise 7: Information on significant people Follow-up activity: large pieces of paper

WARMER 1

If you set the homework from the previous lesson, students tell each other their predictions for the future and discuss whether they agree or disagree.

WARMER 2

Game *Twenty questions* Tell students you are thinking of a person who changed the world, e.g. the Scottish scientist, Alexander Fleming, who discovered penicillin in 1928. They can ask a maximum of 20 questions to find out who it is but you can only answer *yes* or *no*.

1 OPENER

- The aim is to set the scene and generate interest in the reading.
- Discuss the question as a whole class.

2 READING

- Ask students to look quickly at the three people in the text to see if they were mentioned in exercise 1. Students read through the text quickly and find out how each person changed the world (*Pasteur invented pasteurisation and vaccinations, Carson started the modern environmental movement, Marconi invented the radio transmitter*).
- Give students a further five minutes to read the text more carefully and complete it with the correct phrases. Point out that two of the phrases are not needed. With a less confident class, do the first one as an example, showing students how to make connections between the text and the sentence, e.g. *liquids* and *the liquid*.
- Students listen and check their answers. Ask students which words helped them to complete the text.

 1.35 Recording

People who changed the world
The French chemist and biologist **Louis Pasteur** *(1822–1895) made one of the most important discoveries in medical history. He discovered that there were germs called bacteria in the air which caused liquids to turn sour, so he developed the process called 'pasteurisation': killing the bacteria* **by boiling and then cooling the liquid**. *Because of Pasteur's research, most dairy products today are pasteurised. Pasteur then realised that most infectious diseases are caused by germs in the air,* **which led to his 'germ theory of disease'**. *He used this theory to explain how vaccination worked and showed how doctors could prevent some illnesses by injecting weak forms of the disease. Pasteur's pioneering work has protected millions of people from disease, thanks to pasteurisation and vaccination.*

The American writer and biologist **Rachel Carson** *(1907–1964) started the modern environmental movement when she wrote a controversial book about the destructive effects of pesticides on the chain of life. Silent Spring,* **published in 1962**, *is one of the few books that have changed the way people view the natural world. Its impact was so enormous that it was compared with Charles Darwin's theory of evolution. As a result, Carson was attacked by the chemical industry, but Silent Spring also caused a massive protest against environmental pollution. Consequently, the US government started to take action to control the use of pesticides in agriculture* **and to reduce environmental damage**. *And thanks to Rachel Carson, there is now a worldwide movement to protect the environment.*

The Italian physicist, **Guglielmo Marconi** *(1874–1937) made the first ever transatlantic radio transmission on 12 December 1901. A transmitter in south-west England signalled the letter S – three dots in Morse code – and the signal was picked up in Newfoundland, 3,500km away. This achievement was so extraordinary that at first people didn't believe it. Marconi had already successfully transmitted a message over 50km* **from England to France in 1899**. *But most scientists believed that radio waves would not follow the curve of the Earth and could, therefore, never transmit signals across an ocean. It was such a long way that it seemed completely impossible. Marconi proved them wrong. As a result of his achievement, we have seen the development of broadcasting, communications satellites, radar, the telephone and the Internet. Marconi's genius has also* *helped to save thousands of lives on land, **in the air and at sea** – when the Titanic sank in 1912, an estimated 700 lives were saved thanks to SOS signals from a Marconi transmitter.*

Answers and key words
1 e (liquids, the liquid)
2 b (germ theory, this theory)
3 f (book, published)
4 a (take action, control pesticides, reduce environmental damage)
5 h (transmit, over 50km)
6 d (land, air, sea)

3

• Students search the text for words that match the definitions. Tell students that the definitions are in the same order as the words in the text. With weaker classes, tell students which part of the text the words are in (1–2: Pasteur, 3–7: Rachel Carson, 8–10: Marconi).

Answers
1 infectious   2 theory   3 controversial   4 pesticides
5 impact   6 (environmental) pollution   7 agriculture
8 physicist   9 transatlantic   10 transmit

Optional activity

Students copy the new vocabulary onto cards and write the definitions on the back. Add these to the Vocabulary Box.

4

• Before looking at the phrases in the box, write these sentences on the board: *The achievement was extraordinary. People didn't believe it.* Elicit which is the cause and which is the result. Elicit some words/phrases that could be used to connect the two sentences.
• Students then look at the phrases in the two boxes, find examples in the text and notice how they are used. Check students have noticed the grammar of these words by asking: *Which ones are followed by a noun?* (*as a result of, because of, thanks to*) *Which ones link the cause and result in a single sentence?* (all of them except *as a result* and *consequently*).

Answers
Pasteur:
…, so he developed the process
Because of Pasteur's research, most dairy products
…, thanks to pasteurisation and vaccination
Carson:
Its impact was so enormous that
As a result, Carson was attacked
Consequently, the US government started
And thanks to Rachel Carson, there is now a worldwide movement
Marconi:
This achievement was so extraordinary that
… and could, therefore, never transmit
It was such a long way that it seemed impossible
As a result of his achievement, we have seen the development

Optional activity

Write the following sentences on the board: *It was a long way. It seemed completely impossible.* Ask students to work in pairs and connect these ideas using some of the linking phrases. Ask students to read out their sentences and correct any errors. As a class, make sentences with any linking phrases students have not already used.

5 LISTENING

• Ask students to look at the pictures and guess how Harrison changed the world. Give students one minute to read the text and check their predictions (*He invented a clock which allowed sailors to calculate longitude*).
• Students read the text again and try to find ten mistakes.
• Play the recording for students to listen and check.

🔘 1.36 **Recording and answers**
*The English engineer John Harrison (1693–1776) solved a major scientific problem. Ships sailing across **oceans** didn't know their exact position at sea because they couldn't measure longitude – the distance east or west from an imaginary line (called the meridian) from the top of the Earth to the **bottom**. Longitude is measured in degrees, and for every 15 degrees that you travel east, the local time is one hour ahead. If you travel west 15 degrees, the local time is one **hour** behind, Therefore, if we know the exact time at two points, we can work out **where** we are. But early sailors couldn't do this because the movement of the **sea** made their clocks inaccurate.*
*In 1714 the British government offered a prize of £20,000 (a **huge** amount then) for a clock which would tell the time accurately at sea. Thanks to John Harrison, the 'longitude' problem was solved, but it took him most of his life. His **first** attempt was a clock called H1, which he built between 1730 and 1735. His next attempts from 1737 to 1759 resulted in H4, a **smaller** pocket watch. This was tested on a voyage to the West Indies in 1764 and worked perfectly. But Harrison was given only half the prize and told to make **two** more watches. This he did and, as a result of complaining to the King and Parliament, received the rest of his money in 1773, at the age of **80**!*

6 SPEAKING

• Students discuss the question in pairs and then as a whole class.

7 GUIDED WRITING

• Students may need to research this, in which case it could be set as homework. Alternatively, bring in basic information on people who changed the world, e.g. Albert Einstein, Mahatma Gandhi, Martin Luther King.
• Set a time limit for students to write about the person of their choice. Encourage them to use the texts in this lesson as a guide and to include some of the linking words/phrases from exercise 4. Monitor and help as necessary.
• Display the pieces of writing around the room. Students walk round and read the information. At the end, take a class vote on who changed the world the most.

8 LEARNER INDEPENDENCE

- The aim is to raise students' awareness of their own strategies for remembering vocabulary and possibly introduce a new strategy. The exercise also consolidates vocabulary from this unit.
- Allow students two minutes to look at the list of nouns and try to remember them. Covering the list, each student writes down the words they can remember and then compares with a partner.
- Discuss which words were easier to remember with the whole class. It is likely that students found the concrete nouns easier. Students read the advice on how to remember abstract nouns. In pairs, students think of a thing you can see or touch to associate with each of the abstract nouns.

9 WORD CREATION

- The aim is for students to learn ways in which nouns can be formed from verbs and to extend their vocabulary. Warn students that the spelling of the word changes sometimes when the ending is added.
- Students make nouns from the verbs in the box. Allow students to use dictionaries to help them if necessary.
- Check the answers and the spelling of the nouns with the whole class.
- Tell students to think about the pronunciation of the nouns. Ask *What is the rule?* (The main stress is always on the syllable before the *-sion/-tion* ending.)
- Students then complete the sentences individually and compare in pairs. Check answers by asking different students to read the sentences aloud.

> **Answers**
>
> *action   creation   decision   discussion   evolution*
> *pasteurisation   permission   pollution   possession*
> *production   revision   solution   transmission*
> *vaccination*
> *1 pollution   2 discussion   3 vaccination*
> *4 permission   5 transmission   6 action*

EXTRA PRACTICE

If you would like to give your students more practice in forming nouns from verbs, please see the Vocabulary EXTRA! Worksheets on the Teacher's Resource Site (www.macmillanenglish.com/inspiration).

10 PHRASEBOOK

- Ask students to look through the unit to find the expressions, and look at how they are used. Be ready to help with explanations or translation as necessary.
- Play the recording, pausing after each expression for students to repeat.

1.37 Recording and answers

Lesson 2, exercise 2	**Lesson 3, exercise 2**
What a fantastic sight!	*How exciting!*
It's so unexpected!	*Hang on.*
The most incredible thing is …	*Forget it!*
What has this got to do with …?	

- Ask students to work individually and write down one or two situations when you could use the four exclamations. Students then read their situation to their partner who says the correct exclamation for that situation. Monitor and help as necessary.
- Students can add expressions they like to their Personal Phrasebooks.

Follow-up activities

- Draw a word map on the board. Write *SCIENCE* in the centre. Elicit different categories from the class and write them on the word map, e.g. *Earth, sea, space, future, discovery, invention.* Divide students into small groups to draw their own word map on a large piece of paper or card. Students choose categories for their word map and add as many words as they can. Set a time limit and give out bilingual dictionaries if available. The word maps can be displayed in the classroom.
- Tell students that the local town has decided to put up a statue to a person who has changed the world in some way. Students will debate in favour of one person of their choice. Organise students into teams of two or three. Make sure that every team chooses a different person. Write the names on the board. Give teams 10 minutes to prepare their argument and think about weaknesses in the other candidates. Chair a whole class debate, or divide each team AAA, BBB, CCC, DDD so they work in groups ABCD and each group makes its own decision.
- **Game** *Noughts and crosses*   See Review Units 1–2, Follow-up activities for instructions and example grid. Use the following categories: *comparative adverb, present simple for future, such, going to, three adjectives to describe a fish, irregular comparative adverb, future simple, so, present continuous for future.*

HOMEWORK

Students write a paragraph about a person or thing that changed their life for the better. Students should include at least one linking word or phrase.

WEBLINK

Students may like to visit www.bbc.co.uk/news/science_and_environment to read about developments in science and the environment.

Revision and Extension p45

Workbook Unit 3 Lesson 4 pp32–33

Inspiration EXTRA!

LANGUAGE LINKS

- Focus on the picture and ask students what it is for (making coffee).
- Focus on the instructions and point out that there are two instructions in each language. Ask students to work in pairs to match the headings to the instructions.
- Students then find the words for the parts of the cafetière in each language and label the diagram.
- Check answers and ask students what words helped them choose the correct headings.
- Ask students which instruction is different and in what way.

Answers

F, C, B, D, E, A
1 E plunger, F piston, G Stempel
2 E jug, F pichet, G Kanne
3 E filter, F filtre, G Filterteller
4 E lid, F couvercle, G Deckel

GAME   MYSTERY WORD

- Organise students into pairs. Ask students to read the instructions carefully. Check comprehension by asking: *Where do you find the word?* (in this unit) *Is it OK to choose a word with eight letters?* (No, four to six letters)
- Choose a word, e.g. *Earth* and demonstrate the game with the whole class. Students play the game in pairs.

Optional activity

Make the game more competitive by giving a time limit, e.g. students see how many of their partner's words they can get in five minutes.

SKETCH   SPACE TALK

- The aim is for students to enjoy using their English while also reviewing language presented in this unit and getting valuable stress and intonation practice.
- Ask the students to look at the title and the cartoon. Ask students to describe the scene in the cartoon. Ask *Why do you think the man is carrying so much equipment? Do you think this will be a problem?*
- With a more confident class, play the recording with books closed. With a less confident class, play the recording while the students follow in their books. Check the answers (*He needs the equipment to record them breaking the spacewalk record. It means he can't get back in and so is left in space!*).

🔘 1.38 Recording
See text on page 44 of the Student's Book.

- Divide the class into two equal groups and play the recording again, with one group repeating the Captain's role in chorus and the other group repeating Number 1's role. Encourage students to exaggerate stress and intonation.

Language File pp114–115

- Ask the students to close their books and play the recording again. Then ask the students to work in pairs and practise the sketch. Choose several pairs to act out the sketch in front of the class.

REVISION

Lessons 1–3
Students' own answers.

EXTENSION

Lessons 1–3
Students' own answers.

YOUR CHOICE!

- The aim is to give students more learner independence and help them to identify their preferred way of learning. Encourage students to choose an activity that they feel less comfortable with if they want a challenge or are aware that they need practice in a particular area.
- Monitor and help groups. Check answers if necessary, or provide written answers for groups to check their own.

CONSTRUCTION

Answers

1 uncomfortable small round
2 modern round American; famous old
3 spectacular, long, red and white; strange, small, pink; unusual white
4 unknown giant black; 5cm-long white

REFLECTION

Answers

such … adjective   so … a/an.   So   so   Such   such

ACTION

- Students work in groups of five or six. They find a suitable paragraph from this unit and copy the first five sentences onto separate pieces of paper.
- Students do the activity one group at a time. If any groups are smaller than five, students can take two sentences each.

INTERACTION

- Students work in small groups. Allow students two minutes to think about what they would like their life to be like one, three and ten years from now.
- Groups choose a fortune teller who finds out what the other students want to happen and then predicts this.

Workbook Unit 3 Inspiration EXTRA! pp34–35

Young scientists

Focus on the photos and explain that the people are all young scientists. Ask *What things have scientists discovered recently? What are the most important discoveries of the last twenty years? What would you most like to discover?* Elicit a range of answers.

1 READING

- Pre-teach *flippers, humpback whale, method, magnet/magnetic* and *sensors*. Ask students to read the text quickly and answer the questions.
- Allow students time to compare their answers in pairs before you check with the class.

  🔘 1.39 Recording
  See text on pages 46–47 of the Student's Book.

  Answers
  1 *Humpback whales use their flippers in water like wings.*
  2 *The flippers of humpback whales are more efficient than aircraft wings.*
  3 *So that they didn't lose touch with their cultural heritage.*
  4 *They were put on CD.*
  5 *They are discovered using special equipment in a hospital.*
  6 *It was nearly as successful as the normal method.*
  7 *The leaves on plants.*
  8 *They wouldn't need windscreen wipers.*
  9 *They used electromagnets.*
  10 *It could be used when steel is being painted or is contaminated.*

Optional activity

More confident students can choose one of the texts and read it again carefully. Tell them they are going to explain it in their own words. Students work in small groups and, with books closed, tell each other about the invention they chose.

2 VOCABULARY

- Students work individually or in pairs to find the vocabulary in the text.

  Answers
  1 *oral*   2 *coated*   3 *detecting*   4 *evolved*   5 *optical*
  6 *prevent*   7 *transporting*   8 *standard*   9 *applications*

Optional activity

Fast-finishers can find three more words that are new to them in the texts and look them up in a dictionary.

3 SPEAKING

- Allow students a few minutes to read the questions and prepare their ideas individually.
- Students work in small groups to discuss the questions. Monitor and note down errors to deal with in a brief feedback session at the end.
- Ask each group to report back to the class on which things they agreed and disagreed about. Continue as a class discussion if students are interested.

4 MINI-PROJECT WOMEN AND SCIENCE

- Read the statistics on women and science with the class. Put students into pairs to discuss the questions. Students might like to use the Internet to do research on women and science in their country.
- In pairs, students write about their views. With weaker classes, revise or teach some written expressions for giving opinions, e.g. *We believe that ... We would suggest that ... It is our view that ...*
- Students write their views individually. Encourage them to illustrate their work with photos or drawings from the Internet. When students have written their views, ask them to check their work carefully for errors. Students could also swap their work with another pair for peer-correction.
- Pin the work around the classroom so that students can read all the views.
- Ask students if they have read any views which have changed their opinions.

WEBLINK

Students may like to visit www.wikipedia.org/wiki/women_in_science to find links to information on important women scientists.

Workbook Culture pp36–37

GETTING IT RIGHT

Some things won't have changed

Communicative aims	Language	Pronunciation	Vocabulary	Optional aids
Discussing possible future lifestyles	Future continuous Future perfect	List intonation	Technology Phrasal verbs with *out*	Warmer 1: a few objects which show change over time Exercise 3 Optional activity: cards for the Vocabulary Box

WARMER 1

Bring in objects which illustrate change over time, e.g. an audio cassette, a CD and a modern music player. Write the categories *Past, Present* and *Future* on the board and ask students under which category they would put each object. Invite students to speculate on what will fill the *Future* category. Brainstorm other topics as a class, e.g. *transport, medicine, communication, education.* Students then work in small groups to try to think of examples for each topic, speculating each time about the objects or technologies of the future.

WARMER 2

Game *Year race*   Write about 20 different years on the board, e.g. *2020, 1963.* Divide the class into two teams and give one student in each group some coloured chalk or a board pen. Say a year from the board. The two students race to the board to circle the given year. The fastest wins a point for the team. They then choose a new student from each team to be the runner.

1 OPENER

- The aim is to introduce the context for the reading.
- Ask the class if they think it is possible to predict the future. They read the bad predictions in the box and discuss with a partner what really happened. Students also discuss what they think life will be like in 2020, using the photographs on the page for ideas. Ask each pair to report back to the class on their ideas.

2 READING

- Students read and listen to the text and compare their own predictions with those of the experts. Encourage them to guess unfamiliar words from context. Clarify the meaning of *pulse* by showing a pulse point, e.g. *wrist.* Be prepared to translate *wireless, vaccine* and *gadget.*
- Ask students how similar their own predictions were to the text and also what they learnt about the objects in the photographs.

  🔘 2.01 Recording
  See text on page 48 of the Student's Book

3 AFTER READING

- Students read the text again and answer the questions individually. Check the answers together as a class.

  Answers
  1 People will still have to work.
  2 No, they will be retiring later.
  3 Diseases.
  4 It will contain vitamins and vaccines.
  5 Wireless technology will have continued to develop.
  6 Gadgets which will combine the functions of phone, camera, MP3 player and computer.
  7 It will communicate by wireless networks.
  8 Keys.

  Optional activities
  - Fast-finishers can write new words from the text on cards with a definition or example sentence on the reverse, for the Vocabulary box.
  - Ask students to close their books. Write one half of some two word expressions from the text on the left of the board and the other half on the right, in a jumbled order. Ask students to remember the combinations. Examples could include *pulse rate, life expectancy, wireless technology, household equipment, keyless cars, bright future, health problems.*

  Your response

  Ask students to work in pairs to discuss the questions. Ask some pairs to report back to the class.

4 VOCABULARY

- Ask students to look back at the text on page 48 and find some of the phrasal verbs, e.g. *wipe out, carry out, point out.* Ask students to match the phrasal verbs with the definitions 1–5.
- Check the answers together as a class.

  Answers
  1 work out   2 wipe out   3 carry out   4 miss out on
  5 point out

Optional activities

♦ Students write example sentences using the phrasal verbs in their notebooks.

♦ On the board, write some nouns which commonly collocate with these phrasal verbs, e.g. *a project, an opportunity, the answer to a maths problem, an interesting building, company profits.* Ask students which nouns go with which phrasal verbs. Students can then use the nouns to write example sentences.

5 PRONUNCIATION

• Before the students look at the list, ask if they can remember how life will have changed by 2020 and what will have caused these changes. Elicit ideas that students can remember.

• Students listen and repeat the list, trying to copy the stress and intonation patterns. Highlight the rising intonation on most items in the list, but the falling intonation on the final item.

 **2.02** Recording

Life in 2020 will have changed because of better medicine, later retirement, less disease, fewer health problems, wireless technology, more microchips and improved household equipment.

Optional activity

Dictate some prompts for students to write down, e.g. *My favourite foods are…, The best things in life are …* Ask students to complete each sentence with a list of at least three items and then compare their lists with a partner, using the correct list intonation.

LANGUAGE WORKOUT OPTION

If you want to pre-teach the language students will use in the following activities, you may like to go to the Language Workout box now.

6 SPEAKING

• Tell students that they are going to interview two other students about what they will be doing in three months' time.

• Students read through the questions and think about their answers.

• Choose two confident students to ask each other an example question from the lists, encouraging them to ask *So what/who will you be …ing?* if the first answer is *no*.

• Students work in groups of three to ask and answer the questions. Remind them to note down the answers of the other two students.

• Ask one or two students to tell the class what they learnt about one of the students they spoke to.

7

• Tell students that they are going to do the same activity again but this time asking about what people will have done in three months' time.

• Follow the steps in exercise 6.

Optional activities

♦ Students write down two answers given to them by one of their partners. They give the answers to a new partner, who decides which question had been asked, e.g. *Monica will have been to Switzerland (Will you have been on holiday?).*

♦ Write some of the key words from the questions on the board, e.g. *same clothes.* Ask students to try to remember the full questions, e.g. *Will you be wearing the same clothes?*

Extension Ask students to work individually or in pairs to write five more questions. Be prepared to feed in ideas, e.g. *Will you be doing the same sports? Will you be studying the same subjects? Will you have learnt a new skill?* Students interview two more students. Ask them to report back to the class on what they learnt.

8 WRITING

• Ask students to look back at the questions in exercises 6 and 7 and write two paragraphs about themselves, saying what they will be doing and will have done in three months' time. Encourage students to link their ideas into coherent paragraphs rather than just giving a list of answers to the questions.

• Monitor and help as necessary.

• Students check their own work for spelling, grammar and punctuation, before exchanging writing with a partner to read and check each other's work.

Optional activity

Fast-finishers can write a third paragraph about what they will be doing/will have done in three years' time.

LANGUAGE WORKOUT

- Ask students to look at the Language Workout box and complete the examples. Confident students can complete first and then check, while others can look back at exercises 2 and 3 and then complete.
- Students turn to page 115 of the Language File to check their answers.

  Answers
  They'll be working   won't be treating
  Will ... be living   will ... invented
  won't have got   Will we have created
  continuous   perfect

- Highlight that future continuous is formed by *will + be* + verb + *-ing* and future perfect by *will + have* + past participle.
- Show the difference between the two tenses by drawing a timeline. Check students' understanding by asking questions about the examples, e.g. Scientists will have invented earrings which take our pulses: *Will 'inventing earrings' be in progress or finished?*
- Drill the examples in chorus for pronunciation, highlighting the *'ll* contraction, the weak pronunciation of *have* /ə/ and the stress on the verb in the *-ing* form or the past participle.

Optional activities

- To help students practise formulating and pronouncing these tenses, do a substitution drill, e.g. You say *he-work-future continuous* and students reply *He'll be working*. Repeat with other variations.
- Ask students to look back at the text on page 48 and find more examples of the future continuous and future perfect.

PRACTICE

- Students do Practice exercise 11 on page 115 of the Language File. They complete the predictions with the future continuous or future perfect of the verbs in the box. Remind the students to choose the tense suggested by the text in exercise 2.
- Check the answers by asking different students to read out each prediction to the class.

Answers
1 will have created / will be creating   2 will be talking
3 will have become   4 won't be retiring
5 will be wearing   6 will be living   7 will we have learnt

Optional activity

- Fast-finishers can write two more of their own sentences using future perfect or continuous to predict the future.
- Students discuss with a partner whether or not they agree with the predictions 1–7 in Practice exercise 11 and whether the changes will have positive or negative effects on our lives. Ask pairs to report back to the class and continue with a class discussion if students are interested.

Follow-up activities

- **Game** *Memory chain*   Divide the class into groups of 8–10 students. On the board, write *By the end of the year, I'll have …* The first student in each group says the sentence aloud, adding an activity they will have done. The second student repeats the words of the first student and then adds an extra activity, e.g. *I'll have visited England and I'll have taken my exams.* Subsequent students repeat the sentences, adding an extra activity each time. Students who forget any of the activities in the chain are out of the game. Groups keep going until only one winning student is left in each.
- Ask students to imagine that they are going to have a school reunion in the year 2020. Divide the class into groups of 6–8 students. Students work individually to imagine what each person in the group, including themselves, will have done or will be doing by the time of the reunion. Give students some ideas, e.g. *Marco will be playing football in the national team, Emma will have bought a house in New York.* Students then share their predictions with their group to see if they agree with each other.

HOMEWORK

Ask students to write a paragraph for the class magazine about what will have happened or will be happening in the year 2020. Give students a selection of topics and ask them to choose one as the subject of their predictions, e.g. food, shopping, fashion, music, holidays, family life, politics.

WEBLINK

Students may like to visit www.guardian.co.uk/2020 for a special report on life in 2020.

Revision and Extension p57

Language File p115

Workbook Unit 4 Lesson 1 pp38–39

Photocopiable worksheet p172, notes p157

We won't halt global warming until ...

Communicative aims	Language	Pronunciation	Vocabulary	Optional aids
Talking about future possibility	First conditional with *if* and *unless* Future time clauses with *when*, *as soon as* and *until*	Two syllable words stressed differently as nouns and verbs	Global warming	Follow-up activity: first conditional/time clause sentences

WARMER 1

If students did the homework from the last lesson, they can read each other's paragraphs and discuss in groups whether or not they agree with the predictions and then agree on the five predictions most likely to come true.

WARMER 2

Divide the class into two groups. Ask one group to think of any environmental problems they know and the other to brainstorm things we can do to look after our environment. After a few minutes, the two groups share their ideas. Write useful vocabulary on the board.

1 OPENER

- The aim is to introduce the context for the lesson.
- Read the title of the lesson with the class. Students work in pairs to decide which words they think will be in the lesson. Encourage students to look up any words they don't understand.

2 LISTENING

- Set the context of the radio phone-in programme by asking students if they listen to this kind of programme and what subjects are typically discussed.
- Ask three confident students to read out the statements. Ask students which one they agree with the most.
- Students listen and complete the chart and check their answers with another student.
- Check the answers together as a class.
- In pairs, students interview each other and complete the chart with their opinions. Ask some pairs to report back to the class.

2.03 Recording

INTERVIEWER — *We're asking people if they agree with three statements about global warming. And I'm going to talk to Adam, Montse and Claudia. Can I start with you, Adam?*

ADAM — *Sure. Looking at statement 1 – well, I don't really believe in global warming – last winter was really cold. So that's a 'no' I'm afraid.*

INTERVIEWER — *You know a lot of people would say that the facts are against you!*

ADAM — *Well, that's my opinion. And as I don't believe in global warming, I don't think it will make any difference if I travel by plane. So I agree with statement 2. And I also think statement 3 is right – it makes more sense to produce our own food.*

INTERVIEWER — *And you, Montse?*

MONTSE — *Hello. I'm really glad you asked me because I think that global warming is the greatest problem we face, and the sooner we do something about it the better.*

INTERVIEWER — *And statement 2?*

MONTSE — *We have to start somewhere, and individual decisions by individual people will add up. So travelling by plane will make a difference – I disagree with that statement. I'm not so sure about statement 3 – I don't know enough about it. But I guess it's correct.*

INTERVIEWER — *Many thanks. And now you, Claudia.*

CLAUDIA — *Yes, thanks for asking me. Like my friend Montse, I'm worried about global warming and I believe that we must do something about it now. If flying is a problem, then we'll have to fly less, so I think statement 2 is wrong. As for the question about food, I think we need to look at both sides of the argument – it can take more energy to grow food in a cold climate and this will produce greenhouse gases. So I'm afraid I don't agree.*

INTERVIEWER — *Many thanks to all three of you for sharing your views. And now back to the studio.*

Answers

Statement	Adam	Montse	Claudia
1	✗	✓	✓
2	✓	✗	✗
3	✓	✓	✗

Optional activity

Students work in groups of three and have similar conversations about the statements.

3 READING

- Ask students to read and listen to the text and to check which of the statements in exercise 2 Gina agrees with. Check that students have understood *carbon emissions* and *global warming*. Explain that a *tonne* is a quantity measure. Be prepared to translate *import, export, greenhouse gases, offset, campaigner* and *halt*.

🔘 2.04 **Recording and answer**

See text on page 50 of the Student's Book.
Gina agrees with statement 1.

4 AFTER READING

- Students read the text again and decide if sentences 1–8 are true or false.
- Check the answers before students write corrections for the false sentences. Monitor and help where necessary.
- Ask students to read their answers to the class.

Answers

1 False. When carbon emissions decrease, air pollution will decrease too.
2 True
3 False. We will reduce carbon emissions if we fly less often.
4 False. If we travel by train we'll only produce 12.5% of the emissions of a flight.
5 True
6 True
7 False. They won't solve the problem of global warming.
8 True

Optional activity

Ask students to look through the text again and find as much vocabulary to do with the environment as they can. Elicit words, write them on the board and explain them if necessary. Students can then write the vocabulary in their vocabulary notebooks.

Useful information

A 'carbon footprint' is the amount of carbon emissions that each individual is responsible for producing, for example through transport, leisure activities, home electricity usage, clothing and food. On average, 6% of an individual's carbon footprint comes from holiday flights. We can reduce carbon emissions by flying less, using public transport, choosing renewable energy sources and locally produced goods.

Your response

Have students work in pairs or groups to make a list of things they can do to help reduce globabl warming. Then conduct a class feedback session.

5 PRONUNCIATION

- Elicit *decrease* from the students by asking what we need to do to carbon emissions. Ask students if it is a verb or a noun and establish that it can be both, showing the different stress in each case.

- Go through the rule with the students, drilling the words in the box as both nouns and verbs. Point out that this is true just for a small group of English words.
- Students look at sentences 1–6 to decide whether the highlighted word is a noun or a verb and mark the stress accordingly.
- Play the recording for students to check their answers. Play the recording again, pausing between sentences for students to repeat them.

🔘 2.05 **Recording and answers**

1 There will be a decrease in pollution when carbon emissions decrease.
2 Our problems increase with the increase in global warming.
3 The soldier deserted the army in the desert.
4 The UK imports a lot of food but also sells food exports.
5 The police suspect the money was stolen and are questioning a suspect.
6 You aren't permitted to work there without a work permit.
1 noun, verb   2 verb, noun   3 verb, noun   4 verb, noun
5 verb, noun   6 verb, noun

Optional activity

Read out some of these two-syllable words either alone or in a sentence. Students raise their right hand if they think it was the verb and their left if it was the noun.

Extension Students find the words in the lesson and decide if they are nouns or verbs. (*A question of Balance: decrease* (v), *increase* (n), *produce* (v), *export* (n), *import* (v))

LANGUAGE WORKOUT OPTION

If you want to pre-teach the language students will use in the following activities, you may like to go to the Language Workout box now.

6 ROLE PLAY

- Set the context for the role play by asking students if they have any travel plans this year.
- Divide the class into two groups, A and B. Students work with a partner from the same group to read the conversation guidelines and think about what they will say. Encourage students to look back through the lesson for useful language. Students can make notes, but should avoid writing a complete script. Monitor and help where necessary.
- Organise students into A/B pairs to do the role play.
- Ask confident students to perform the dialogue in front of the class.

LANGUAGE WORKOUT OPTION

If you want to pre-teach the language students will use in the following activities, you may like to go to the Language Workout box now.

7 WRITING

- Ask students to complete the paragraph in their own words to explain why we should reduce carbon emissions. Remind them to look back through the lesson for useful language and ideas. Be prepared to translate or explain *droughts*, *floods* and *melt*.
- Monitor and help with vocabulary and grammar.
- When they have checked their own work, students exchange writing with a partner to check each other's work and compare with their own.

LANGUAGE WORKOUT

- Ask students to look at the Language Workout box and complete the examples. Confident students can complete first and then check, while others can look back at exercises 3 and 4 and then complete.
- Students turn to page 115 of the Language File to check their answers.

  Answers
  *don't fly ... we'll reduce   stop ... we'll make
  won't improve ... work   will look ... agree
  decrease ... will decrease
  won't halt ... stop*

- Highlight that:
  - the clause beginning *if/unless/when/as soon as/until* has the verb in the present simple, not the *will* form.
  - first conditional sentences refer to possible, real situations in the future.
  - it is possible to reverse the order of the condition and result clauses, as shown in the first two conditional sentences. There is no comma when the sentence starts with the result clause.

- Check students' understanding by asking questions about the examples, e.g. *Is it possible to reduce carbon emissions? How?* Ask students to transform the *unless* sentence into an *if* sentence, i.e. *The situation won't improve if we don't all work together./The situation will improve if we all work together.*
- Drill the examples in chorus for pronunciation, highlighting the *'ll* contraction, the pronunciation of *won't* and the natural rhythm of the sentences.

PRACTICE

- Students do Practice exercise 12 on page 115 of the Language File. They complete the gaps with the present or future simple form of the verb.
- Check the answers with the class.

  Answers
  *1 continue, will get   2 won't stop, becomes
  3 get, will use   4 will have, want   5 will be, take
  6 takes, will improve*

Optional activity

Fast-finishers try to rewrite one or two of the sentences, using *unless* instead of *if* and vice versa and making the other necessary changes.

Follow-up activity

Game *Telepathy*   Before the lesson, prepare some first conditional sentences and sentences with time clauses from the lesson. Read out the first half of one of the sentences, either the condition or the result clause. See Unit 3, Lesson 2 Follow-up activities for further instructions.

HOMEWORK

Ask students to write a short letter to a politician to explain their concerns about the environment and suggest that action be taken by the government, for example working with politicians from other countries, publicising carbon offsetting and developing environmental projects.

WEBLINK

Students may like to visit www.carbonfootprint.com. They can follow the links for 'Individuals' to work out their own carbon footprint and get tips on how to reduce it.

Revision and Extension p57

Language File p115

Workbook Unit 4 Lesson 2 pp40–41

Photocopiable worksheet p173, notes p157

3

If you could choose ...

Communicative aims	Language	Pronunciation	Vocabulary	Optional aids
Talking about imaginary or unlikely situations Expressing wishes about the present	Second conditional *wish/if only* + past simple	Sentence stress and intonation	Tourism and travel	Warmer 1: world map Follow-up activity: a few blank slips of paper per student

Useful information

Nepal is situated between India and China (Tibet) and its capital is Kathmandu. It's famous for its spectacular scenery, notably the Himalayas, which include the world's highest mountain, Mount Everest, along with seven of the world's other highest peaks. The main language spoken is Nepali and tourism is the largest industry.

WARMER 1

Show students a world map and ask *Where is Nepal?* Find out if the students know anything about Nepal, e.g. the capital, the landscape, the neighbouring countries, etc.

WARMER 2

Game *A place I'd like to visit*   Give students clues about a city or country you would like to visit, but haven't yet, e.g. *There's lots of water, You can eat good pizza there, You can see great art there* (Answer: *Venice*). Ask students to play the game in pairs.

1 OPENER

- The aim is to introduce the context for the reading in exercise 2.
- Tell students they are going to read about travel. Ask students to look at the words in the box and predict which they will find in the text.
- Ask students to share their ideas with the rest of the class. Clarify or translate words that they are unsure of, but do not confirm which are in the text yet.

2 READING

- Students read and listen to the text to find out whether Vic has been to Nepal before. Encourage students to read quickly and guess unfamiliar words from context. Be prepared to translate *hand-carved*. Explain that *hippies* were famous in the 1960s as people who believed in love and peace. Check the answer to the question, then check which words from the Opener students found in the text (*guesthouse, hostel, overland, traditional, trekking*).

2.06 **Recording and answers**
See text on page 52 of the Student's Book.

Yes, Vic has been to Nepal. He went last year.

3 AFTER READING

- Students re-read the text and match the beginnings 1–8 with the endings a–k. Ask students to compare with a partner before checking the answers together as a class.

  Answers
  1 k   2 f   3 d   4 j   5 i   6 e   7 h   8 b

Your response

Put students into pairs to discuss the questions. Ask pairs to report back on their discussion and their ideas of paradise on earth.

Optional activities

- Students read out the dialogue in pairs, taking the role of Vic and the interviewer.
- In pairs, students discuss if they would like to visit Nepal and why. They discuss whether they would enjoy trekking and why/why not.

LANGUAGE WORKOUT OPTION

If you want to pre-teach the language students will use in the following activities, you may like to go to the Language Workout box now.

4 LISTENING

- Set the context of the radio phone-in programme and explain that the four callers have problems and secret wishes. Ask the students to look at the chart and see if they can guess any of the missing information.
- Students listen and complete the chart. Check the answers with the whole class.
- Students work in pairs to say what the callers' secret wishes were and what the callers believe, following the examples. Ask some students to say their sentences to the class.

🔘 2.07 **Recording and answers**

PRESENTER Hi, is that Karen? You're through to Secret Wishes and I'm Jane. So what's your secret wish, Karen?

KAREN Well, I know you can't do anything about it – no one can. And it's a terrible thing to say … It's hard. Really hard.

PRESENTER Go on, Karen, you can tell me. It'll be good to get it off your chest.

KAREN It's my sister, you see. She's much quicker and cleverer than me. So when we have friends around people don't talk to me. They ignore me and all talk to my sister.

PRESENTER And your wish?

KAREN I wish I was an only child. I wish I didn't have a sister. There, now I've said it. If my sister wasn't there, people would talk to me.

PRESENTER Have you tried discussing this with …

*****

PRESENTER Will, I'm Jane and you're live on Secret Wishes. What can we do for you?

WILL I'm not sure you can do anything. I know it sounds silly, but my problem is that I seem to spend all my time on buses. We live a long way from school and I have to take two buses to get there. That's an hour and a half each way every day. It takes ages. Absolutely ages.

PRESENTER That's a long journey – fifteen hours a week on a bus. Plenty of time to do your homework though!

WILL No, the worst part is that I can't read on buses. If I read, I feel sick.

PRESENTER Oh, dear. And what do your parents think?

WILL They don't see the problem. You see my dad's a bus driver and …

PRESENTER So what's your wish?

WILL It's simple. I wish I lived nearer the school and never had to get on a bus again ever!

PRESENTER Is there another …

*****

ALICE Hello? Is that Secret Wishes?

PRESENTER Yes, it is. You're Alice, aren't you? I'm Jane, all ready to help you with your problem if I can.

ALICE OK – it's this. I have too many friends. They're always on the phone or coming round to see me. It sounds silly. Extremely silly. But …

PRESENTER Too many friends? People usually ring us when they don't have enough friends!

ALICE It's nice of course, and I try to be polite and listen to them. But they go on and on – if it's not one thing, it's another. I never have any time for myself.

PRESENTER So you would like to …

ALICE Be more unpopular. If I weren't so popular, I'd have more time for myself.

PRESENTER Well, have you thought of …

*****

PRESENTER Hello? I believe there are two of you on the line – Sally and Frank. Is that right?

FRANK That's right, but I'll let Sally do the talking.

SALLY Frank and I have been going out together for nearly a year now, but there's a problem with our parents – his parents and mine. They say they aren't happy with our relationship – they think we're too young. They get angry. Very angry.

PRESENTER I see.

SALLY We just wish they understood what we mean to each other. If they understood what we meant to each other, they'd be happy with our relationship.

FRANK That's right.

PRESENTER It's very difficult when …

Name	Problem	Secret Wish
Karen	People all talk to her sister not her.	to be an only child
Will	Spends all his time on buses. Feels sick when he reads on buses.	to live nearer the school
Alice	Has too many friends, never has time for herself.	to be more unpopular
Sally and Frank	Their parents aren't happy with their relationship.	parents to understand what they mean to each other

Extension Students complete the presenter's final sentences to each caller with their own ideas. Elicit answers from the class and get the class to decide which is the best advice.

LANGUAGE WORKOUT OPTION

If you want to pre-teach the language students will use in the following activities, you may like to go to the Language Workout box now.

5 SPEAKING

- With weaker classes, give some examples yourself or brainstorm some ideas with the whole class before students work individually to complete the sentences.
- Students work in pairs to tell their partner their ideas. Ask some pairs to report back to the class.

6 PRONUNCIATION

- Tell students that they will hear some sentences from exercise 4 and that they should mark the stressed words.
- Play the recording, pausing after each sentence.
- Check answers, and remind students that we stress these words to convey a strong meaning.
- Play the recording again, pausing for students to repeat.

2.08 Recording and answers

It's hard. _Really_ hard.

It takes ages. _Absolutely_ ages.

It sounds silly. _Extremely_ silly.

They get angry. _Very_ angry.

LANGUAGE WORKOUT OPTION

If you want to pre-teach the language students will use in the following activities, you may like to go to the Language Workout box now.

7 SPEAKING

- Tell students that they are going to interview three students using the questions from exercise 2.
- Students read the questions and think about their own answers. Monitor and help with vocabulary at this stage.
- Students work in groups of four to ask and answer the questions and note down the answers.
- Ask some students to tell the class what they learnt about the students they spoke to.

8 WRITING

- Students write a paragraph about two of the interviews from exercise 7. Encourage students to link their ideas into coherent paragraphs rather than listing answers.
- Students check their own work for spelling, grammar and punctuation, before exchanging writing with their interviewees to read and check each other's work.

LANGUAGE WORKOUT

- Ask students to look at the Language Workout box and complete the examples. Confident students can complete first and then check, while others can look back at exercises 2 and 3 and then complete.
- Students turn to page 115–116 of the Language File to check their answers.

    Answers
    had ... I'd   was ... I wouldn't
    could ... would   could   were
    second   if   wish

- Highlight that:
  - Second conditional sentences are formed If + past simple + would + infinitive.

- The second conditional expresses an imaginary or unreal situation. Contrast this with the first conditional which expresses a possible or likely future situation.
- The condition and result clauses can be reversed, but no comma is used in this case.
- If only and wish are followed by the past simple, to express a hope or desire for a situation in the present to be different.
- The use of the past tense expresses a hypothetical meaning, rather than past time.
- Both was and were are possible after I/he/she/it, but were sounds more formal.
- Check students' understanding by asking questions about the examples, e.g. Is it possible for him to take all his friends?
- Drill the examples for pronunciation, highlighting the 'd contraction, and the stress on wish and only.
- Wish can be used in a variety of ways, but it may be helpful to point out that:
  - we don't use wish to refer to things which we feel are possible in the future. Instead we use hope, e.g. I hope I pass the test.
  - wish + would is used, instead of past simple, to express annoyance with someone else's actions, e.g. I wish you would stop laughing.

PRACTICE

- Students do Practice exercise 13 on page 116 of the Language File. They complete sentences 1–8 with the correct form of the verbs in the box.
- Check the answers by asking different students to read a sentence, correcting pronunciation where necessary.

    Answers
    1 had   2 was/were   3 knew   4 had   5 knew   6 could
    7 had   8 was/were

Follow-up activity

Game Who would …?   Divide students into groups of eight. Give each student some blank slips of paper. Read out a question using the second conditional, e.g. What would you buy with a million pounds? Students write each answer on a separate piece of paper, then collect their group's papers. The papers are mixed and passed to another group, who guess who wrote which answer, e.g. We think Simon would buy a Ferrari.

HOMEWORK

Students interview a friend or family member using the questions in the interview in exercise 2.

WEBLINK

Students may like to visit www.welcomenepal.com for more information about Nepal.

Revision and Extension p57

Language File pp115–116

Workbook Unit 4 Lesson 3 pp42–43

Photocopiable worksheet p174, notes p157

81

Integrated Skills Debating an issue

Skills		Learner independence	Vocabulary
Reading For and against: Direct Action	*Speaking* Debate	Thinking skills	Politics
Direct Action	*Writing* A balanced account	Word creation: noun prefixes	Formal debate
Listening Completing notes on a debate	of a controversial issue	*anti-* and *non-*	Useful expressions

WARMER 1

Game *Password*   See Unit 3, Lesson 3 Follow-up activities for instructions. Use words from the Vocabulary box.

WARMER 2

Write the names of some famous people who have changed the world on the board. You could use the examples in exercise 2 or others your students will know. Ask students to discuss what they know about these people.

1 OPENER

- The aim is to set the context for the reading.
- Ask students what is happening in the photo. Elicit *protest* and ask students what other issues people protest about. Be ready to give some examples: *animal testing, nuclear power, war*. Explain that *direct action* has a similar meaning to *protest*.

Optional activity

Ask students what issues in the world today they feel strongly about. Ask *What can you do to change things? What's the best way to protest?* Elicit students' ideas in a class discussion.

2 READING

- Students read the text and complete it with phrases a–g. Encourage them to guess unfamiliar words from context and tell them that the meaning of the highlighted words will be dealt with in exercise 3. Be prepared to translate *democracy, generate, publicity* and *anti-globalisation*.
- Play the recording for students to check their answers. Ask students which words in the phrases helped them complete the gaps.

(2.09) Recording
Direct action
For three famous people, Mahatma Gandhi, Emmeline Pankhurst and Martin Luther King, direct action was the only way to achieve their aims. They organised demonstrations and marches, sit-ins and hunger strikes, and generated enormous publicity. Largely as a result of their direct action, India became independent (1947), women in Britain got the vote (partly in 1918 and fully in 1928), and racial segregation ended in the USA (1964 and 1965).

So what are the arguments for and against direct action? Supporters of direct action say that their methods get results. For example, they claim that anti-GM food demonstrations have made people aware of the dangers of genetically modified food. And the world knows about the cruelty of whale hunting thanks to direct action against Japanese and Norwegian whaling ships. They also argue that direct action involves people who can't, or don't, vote in elections, such as those who are not registered or who are too young to vote. What's more, they say that when the media report direct action, for instance a million people on an anti-war march, politicians have to take notice.

Opponents of direct action point out that non-violent protest can lead to violence as protesters and police clash, as has happened in the recent anti-globalisation demonstrations. They also claim that it is easy for small groups of protesters who feel strongly about a particular issue to 'hijack' demonstrations. In addition, they argue that the whole point of a democracy is that we elect representatives to take decisions for us. If we feel strongly about an issue, we should make our case with the elected representatives and not on the streets.

Answers
1 g   2 a   3 c   4 b   5 f   6 d

3

- The aim is to encourage students to deduce the meaning of unknown words from context. Ask students to match the highlighted words in the text with definitions 1–10.

Answers
1 moral   2 hijack   3 demonstrations   4 crucial
5 genetically modified   6 hunger strikes   7 clash
8 racial segregation   9 in harmony   10 sit-ins

4

- Ask students to discuss in pairs if they agree with the ideas in the quotations. Pairs report back to the class.

5

- Ask the students to find an example of *also, in addition* and *what's more* in the text. They should use the examples to decide which two usually come at the start of a sentence.

- Students then find *for example, for instance* and *such as* in the text. Ask which of the expressions cannot come at the start of a sentence.

Answers

***What's more**, they say there is evidence*
*They **also** claim that it is easy for small groups*
*They **also** argue that direct action*
***In addition**, they argue that*
***For example**, they claim that anti-GM food*
*the media report direct action, **for instance** a million people*
*… vote in elections, **such as** those who are not registered*
***What is more** and **in addition** usually come at the start.*
***Such as** cannot come at the start.*

Optional activity

Write *We need to act now, to prevent global warming* on the board. Ask students to give opinions and examples. Write these on the board in two columns. Students then work in pairs to organise the ideas into a paragraph, using the linking expressions.

6 LISTENING

- Explain to students that they are going to listen to a debate. Ask them to read the introduction and find out the subject (Answer: taking direct action to protect the environment). Explain that an *eco-warrior* is someone who takes protest action to protect the environment.
- Play the recording and ask students to listen for the result.
- Check the answer with the whole class.

2.10 Recording and answer

CHAIR *Hello, my name's Jan and I'm chairing this debate. The motion today is: 'If necessary, we should take direct action to protect the environment'. Tim is proposing the motion and Helen is opposing it. Tim, would you like to start?*

TIM *What I'm going to argue is that direct action can be necessary. Firstly, because big business is so powerful that even governments can't stop it. Secondly, because direct action makes people aware of problems, take whales for example. And thirdly, because it is often the only way to save an animal or the environment before it is destroyed. The first argument for direct action is the power of big business. Large multi-national companies more money and influence than many small governments. It can be hard for a government to oppose, for example, exploration for oil by a big company, even though it may damage the environment. This is where ordinary people have a role in stopping harmful development. Secondly, direct action is reported in the media and this makes people aware of environmental problems. A very good example of this is the Greenpeace campaign to save the whale. If Greenpeace didn't take direct action, many people around the world wouldn't know the danger whales are in. The third point is to do with time. Governments act slowly but individuals can act quickly. Take road building for instance. Protesters can stop*

a new road from damaging the environment by living in trees or tunnels along its route and by lying down in front of equipment – simple but very effective action. What I've argued is that direct action can be necessary. Firstly, I pointed out that big business is so powerful that even governments can't stop it. Secondly, I showed how direct action can make people aware of problems. And thirdly, I showed how it is often the only way to save an animal or the environment before it is destroyed.

CHAIR *Thank you, Tim. Now Helen to oppose the motion.*

HELEN *What I'm going to argue is that there are better ways than direct action. Firstly, if everyone looks after their own environment we won't need direct action. Secondly, many protesters are better at getting publicity than actually changing anything. And thirdly, political action is better than direct action – the environment is too important to be left to protesters. To start with, it's clear that if everyone did what they could to protect the environment, by recycling, for example, or saving energy, then there would be no need for direct action. We must take responsibility for the environment in our daily lives.*
Then we have to look at the effects of direct action. Tim claims that it brings issues to people's attention. However, in my opinion, many of these environmental protesters get publicity for themselves but they don't really help protect the environment.
Finally, what is the point of having elections and voting if we don't let the politicians do the job we chose them for. I believe democracy is the best protection for the environment.
So what I've argued is this. Firstly, if everyone looked after their own environment we wouldn't need direct action. Secondly, many protesters are better at getting publicity than actually changing anything. And thirdly, that political action is better than direct action – the environment is too important to be left to protesters.

CHAIR *Thank you both very much. Now you have one sentence each to sum up your argument before we have a vote.*

TIM *We've only got one world. Let's use direct action to save it.*

HELEN *Show by the way you live your life that you care about the environment.*

CHAIR *And now raise your hands to vote. Those in favour of the motion? Thank you. And those against? Thank you. The result is **ten** votes for the motion and **ten** votes against!*

- Ask the students to listen to the recording again and complete the speakers' notes. Check the answers.

Answers

1 powerful   2 whales   3 destroyed   4 everyone
5 publicity   6 protesters   7 ten   8 ten

Optional activity

Students discuss with a partner how they would vote in this debate. You could do a class vote on the debate to see which way the class would vote.

7 SPEAKING

- Divide the students into two or three groups, each to have a debate.
- Give the group(s) a few minutes to agree on which topic they would like to debate.
- Choose three confident students per group to be the Chair and the two speakers. Give the speakers a few minutes to prepare their speech, encouraging other students to help them. Remind them to use the linking expressions from exercise 5 to help present their opinions and examples.
- The groups have their debates. Ensure the Chair gives each speaker a chance to speak and then summarise what he/she has said.
- The Chair organises a final vote among the students in the group. Students tell the other group(s) the result of their debate.

8 GUIDED WRITING

- Students write two paragraphs giving the arguments for and against the topic of their debate in exercise 7. Remind students to look back at the text in exercise 2 for useful language, and to use the linking expressions in exercise 5.
- Monitor and help with vocabulary as necessary.
- Students check their own work and then exchange writing with a partner to read and check each other's work.

9 LEARNER INDEPENDENCE

- The aim is to encourage students to think more about their learning.
- Ask students if they know any ways of learning and remembering new words and phrases. Ask them to read the suggested procedure. Find out if any students have already used the technique.
- If there is time, students can try the technique in the classroom. Otherwise they can do so at home and report back next lesson on which words and phrases they managed to remember.

10 WORD CREATION

- Ask students if they can remember the expression from the text meaning being against war (Answer: *anti-war*). Write the prefixes *anti-* and *non-* on the board and elicit other examples of words starting with each.
- Students add the prefix *anti-* or *non-* to the nouns in the box. Explain that *spam* is unwanted email messages.
- Students use the words to complete the sentences. Check the answers as a class.
- Ask students to copy the words into their vocabulary notebooks.

Answers

1 anti-terrorism   2 non-iron   3 non-fiction
4 non-violent   5 anti-war   6 anti-spam

Optional activity

Dictate other words that can be prefixed by *anti-* or *non-*. Students decide which go with each prefix. Examples could include *smoker, clockwise, social*.

EXTRA PRACTICE

If you would like to give your students more practice in forming words which start with *anti-* or *non-*, please see the Vocabulary EXTRA! Worksheets on the Teacher's Resource Site (www.macmillanenglish.com/inspiration).

11 PHRASEBOOK

- Students look through Unit 4 to find the expressions, noting how they are used.
- Play the recording for students to listen and repeat the expressions.
- Check students understand the expressions by asking them to write a five-line dialogue using three of them.
- Students exchange their dialogues, then read and underline the three expressions their partner chose to include.

2.11 Recording and answers

Only time will tell. (Lesson 1, exercise 2)
But what if I …? (Lesson 2, exercise 3)
Not necessarily. (Lesson 2, exercise 3)
If only people were like that … (Lesson 3, exercise 2)
You meet the most amazing people. (Lesson 3, exercise 2)
The whole point is … (Lesson 3, exercise 2)
It takes ages. (Lesson 3, exercise 4)
It sounds silly.   (Lesson 3, exercise 4)
What's more … (Lesson 4, exercise 2)

Follow-up activities

- Ask students to choose a topic they feel strongly about and design a protest poster. They should choose a memorable slogan and include their reasons for opposition. Titles could be serious or light, e.g. *Stop animal testing, Peace not war, Say no to homework.* Students present their posters to a small group, explaining why they chose the issue.
- Roleplay *Good cop, bad cop.* Students work in A/B pairs. Read out a subject which has both pros and cons, e.g. *single sex schools, air travel.* Student A thinks of the pros and student B thinks of the cons. Set a short time limit. Students A and B then say their arguments to each other. Ask students who had the stronger arguments, before changing to a new subject.

HOMEWORK

Ask students to research and write a paragraph about a famous person who took direct action, e.g. those mentioned in exercise 2 or someone else of their choice.

WEBLINK

Students can find out more about a range of Greenpeace protest campaigns at
www.greenpeace.org/international/en/campaigns

Revision and Extension p57

Workbook Unit 4 Lesson 4 pp44–45

Inspiration EXTRA!

PROJECT FUTURE PREDICTIONS

1 • Explain to students that the aim of the project is to write their predictions about life in the future. Ask students to read the model text, ask *Do you agree with these predictions?*

 • Divide the students into groups and tell them to work together to choose a year in the future, and decide what topics they are going to write about.

2 • Different students within the group make notes about each topic, using the questions in the box as a guide.

 • Remind students that they can use the future tenses covered in Lesson 1.

3 • Students work together to write their future predictions. Tell them they can use the example text as a model.

 • Students read their work carefully to correct any mistakes. They then copy their writing out neatly and the editor chooses the order of the material, whilst other students work on illustrating the work with pictures or images from magazines and newspapers.

 • Students show their predictions to other groups. Display them on the classroom wall if possible.

Optional activity

Students can look at all the predictions and decide in pairs which they think are most and least likely. Put pairs into groups of four to compare their ideas, then ask each group to report back to the class.

GAME WORD SQUARE

 • Tell students to work in pairs to write down as many English words as possible, using pairs of letters from anywhere in the square. Point out the examples and remind students that the letters do not have to be next to each other in the square.

 • Tell students that four-letter words score one point, six-letter words score two and eight-letter words score four.

 • The pair with the highest score are the winners. Ask the winning pair to read out their list of words to the rest of the class.

Suggested answers

port, test, heat, coal, meat, action, energy, reaction, threat(en) full(er), coat, health, (re)heat(er), here, hell, heal, polite, fell, future, nature, then, meal, real, (re) port(er), teen, tell(er), that, nation(al), (re)fuel, (re)tire, cost, list(en)(er), post(er), rest, life, come, actual, feel(er), carton, (re)call(er), care(er), cart, cafe, came, cast, time, (re)name.

REVISION

Lesson 1
Students' own answers.

Lesson 2
Students' own answers.

Lesson 3

Suggested answers

I wish I lived nearer the school. If I lived nearer school, I wouldn't have to take a long bus journey every day.
I wish I wasn't so popular. If I had fewer friends, I'd have more time for myself.
I/We wish my/our parents understood what we meant to each other. If they understood, they'd be happy with our relationship.

EXTENSION

Lesson 1
Students' own answers.

Lesson 2
 • Remind students not to use *will* in the clause beginning *if/unless/when/as soon as.*
Students' own answers.

Lesson 3
 • Remind students to use the past simple where necessary after *I wish* and *If only ...*
Students' own answers.

YOUR CHOICE!

 • The aim is to give students more learner independence and help them to identify their preferred way of learning. Encourage students to choose an activity that they feel less comfortable with if they want a challenge or are aware that they need practice in a particular area.

 • Monitor and help groups. Check answers if necessary, or provide written answers for groups to check their own work against.

CONSTRUCTION

Answers

1 You won't catch the train if you don't run.
You won't catch the train unless you run.
2 I wouldn't buy a car if I didn't pass my driving test.
I wouldn't buy a car unless I passed my driving test.
3 We won't have a picnic if the weather isn't fine.
We won't have a picnic unless the weather is fine.
4 They won't see the Pyramids if they don't go to Cairo.
They won't see the Pyramids unless they go to Cairo.
5 He wouldn't have Greek lessons if he didn't go to Greece.
He wouldn't have Greek lessons unless he went
to Greece.
6 I won't phone you if I don't need help.
I won't phone you unless I need help.
7 She won't go to the party if she doesn't feel better.
She won't go to the party unless she feels better.
8 They wouldn't call the police if they weren't
really worried.
They wouldn't call the police unless they were really
worried.

REFLECTION

Answers

We form the future continuous with will/won't be +
***present** participle.*
*This time tomorrow, she'll be on a plane. She'll **be flying***
to Australia!
*We form the future perfect with will/won't have + **past***
participle.
*I'm sorry, but I won't **have finished** my homework*
by tomorrow.
In first conditional sentences, the verb in the if clause is in
*the **present** tense.*
*If you **smile** at people, they'll smile back at you.*
In second conditional sentences, the verb in the if clause is
*in the **past** tense.*
*We wouldn't be lost if we **had** a map.*

Language File pp115–116

Song – photocopiable worksheet p188, notes p162

ACTION

- Students work in small groups.
- They follow the instructions in the box, taking it in turns to mime. Point out the example *HALT* as a model.
- The other students in their group guess and write down each letter until they have the complete word.

INTERACTION

- Students work in small groups.
- They first read the instructions and think about what they are going to say. They then tell each other their answers. Encourage them to explain the reasons for their wishes and to ask further questions to each other.
- Students could report back to the rest of the class on any common or unusual wishes in their group.

You may now like students to do the song *Every Breath You Take*. See p162 for the notes and p188 for the worksheet.

Workbook Unit 4 Inspiration EXTRA! pp46–47

Units 3–4

1 Ask students to look at the picture and the headline and predict where the boy is and what sort of life he has. Students read the story and check their predictions (Answer: He's in Mumbai, India and his life is likely to be uncomfortable, living in poor, overcrowded conditions). Explain that *slums* are poor areas of housing in very bad condition. Students read the story again and choose the appropriate word for each space. Do the first one together as an example. This can be done in pairs or individually as a short test. Check the answers together as a whole class.

> **Answers**
>
> *1 B   2 C   3 A   4 C   5 A   6 B   7 C   8 B   9 A*
> *10 B*

> **Optional activity**
>
> Confident students can attempt the task before looking at the word options.

2 Students complete the sentences with the correct adverbs, using the information in *Expanding Cities* where necessary.

> **Answers**
>
> *1 incredibly quickly   2 faster   3 more seriously*
> *4 the most rapidly   5 extremely miserably   6 better*

3 Students complete the sentences 1–5 with *so* or *such* and match them with an ending a–e.

> **Answers**
>
> *1 so; e   2 such; d   3 so; c   4 so; b   5 such; a*

> **Optional activity**
>
> Fast-finishers try to recall the rules for when we use *so* and *such* and prepare to explain their choices in the exercise.

4 Students complete the dialogue with the correct form of the verb in brackets.

> **Answers**
>
> *1 will fly   2 will have   3 are you doing   4 'm flying*
> *5 does it leave   6 gets   7 will be   8 will be   9 will be*
> *10 'm only going   11 'm coming   12 does that leave*
> *13 will arrive   14 are you doing*

5 Students complete the sentences with the correct form of the verb in brackets.

> **Answers**
>
> *1 will be injecting   2 will have eaten   3 will have eaten*
> *4 will still be sending   5 will have passed*
> *6 won't be using*

6 Students complete the questions with the past simple of the verb or *would*, and answer the questions for themselves.

> **Answers**
>
> *1 would you do, dropped*
> *2 arrested, would you phone*
> *3 would you get, didn't have*
> *4 had to, would you give up*
> *5 were, would you ask*
> *6 would you do, were*
> *7 had to, would you take*
> *8 would you have, had to*
> *9 would you say, asked*
> *10 Would you panic if you were, heard*

> **Optional activity**
>
> Fast-finishers write another everyday nightmare question using the second conditional.

7 Students complete the wishes with the correct form of the verbs in the box.

> **Answers**
>
> *1 tried   2 was/were   3 could   4 spent, grew   5 realised*
> *6 had*

> **Optional activity**
>
> Fast-finishers write a second conditional to say how things would be different if the 'wish' came true, e.g. *If people understood each other better, there would be less conflict.*

VOCABULARY

8 Students complete the sentences with the correct word from the box. Point out that there are four words that students don't need. Confident students can cover the words and guess which words are missing before checking against the list.

> **Answers**
>
> *1 expectancy   2 protesters   3 atmosphere*
> *4 wireless   5 retire   6 rotate   7 march   8 flood*
> *9 balance*

9 Students match the words in the box with definitions 1–6. Confident students can attempt the task without looking at the words in the box and then look to check.

> *1 hoax   2 absorb   3 pulse   4 crisis*
> *5 glow   6 decrease*

> **Optional activity**
>
> Fast-finishers try to remember where in the lesson they saw each word, and write an example sentence including each word.

10 Students match the verbs in list A with the words and phrases in list B. They then write sentences using four of the expressions.

| Answers

1 *achieve an aim*   2 *fund a project*   3 *generate publicity*
4 *make a case*   5 *play a part*   6 *vote in an election*

Optional activity

In pairs, students write questions using four of the verbs and phrases. They can then join with another pair and ask and answer their questions.

LEARNER INDEPENDENCE SELF ASSESSMENT

- Explain to students that the aim of the self-assessment is to encourage them to check their own progress and take any necessary action to improve. Point out that the list 1–8 covers areas of functional language from Units 3–4. Students tick the 'Fine' box for functional language that they feel confident using, but put a question mark in the 'Not sure' box for functional language that they have difficulties with or still cannot use confidently.

- Encourage students to look at the Language File and re-do exercises from the Workbook in areas where they have problems. They may also like to re-do exercises from the lessons and from the Revision and Extension sections in Units 3 and 4.

- Students write an example sentence for each language area in the list. You may like to elicit grammar students need for each example before students write their sentences, e.g. *Describing and comparing the way things happen: comparison of adverbs.* Students can refer back to the lessons and the Language File.

- Ask students to compare their sentences with a partner and discuss and correct any mistakes.

- Check students' sentences and note down any language areas for further practice.

Follow-up activities

- ◆ Tell students that they are going to make lists similar to the one in exercise 7, based on their own wishes. Give a selection of titles to choose from, e.g. *Eight wishes for a better school/town/life for teenagers.* Students work individually to write their list of wishes for their chosen title, e.g. *I wish we could study film and media rather than science.* Students share their wishes in small groups, explaining how things would be different if their wish came true, e.g. *If we could study media, we'd have better job opportunities.*

- ◆ **Game** *Cross the river*   On the board, draw a picture of three stepping stones across a river. Divide the class into two teams and tell them that for their team to score a point, they must 'cross' the river by successfully answering one vocabulary question, one grammar question and one pronunciation question. For the first, ask students to guess the word from a definition from the vocabulary box. For the second give a 'grammar' structure (future perfect, *unless, if only*) for students to put in an example sentence, and for the last, write a word from the unit and ask students to identify the stressed syllable. Teams take it in turns to attempt to 'cross the river' as many times as possible.

HOMEWORK

Now that they are half way through the book, ask the students to write a paragraph about their learning experience so far. They should mention what they've enjoyed, what they've learnt, what they've found difficult and which learning style they are most enjoying in the *Your Choice!* sections.

WEBLINK

Students may like to visit www.wikitravel.org/en/Mumbai for information on the more positive aspects of Mumbai as a city to visit.

Language File pp114–116

Workbook Review Units 3–4 pp48–49

Activities		Project	Vocabulary
Identifying the function of communicative language	Categorising vocabulary Contextualising listening extracts	Extraordinary people	Aviation Restaurant Sport

WARMER 1

Game *Vocabulary guessing* Put students into pairs and ask them to look at the pictures. Tell them they should write down five items of vocabulary that have a connection with each one. They cannot write words for anything they can see in the pictures, but they should write words that have an association with the picture, e.g. for picture A they might write *dangerous*. Students write their words in pairs.

Ask pairs in turn to read out their five words for one of the pictures, without saying which one it is for. Other students guess the picture.

WARMER 2

Game *What are they saying?* Put students into pairs and ask them to imagine a speech bubble coming from the mouth of one of the people in each picture. They try to think of something amusing that each person is saying. Ask students in turn to read out their quotes, and get the class to choose the most amusing/original for each picture.

1 • The aim is to introduce students to the main areas of communicative language they will cover in Units 5 and 6.
• Focus on the two boxes and explain that they show the communicative language and topics/vocabulary that students will learn in Units 5 and 6. Students match six of the communicative aims 1–8 with the pictures A–F.

> **Answers**
> *1 -   2 D   3 A   4 E   5 C   6 F   7 -   8 B*

Optional activity

Students write another example sentence for each of the communicative aims 1–8. Monitor and help where necessary. Ask students to read out some of their sentences, and ask the class to decide which aim they go with.

2 • Give students two minutes to complete the words and write them in the correct categories.
• Allow students time to check their answers in pairs before you check with the whole class.

> **Answers**
> *Aviation: aircraft, flight, landing, passenger, pilot, plane*
> *Restaurant: fork, glass, menu, plate, soup, waitress*
> *Sport: club, game, goal, match, player, team*

Optional activity

Students work in pairs or small groups and add as many words as they can to the *Restaurant* category. Bring the vocabulary together on the board and ask students to write example sentences for five of the words.

3 • The aim of the activity is for students to contextualise short listening extracts by working out what kind of listening text each is from. Remind students that for this type of activity they should listen for the main gist, and should not worry if they don't understand every single word. Remind them that there is one text type they do not need.
• Play the recording. Students match the extracts 1–3 with A–D.

> ⊙ 2.12 **Recording**
> *1*
> *Kinsey works at Madame Tussaud's in London. Starting at 7.30am, two hours before the crowds arrive, she moves through the museum, checking that all the models are undamaged. 'Richard Branson had a broken nose this morning,' she says. 'And Hitler had a broken ear. He's had several lately, I don't know why.'*
> *2*
> *Bill Bryson, an American writer who had lived in Britain for ten years, returned to the USA to rediscover his homeland. He borrowed his mother's old Chevrolet and drove 13,978 miles through 38 states, keeping mainly to side roads and small towns. This is Bryson's description of a meal in a town called Littleton in New Hampshire.*

3

INTERVIEWER What's the best holiday you've ever had?
BEN It was in Canada three years ago. Some friends invited us to stay in Nova Scotia – that's the east coast of Canada. So we went for two weeks, and while we were there we went whale-watching. We saw all kinds of whales and dolphins, and they came really close to the boat. It was magic.

Answers

1 C   2 D   3 B

Optional activity

Play the recording again and ask students comprehension questions, e.g. *Where does the person work?* (In a museum in London) *Where is the travel book about?* (the USA) *Where was the holiday to?* (Canada).

4 • Give students a few minutes to look through the *Extraordinary People Survey*. Deal with any vocabulary issues.
   • Students do the survey in groups of four, noting down any interesting or surprising answers.
   • Divide each group into pairs, and put pairs together into new groups of four. Students report on anything interesting or surprising that came up in their discussions.
   • Point out the 'Believe it or not!' fact at the bottom of the page. Ask students if they know any other strange or surprising facts like this about travel, or people who have travelled a lot.

Extraordinary people project

   • Ask students to work individually and make a poster about an extraordinary person they would like to meet. It can be someone from history, a real person, or a fictional character. They should write a paragraph about why the person is extraordinary and why they would like to meet them. They should also illustrate their poster with illustrations or photos. Display the posters in class so that students can look at each others' work.

Follow-up activities

   ◆ Put students into pairs and ask them to choose three other vocabulary categories in the Topics and vocabulary box on page 60 and brainstorm vocabulary for them. Put pairs together to form groups of four, and ask them to compare their lists and add any more words that they can.
   ◆ Ask students which of the topics in the list they would like to learn more about at school. Students can discuss the question in pairs and choose one or two topics, then compare their answers in small groups and discuss any similarities or differences.

HOMEWORK

Ask students to interview someone else for the *Extraordinary People Survey* and to write down the person's answers. They can report back to the class in the next lesson.

If the plot had succeeded ...

Communicative aims	Language	Pronunciation	Vocabulary
Talking about unreal or imaginary past events	Expressing regret about the past	Third conditional *wish/if only* + past perfect	Sentence stress and weak forms	Historical events

WARMER

Game *Date game*   Write some important dates on the board, e.g. *5 November, 25 December, 14 February*. Include some national holiday dates from your own country. Give some information about one of the dates to the whole class, e.g. *It's a day when men give women red roses. It's called Valentine's Day.* The first student to shout out the correct date (14 February) wins a point for their team.

Useful information

On 5 November, there are large organised firework displays in major parks and some friends/families gather in their gardens for smaller firework parties. Many have bonfires and children make a model of Guy Fawkes to be thrown on to the bonfire and burned. Children learn the rhyme:

Remember, remember
The fifth of November,
Gunpowder, treason and plot.
I see no reason
Why gunpowder treason
Should ever be forgot.

1 OPENER

- The aim is to set the scene for the text in exercise 2.
- Ask the students to look at the pictures on the page and elicit that they show Guy Fawkes and fireworks. Ask students if they know anything about this event.
- Focus on the words in the box. Explain any words they didn't know. Ask students to work with a partner and predict which words will be in the text. Don't confirm answers at this stage.

2 READING

- Students read and listen to the text. Encourage students to read quickly and guess unfamiliar words from context. Explain that *catch someone red-handed* means to catch someone in the middle of doing something wrong and that if you *get away with something*, you are not caught or punished for your wrong-doing. Be prepared to translate *attempted, persecuted, conspirators, executed* and *poll*. Elicit the answer to the question, and check with the class which words from exercise 1 occur in

the text. (All the words are in the text except *electricity, environment, flood*.)

2.13 Recording
See text on page 62 of the Student's Book.

Answers
5th November is celebrated because a plot to blow up the British Houses of Parliament was prevented on that day in 1605.

3 AFTER READING

- Students read the text again and match the beginnings and endings of the sentences. Remind them that there are two extra endings.

Answers
1 c   2 d   3 i   4 j   5 a   6 g   7 f   8 b

Optional activities

- Read out the story of Guy Fawkes, but include some incorrect information, e.g. *He attempted to blow up King William I*. Students shout *Stop!* every time they hear a mistake and correct the information.
- Write *The plot, The possible results, The actual results, Then and today* on the board. In pairs, students try to remember two pieces of information about each subject, with books closed.

Your response

Ask students to work in pairs to discuss the questions. Ask some pairs to report back to the class.

LANGUAGE WORKOUT OPTION

If you want to pre-teach the language students will use in the following activities, you may like to go to the Language Workout box now.

4 WRITING

- Tell students they are going to complete some famous quotations. Ask students to look at the names of the people the quotes are from, and elicit any information they know about the people.

- Tell students the quotes are all about imaginary events in the past. Do the first one with the class as an example. Students then work individually or in pairs to complete the quotations.

Answers

1 had intended, would have given
2 had known, would have taken
3 hadn't started, would have raised
4 hadn't been, wouldn't have sent
5 would have happened, hadn't been
6 hadn't been, would have ended

5 PRONUNCIATION

- Play the recording for students to listen and repeat the conditional sentences from Exercise 4. Ask students to underline the stressed words in each sentence. Pause the recording between sentences to check the stress and for students to repeat. Ask *What kind of words are stressed: content words or grammar words?* (content).
- Ask students about the pronunciation of *have* and *had* in the sentences. Highlight the weak pronunciation of *have* /əv/ and the contraction of *had* to *'d*.

2.14 **Recording and answers**

1 If *God* had *intended* us to *fly*, he would have *given* us *wings*.
2 If I had *known* I was going to *live* this *long*, I would have *taken* better *care* of *myself*.

LANGUAGE WORKOUT OPTION

If you want to pre-teach the language students will use in the following activities, you may like to go to the Language Workout box now.

6 SPEAKING

- Ask students to look at the pictures and work with a partner to decide what the people might be thinking. Do the first one together as a whole class as an example. Remind students to use the past perfect.
- Ask different students to share their suggestions with the rest of the class. Accept a range of suggestions.

Suggested answers

1 If only I'd saved the penalty.
2 I wish I hadn't had the accident.
3 If only I'd turned off the iron.
4 If only I'd brought a mobile phone.
5 I wish I'd filled up the car with petrol before.

Extension Give one or two examples of sentence endings yourself, e.g. *I wish I'd known about the concert last weekend. If only I hadn't forgotten about the party!* Allow students time to complete the sentences individually. They then tell a partner. Ask some students to read their sentences to the class.

7 LISTENING

- Ask students to say what they would do/buy if they won the lottery, reminding them of second conditional forms.
- Ask students to guess what Sally King did with her lottery money, using the photo for ideas. Explain that students will hear her talking about how her life changed.
- Allow students time to read through the things in the list, then play the recording. Students tick the things in the list that Sally did and put a cross by the things that she didn't do.
- Students check their answers with another student, explaining how things would have been different if she hadn't won the lottery, as in the example.
- Ask a few students to say their answers to the whole class. Correct pronunciation as necessary.

2.15 **Recording**

Sally:
When I won the lottery, it changed my life completely. Two years ago, I was living in a small flat in Manchester, and I was working as an accountant. And that was how I saw my life – I expected to stay in Manchester and be an accountant for the rest of my life. I'd always wanted to be an artist, to paint pictures, but I had to earn a living. And then I won two and a half million pounds – I still find it hard to believe.
I gave up my job immediately. Then I thought – I don't have to stay in Manchester, I can go anywhere in the world. In the end I decided to move to Italy because I love Italian food. So I sold my flat and bought an old farmhouse in the hills near Florence. And a few months later, I met Giorgio. We started going out together, and we got married last year. I'd never have met Giorgio if I hadn't won the lottery. Oh, and my dream has come true – I've taken up painting, and I sold my first picture last week! As I say, winning the lottery has changed my life.

Answers

a give up her job ✓	*e stay in Manchester* ✗
b carry on working ✗	*f moved to Italy* ✓
c sell her flat ✓	*g meet Giorgio* ✓
d buy a farmhouse ✓	*h take up painting* ✓

a She wouldn't have given up her job if she hadn't won the lottery.
b She would have carried on working …
c She wouldn't have sold her flat …
d She wouldn't have bought a farmhouse …
e She would have stayed in Manchester …
f She wouldn't have moved to Italy …
g She wouldn't have met Giorgio …
h She wouldn't have taken up painting …

Optional activity

Students write a paragraph as if they were Sally, explaining how their life would have been different if they hadn't won the lottery. Give them the starter sentence: *Two years ago I won the lottery and it completely changed my life. If I hadn't won …*

If you want to pre-teach the language students will use in the following activities, you may like to go to the Language Workout box now.

8 WRITING

- Ask students to remember how history would have been different if the Gunpowder Plot had succeeded. Elicit some ideas, and check that students are using the third conditional correctly.
- Look at the examples in the Student's Book and, as a whole class, brainstorm and write on the board other important events, e.g. *the attack on the World Trade Centre, World War I/II, the invention of the microchip.*
- Students choose one of the events and write sentences saying what would/wouldn't have happened if things had been different. Monitor and help with vocabulary.
- Students check their own work for spelling, grammar and punctuation, before exchanging writing with a partner to read and check each other's work.

LANGUAGE WORKOUT

- Ask students to look at the Language Workout box and complete the sentences. Confident students can complete first and then check, while others can look back at exercises 2 and 3 and then complete.
- Students turn to page 116 of the Language File to check their answers.

  Answers
  had, would have
  would have, had
  had
  had got
  hadn't caught
  third   if   wish

- Highlight that:
  - third conditional sentences are generally formed with *if* + past perfect, + *would* + *have* + past participle. They often express regret or inability to change a past situation or event. Both the main and the conditional clauses refer to the past. The conditional clause can follow the main clause, but no comma is used in this case.
  - *If only/wish* + past perfect also express regrets about the past.
- Check students' understanding by asking questions about the examples, e.g. *Did the plot succeed? Did the King die as a result of the plot?*

Optional activity

Ask students to find more examples of the third conditional in the text on page 62.

PRACTICE

- Students do Practice exercise 14 on page 116 of the Language File. They rewrite the sentences using the words in brackets.

  Answers
  1 If only he hadn't failed his exams.
  2 She wishes she'd got the message in time.
  3 I wish I hadn't eaten so much!
  4 If only you'd listened to me!
  5 He wishes he'd learnt to play an instrument.
  6 If only he hadn't lost his job.

- Students do Practice exercise 15 on page 116 of the Language File. They complete the sentences with the correct form of the verbs. Allow students time to check their answers in pairs before you check with the class.

  Answers
  1 had had, would have won
  2 had charged, wouldn't have missed
  3 would have got, had booked
  4 had listened, wouldn't have misunderstood
  5 would have been able, hadn't lost
  6 wouldn't have lost, had played

Follow-up activities

- Ask students to think of three important events or situations in their life so far and write them down, e.g. *I moved to this town seven years ago, I chose to study physics.* Students then mingle, asking questions, e.g. *How would your life have been different if you hadn't …?*
- Remind students that Guy Fawkes was recently listed in the top 100 Great Britons. Tell students that they are going to make a list of the top ten people (living or dead) from their own country. Students make their lists individually, then share with a partner, and try to reach a new agreement on the top ten people. They then work in a group of four, a group of eight and eventually as a whole class.

HOMEWORK

Students choose a special date from their own country and research what originally happened on this day and why it is remembered. They then write a paragraph explaining their findings and saying how things would have been different in their country if this event had not happened.

WEBLINK

Students may like to visit www.bonfirenight.net for more information on bonfire night and Guy Fawkes.

Revision and Extension p71

Language File p116

Workbook Unit 5 Lesson 1 pp50–51

Photocopiable worksheet p175, notes p158

2 You have to be careful

Communicative aims	Language	Pronunciation	Vocabulary	Optional aids
Expressing obligation and lack of obligation	*must(n't), have to* and *need to* *don't have to, don't need to* and *needn't*	Contrastive stress	Routines Qualifications	Follow-up activity 1: sticky labels with job titles, one per student

WARMER 1

Students see how many words they can make from the unit title *Extraordinary people*. Students may not use a letter more than once unless it appears more than once in the title itself. The student with the greatest number of words wins.

WARMER 2

Tourist attractions. Elicit suggestions for the world's most visited cities, e.g. *Paris, London, New York, Sydney*. Write these on the board. Students then discuss with a partner what the most famous tourist attractions are in each. After a few minutes, nominate a student to describe one of the cities and its attractions, without saying the city's name. Other students listen and identify the city.

Useful information

Madame Tussaud was a French model-maker born in 1761 who worked with the French court and then came to England at the time of the French Revolution. She eventually set up her collection of wax models in Baker Street, London. This developed into Madame Tussaud's waxwork museum, one of London's top attractions, which includes models of historical figures as well as current stars. The Jorvik Viking Centre was set up after an archaeological dig in the centre of York unearthed well-preserved remains of 10th century Viking buildings. The Centre is a living museum where visitors can experience life at that time through these archaeological finds. The London Aquarium is on the South Bank of the Thames, near the London Eye, and has 350 species of fish in 2.5 million litres of water.

1 OPENER

- The aim is to set the scene for the text in exercise 2.
- Ask *Do you recognise these famous British tourist attractions? What are they called and where are they?*

    Answers
    A Madame Tussaud's   B Jorvik Viking Centre
    C London Aquarium

2 READING

- Students read and listen to the text. Encourage them to guess unfamiliar words from context and set a short time limit, so that students read for gist only

at this stage. Explain that *wax* is the material from which candles are made. Students decide which job is dangerous (working at the London Aquarium).

⊙ 2.16 Recording

See text on page 64 of the Student's Book.

3 AFTER READING

- Students read the text again and answer the questions.

    Answers
    1 Because he is a wax model.
    2 She checks that the models are undamaged.
    3 She doesn't want to melt the wax.
    4 Smells.
    5 No, two or three times a week.
    6 Because a machine does it.
    7 George is a male name for a female shark.
    8 Because there are other people with her and she's never had any scary moments.
    9 So that visitors can see the fish clearly.

Your response

Ask students to work in pairs to discuss the questions. After a few minutes, put pairs together into groups of four to compare their answers. Ask a student from each group to report back on their discussions.

Optional activity

Students choose one of the people from the text and write three questions that they would like to ask them. They then role play an interview with another student taking the role of Jo, Mark or Jeanette.

4 PRONUNCIATION

- Ask students to make sentences correcting the statements 1–6 about the text in exercise 2. Point out the example given for number 1.
- Play the recording of the first sentence only and ask students to identify the stressed word (*London*). Establish that we stress the new, corrected or contrasting information.
- Ask students to predict the stressed words in the other sentences. Then play the recording, pausing between each sentence to check the stress. Play the recording

again, pausing after each sentence for students to repeat.

🔘 2.17 Recording

1 *Jo Kinsey works in* <u>London</u>, *not* <u>York</u>.
2 *Richard Branson had a broken* <u>nose</u>, *not a broken* <u>leg</u>.
3 *There are* <u>400</u> *photographs of each model, not* <u>200</u>.
4 *Mark Shepherd creates* <u>smells</u>, *not* <u>sounds</u>.
5 *George is the* <u>largest</u> *shark, not the* <u>smallest</u>.
6 *Jeanette Ewart is* <u>23</u> *years old, not* <u>25</u>.

Extension Students write down a further sentence about each job which contains a false fact. They then swap sentences with a partner and correct their partner's sentences. Correct their pronunciation if necessary.

Optional activity

Students write a sentence about themselves, containing one false fact. Ask students in turn to read out their sentence, and see if anyone can correct it.

LANGUAGE WORKOUT OPTION

If you want to pre-teach the language students will use in the following activities, you may like to go to the Language Workout box now.

5 LISTENING

- Focus on the three pictures and job titles, and check that students understand them. Allow students time to read through the list of qualifications.
- Point out the system of ticks and crosses students must use, then ask them to work in pairs to guess which qualifications are necessary for each job.
- Play the recording for students to check their predictions and complete the chart with a tick for *have to*, a cross for *needn't* and two crosses for *mustn't*.

🔘 2.18 Recording

Radio presenter:
Hello and welcome to Where next?, the programme which answers your questions about interesting and exciting jobs for when you leave school. Today we're going to look at three jobs: flight attendant, yacht crew and, believe it or not, human cannonball!

First, we've had lots of emails asking about jobs as flight attendants. Flight attendants look after passengers on planes, serving food and drinks and being responsible for safety. Lots of young people would like this job and competition is quite strong. You must be over 21 and you must be over 1.5 metres tall – so you can put baggage above the seats on the plane. But you mustn't be over 1.88 metres or you'll hit your head on the ceiling! Flight attendants work long hours – up to 16 hours a day – and have to open and close heavy doors, so you must be physically fit.

A driving licence isn't needed but you must speak two foreign languages. Many flight attendants have a university degree but it's OK without one. As you're responsible for safety you must have safety training and of course it goes without saying that you must be willing to travel.

The next job is as a member of the crew of a yacht, helping to sail it and keep it clean. Many yachts are in great places in the Mediterranean and the Caribbean and if you like sun and sea, it's the job for you. One problem is that obviously there are more jobs in the summer than in the winter! There isn't an age limit so teenagers can apply. Your height doesn't matter either but you have to be quite strong to help sail the yacht, so top physical fitness is essential. A driving licence isn't important but you must be able to speak at least one foreign language. A university degree isn't needed but safety training is. You must have done a five-day safety training course. And the job is about travelling so you will never be in the same place two days in a row.

And our third job is working in a circus as a human cannonball. Not the first job people think of but we have had emails asking about work in a circus. It doesn't matter what age you are, and if you're short that's OK. But you can't be over 1.88 metres or you won't be able to get into the cannon! Physical fitness is essential as you will fly through the air across the circus tent. You usually must be able to drive so that you can help the circus move from town to town. It's not necessary to be able to speak a foreign language or have a degree. Safety is of course important but there aren't any special training courses. And like our other two jobs this is one where you move from place to place. So if the circus is for you, we hope your career as a human cannonball goes with a bang! For more information on how to apply for these jobs please go to our website www. …

Answers

	Flight attendant	Yacht crew	Human cannonball
Be over 21 years old:	✓	✗	✗
Be over 1.5 metres tall:	✓	✗	✗
Be over 1.88 metres tall:	✗✗	✗	✗✗
Be physically fit:	✓	✓	✓
Have a driving licence:	✗	✗	✓
Speak a foreign language:	✓	✓	✗
Have a degree:	✗	✗	✗
Have safety training:	✓	✓	✗
Be willing to travel:	✓	✓	✓

- Students then talk with a partner about the qualifications for the three jobs. Encourage them to use a range of expressions to express obligation and lack of obligation, e.g. *have to, must, don't have to, needn't, mustn't*. Ask individual students to tell the class what qualifications are and aren't necessary for each job.

LANGUAGE WORKOUT OPTION

If you want to pre-teach the language students will use in the following activities, you may like to go to the Language Workout box now.

6 WRITING

- Tell students that they are going to write two paragraphs for the class magazine, about the qualifications needed for two of the jobs from exercise 5. Give them a ten-minute time limit to produce their paragraphs.
- Monitor, help with vocabulary and note down any errors or examples of good language. With fast-finishers, highlight where they have made mistakes and encourage them to self-correct. Fast-finishers can also think of a suitable title for their writing.
- Students check their own work for spelling, grammar and punctuation, before exchanging with a partner to read and check each other's work, and selecting the best paragraphs for the magazine.
- Go through a few examples of good language or errors with the whole class, writing corrections on the board for students to copy down.

Extension Students can work individually or in pairs to choose another unusual job and write a paragraph about the qualifications needed for it. With weaker classes, brainstorm ideas for unusual jobs with the whole class first.

LANGUAGE WORKOUT

- Ask students to look at the Language Workout box and complete the sentences. Confident students can complete first and then check, while others can look back at exercises 2 and 3 and then complete.
- Students turn to page 116 of the Language File to check their answers.

    Answers
    must   have to   needs to   had to
    doesn't, have to   needn't

- Highlight that:
    – *must, have to* and *need to* all indicate obligation; *don't have to, don't need to* and *needn't* indicate lack of obligation; *mustn't* means you're not allowed to do something.
    – *must* has no past form. Use *had to* or *needed to*.
    – *needn't* is followed by the bare infinitive, without *to*, although *need* is followed by the full infinitive with *to*.
    – We use *didn't need to/didn't have to* to talk about lack of obligation in the past.

- Check students' understanding by asking questions about the examples, e.g. *Is it necessary for Mark to heat the oil himself?*
- Drill the examples from the Language Workout box for pronunciation practice. Highlight the weak pronunciation of *must*, the pronunciation of *(don't) have to* /hæftə/ and the weak pronunciation of *to* /tə/.

PRACTICE

- Students do Practice exercise 16 on page 116 of the Language File. Introduce the theme of sayings/proverbs by giving an example from your own country or sentence 1 from the exercise. Elicit the meaning of the saying and find out if students agree or disagree.
- Students complete the remaining sentences with the correct form of the verbs in brackets. Encourage them to think about the wider meaning of each sentence to guide their choices.
- Check the answers by asking different students to read out each sentence. Correct pronunciation as necessary.

    Answers
    1 must   2 don't have to   3 mustn't
    4 needn't / don't need to   5 don't have to
    6 had to   7 needed to   8 needn't / don't need to

Follow-up activity

Game *Guess your job*   Before the lesson, prepare some job names on sticky post-it notes, enough for one per student. Stick one on each student's back, so that they cannot see it but other students can. Students must guess their own job by walking around the room, asking *yes/no* questions, e.g. *Do I have to be physically fit? Do I have to wear special clothes? Do I need to help other people?* With a less confident class, brainstorm possible questions first and write them on the board. With a confident class, include some unusual jobs, e.g. *personal shopper, funeral director, film extra, food taster, yoga teacher.*

HOMEWORK

Students interview someone they know about their job and qualifications, using the chart in exercise 5 and their own ideas. They could choose a friend, relative or person working in the school. They should bring their interview questions and answers to the next lesson.

WEBLINK

Students may like to visit these sites for more information www.madame-tussauds.co.uk, www.visitsealife.com/london, www.jorvik-viking-centre.co.uk

Revision and Extension p71

Language File p116

Workbook Unit 5 Lesson 2 pp52–53

Photocopiable worksheet p176, notes p158

EXTRAORDINARY PEOPLE

What could have happened to them?

Communicative aims	Language	Pronunciation	Vocabulary	Optional aids
Making deductions Speculating about the past	*must have* and *can't have* *could/may/might have*	Sentence stress and weak forms	Aviation Phrasal verbs with *up*	Exercise 6 Optional activity: small cards Follow-up activity 1: descriptions and explanations of 'unusual' situations

WARMER 1

If the students did the homework from the last lesson, they can show or talk about their interviews to other students, explaining who they interviewed, what the person's job requirements are and whether or not they would like to do their job.

WARMER 2

Focus on the pictures and the title of the text. Ask students what they know about Amelia Earhart and the history of aviation. Ask *When was the first flight?* (the Wright brothers, 1903), *When was the first flight across the Atlantic?* (Charles Lindbergh, 1927). Elicit other information that students know.

WARMER 3

Tell students that they are going to read a text about flying. Give them one minute to write a list of six words or phrases they expect to find in the text. Write their ideas on the board as a word map with *FLYING* in the centre. After students have read the text in exercise 2, check how many of their words they found. The winning student is the one who found the most words.

1 OPENER

- The aim is to introduce the context for the reading in exercise 2.
- Ask students to look at the photo and map and guess what the woman pilot did. Accept all suggestions but don't confirm the answer yet.

2 READING

- Students read and listen to the text, checking their predictions and answering the question. Encourage them to guess unfamiliar words from context. If you did Warmer 3, ask students how many of their words they found. Check that students understand *solo* by asking *How many people?* Explain that you *set* or *break a record* by being the best/fastest, etc. in a particular task and *to be short of* means having very little left. Be prepared to translate *attempt*, *no trace*, *fuel* and *abduct*.

2.19 Recording

See text on page 66 of the Student's Book.

Answers

Ex1: She was the first woman to make a solo flight across the Atlantic, in 1932.
Ex2: They didn't complete the flight because they went missing. No-one knows what happened to them.

3 AFTER READING

- Students read the text again and decide if the sentences are true, false or if no information is given. Ask them to underline or write down the words in the text that helped them decide on their answers.
- Check the answers as a class before students write corrections for the false sentences. Monitor and help where necessary.

Answers

1 False. She was the first woman to fly solo across the Atlantic.
2 True
3 No information
4 No information
5 False. They disappeared over the Pacific Ocean.
6 True
7 True
8 False. It can't have blown up in mid air because it had used up most of its fuel.
9 False. They were possibly US spies. (They may have been.)
10 True

Optional activity

Fast-finishers can find and write down words to do with flying in the text, e.g. *pilot, solo flight, crash, landing.*

Your response

Put students into pairs to discuss the questions. Ask pairs to report back to the class.

4 WRITING

- Focus on the example sentence, and do another example with the whole class if necessary. Students then work individually or in pairs to rewrite the remaining sentences.

Answers

1 She must have been very brave.
2 She can't have slept during her solo flight.
3 They might have survived.
4 They could have landed on a desert island.
5 Aliens can't have abducted them.
6 The plane could have come down in the sea.
7 They may have got lost.
8 She must have loved flying.

Optional activity

Students underline the expressions in the original sentences 1–8 which indicated certainty or lack of it, e.g. *I'm sure*, *perhaps*.

Extension Ask students to use the structures in exercise 4 to give their own ideas about what happened to Earhart and Noonan.

5 PRONUNCIATION

- Play the recording for students to listen and repeat the sentences and identify the stressed words in each sentence.
- Pause the recording between sentences to check the stress. Ask students *What happens to 'have'?* Establish that it is pronounced as a weak form /əv/. Drill *must have, can't have, might have, could have* and *may have* as single units.

🔘 **2.20** Recording and answers

1 She <u>must</u> have been <u>very brave</u>.
2 She <u>can't</u> have <u>slept</u> during her <u>solo flight</u>.
3 They <u>might</u> have <u>survived</u>.
4 They <u>could</u> have <u>landed</u> on a <u>desert island</u>.
5 <u>Aliens can't</u> have <u>abducted</u> them.
6 The <u>plane could</u> have come down in the <u>sea</u>.
7 They <u>may</u> have got <u>lost</u>.
8 She <u>must</u> have <u>loved flying</u>.

Optional activity

Students can practise saying their own sentences from the Extension activity with the correct pronunciation.

6 VOCABULARY

- Tell the students to complete sentences 1–8 with the verbs from the box. Remind students that they may have to change the form of the verbs. Point out that these are all phrasal verbs with *up*.
- Ask students to read out their sentences to the whole class to check the answers.
- Students identify which of the phrasal verbs were in the text in exercise 2. Check that students understand the meaning of the verbs by asking them to explain or translate, e.g. *blow up = explode*.

Answers

1 used   2 grows   3 blow   4 made   5 ended
6 sum   7 woke   8 took   9 looked
In exercise 2: blow up, use up, end up

Optional activities

♦ Fast-finishers put the phrasal verbs on cards for the Vocabulary box, writing a definition or example sentence on the reverse.

♦ **Game** *Phrasal verb tennis* Write the phrasal verbs on the board and divide the class into two teams. One team 'serves' a phrasal verb to the other team, i.e. chooses one for the other team to put into a sentence. The other team wins a point for making a correct sentence, before in turn 'serving' a different phrasal verb to the other team. Erase phrasal verbs from the board as they are used. With stronger classes, you could include and revise phrasal verbs with *down* from page 41.

7 SPEAKING

- Tell students that they are going to read about four more unexplained mysteries and suggest explanations.
- Focus attention on the four pictures and ask students to describe what they can see. Give students a few minutes to read the mysteries and think about any possible explanations, making brief notes if they like. Elicit that the *crew* are the people working on a plane or ship.
- Students work with a partner to discuss their ideas for what might have happened. Point out the example sentence beginnings to remind students to use the grammar from the lesson.
- Ask a few students to share their ideas for each mystery with the whole class. You could have a class vote on who has the most plausible explanation.

8 WRITING

- Tell students that they are going to write about an unexplained mystery, from this lesson or elsewhere, for the class magazine. Remind students that they can make one up if they prefer and that they should describe the event and what they think happened. With weaker classes, you could brainstorm ideas for other unexplained mysteries with the whole class before students start writing.

- Monitor, help with vocabulary and note down any errors or examples of good language.
- Students check their own work for spelling, grammar and punctuation, before exchanging their writing with a partner to read and check each other's work. Encourage discussion of alternative explanations for the mystery.
- Go through a few examples of good language or errors with the whole class, writing corrections on the board for students to copy down.

LANGUAGE WORKOUT

- Ask students to look at the Language Workout box and complete the sentences. Confident students can complete first and then check, while others can look back at exercises 2 and 3 and then complete.
- Students turn to page 117 of the Language File to check their answers.

  Answers
  *must have   can't have   have   have ended
  have been   might have
  must have   can't have*

- Highlight that:
  - *must have* and *can't have* both indicate that the speaker feels sure, either that something happened or didn't happen.
  - we don't use *mustn't have* to say we are sure something didn't happen. Instead we use *can't have.*
  - *could/may/might have* can all be used to speculate about what possibly happened.
- Check students' understanding by asking questions about the examples, e.g. *Is it possible that the plane ran out of fuel? Is it possible that they were spies?*

PRACTICE

- Students work individually to do Practice exercise 17 on page 117 of the Language File.

  Answers
  1 *It must have been a mistake.*
  2 *She can't have seen me.*
  3 *She might have looked the other way.*
  4 *She could have fallen over something.*
  5 *She may have wanted to talk to me.*

Follow-up activities

- **Game** *Telepathy*   Before the class, prepare a few 'unusual' past situations and an explanation for each, e.g. *A farmer found a 'crop circle' on his land* (aliens must have landed there during the night), *There was no one in the street in London in the middle of the day* (England must have been playing in the World Cup final and everyone was at home watching). Read out a situation and ask students to work with a partner to write down their explanation. Then read the actual explanation. If they match, students score a point. Repeat with other situations. The pair with the most points are the winners.
- Divide students into groups of eight students. Ask them to imagine that they are producing a television documentary about an unsolved mystery. It could be a mystery from the lesson or another that might attract media coverage. Students decide on their roles in the show, e.g. director, presenter, writers, experts to be interviewed, witnesses to be interviewed. They then rehearse their show, including presentation and analysis of the mystery, before performing to the other groups.

HOMEWORK

Students choose five of the phrasal verbs from exercise 6 and write sentences using them. They then use dictionaries to find three new phrasal verbs with *up* and their meanings, and use them in three more sentences.

WEBLINK

Students may like to visit www.unexplained-mysteries.com to read about more mysteries.

Revision and Extension p71

Language File p117

Workbook Unit 5 Lesson 3 pp54–55

Photocopiable worksheet p177, notes p158

5 EXTRAORDINARY PEOPLE

4 Integrated Skills
Contrasting facts and ideas

Skills

Reading Connecting ideas: magazine article about women's football
Listening Completing a text

Speaking Discussing male/female equality
Writing Paragraphs contrasting male and female situations

Learner independence

Thinking skills
Word creation: adjective suffix *-ous*

Vocabulary

Sport
Useful expressions

WARMER 1

Draw a word map with the word *FOOTBALL* in the centre on the board. Ask students to brainstorm vocabulary on the theme and add it to the word map. You could include *score a goal, take a penalty, player, goalkeeper, referee, match, team, defence, supporter.*

WARMER 2

Game *Play or pass* Organise students into teams. Read out a word and ask team A to spell it. Possible words include: *succeeded, destruction, strength, aquarium, regularly, physically, flight, fuel, disappearance.* Team A can choose to spell it or pass it to another team. If team A spells it correctly, they win a point. If they spell it incorrectly, they get no points. If they pass it to team B, team B has to spell the word – they can't pass it on. If team B gets the spelling right, then team B gets the point. If team B gets the spelling wrong, then team A gets the point. Continue with the next word, starting with a different team. The winner is the team with most points.

1 OPENER

- The aim is to set the scene for the text in exercise 2.
- Ask students *What does the photo show?* They discuss the questions about women's sport. Ask a few students to share their ideas with the class.

2 READING

- Students read the text and match the paragraphs with the topics. Encourage them to guess unfamiliar words from context and not worry about the highlighted words, which will be dealt with in exercise 3. Be prepared to translate *tricked* and *have a nose for something.*
- Check the answers as a class, asking students to justify their choices where appropriate.

◎ 2.21 Recording
See text on page 68 of the Student's Book.

Answers

1 Introducing Marigol   2 Early days   3 A discovery
4 Her career   5 A review   6 A surprise decision
7 A new continent   8 The future

Optional activities

- ♦ Students add any extra football vocabulary from the text to their word map from Warmer 1.
- ♦ Write the paragraph topics on the board. With books closed, students try to remember one piece of information from each paragraph. They can compare answers with a partner.

3

- Ask the students to match highlighted words in the text with definitions 1–9.

Answers

1 female   2 confesses   3 round   4 male   5 wasteland
6 quarter-finals   7 knocked out   8 courageous
9 division

Optional activity

Fast-finishers can mark the stress on the words with more than one syllable, then check in a dictionary. They can say the words to the class with the correct stress when other students have finished.

4

- Ask the students to find an example of *whereas* and *while* in the text. Establish that they are used to contrast facts or ideas.

Answers

Maribel got £600 a month, <u>whereas</u> a top male player got £60,000.
The Mexican women's team reached the quarter-finals, <u>while</u> the men's team were knocked out in the first round.

Optional activity

Ask students to talk to a partner about themselves, their likes and dislikes to find three differences between them. Suggest they can talk about the sports, music or TV programmes they like. They then tell a different partner about the differences, using *while* and *whereas*, e.g. *I like soap operas whereas Julia doesn't like them.*

5 LISTENING

- Ask students to read the text about Maribel and another female footballer, Hanna Ljungberg, and complete any gaps that they can for Maribel. For those that they can't yet complete, they should guess what sort of information is missing, e.g. a number or an adjective. Give students time to compare their ideas in pairs.
- Play the recording. Students listen and complete the remaining gaps.
- Check the answers together as a class.

🔊 2.22 Recording and answers

The most famous woman footballer in Sweden is called Hanna Ljungberg and she played for Umeå IK in the north of the country where she was born in 1979. Hanna started playing football when she was seven years old in the Umeå Football Festival. She joined the national team in 1996 when she was seventeen and her first match was against Spain. She has played in 97 international matches and scored 54 goals. Hanna missed the 1999 World Cup through injury and has often been injured. In April 2006 she was taken to hospital when the French goalkeeper knocked her unconscious in the Algarve Cup. 'Football can be dangerous sometimes,' she says. Hanna also has a great sense of humour. When her team were playing in the UEFA Women's Cup Hanna and another player hid in the wardrobe of the room where the team coach and assistant coach were staying. When the men were asleep the players jumped out of the wardrobe and poured cold water over them! 'We must have been there for three hours,' Hanna said, 'before we got them.' In 2005 Perugia, an Italian men's team, asked her to join them but she refused. 'I prefer to play in Sweden,' she said. 'And I'm not sure I would be allowed to play in a men's team.' And her dream? 'Playing in one of the big competitions is great and winning a big championship would be really nice.' Hanna retired from football in 2009 because of injury.
*Both Maribel Dominguez and Hanna Ljungberg are well known international **footballers**. Maribel has scored **46** goals in **49** international matches, whereas Hanna has scored **54** goals in **97** internationals. Maribel started playing when she was **nine**, while Hanna started when she was **seven**. Maribel joined the Mexican team when she was **20**, whereas Hanna joined the Swedish team when she was **17**. Maribel played in the **1999** World Cup in the USA but Hanna **didn't**. Both women are **professional** footballers and both were asked to play for **men's** teams. Neither did. Hanna retired in **2009**, whereas Maribel continues to play in Spain.*

6 SPEAKING

- Divide students into small groups to discuss the questions about male and female footballers and other differences in opportunities for men and women. Try to ensure a mix of male and female students in each group. Ask each group to report back to the class and encourage other students to agree and disagree with each group's ideas. Continue with a class discussion if students are interested.

7 GUIDED WRITING

- Tell students that they are going to write three paragraphs for the class magazine contrasting the situation of men and women in their country. They could choose three topics from their discussion in exercise 6 and write a paragraph on each. Tell them to mention the advantages/disadvantages of each gender and try to decide which it is easier to be. Remind students to use *whereas* and *while* for contrast.
- Monitor and help with vocabulary and use of *whereas* and *while*. Note down any errors or examples of good language.
- When they have checked their own work, students read that of other students, noting which gender most students felt it was easier to be.
- Go through a few examples of good language or errors with the whole class, writing corrections on the board for students to copy down.

8 LEARNER INDEPENDENCE

- The aim is to encourage students to think about their learning and how to revise groups of words or phrases.
- Students make their word map. Remind them of the football word map if you did Warmer 1. Ask students to take their word maps home, try the technique and report back on how it went.

Optional activity

In later lessons, students can bring in their word maps, show and explain any new words on them to other students and swap word maps to take home.

9 WORD CREATION

- Ask students if they can remember the adjective from the text in exercise 1 meaning *brave* (Answer: *courageous*). Write the suffix *-ous* on the board and elicit other adjectives ending in this suffix.
- Students use the suffix *-ous* to make adjectives from the nouns in the box. Check the spelling of the adjectives and explain that *superstitious* people believe in good and bad luck. Drill the adjectives.
- Students use the adjectives to complete the sentences. Check the answers as a class.

Answers

1 courageous   2 luxurious   3 dangerous   4 superstitious
5 infectious   6 nervous   7 spacious   8 poisonous

Optional activity

Students choose four of the adjectives and write personalised sentences using them, e.g. *I always get nervous before exams.* Ask some students to read their sentences to the class and correct any mistakes.

EXTRA PRACTICE

If you would like to give your students more practice in forming words with endings in *-ous*, please see the Vocabulary EXTRA! Worksheets on the Teacher's Resource Site (www.macmillanenglish.com/inspiration)

10 PHRASEBOOK

- Students look through Unit 5 to find the expressions.
- Play the recording for the students to listen and repeat the expressions. Check with students where in the unit each expression was used.
- Students write a six-line dialogue using at least three of the expressions.

2.23 Recording and answers

I don't know why. (Lesson 2, exercise 2)
Which isn't a good thing, really. (Lesson 2, exercise 2)
You needn't worry. (Lesson 2, exercise 2)
What could have happened? (Lesson 3, exercise 2)
In other words … (Lesson 4, exercise 2)
I just wanted to be given the chance. (Lesson 4, exercise 2)

Optional activities

♦ Students think of another sentence in which they might use each expression, e.g. *I don't know why I find maths so difficult.*
♦ Students can add expressions which they like to their Personal Phrasebook. Be ready to help with translation if necessary.

Follow-up activities

♦ Students work in small groups to design a questionnaire for both males and females to see if there are differences between the sexes. Questions might include *What is your favourite possession? What do you think is a good age to get married? How important is sport for you?* Students then interview at least five males and five females, analyse their results and report back to other groups on any interesting results.
♦ Ask students to brainstorm ideas for features that could be included on a website about football, e.g. *football vocabulary lists, interviews with players, reports on matches, football quizzes.* Different groups of students create different material for the website, before pooling their work. This can be displayed in the classroom or made into computer files.

HOMEWORK

Ask students to make a list of ten words that they associate with females and ten with males. They could be gender specific words, e.g. *waiter/waitress* or words which they personally consider more male or female. Ask them to bring them to the next lesson to share their ideas.

WEBLINK

Students may want to visit www.thefa.com for information about British football, including women's football.

Revision and Extension p71   **Workbook Unit 5 Lesson 4 pp56–57**

Inspiration EXTRA!

Optional aids

Action: magazine pictures on card, one per student

LANGUAGE LINKS

- Focus on the picture. Ask *Do you find it easy to learn languages? Why do some people learn languages more easily than others?* Elicit students' ideas.
- Read the questions about the text with the class, and ask students to discuss the questions with a partner. Explain the word *hemisphere*. Ask students to read the text to check their ideas. Check answers with the class.

Answers

We use the front part of the left hemisphere to produce speech, and the back part of the left hemisphere to understand it.

Optional activity

Ask students to read the text again and answer comprehension questions, e.g. *When did humans start to develop language?* (100,000 years ago) *When did different languages start to develop?* (30,000 years ago) *What natural ability do all children have?* (the ability to speak) *What language skills do children have to learn?* (reading and writing).

- Ask students what languages they know that we read and write from right to left, e,g. *Arabic, Chinese, Japanese* and *Hebrew*.

GAME   LINK-UP

- The aim of the game is to recycle vocabulary from Unit 5. Draw the grid in the Student's Book on the board.
- Go through the instructions with the class and draw their attention to the example. Show how teams could link e.g. *C to A, B or J* and point out that they can zigzag. Emphasise that teams should try to block each other.
- Divide the class into two teams and play the game. Each time a team wins a square, circle the letter (in a different colour for each team) on the grid.
- Questions to ask (answers in brackets):
  What A is a fish tank? (aquarium)
  What B is a large fire outside? (bonfire)
  What C is a room under a building? (cellar)
  What D is measured in metres or kilometres? (distance)
  What E means blow up? (explode)
  What F is the opposite of success? (failure)
  What G is a group of people who may cause trouble? (gang)

What J reports the news on TV, the radio or in the press? (journalist)
What M is the opposite of female? (male)
What P is a secret plan to do something bad? (plot)
What Q is the last four games in a competition? (quarter-finals)
What R is on top of a building? (roof)
What S means alone? (solo)
What T means across the Atlantic? (transatlantic)
What W are models made of at Madame Tussaud's? (wax)
What Y is a large expensive sailing boat? (yacht)

SKETCH   THE BREAK-IN

- The aim is for students to enjoy using their English while also getting valuable stress and intonation practice. Ask the students to look at the cartoon. Ask *How does the apartment look? What do you think has happened? How do the people feel?*
- With a more confident class, play the recording with books closed. Then play it again with books open. With a less confident class, play the recording once while the students follow in their books, and then once again with books closed.

🔘 2.24 Recording
See text on page 70 of the Student's Book

- Check that students understand that the mess is due to the son and his friends, and not to a burglary! Ask students if they have ever been in a similar situation with their own family.
- Divide the class into three equal groups and play the recording again, with one group repeating in chorus as *Woman*, one as *Man* and the other as *Sam*. Encourage students to produce weak forms of *have* /əv/ in *can't have, must have,* etc.
- Ask the students to close their books and play the recording again. Then ask the students to work in groups of three and perform the sketch aloud. Choose several groups to act out the sketch in front of the class.

Optional activities

- Make an audio or video recording of students performing the sketch.
- Students discuss in pairs what rules, if any, they have for tidiness/parties/inviting friends in their own homes.

REVISION

Lesson 1

Answers

1 If only he hadn't failed his exams.
2 She wishes she hadn't got the message.
3 I wish there had been more food.
4 If only I hadn't taken your advice.
5 She wishes she had backed up her computer.
6 If only he hadn't stayed in his job.

Lesson 2
Students' own answers.

Lesson 3

Answers

1 What can have happened to him?
2 He must have been tired of the publicity.
3 He may have gone to stay with friends.
4 He might have had an accident.
5 He could have wanted a holiday.
6 He can't have decided to give up football.

EXTENSION

Lessons 1–3
Students' own answers.

YOUR CHOICE!

- The aim is to give students more learner independence and help them to identify their preferred way of learning. Encourage students to choose an activity that they feel less comfortable with if they want a challenge or are aware that they need practice in a particular area.
- Monitor and help groups. Check answers if necessary, or provide written answers for groups to check their own work against.

Language File pp116–117

CONSTRUCTION

Answers

1 needn't   2 don't have   3 needn't   4 don't have
5 needn't   6 don't have   7 needn't   8 needn't

REFLECTION

Answers

1 a, c, f   2 g, i   3 d   4 b, e, h

ACTION

- Students work in small groups.
- A student holds a picture up and flashes it at the other students, who speculate on what they think they saw.
- The student who guesses correctly takes the next picture and repeats the activity.

INTERACTION

- Students work in small groups.
- They think of five English words which have special meaning for them. They share their words with the other group members, describing why they are special. Encourage students to ask each other further questions about the words.
- Students could report back to the rest of the class on any interesting or common words in their group.

Workbook Unit 5 Inspiration EXTRA! pp58–59

Saying the right thing

Useful information

With most shops in the UK now open on Sundays, and a number of shops offering 24-hour opening during the week, shopping is probably Britain's favourite hobby. London's Oxford Street is Europe's longest shopping street and it includes the largest fashion store, Topshop, which sells clothes for men and women and even has its own radio station, Radio Topshop. Top London department stores are Selfridges, Harrods and Harvey Nichols. Britons, like Americans, are increasingly shopping in out-of-town shopping centres, where supermarket chains such as Tesco and Sainsbury's sell clothing, music and electrical goods alongside food.

WARMER

Ask *Do you enjoy shopping? How often do you go shopping? What things do you enjoy buying?* Ask students to discuss their shopping habits in pairs. Ask some students to report back to the class and encourage them to use *while* and *whereas* to show differences between them and their partner.

1 READING

- Ask students to look at the photo. Ask *What does it show? Who might shop here? What could they buy? What phrases do we often use when shopping?*
- Tell students to read the questionnaire about shopping skills and choose the best answers for each question.
- Encourage students to deduce the meaning of unknown vocabulary from context or ask *What does ... mean?* Be prepared to translate or explain *fit, tight* and *lime green*. A *fiver* is a colloquial expression for a five-pound note.
- Students compare their choices with a partner.
- Play the recording for students to check their answers. Pause between questions and elicit why the other two answers are less appropriate, focusing on register/ formality, use of vocabulary and intended meaning.
- Students turn to page 120 to read the explanations and compare them with their own.

2.25 Recording

1

ASSISTANT	*Hello – do you want any help?*
CUSTOMER	*No, thank you, I'm just looking.*

2

CUSTOMER	*Oh – I need some new jeans. Excuse me, could I try these on, please?*
ASSISTANT	*Yes, of course. The fitting rooms are over there.*

3

CUSTOMER	*They're a bit tight. Do you have them in a larger size?*
ASSISTANT	*Yes, I think so – here you are. Try this pair.*

4

ASSISTANT	*Here's a lovely jacket. It's the latest colour.*
CUSTOMER	*It doesn't really suit me. Green isn't my colour. Have you got a blue one?*
ASSISTANT	*How about this one?*
CUSTOMER	*It's very smart. How much is it?*
ASSISTANT	*Er, it's £150.*
CUSTOMER	*Sorry, that's a bit too expensive for me.*

5

CUSTOMER	*Oh dear, I haven't got enough money. Would you mind lending me five pounds?*
FRIEND	*Not at all – here you are.*

Answers

1 C   2 B   3 A   4 A   5 B   6 C

Optional activity

Students could practise reading the dialogues with the correct answers, making an effort to sound polite, or even act out the dialogues in pairs.

2 VOCABULARY

- Students complete the sentences with verbs from the questionnaire.

Answers

1 put   2 fit   3 match   4 wear   5 suit   6 try

3 SPEAKING

- With books closed, elicit phrases for making requests. Students then look at the box to see if the phrases for making requests match their own suggestions.
- Drill the example request and some of the phrases used in requests, modelling polite intonation in requests and enthusiastic intonation (or lack of it) in the responses.
- Students work with a partner to make requests for 1–9, using the phrases. Their partner responds appropriately. They then change roles and practise again.
- Ask one or two pairs to repeat one of their requests and responses to the rest of the class.

4 LISTENING

- Set the contexts for the listening by asking students to look at the photos.
- Students work with a partner to predict if the phrases in the list would be heard in a hostel, railway station or bank.
- Students then decide whether a tourist would hear or say each phrase.
- Play the recording for students to check their predictions.

- Drill some of the phrases for pronunciation practice, highlighting question intonation where appropriate.

2.26 Recording

Bank

TOURIST Could I change 100 dollars into euros?
CLERK Yes – can I see your passport?
TOURIST Yes, of course.
CLERK Right – how would you like the money?
TOURIST Tens and twenties, please.
CLERK Here you are – and here's your receipt for the exchange.
TOURIST Thank you.

Railway station

TOURIST Can I have a ticket to Oxford, please?
CLERK Single or return?
TOURIST A day return, please.
CLERK That'll be £19.50 – thank you. Here's your change.
TOURIST When's the next train?
CLERK There's one in five minutes.
TOURIST Which platform does it leave from?
CLERK Platform 10.
TOURIST Do I have to change?
CLERK No, that's a direct train.
TOURIST Thank you very much.
PA The next train to depart from platform 10 is the 9.15 to Oxford – calling at Reading, Didcot Parkway and Oxford. Platform 10 for the 9.15 to Oxford.

Hostel

TOURIST Good evening – I'd like a room for tonight, please.
RECEPTIONIST Have you made a reservation?
TOURIST No, I'm afraid not.
RECEPTIONIST That's no problem. Single or double?
TOURIST Sorry?
RECEPTIONIST Would you like a single or a double room?
TOURIST Oh, single please, with a shower if possible.
RECEPTIONIST That's fine – would you mind filling in this form, please?
TOURIST No, of course not.

Answers
1 B   2 C   3 A
Tourist says sentences 1, 2, 7, 8, 9, 13, 15.
Tourist hears sentences 3, 4, 5, 6, 10, 11, 12, 14.

5 ROLE PLAY

- Students work with a partner to choose one of the situations in exercise 4 and act out a similar conversation. With a less confident class, give students plenty of time to prepare what they are going to say before doing the role play.
- Students change roles and act out another situation.

6 MINI-PROJECT ADVERTISING

- With weaker classes, brainstorm ideas with the whole class first. Talk about advertisements students know and why they are successful, e.g. using celebrities, using popular music. Students then discuss and prepare their own ideas and look for advertisements in magazines or online. Students can do this in class or for homework.
- Students then write a paragraph about each advertisement they have chosen. Monitor and help with vocabulary. With fast-finishers, point out errors and encourage them to self-correct.
- Ask students to present their work with the advertisements they have written about. Pin students' work around the classroom for everyone to look at. You could have a class vote to decide on the most popular or successful advertisement.

WEBLINK

Students may like to visit www.oxfordstreet.co.uk for more information about Europe's longest shopping street.

Workbook Culture pp60–61

106

6 ON THE MOVE

1 I promised I wouldn't forget!

Communicative aims	Language	Pronunciation	Vocabulary
Reporting what people said	Reported speech with various reporting verbs	Stress in two-syllable verbs	Travel Reporting verbs

WARMER 1

Game *Word association* Divide students into small groups. Student A thinks of a word from the previous unit, e.g. *flight*. Student B says a word associated with *flight*, e.g. *pilot*. Student C says a word associated with *pilot*, e.g. *job* and so on. If a student cannot think of a word or they are challenged to explain the connection between the two words and cannot do so, they are out. The game continues until there is one winner in each group.

WARMER 2

Tell students that the topic of the lesson is *travel*. Students race to write as many words related to travel as they can in one minute. Ask the student with the most words to read them out. Other students listen and then add any other words they wrote to the list.

Useful information

The 2001 census showed that approximately 8% of British citizens at that time were from ethnic minorities. More recent census statistics are not available yet, but predictions suggest that the percentage of the population from ethnic minorities will rise to 20% by 2051. Asians from the Indian subcontinent are the largest ethnic minority group in the UK. Nearly half the total ethnic minority population live in London. Interestingly, Asian youngsters outperform all ethnic groups (include white British) in education.

1 OPENER

- The aim is to set the scene for the text in exercise 2.
- Students look at the photos. Ask *Would you like to go there? Why (not)?* Discuss the advice they would give someone travelling there. If necessary, prompt students with topics, e.g. *food, water, clothes, transport, language, money, safety*. Pre-teach *have an injection* and *malaria*.

Optional activity

Make a note on the board of who gives what advice for use in exercise 5.

2 READING

- Students read and listen to the email to answer the question about Laura.

🔘 2.27 Recording
See text on page 74 of the Student's Book.

| Answer
Yes, her parents agree to her holiday.

3 AFTER READING

- Students read the direct speech and match it to the reported speech in the email. Do the first one together as a class. Students then number the sentences in the right order. Play the recording for students to listen and check.

🔘 2.28 Recording

NISHA	*Would you like to go to India with me in the holidays?*
LAURA	*Oh wow! I'll have to ask my parents – I hope they'll say yes.*
MOTHER	*No, you can't go to India.*
FATHER	*It's out of the question – two young girls travelling halfway round the world on their own.*
LAURA	*We won't be on our own – Nisha's parents are going too.*
MOTHER	*But you don't like Indian food. Last time we had an Indian meal, you complained it was too spicy.*
LAURA	*I've changed my mind, I love Indian food. Please let me go.*
FATHER	*Oh, all right …*
MOTHER	*… you can go.*
FATHER	*But you must keep in touch.*
LAURA	*Of course, I'll send loads of emails.*
MOTHER	*Remember, you must have injections before you leave. And you need to take malaria tablets.*
FATHER	*Yes, you could get malaria if you forget to take them regularly.*
LAURA	*I promise I won't forget.*
MOTHER	*Why don't we invite Nisha and her parents for dinner? Then we can talk it over with them.*
LAURA	*Great!*

Answers

7a   *I told her I'd changed my mind and I loved it.*

5b   *I explained that we wouldn't be on our own because Nisha's parents were coming too.*

12c *I promised Dad I wouldn't forget!*

1d   *She invited me to go with her.*

6e   *Mum pointed out that I didn't like Indian food.*

13f *Mum suggested inviting Nisha and her parents for dinner to talk it over.*

3g   *At first they refused to let me go.*

10h *Mum reminded me that I had to have injections before I left, and that I needed to take malaria tablets.*

8i   *In the end they agreed to let me go! Dad told me to keep in touch.*

2j   *I replied that I'd have to ask my parents, and I hoped they'd say yes.*

11k *Dad warned me that I could get malaria if I forgot to take them regularly.*

4l   *Dad said it was out of the question.*

9m   *I promised to send loads of emails.*

Optional activity

Tell students that a reporting verb is used to express what someone said without using the exact words. Students identify the 13 reporting verbs in the email: *invited, replied, hoped, refused, said, explained, pointed out, told, agreed, promised, reminded, warned, suggested.* Check students understand the meaning of these verbs by asking questions, e.g. *Which verb means 'say you will not do something'?* (refuse) *Which verb means 'tell someone something that they already know'?* (remind) *Which verb means 'tell someone that something bad or dangerous might happen'?* (warn)

Your response

Ask students to work in pairs to discuss the questions. Ask some pairs to report back to the class.

4   PRONUNCIATION

- In pairs, students say the verbs in the box aloud and mark where they think the stress is on each one. They then listen to the recording to check. Check the answers as a whole class.
- Play the recording again, pausing after each one for students to repeat.

🔘 2.29   **Recording and answers**

ad·*vise*   a·*gree*   com·*plain*   ex·*plain*   in·*vite*   *of*·fer

prom·ise   re·*fuse*   re·*mind*   re·*ply*   sug·*gest*

Offer and promise are different: the stress is on the first syllable.

LANGUAGE WORKOUT OPTION

If you want to pre-teach the language students will use in the following activities, you may like to go to the Language Workout box now.

5   SPEAKING

- Students read the replies to Laura's request. Ask students which advice they think is useful. Focus on the first question and the example answer. Do another example with the whole class, pointing out that each question uses a different verb, and students should use the same verb in their answer.
- Put students into pairs to continue asking and answering the questions. Check answers.

Answers

1 *Jackie told Laura to take more money and fewer clothes than she thought she would need.*

2 *Kim explained that it was best to book an aisle seat on the plane so she could easily get up and walk around.*

3 *Sandy warned Laura not to take more luggage than she could run with.*

4 *Roger advised her to carry a local newspaper under her arm so she didn't look like a tourist.*

5 *Sara suggested buying a cotton sarong in India.*

6 *Peter reminded her to take some insect spray.*

Optional activity

Write the reporting verbs on the board. Fast-finishers close their books and try to recall the sentences.

Extension   Students work individually to write their travel tips. They then exchange tips with a partner and write sentences saying what their partner advised them to do. Encourage students to use a range of reporting verbs in their writing.

6

- Students read the situations and think about what they would say in each situation. Tell them they must think of the exact words they would say, e.g. for number 1: *OK, I'll turn it down.*
- Ask two students to demonstrate the interview. Make sure the student responds with their exact words and that their partner notes the response.
- Each student interviews two other students and notes their answers. Monitor and help as necessary.

LANGUAGE WORKOUT OPTION

If you want to pre-teach the language students will use in the following activities, you may like to go to the Language Workout box now.

7 WRITING

- Students report their interviews. Do one or two examples with the whole class using answers from exercise 6. Encourage students to use a variety of reporting verbs. Monitor and help as necessary.
- Make a note of any errors, particularly with the use of the reporting verbs. Write these on the board for students to correct when they have finished writing.

LANGUAGE WORKOUT

- Ask students to look at the Language Workout box, look at the verb patterns and complete the sentences. Confident students can complete first and then check, while others can look back at exercises 2 and 3 and then complete.
- Students turn to page 117 of the Language File to check their answers.

  Answers
  to let   to send   me to go   me to keep
  didn't   was   me, had   inviting

- Highlight that:
  - after a reporting verb in the past, the other verbs usually move one tense back into the past, e.g. *You don't like Indian food → She pointed out that I **didn't** like Indian food*. With a less confident class, review these changes: present simple → past simple, present continuous → past continuous, past simple/present perfect simple → past perfect simple, past continuous/present perfect continuous → past perfect continuous, *must → had to, can → could, will →would*.
  - the negative form of the infinitive is *not to* + verb. Elicit some negative examples, e.g. *I promised not to go out on my own, Her father told her not to drink the water*.
  - some verbs can be followed by two different forms, e.g. *agree* + infinitive and *agree* + *(that)* clause.

Optional activity

Ask students to look at the other examples of reported speech from exercise 3 and match them to the right pattern.

PRACTICE

- Students do Practice exercise 18 on page 117 of the Language File. Students write the sentences in reported

speech, using the reporting verbs in brackets. With a less confident class, students can work in pairs. With a confident class, students work individually and then compare in pairs. Monitor and help as necessary. Be prepared to explain that time expressions, like *tomorrow* in number 6, need to change in reported speech. Check answers with the whole class.

Answers
1 Laura invited Nisha to dinner.
2 Her father pointed out that the plane ticket would be quite expensive.
3 Nisha reminded Laura not to forget her passport.
4 Her mother warned her not to get sunburnt.
5 Laura promised to be very careful/Laura promised that she would be very careful.
6 Nisha suggested going to the travel agency the next/following day.
7 Laura explained that Kerala was in the south-west of India.
8 Her father said that Laura was a very lucky girl.
9 Nisha offered to lend Laura a book about India.
10 Laura complained that she hadn't got any nice clothes to wear.

Optional activity

Students recall the advice they suggested in exercise 1. They work in pairs, giving their advice to their partner and reporting the advice their partner gave them, e.g. *Marta suggested taking a phrasebook*.

Follow-up activity

Students work in pairs. Each pair chooses eight words related to travel and writes them in an interlocking crossword layout. Encourage students to choose challenging words from this lesson and from their own knowledge. They then create a blank crossword grid to represent their layout, numbering the start of each word and write clues. Monitor and help as necessary. Pairs then exchange blank crosswords and give each other clues to complete them. This could be run as a competition with the winner being the first group of four to complete both crosswords.

HOMEWORK

Students write travel tips for a website for tourists visiting their country. They should include at least six pieces of advice. (These can then be used in a following lesson to revise the reporting verbs.)

WEBLINK

Students may like to visit www.lonelyplanet.com/england to read about holiday destinations and get travel advice.

Revision and Extension p83

Language File p117

Workbook Unit 6 Lesson 1 pp62–63

Photocopiable worksheet p178, notes p159

ON THE MOVE

The waitress wanted to know if ...

Communicative aims	Language	Pronunciation	Vocabulary	Optional aids
Reporting what people asked	Reported questions	Sentence stress and intonation	Restaurant Food	Follow-up activity 1: small cards

WARMER 1

If you set the homework in the previous lesson, ask students to exchange their travel tips, then summarise their partner's tips using reported speech, e.g. *Pedro advised visitors to our country to bring warm clothes.* Write *advise, explain, remind, say, suggest, tell, warn* on the board as prompts.

WARMER 2

Write anagrams for these words on the board: *waitress, knife, fork, customer, glass, tray, menu.* Students race to solve the anagrams and work out where you might hear these words: *a restaurant.*

Useful information

Bill Bryson is a best-selling American-born author of humorous books on travel, as well as books on the English language. He's written travel books about his homeland, the United States (in *The Lost Continent*, where this excerpt is taken from), Britain, where he has lived for most of his adult life (in *Notes from a Small Island*) and Australia (in *Down Under*).

1 OPENER

- The aim is to set the scene for the text in exercise 2.
- Discuss the questions with the whole class. Ask students if there are parts of their country that they haven't visited and would like to visit. Ask if there are parts of their own country that they know nothing about. Elicit ways to find out more about your own country, e.g. *go to the national museum, read books, take holidays in your own country.* Then ask students to say which they think is best and why.

2 READING

- Ask students to read and listen to the introduction about Bill Bryson and find out where he is from and how he discovered more about his country. Pause the recording after the introduction and check the answers (*USA, he drove around the country*).
- Read the question with the class and ask students to speculate on the answer. Students then read and listen to check the answer.

🔘 2.30 Recording and answer
See text on page 76 of the Student's Book.
He couldn't stop saying thank you.

3 AFTER READING

- Students match the beginnings and endings. Confident students can match first and then re-read the extract to check. Less confident students can find the answers in the extract. Point out that two of the endings are not used.

Answers

1k 2h 3b 4i 5c 6l 7d 8a 9f 10g

Optional activities

- ◆ Students cover the endings and finish the sentences in their own words. They then check their ideas with the endings given.
- ◆ With stronger classes, students read the story again and try to remember it. In groups, students retell the story. If a student remembers a detail that the speaker has omitted then they stop the speaker, add the detail and continue.

Your response

Ask the question to the whole class and elicit a range of suggestions. Make sure that students use the correct form *I would have ...*

4 VOCABULARY

- Ask students to find the words and phrases in the lesson. Remind students that the *n* means noun (which may surprise them for *special*). Students use the context to match the words to the definitions.

Answers

1 *special*   2 *cutlery*   3 *bread roll*   4 *ketchup*
5 *dressing*   6 *cash register*   7 *gravy*   8 *tray*   9 *napkin*

Optional activities

- ◆ In pairs, one student reads the definition and the other student says the word from memory.
- ◆ Give definitions of more words in the lesson, e.g. *homeland, plump, menu, wipe, starving, push off.* Students race to find the words.

5 PRONUNCIATION

- Ask students to read the sentences and underline the word they think is most important in each sentence. Explain that the main stress in a sentence usually falls on the most important word. Students listen and check their ideas. Play the recording again, pausing for students to repeat.

🔘 **2.31** **Recording and answers**

1
Would you like some more <u>chicken</u>?
No thank you, but I'd like some more <u>chips</u>.
2
Have you got enough <u>gravy</u>?
Yes thanks, but I'd like some more <u>bread</u>.
3
Would you like some <u>ketchup</u>?
No thank you, but I'd like some <u>dressing</u>.
4
How about some <u>coffee</u>?
Yes please, and some <u>cake</u>.

LANGUAGE WORKOUT OPTION

If you want to pre-teach the language students will use in the following activities, you may like to go to the Language Workout box now.

6 LISTENING

- Allow students time to read through the statements. Students listen and decide if the statements are true or false. Check answers before students correct the false statements.

🔘 **2.32** **Recording**

INTERVIEWER	Hi Lizzie – I'm interviewing people for the school magazine. Can I ask you some questions about your last holiday?
LIZZIE	Sure, go ahead.
INTERVIEWER	OK – when did you last go on holiday?
LIZZIE	I had a holiday at the beginning of this year, in January.
INTERVIEWER	And where did you go?
LIZZIE	Switzerland. I went to the Swiss Alps for a week. It was a school trip, so I went with my friends.
INTERVIEWER	Cool. And what did you do there – winter sports?
LIZZIE	Yeah, I did lots of snowboarding, it was great.
INTERVIEWER	Did you go skiing as well?
LIZZIE	I tried it, but I didn't like it as much as snowboarding.
INTERVIEWER	What was the food like? What did you eat?
LIZZIE	We had delicious cakes … and I really enjoyed cheese fondue. And when we were out on the mountain, we took packed lunches, with sandwiches, fruit and chocolate.

INTERVIEWER	Did you like Swiss chocolate?
LIZZIE	Of course – yummy!
INTERVIEWER	What did you enjoy most while you were on holiday?
LIZZIE	Doing jumps on the snowboard – it's really exciting.
INTERVIEWER	And what did you enjoy least?
LIZZIE	Falling over in the snow!
INTERVIEWER	Know the feeling – it's not much fun, is it? Well thanks very much, Lizzie …

Answers

1 False. He asked when she had last been on holiday.
2 True
3 False. She said she had been for one week.
4 False. She went with her friends.
5 False. He wondered if she had done winter sports.
6 True
7 False. They took sandwiches, fruit and chocolate.
8 True
9 False. She said it was really exciting.
10 False. He agreed that it wasn't much fun.

LANGUAGE WORKOUT OPTION

If you want to pre-teach the language students will use in the following activities, you may like to go to the Language Workout box now.

7 SPEAKING

- Students look at the prompts for talking about their last holiday. Elicit the first question *When did you last go on holiday?*
- Students prepare their questions using the prompts. In pairs, students interview each other and note the answers. Tell students that if they prefer, they can invent a holiday and talk about that.

Optional activity

Students can prepare and ask two more questions of their own.

8 WRITING

- Students use their notes from exercise 7 to write sentences reporting the questions and answers. Encourage students to use a range of reporting verbs. Students can swap with a partner and peer correct.

Extension Students choose a famous person and invent an interview with them on the same subject. They then write a report of the interview using reported speech.

LANGUAGE WORKOUT

- Ask students to look at the Language Workout box and complete the sentences and the rules. Confident students can complete first and then check, while others can look back at exercises 2 and 3 and then complete.
- Students turn to page 117 of the Language File to check their answers.

  Answers
  if, was   if, could   if, would   don't   would

- Highlight that:
  - after the reporting verb, the main verb moves back one tense into the past in the same way as with reported statements.
  - *wondered* is often used when you don't actually ask the question aloud, you just think about it.
  - in reported *yes/no* questions, we use *if* before the reported question.
  - in other reported questions, we use the question word, but the word order changes to statement word order, e.g. *What would you like? She asked me what I would like.*

Optional activity

In pairs, not looking at the extract, students recall the seven questions the waitress asked Bill Bryson, then see if they can remember how they are reported in the text. They can look at the text again to check their answers.

PRACTICE

- Students do Practice exercise 19 on page 117 of the Language File. They match the direct questions with the reported questions.

  Answers
  1 d   2 b   3 e   4 c   5 a

- Students then interview another student and note their answers to the five questions. Encourage confident students to ask follow-up questions, e.g. *When did you go there? Did you like it?* and provide more information in their answers.

- Students then write their notes out in complete sentences, reporting the questions and the answers. Encourage students to use a variety of ways to report the questions, e.g. *ask, want to know, wonder*, and a variety of verbs for the responses, e.g. *say, tell, reply, explain.*
- Ask different students to read a reported question and answer to the class.

Follow-up activities

- ♦ **Game** *What did they say?* Write the names of people on cards, e.g. *you, student, teacher, mother, father, sister, bank manager, police officer.* Write reporting verbs on another set of cards. Put the cards face down on the table. Students work in teams. Each team takes two people cards and one reporting verb card. They must then make two sentences reporting what one of the people asked and how the other responded using the reporting verb, e.g. *The police officer asked where my father was going. My father explained that he was going to work.* For each grammatically accurate sentence, they win one point. If the exchange seems likely, they win an extra point. So each team can win a maximum of three points per go. The winners are the team with the most points.
- ♦ Each student writes down one question they would like to ask all the class. It can be about any subject, e.g. sport, food, school. Students move around, asking every student their question and making a note of answers. Each student then reports back on their findings. They say what they asked and how the students in the class responded, e.g. *I asked what their favourite time of day was. Most of them said that they preferred the evening, after 7 o'clock. Some of them said they liked the morning because they had a lot of energy then.*

HOMEWORK

Students interview a friend or member of the family about eating out, e.g. *Do you prefer eating out or staying at home? What's your favourite dish? What's your favourite restaurant? What's it like?* They then write up their report of the interview, reporting the questions and the answers.

WEBLINK

Students may like to visit www.randomhouse.com/features/billbryson, the official website for Bill Bryson, to find out more information about him.

Revision and Extension p83

Language File p117

Workbook Unit 6 Lesson 2 pp64–65

Photocopiable worksheet p179, notes p159

Would you get it repaired?

Communicative aims	Language	Pronunciation	Vocabulary	Optional aids
Describing problems Suggesting solutions	*get/have something done* *It's time* + past simple	Strong and weak forms of *have*	Shops and services Appearance Phrasal verbs: *in/into*	Follow-up activity 1: small blank cards for Vocabulary box

WARMER

Tell students that the topic of the reading in this lesson is *tourism*. Tell students you have a list of six things you should always do before you go on a long holiday. Elicit some possible ideas, e.g. *find your passport*. In teams, students write down six ideas of their own. Ask teams to read their ideas to the class. They win a point for each idea which is the same as one of yours. Possible ideas: *buy suncream, find your passport, pack your suitcase, go to the dentist, learn the language, buy some local currency, get a visa, have injections.*

1 OPENER

- The aim is to set the scene and generate interest in the topic of the questionnaire. Read the question and give some examples of things you do yourself, e.g. *clean your house,* and things you get others to do for you, e.g. *repair your car.* Discuss the question with the whole class.

2 SPEAKING

- Tell students that this is a questionnaire to find out how much they do themselves and how much they get others to do things for them. Students read and answer the questions for themselves.
- Students work in groups of three and compare answers. Encourage students to ask and answer the question fully and not to refer to the different actions as A, B, C. Ask one group to demonstrate. Encourage confident students to say why they chose their answer. Students note each other's answers. Monitor and help/correct as necessary.
- Ask each group to report back on who did things themselves and who got other people to do things.
- Questions 4, 5 and 6 are mixed conditionals. The first part of the question is an imaginary past situation (*if* + past perfect) and the second part is an imaginary present reaction (*would* + base infinitive without *to*). There is no need to draw attention to this unless students query it.

3 READING

- Read the question and ask students to predict the answer. With weaker classes, pre-teach or review *rude* and *tip.* Students then read and listen to check their ideas (*the British were the worst at learning the local language*). Ask students if they agree that the British are the world's worst tourists.

🔘 2.33 Recording
See text on page 78 of the Student's Book.

4 AFTER READING

- Students read the statements and then re-read the article more carefully and decide if they are true, false, or there is no information given. Students correct the false sentences.
- Students compare answers in pairs. Then check the answers with the whole class.

Answers
1 False. There were 24 countries in the survey.
2 No information
3 True
4 False. He thinks it's time the British woke up to reality.
5 False. They expect to have everything done for them.
6 True
7 True
8 No information
9 False. He wants the British to be more like the Germans.

Your response

Students discuss the questions in pairs, and then as a class.

Optional activity

If your students come from one of the countries on the list of top tourists, ask them if they agree with their ranking. If not, ask them where they think their country would be in the list and why.

5 PRONUNCIATION

- Write *have* on the board and tell students that there are two ways that this can be pronounced: /**haev**/ (strong) and /əv/ (weak).
- Students read the sentences and choose whether the pronunciation of *have* in each sentence is strong or weak. Students then listen to check.
- Elicit the rule from students: when *have* is important to the meaning, e.g. in *have something done* it is strong, when *have* is used as an auxiliary, e.g. third conditional or present perfect, it is weak.

🔘 2.34 Recording and answers
1 They expect to have everything done for them.   strong
2 What would you have done?   weak
3 Are you going to have it installed?   strong
4 I'd like to have some flowers sent.   strong
5 I have had some photos taken.   weak
6 It would have been fun.   weak

6 VOCABULARY

- Students look for the phrasal verbs in the text in exercise 3 (*fill in*, *take in*, *turn into*). Encourage students to use the context to work out the meaning of these verbs. Students then match the remaining three verbs to their meanings.

Answers

1 look into   2 break into   3 take in   4 turn into
5 fill in   6 give in

Extension Ask students to write sentences using the phrasal verbs from exercise 6.

LANGUAGE WORKOUT OPTION

If you want to pre-teach the language students will use in the following activities, you may like to go to the Language Workout box now.

7 WRITING

- Put students into groups of three to compare their answers to the questionnaire.
- Elicit expressions that students can use to compare their answers with the other students, e.g. *Two of us would ...,* *whereas ...; All of us would ....*
- Students write the paragraph. Monitor and help as necessary. Students exchange their writing and correct each other's work for spelling, grammar and punctuation.

LANGUAGE WORKOUT

- Ask students to look at the Language Workout box and complete the sentences. Confident students can complete first and then check, while others can look back at exercise 3 and then complete.
- Students turn to page 118 of the Language File to check their answers.

  Answers
  tested   serviced   time, woke

- Highlight that:
  - the form is *get/have* + object + past participle.
  - to use this structure in the past or the future, you only need to change the form of *get/have*. Ask students to put the first example in the past (*You had your car serviced*) and the future (*You are going to have your car serviced*).

- Check students understand by asking questions about the examples:
  get/have something done: *Do you service your car/test your eyes/yourself?* (No) *Do you pay someone else to do it?* (Yes)
  It's time + past simple: *Is this about the past or the present?* (present) *It's time* + past simple = *You ... do this soon* (should). Point out that this is more often used as obligation than advice.

PRACTICE

- Students complete exercise 20 on page 118 of the Language File. They complete the sentences using the words in brackets. Do the first one together as an example. Point out that students need to use the correct form of *have/get*. Check answers.

Answers

1 He's going to have a passport photo taken.
2 She's having her hair done.
3 He's going to get his eyes tested.
4 She's just had a tooth filled.
5 He's going to get a new key cut.
6 She's just had her car serviced.

Follow-up activity

Game *What's the word?*   Students write new vocabulary from the lesson on cards. Collect the cards and divide the class into teams of three or four. One student from each team comes to the front of the class. Choose a card and show it to the students at the front. These students then mime or draw the meaning of the word for their team. They must not speak. The first team to shout out the word wins a point. Repeat with different students. Add the cards to the Vocabulary box.

HOMEWORK

Students write about the typical day of a famous person, e.g. a member of a royal family, a politician, a singer, an actor. They should include at least four examples of *get/have something done*. You could also use this to review *before/after* + *-ing*.

WEBLINK

Students may like to visit www.telegraph.co.uk/travel/travelnews/5788582/Britons-are-worst-tourists-in-Europe.html to read another article about a survey that gave slightly different results.

Revision and Extension p83

Language File p118

Workbook Unit 6 Lesson 3 pp66–67

Photocopiable worksheet p180, notes p159

Integrated Skills Reporting and summarising what people said

Skills		Learner independence	Vocabulary	Optional aids
Reading Topics: Family Holidays interview *Listening* Note-taking *Speaking* Interviewing and reporting an interview	*Writing* A report summarising an interview	Thinking skills Word creation: adjective prefix *well-*	Holidays Useful expressions	Exercise 3 optional activity: cards for vocabulary box

WARMER 1

Game *It's a race!* Write 10–15 words you would like to review on the board. If you have a Vocabulary box, choose words from the box. Students work in teams. Each team chooses one student to answer. Give a definition for one of the words on the board. The chosen student from each team shouts the correct word. The first team to shout the right word wins a point. Repeat with different students.

WARMER 2

Write the words from the following sentences on the board in a jumbled order: *It's time he went to the optician's. He can't see a thing. Don't worry, he's having his eyes tested tomorrow.* Students race to organise the words to make three sentences which make sense.

1 OPENER

- The aim is to set the scene and generate interest in the text in exercise 2. Discuss the question as a class.

2 READING

- Ask students to look at the photo and guess where Isabel went. Read through the questions with the class and make sure students understand the task. Encourage students to read for general understanding by setting a short time limit for students to match the questions and answers. Students then listen and check their answers.

  🔘 2.35 Recording
  See text on page 80 of the Student's Book.

  Answers
  1 c 2 e 3 a 4 f 5 b 6 d

3

- Students search the text for words or phrases that match the definitions. Tell students that the definitions are not in the same order as the words in the text.

Answers

*1 games console 2 groceries 3 gap year 4 well off
5 lazing around 6 rented 7 obvious 8 relatives
9 packed*

Optional activities

- ♦ Ask students to write their own example sentences for the new words.
- ♦ Students copy the new vocabulary onto cards and write the definitions on the back. Add these to the Vocabulary box.

4

- The aim is to raise students' awareness of the use of general nouns, pronouns and ellipsis (leaving out words when the meaning is clear without them) to link ideas in a text. Do the first one together as an example.

Answers
*1 to Argentina; his parents
2 me and my parents
3 sunbathing and swimming
4 travelling by train
5 Lo siento, no entiendo
6 one of my cousins called Mariela*

5 LISTENING

- Students look at the photos. In pairs, students discuss *Where was his best holiday? What did he do there?*
- Tell students that they will hear Ben answering the six questions from exercise 2. The questions are asked in the same order as in the listening in exercise 2. Students should listen and note Ben's answers.
- Play the recording to students to listen and take notes. If necessary, pause the recording after each answer to allow students time to write their notes.
- Students compare their answers in pairs. If necessary, play the recording again and pause after each answer for students to confirm their ideas with their partner. Check the answers as a class but don't ask students to give complete sentences at this stage; they just need the key ideas.

🔘 2.36 Recording

INTERVIEWER *What's the best holiday you've ever had?*
BEN *It was in Canada three years ago. Some friends invited us to stay in Nova Scotia – that's the east coast of Canada. So we went for two weeks, and while we were there we went whale-watching. We saw all kinds of whales and dolphins, and they came really close to the boat. It was magic.*

INTERVIEWER *Do you help decide where you go?*
BEN *Not really, because we go to the same place nearly every summer, but that's cool. We rent a house in Wales with another family – friends of ours – and it's great. It's an old house near the beach with lots of rooms and a big garden.*

INTERVIEWER *What do you enjoy doing most on holiday?*
BEN *I like water sports – surfing, snorkelling, swimming, all that stuff. And now I'm learning to sail. I don't like just lying on the beach. And in the evening I like having barbecues on the beach – as long as it's not raining!*

INTERVIEWER *What's your favourite way of travelling?*
BEN *You can't beat travelling by sea – I love sailing. But it isn't exactly fast. Like, it would have taken ages to get to Canada by sea. If you're in a hurry, flying is fun. Especially the moment when the plane takes off, it's wicked.*

INTERVIEWER *Do you have any advice for people going on holiday with their parents?*
BEN *Don't tell us when to go to bed! It wouldn't matter if we stayed up all night – we haven't got school the next day. Parents are far too bossy on holiday – they don't need to tell us what to do all the time.*

INTERVIEWER *Where are you going next?*
BEN *I'm going to Holland at half term for a week with the school football team. We're playing matches against schools in different towns, starting with Amsterdam. I've never been to Holland before and I'm really looking forward to it.*

Answers

1 *East coast of Canada, three years ago, for two weeks, whale watching*
2 *Not really, same place nearly every year, house, Wales, with another family, near beach*
3 *Water sports, not lying on the beach, barbecues*
4 *By sea, sailing, also flying is fun*
5 *Parents – don't tell children when to go to bed, don't tell them what to do all the time*
6 *Holland, school football team, starting in Amsterdam*

Optional activity

♦ Students discuss which holiday, to Argentina, Wales or Canada, they would prefer to go on and why. Stronger classes could use the questions in exercise 2 and role play the interview with Ben from memory.

6 SPEAKING

- Students use their notes to report what Ben said. Make a note of any errors that are made, particularly with reported speech, and write these on the board for students to correct. If necessary, stop the activity and revise the basic rules for reported speech before students continue.
- Tell students they are now going to interview each other using the same six questions. Be prepared to provide any specific vocabulary that students need to talk about holidays. Set a time limit for students to interview each other and note down each other's answers. Monitor and help as necessary.

7 GUIDED WRITING

- Use the notes from Ben's interview in exercise 5 to demonstrate summarising. Look at the answers to the first two questions and consider together how to summarise them. Guide students towards *He said his best holiday had been on the east coast of Canada where he had gone whale-watching. He said he didn't really have a say in where they went because they usually did the same thing every year.*
- Write a list of reporting verbs on the board and elicit examples using them. Remind students that different reporting verbs use different patterns. If necessary, refer them to page 117 of the Language File. Students then write their report on the student they interviewed. Monitor and help as necessary. Students can exchange reports and peer correct.

8 LEARNER INDEPENDENCE

- The aim is to get students thinking about how to improve their listening and note-taking skills.
- Write the following questions on the board for students to discuss: *What can you do before you listen to make the listening easier? What kind of words should you focus on when you are listening? What kind of words do you need to note down?* Students then read the advice and check their ideas.

Optional activities

♦ Use some sentences from the recording script in exercise 5 to show students that they only need to focus on the words that are stressed: Write the following sentences on the board: *It was in Canada three years ago. Some friends invited us to stay in Nova Scotia – that's the east coast of Canada.* Ask students to identify the stressed words: *Canada, three years ago, friends, invited, stay, Nova Scotia, east coast, Canada.* Ask if this is enough to understand the sentence (*yes*).

♦ Use the recording from the listening on page 77 to give students more practice of listening and taking notes. With books closed, play the recording once for students to note down the questions in the interview, then play the recording again for students to listen and take notes of Lizzie's answers.

9 WORD CREATION

• The aim is for students to learn which words the prefix *well-* is most frequently combined with.
• Students complete the sentences with the correct adjectives. Point out that *well-* and the adjective are sometimes hyphenated.

Answers

1 dressed   2 paid   3 balanced   4 done   5 behaved
6 off   7 known

EXTRA PRACTICE

If you would like to give your students more practice in forming words which start with *well-*, please see the Vocabulary EXTRA! Worksheets on the Teacher's Resource Site (www.macmillanenglish.com/inspiration).

10 PHRASEBOOK

• Ask students to look through the unit to find the expressions and look at how they are used. Be ready to help with translation if necessary.
• Play the recording, pausing after each expression for students to repeat.

🔘 2.37 Recording

You'll never guess what! (Lesson 1, exercise 2)
I've changed my mind. (Lesson 1, exercise 3)
It's out of the question. (Lesson 1, exercise 3)
You're welcome. (Lesson 2, exercise 2)
It's time that people realised … (Lesson 3, exercise 3)
Let me explain. (Lesson 4, exercise 2)
I'm not a great one for … (Lesson 4, exercise 2)
In fact, it was the opposite. (Lesson 4, exercise 2)

• Ask students to work in pairs to make up the five-line dialogue. Invite some pairs to act out their dialogues in front of the class.

Optional activity

Students can add expressions they like to their Personal Phrasebooks.

Follow-up activities

♦ **Game** *What comes next?* Students close their books. Read *Family Holidays* aloud to the students. Stop occasionally before a key word. The first student to shout out the next word in the text wins a point, e.g. *It was a trip to Argentina six … ago. What? You're going on holiday with your …?*

HOMEWORK

Students write a leaflet entitled *Tips for parents on holiday with teenagers.* They can use Isabel and Ben's ideas if they agree with them and include some of their own.

WEBLINK

Students may like to visit www.guardian.co.uk/travel/activities/family/story/0,7447,1577087,00.html to read a similar article to the ones in this lesson.

Revision and Extension p83

Workbook Unit 6 Lesson 4 pp68–69

Inspiration EXTRA!

Optional aids

Your choice! Interaction: pictures from magazines and newspapers

PROJECT   IDEAL HOLIDAY

1
- Ask students to look at the photos. Ask *What can you see in the photos? What kinds of holiday are shown?* (cycling holiday, adventure holiday) *Would you like to go on this kind of holiday?*
- Explain that the aim of the project is to write about an ideal holiday.
- Divide the students into groups and appoint a 'secretary' for each group. The 'secretary' is responsible for taking notes for the group.
- Students add to the list of kinds of holiday, e.g. *sightseeing, camping, cycling, city break, cruise*. Each group then chooses one that everyone in their group would like to go on.

2
- Students make notes about their ideal kind of holiday using the questions to help them.
- Students find more information from brochures, magazines and the Web. If this is not possible, print out information from the Internet. A website you could recommend/use is www.lonelyplanet.com where you can browse all kinds of holiday. Alternatively, search for the kinds of holiday they have chosen using a search engine such as www.google.com. Encourage students to bring pictures to class to illustrate their work.

3
- Working together in a group, students compare the information they have found. They decide in which order to put the information. Students write their texts and then read them through carefully to correct any mistakes. Monitor and help as necessary. They copy their texts out neatly and illustrate their work with photos, pictures from magazines or newspapers or their own drawings
- Students show their *Ideal Holiday* to other groups. Display the files in the classroom if possible.

Optional activities

♦ Students prepare and give an oral presentation on their holidays. The class decide which they would most like to go on. Tell students they cannot choose the holiday they wrote about.
♦ Give examples of different kinds of people, e.g. *a couple in their 50s, a family with two young children*. The class discusses which of the holidays would be suitable for the people and why.

GAME   QUESTION GAMES

1
- Students work in two teams and choose a question master. Ask students to read the instructions carefully. Check comprehension by asking: *What does the question master write on the board?* (an answer) *How many questions do you write?* (as many as they can think of).
- Students look at the examples. Point out that the questions must be realistic questions for the answer, it cannot be impossible, e.g. *How many children do you have?* 150 is not acceptable!

2
- Students work in pairs. Tell them to read the instructions carefully. Check comprehension by asking: *How do you start?* (one student asks a question) *How does the other person reply?* (with another question) *How can you lose a point?* (by making a statement or repeating a question). Tell students that the conversation must make sense, and remind them that each player can only lose three points, and then they have lost the game.
- Demonstrate with one student, e.g. T: *How are you?* S: *Why do you want to know?* T: *Why don't you want to tell me?* S: *Are you angry with me?*

REVISION

Lesson 1

| Answers

Who replied that she would have to ask her parents? Laura did.
Who hoped that they would say yes? Laura did.
Who refused to let her go? Laura's father did.
Who explained that they wouldn't be on their own? Laura did.
Who pointed out that Laura didn't like Indian food? Her mother did.
Who agreed to let her go? Her parents did.
Who promised to send loads of emails? Laura did.
Who reminded Laura that she had to have injections? Her mother did.
Who warned her that she could get malaria if she forgot to take her malaria tablets? Her father did.
Who suggested inviting Nisha and her parents for supper? Laura's mother did.

Lesson 2
Students' own answers.

Lesson 3
Students' own answers.

EXTENSION

Lessons 1–3
Students' own answers.

YOUR CHOICE!

- The aim is to give students more learner independence and help them to identify their preferred way of learning. Encourage students to choose an activity that they feel less comfortable with if they want a challenge or are aware that they need practice in a particular area.
- Monitor and help groups. Check answers if necessary, or provide written answers for groups to check their own work against.

Language File pp117–118

Song – photocopiable worksheet p189, notes p162

CONSTRUCTION

| Answers

1 asked   2 reminded   3 suggested   4 warned
5 wondered   6 refused   7 offered   8 replied

REFLECTION

| Answers

1j   2d   3e   4a   5g, i   6f, h   7c   8b

ACTION

- Students work in small groups and mime eating or listening to something.
- This could be made into a competition by setting a time limit and asking groups to record how many they guess right in that time.
- Ask *How many did you guess? Were there any that you didn't guess?**

* 'Sense mimes' was inspired by 'Taste, touch, smell' (p57) in *Drama Techniques* by Alan Maley and Alan Duff (Third edition, CUP, 2005)

INTERACTION

- Students work individually to make their collages. Have them use the pictures from magazines and newspapers that you or they brought in. Remind students not to put their name on them. Give each group five minutes to discuss their collages.
- Students show their collages to the whole class. The class guesses whose they are.*

* 'A collage of myself' was inspired by 'Self-collage' (p158) in *Caring & Sharing in the Foreign Language Class* by Gertrude Moskowitz (Newbury House, 1978)

You may now like students to do the song *Hanging on the Telephone*. See p162 for the notes and p189 for the worksheet.

Workbook Unit 6 Inspiration EXTRA! pp70–71

1 Ask students to look at the picture and the title and predict what the text will be about. Students read the text and check their predictions. Students read the text again and choose the appropriate word for each space. Do the first one together as an example. This can be done in pairs or individually as a short test.

> **Answers**
>
> 1C   2C   3B   4A   5B   6B   7A   8C   9A   10C

Optional activity

> In pairs, students discuss the advantages and disadvantages of this way of living.

2 Students combine the information in the two sentences into one sentence beginning with *If*. Point out that the sentences could be written in reverse, e.g. *The King would have died if the Gunpowder Plot had succeeded.*

> **Answers**
>
> 1 *If Amelia Earhart hadn't been daring, she wouldn't have tried to fly round the world.*
> 2 *If something strange hadn't happened, the plane would have reached the island.*
> 3 *If the boys had realised Maribel was a girl, they wouldn't have called her 'Mario'.*
> 4 *If Maribel hadn't been a brilliant footballer, she wouldn't have played for Mexico.*
> 5 *If FIFA had said Maribel could play for a men's club, she would have played for Celaya.*
> 6 *If Nisha hadn't invited her, Laura wouldn't have gone to India for the holidays.*
> 7 *If the restaurant hadn't looked friendly, Bill Bryson wouldn't have decided to have dinner there.*
> 8 *If Isabel had spoken Spanish, she wouldn't have been worried about meeting her relatives.*

Optional activity

> Students write further sentences in the third conditional on the topics of the lessons in Units 5 and 6.

3 Before students look at the exercise, set the context and ask students to predict what went wrong. They read the sentences to see if they were right. Students then write sentences using *I wish* and *If only*.

> **Answers**
>
> 1 *I wish/If only I had taken the train.*
> 2 *I wish/If only the traffic hadn't been so heavy.*
> 3 *I wish/If only I'd stopped for petrol.*
> 4 *I wish/If only the car hadn't run out of petrol.*
> 5 *I wish/If only I'd got to the airport in time.*
> 6 *I wish/If only I hadn't missed my flight.*
> 7 *I wish/If only I'd had a holiday.*

4 Students complete the sentences with the correct verb and a verb from the box. Do the first one together as an example.

> **Answers**
>
> 1 *needs to have*   2 *needn't book*   3 *mustn't stay*
> 4 *needs to start*   5 *needn't go*   6 *needn't look*
> 7 *mustn't forget*   8 *need to stop*

5 Students work in pairs and use the prompts to discuss what could/might have happened. Monitor and help/correct as necessary.

> **Answers**
>
> 1 A *She could have lost the address.*
>   B *Yes, she might have lost the address.*
> 2 A *She could have forgotten about it.*
>   B *Yes, she might have forgotten about it.*
> 3 A *She could have felt too tired.*
>   B *Yes, she might have felt too tired.*
> 4 A *She could have gone to another gig.*
>   B *Yes, she might have gone to another gig.*
> 5 A *She could have missed the bus.*
>   B *Yes, she might have missed the bus.*
> 6 A *She could have decided not to come.*
>   B *Yes, she might have decided not to come.*

6 Students write the sentences in reported speech. Point out that they will need to change words in the sentence, e.g. the pronoun *this* in *this evening*. Confident students can attempt the task without looking at the words in the box. Do one together as an example.

> **Answers**
>
> 1 *Paul reminded Sue to phone him that evening.*
> 2 *Sally invited Tom to go to the cinema.*
> 3 *Robert explained that you pressed the red button to turn on the DVD player.*
> 4 *Marta refused to tidy her room.*
> 5 *Dan warned Emma not to drive too fast.*
> 6 *The doctor suggested that Mr Evans took a holiday.*
> 7 *Jenny complained that she couldn't concentrate with all the noise.*
> 8 *Bill offered to carry his mum's suitcase.*

7 Students report the questions. Do one together as an example first.

> **Answers**
>
> 1 *Marion wanted to know when the next train left.*
> 2 *She wondered if she had to change trains.*
> 3 *She asked how long the journey took.*
> 4 *She wanted to know if the hotel was near the station.*
> 5 *She wondered how much a single room cost.*
> 6 *She asked if she could pay by credit card.*

8 In pairs, students use the prompts to ask and answer the questions.

Answers
1 *Did she get a new passport photo taken? Yes, she did.*
2 *Did she have her eyes tested? No, she didn't.*
3 *Did she have her hair cut? No, she didn't.*
4 *Did she get her teeth checked? Yes, she did.*
5 *Did she have her nails painted? No, she didn't.*
6 *Did she get her shoes repaired? Yes, she did.*

• Students write the sentences.

1 *She got a new passport photo taken.*
2 *She didn't have her eyes tested.*
3 *She didn't have her hair cut.*
4 *She got her teeth checked.*
5 *She didn't have her nails painted.*
6 *She got her shoes repaired.*

VOCABULARY

9 Students complete the sentences with the correct form of the verbs. Confident students can cover the verbs in the box, complete the sentences and then check.

Answers
1 *pick* 2 *warned* 3 *tipped* 4 *push off* 5 *collapsed*
6 *supervised* 7 *install* 8 *pointed out* 9 *stuck* 10 *spilt*

10 Students match the words with their definitions. Confident students can read the definitions and attempt to write the words without looking at the box. They can then look at the words in the box to check.

Answers
1 *massive* 2 *defrost* 3 *abduct* 4 *puncture* 5 *blow up*
6 *trace* 7 *aisle* 8 *remote*

11 Students match the verbs from list A with the words and phrases in list B.

Answers
1 *catch someone red-handed*   5 *score a goal*
2 *fly solo*   6 *set light to*
3 *give someone a chance*   7 *take a tablet*
4 *remain a mystery*

LEARNER INDEPENDENCE SELF ASSESSMENT

• Explain to students that the aim of the self-assessment is to encourage them to check their own progress and take any necessary action to improve. Point out that the list 1–8 covers areas of functional language from Units 5–6. Students tick the 'Fine' box for functional language that they feel confident using, but put a question mark in the 'Not sure' box for functional language that they have difficulties with or still cannot use confidently.

• Encourage students to look at the Language File and re-do exercises from the Workbook in areas where they have problems. They may also like to re-do exercises from the lessons and from the Revision and Extension sections in Units 5 and 6.

• Students write an example sentence for each language area in the list. You may like to elicit grammar students need for each example before students write their sentences, e.g. *Talking about unreal or imaginary past events: third conditional.* Students can refer back to the lessons and the Language File.

• Ask students to compare their sentences with a partner and discuss and correct any mistakes.

• Check students' sentences and note down any language areas for further practice.

HOMEWORK

Students bring their vocabulary notebooks up to date. Students interview a friend or relative about their holiday preferences and then write up the report of the interview.

WEBLINK

Students may like to visit www.guardian.co.uk/books/review/story to learn more about the Eveny people.

Language File pp116–118

Workbook Review Units 5–6 pp72–73

Units 7–8

Activities		Project	Vocabulary
Identifying the function of communicative language	Categorising vocabulary Contextualising listening extracts	Telephone conversation	Education Furniture, fixtures and fittings Science

WARMER 1

Game *Who are they?* Put students into pairs and give them five minutes to find out who the people in the photos are, and what they are famous for. They can do this by looking in Units 7–8. Students should then find as much information about the people as they can in the time available. After 5 minutes, put pairs together into groups of four to pool their ideas. Ask each group in turn to read out their ideas about each person, and bring the information together on the board. Ask *Which person do you find most interesting? Which person do you admire the most? Why?* Elicit a range of answers.

WARMER 2

Game *Pictures and words* Put students into pairs and ask them to look at the photos. Tell them they should write down five words that have an association with each picture. Tell students they should be creative and imaginative, because the aim is to think of words that no one else thinks of. When students are ready, ask pairs in turn to read out their words. They get a point for each word that no one in the class has written for that picture. Other students can challenge individual words if they feel there is no association with the picture. The pair must then justify the association. The pair with the most points wins.

1 • The aim is to introduce students to the main areas of communicative language they will cover in Units 7 and 8.
  • Focus on the two boxes and explain that they show the communicative language and topics/vocabulary that students will learn in Units 7 and 8. Students match five of the communicative aims 1–7 with the photos A–E.

  ### Answers
  1 - 2 C 3 E 4 B 5 D 6 - 7 A

Optional activity

Students write another example sentence for each of the communicative aims 1–7. Monitor and help where necessary. Ask students to read out some of their sentences, and ask the class to decide which communicative aim they go with.

2 • Give students two minutes to complete the words and write them in the correct categories.
  • Allow students time to check their answers in pairs before you check with the whole class.

  ### Answers
  Education: curriculum, examination, lesson, timetable, uniform, university
  Music: band, composer, guitar, opera, singer, tune
  Furniture, fixtures and fittings: chair, cupboard, shelf, sink, table, window

Optional activity

Students work in pairs or small groups and add as many words as they can to the *Furniture, fixtures and fittings* category. Bring the vocabulary together on the board and ask students to write example sentences for five of the words.

3 • The aim of the activity is for students to contextualise short listening extracts by working out what kind of listening text each is from. Remind students that for this type of activity they should listen for the main gist, and should not worry if they don't understand every single word. Remind them that there is one text type they do not need.
  • Play the recording. Students match the extracts 1–3 with A–D.

◯ 3.01 Recording

1
PRODUCER *Has the window been repaired?*
DAVE *Yes, that was done yesterday. And a new blind will be hung tomorrow.*
PRODUCER *Have the lights been changed?*
DAVE *Not yet – they'll be changed tomorrow.*
PRODUCER *What about the sink? Has it been replaced?*
DAVE *Yes, it was replaced yesterday. And a new cooker was installed yesterday too.*

2
Although he was often ill and finally became totally deaf, he managed to produce an extraordinary quantity of work, including concertos, symphonies and operas. It has often been said: 'Though Beethoven wasn't able to hear, he was able to listen.'

3
Generally you have to work hard at songwriting. I keep a notebook by my bed and note down things I remember from my dreams. Sometimes the lyrics come first, sometimes the music. You can't make a song happen – you just have to let it take shape.

Answers

1 D   2 B   3 A

Optional activity

Play the recording again and ask students the comprehension questions, e.g *What was put into the kitchen yesterday?* (A new cooker) *What wasn't Beethoven able to do?* (He wasn't able to hear) *Why does the singer keep a notebook by the bed?* (to remember things from dreams).

4 • Read through the instructions with the class. With weaker classes, demonstrate the activity by reading out some spellings yourself in the ways described.
• Students play the game in pairs.
• Read the 'Believe it or not' fact with the class. Ask students how often they send text messages.

Telephone conversation project

• Ask students to work individually and imagine they have a telephone conversation with a famous person. Tell them it can be a living person, someone from history, or a fictional character. Tell students they can look through the Student's Book for ideas of famous people they could interview, or they can think of their own ideas. They should write their conversation, and illustrate it with pictures or photos. Display the conversations and get the class to vote for the funniest or most imaginative. Alternatively, students can work in pairs and role play their conversations.

Follow-up activities

◆ Put students into pairs and ask them to choose three other vocabulary categories in the Topics and vocabulary box on page 86 and brainstorm vocabulary for them. Put pairs together to form groups of four, and ask them to compare their lists and add any more words that they can.
◆ Ask students which of the topics in the list they would like to learn more about at school. Students can discuss the question in pairs and choose one or two topics, then compare their answers in small groups and discuss any similarities or differences.

HOMEWORK

Ask students to find out more about one of the people in the photos. In the next lesson, students can take it in turns to read out one of the facts they learned. The rest of the class can guess which person it relates to.

123

 # Well done – keep it up!

Communicative aims	Language	Pronunciation	Vocabulary	Optional aids
Describing changes and experiences	Passive tenses	*been* and *being*	Idioms Furniture, fixtures and fittings	Exercise 3 Optional activity: cards for Vocabulary box

WARMER 1

Game *Past participle tennis*   Divide the class into two teams. One team chooses a verb and 'serves' it to the other team, who must say (and be able to spell) the past participle within five seconds to win a point. The second team then serves another verb to the first. Encourage teams to choose challenging irregular verbs.

WARMER 2

Game *Call my bluff*   Give students an example of an idiom which you think will be unknown to them, e.g. *I was over the moon*. Tell them three possible meanings, e.g. *I was really pleased* (correct), *I was amazed, I was confused*, and ask them to guess which is correct. Repeat with other idioms.

1 OPENER

- The aim is to set the scene for the reading text in exercise 2.
- Revise the idiom *you're pulling my leg* and elicit the meaning. Ask the students to work with a partner to remember the meaning of the idioms from earlier units.

Answers
caught red-handed: caught in the act of doing something wrong
down-to-earth: realistic and straightforward
touch wood: let's hope we have (or continue to have) good luck
face to face: in each other's presence
learn by heart: learn something by memorising

2 READING

- Ask students to look at the illustrations and describe what they see. Students read and listen to the text. Encourage them to guess unfamiliar words from context and be prepared to translate *nautical*. Ask students which of the idioms they already knew, and which are new to them.

🔘 3.02 Recording
See text on page 88 of the Student's Book.

3 AFTER READING

- Students read the text again and answer the questions. Weaker classes could work in pairs for this activity.

Answers
1 *He has lost his job. It's because workers used to leave a sack of tools with an employer until the job was finished and they were given it back.*
2 *know the ropes, under the weather*
3 *jumbo-sized. It comes from the large elephant named Jumbo.*
4 *Keep it up! It comes from keeping up the shuttlecock in the game of badminton.*
5 *I'm under the weather.*
6 *wicked, cool*
7 *She knows the ropes. It comes from the days of sailing, when sailors had to learn what to do with many different ropes.*

Your response

Ask students to work in pairs to discuss the questions. Bring students' ideas together with the whole class.

Optional activity

Fast-finishers can write the idioms from the text on cards with a definition or example sentence on the reverse for the Vocabulary box.

4 LISTENING

Useful information

Reality TV shows are some of the most popular programmes on British TV. They include:
Changing Rooms: friends or neighbours swap houses for three days and redecorate one of each other's rooms, with the help of a design team.
Supersize versus Super-skinny: someone who over-eats is paired with someone who under-eats, and the two have to swap diets for a week, with the hope that both will learn from the process what is a healthy amount of food to eat each day.
Ten years younger: a team of fashion and beauty experts and plastic surgeons attempt to make someone look ten years younger.

- Set the context for the listening by asking *Have you ever seen any TV shows where people or places are changed? What changed?*
- Explain the context of the phone conversation and ask the students to look at the plan and notes.

- Play the recording and tell students to listen and mark the notes Y (was done yesterday), N (being done now) or T (will be done tomorrow).
- Students compare their answers with a partner, making sentences to say what *was done, is being done* and *will be done*. Check the answers together as a whole class.

🔘 3.03 Recording

PRODUCER	*Hi Dave, how are things going?*
DAVE	*Not too bad, we're getting there.*
PRODUCER	*What's happening at the moment?*
DAVE	*Well, new cupboards are being made …*
PRODUCER	*Right.*
DAVE	*… and the walls are being repainted.*
PRODUCER	*What colour?*
DAVE	*Yellow and white – it already looks much brighter.*
PRODUCER	*I can imagine! Has the window been repaired?*
DAVE	*Yes, that was done yesterday. And a new blind will be hung tomorrow.*
PRODUCER	*Have the lights been changed?*
DAVE	*Not yet – they'll be changed tomorrow.*
PRODUCER	*What about the sink? Has it been replaced?*
DAVE	*Yes, it was replaced yesterday. And a new cooker was installed yesterday too.*
PRODUCER	*Great. What else is on the list?*
DAVE	*Some new furniture is being bought right now …*
PRODUCER	*What – a table and chairs?*
DAVE	*Yes, and also some shelves, which will be put up tomorrow.*
PRODUCER	*So everything is going to plan!*
DAVE	*I think so!*
PRODUCER	*Well done – keep it up!*

Answers

Put up some shelves T
Change the lights T
Hang a new blind T
Repair the window Y
Make new cupboards N
Install a new cooker Y
Repaint the walls N
Buy new furniture N
Replace the sink Y

5 PRONUNCIATION

- Point out that it can be difficult to hear the difference between *been* and *being* and therefore to distinguish which tense is being used.
- Play the recording for students to listen and repeat. Point out that *been* has one syllable and *being* has two and finishes with a light /ŋ/ sound.

🔘 3.04 Recording

A	B
They've been made.	*They're being made.*
It's been bought.	*It's being bought.*
He's been asked.	*He's being asked.*
She's been phoned.	*She's being phoned.*

- Students listen and identify if they hear A or B.

🔘 3.04 Recording and answers

They're being made.	B
It's been bought.	A
He's been asked.	A
She's being phoned.	B

LANGUAGE WORKOUT OPTION

If you want to pre-teach the language students will use in the following activities, you may like to go to the Language Workout box now.

6 SPEAKING

- Ask students to interview two other students, using the questions in *What about you?* Explain that *pocket money* is a small amount of money usually given regularly to young people by parents/family, and that a *chain email* is a message that you are asked to forward to more people and continue the 'chain'. Remind students to note down the other students' answers and ask further questions where possible, as in the example.

Extension Students write three more questions in the passive. They then interview two more students, using their own questions as well as the ones in *What about you?*

7 WRITING

- Give students ten minutes to write a paragraph comparing the two students they interviewed in exercise 6. Remind them to use *both, while, but,* and *whereas* to make contrasts.
- Monitor and help with vocabulary and note down errors or examples of good language. With fast-finishers, highlight where they have made mistakes and encourage them to self-correct.
- Students check their own work for spelling, grammar and punctuation, before exchanging their writing with a partner to read and check each other's work.
- Go through a few examples of good language or errors with the whole class, writing corrections on the board for students to copy down.

LANGUAGE WORKOUT

- Ask students to look at the Language Workout box and complete the sentences. Confident students can complete first and then check, while others can look back at exercises 2 and 3 and then complete.
- Students turn to page 118 of the Language File to check their answers.

  Answers
  was named   I've been given   is kept
  are being added   will be shown   be

- Highlight that:
  - to form the passive in different tenses, we change the tense of *be*, but leave the past participle unchanged. The choice of tense depends on the wider context.
  - we choose the passive when we are not interested in, or do not know, the doer of the verb, e.g. *I've been given the sack* ('*I*' is important, not the person who gave me the sack).
  - if we do want to mention the doer in a passive sentence, we use *by*.
- Drill the examples for pronunciation practice, highlighting that the verb *be* is not stressed. Instead we use contractions, e.g. *'ve, 'll*, and weak forms, e.g. *was* /wəz/, *been* /bln/.

Optional activity

Ask students to find and underline other examples of passive constructions in the text in exercise 2, e.g. *he was sent down below the deck*.

PRACTICE

- Students do Practice exercise 21 on page 118 of the Language File. They write sentences using the correct passive form of the verbs.
- Check the answers by asking different students to read out each sentence to the class. Correct pronunciation as necessary.

  Answers
  1 have been delivered   2 are sent   3 will be transmitted
  4 were arranged   5 are being bought   6 will be taken
  7 have been used   8 is being carried   9 will be done

Optional activity

Fast-finishers can transform some of the passive sentences into active sentences, using *we/people* as the subject when the doer is unspecified. They can read the active sentences to the class when everyone has finished.

Follow-up activities

- Ask students to draw a plan of their own bedroom (or another room if they prefer). They give this plan to their partner, who makes three improvements by drawing on the plan. They then explain to the owner of the room what changes have been made and why (using the present perfect passive). The owner could give them a mark out of ten according to how good an interior designer they consider them to be.
- Students work in small groups. Give each group a different key word, which features in a number of idioms, e.g. *red, under, back, give, cat, lose, eye, down, fast, black, heart*. Students use dictionaries to find at least three idioms including their key word and they design a poster to display these idioms, including illustrations and explanations of the meaning of each. Groups then present their posters to other students and display them on the classroom wall.

HOMEWORK

Ask students to imagine that they were given money to improve their school and to write a report for the class magazine on what was changed, installed, replaced, etc. They should mention at least three changes that were made and two that they didn't have enough money to change, but will do in the future.

WEBLINK

Students may like to visit www.bbc.co.uk/homes/tv_and_radio/cr_index.shtml to find details of the British reality TV show *Changing Rooms*.

Revision and Extension p97

Language File p118

Workbook Unit 7 Lesson 1 pp74–75

Photocopiable worksheet p181, notes p160

She deserves to be awarded a prize

Communicative aims	Language	Pronunciation	Vocabulary	Optional aids
Talking about what's right	Passive infinitive *either ... or* *both ... and*	Syllable stress	Science	Exercise 3 Optional activity: cards for Vocabulary box

WARMER 1

Ask students if they know what DNA is, and what it stands for (*Deoxyribonucleic Acid*). Write other acronyms on the board, e.g. *VIP* (very important person), *MD* (managing director), *EU* (European Union), *UN* (United Nations). Divide students into two teams and award points for identifying what the acronyms stand for.

WARMER 2

Ask students to look back at Unit 3 and find five words to do with science. They then explain their words to a partner, who tries to guess which word they are defining.

Useful information

The Nobel Prize is an international award for achievement in the fields of physics, chemistry, medicine, literature and peace. The founder of the Nobel Prize was Alfred Nobel and it has been awarded every year since 1901. It is organised and presented by the Nobel Foundation in Stockholm, Sweden, who consider nominations from a range of academic and other international institutions. Thirty-three women have been awarded the prize, including Marie Curie and Mother Teresa.

DNA is the genetic material of a cell, found in the cell nucleus. The 'double helix' (pictured) is a model of the DNA molecule, and it is made up of two coiled strands. Half of your DNA comes from your mother and half from your father. The genes therefore occur in pairs, with one coming from each parent. The distribution, however, is random, so brothers/sisters will not be exactly the same. Everything about us, from our eye colour to our likelihood to suffer certain diseases, is determined by our DNA.

1 OPENER

- The aim is to set the scene for the text in exercise 2.
- Ask students to look at the photo on the left and say what they think it shows. Try to elicit that it represents the structure of DNA.

2 READING

- Ask *Who was Rosalind Franklin? What was her great achievement?* Elicit some ideas, then ask students to

read and listen to the text to find the answer (She took photos of atoms, showing the structure of DNA). Encourage students to guess unfamiliar words from context and focus first on the overall meaning of the text. Be prepared to translate *atom, cheat, prejudice, acknowledge, deserve, honour* and *recognise*. Explain that a *degree* is a university qualification.

🔘 **3.05** Recording
See text on page 90 of the Student's Book.

3 AFTER READING

- Students complete the questions with a question word and then match the questions with the answers, re-reading the text to help.

Answers
1 When, i   2 What, f   3 When, a   4 Who, j   5 Why, d
6 How, h   7 When, e   8 What, b   9 When, c
10 Why, g

Optional activity

Fast-finishers can find new vocabulary to do with science in the text and write it on cards, with a definition or example sentence on the reverse, for the Vocabulary box.

Your response

Ask students to work in pairs to discuss the questions. After a few minutes, put pairs together into groups of four to compare their answers. Ask a student from each group to report back on their discussions. See if the class shares the same opinion or has different opinions.

4 VOCABULARY

- Tell students that all the words in the box are also in the text in exercise 2. Ask students to find the words and work out what they mean, then complete the sentences. Point out to students that they will have to change the form of some of the words to fit the context of the sentences.
- Allow students time to check their answers in pairs before you check with the class.

Answers
1 persuaded   2 colleague   3 acknowledge   4 prejudice
5 recognise   6 benefit   7 deserve   8 honour

Extension Ask students to use their dictionaries to find which of the words can be both a noun and a verb (*benefit, honour, prejudice*).

5 PRONUNCIATION

- Write *acknowledge* on the board and ask students to identify the stressed syllable. Mark the stress on the board and ask students to repeat the word.
- Students predict the stressed syllable on the other words in the vocabulary box, comparing with a partner.
- Play the recording for students to listen, check and repeat each word.

🔘 3.06 **Recording and answers**

ack*no*wledge   *be*nefit   *co*lleague   de*serve*   *ho*nour

per*suade*   *pre*judice   *re*cognise

LANGUAGE WORKOUT OPTION

If you want to pre-teach the language students will use in the following activities, you may like to go to the Language Workout box now.

6 WRITING

- Ask students to read the text quickly without completing it yet, and find the three women scientists and what each did (Caroline Herschel – first woman to discover a comet, Lise Meitner – worked on nuclear fission, Jocelyn Bell Burnell – discovered pulsars). Be prepared to translate *comet, nuclear fission* and *astronomer*.
- Students complete the text with the passive infinitive.
- Check the answers together as a whole class.

  Answers
  1 *not be forgotten*   2 *to be given*   3 *be awarded*
  4 *be honoured*   5 *to be given*   6 *be changed*
  7 *to be awarded*   8 *be recognised*

Your response

Ask students to work in pairs to discuss the question and give their own opinions. Ask pairs to report back to the class, and continue with a class discussion if students are interested and have strong opinions.

LANGUAGE WORKOUT OPTION

If you want to pre-teach the language students will use in the following activities, you may like to go to the Language Workout box now.

7 SPEAKING

- Tell students that they are going to make notes about how they think teenagers should be treated, using the headings given. Point out the examples and ask students to write three more things teenagers deserve and should be encouraged to do.
- Students compare their ideas with a partner, adding any new ideas that they agree with to their own lists.
- Ask a few pairs to report their ideas to the rest of the class. If there is time, you could compile a whole class list, pooling the ideas of each pair.

Optional activity

Students could compile similar lists for how parents, teachers, children, animals, etc. should be treated.

Extension Put students into pairs to act out a role play between a parent and a teenager. Allow students time to prepare their ideas. With weaker classes, brainstorm ideas with the whole class about things the teenager and parent might say. Students do the role play, then swap roles and do it again. Ask some confident pairs to do their role play for the class.

8 WRITING

- Students write an article for the school magazine explaining how teenagers want to be treated. Before students start, elicit or point out that a magazine article should be quite informal, and should be written in an interesting way, to engage the reader.
- Monitor and help with vocabulary and note down errors or examples of good language. With fast-finishers, highlight where they have made mistakes and encourage them to self-correct.
- Students check their own work for spelling, grammar and punctuation, before exchanging it with a partner to read and check each other's work.
- Go through a few examples of good language or errors with the whole class, writing corrections on the board for students to copy down.

LANGUAGE WORKOUT

- Ask students to look at the Language Workout box and complete the sentences. Confident students can complete first and then check, while others can look back at exercises 2 and 3 and then complete.
- Students turn to page 118 of the Language File to check their answers.

  Answers
  to be awarded   to be recognised   be used be served   be given   be seen   Both ... and Either ...or

- Highlight that:
  - the full passive infinitive is formed with *to be* + past participle. After some verbs we use the full infinitive, whilst modal verbs are followed by the bare infinitive without *to*.
  - we choose the passive infinitive when there is another verb immediately before the passive form which needs to be followed by an infinitive, e.g. *deserve, begin, should*.
  - to make a negative passive infinitive, we put *not* immediately before it.
  - *either ... or* and *both ... and* are linking words. *Both ... and* refers to the two things mentioned, whilst *either ... or* means one or the other.
- Drill the examples for pronunciation practice, highlighting the weak pronunciation of *to* and *be*, with the stress on the past participle and the previous verb.

Optional activities

- Ask students to transform some of the passive sentences in the Language File into active sentences, e.g. *People could use the picture, People are beginning to recognise her ...*
- Give students a review test on verbs that are followed by the infinitive. Read out example verbs and ask students to identify whether they are generally followed by the full infinitive, the bare infinitive or the *-ing* form. Examples could include *avoid, consider, must, might, want, decide* or others from Unit 1.

PRACTICE

- Students do Practice exercise 22 on page 118 of the Language File. Set the context by asking students to look at the title and predict who is using the Internet to cheat. They then read and check their predictions (students).
- Students complete the text with the passive infinitives of the verbs in the box.
- Check the answers together as a class.

  Answers
  1 be allowed   2 be forbidden   3 be written   4 be marked 5 be done   6 be taught   7 be caught   8 be used

Follow-up activities

- Write a sentence on the board using a passive infinitive to refer to a controversial issue, e.g. *Top footballers deserve to be paid six-figure salaries, Young men and women should be obliged to do military service for their country.* Students divide into two groups, for and against, and debate the issue. Remind students of the debating language from Unit 4, Lesson 4.
- Divide students into groups of 6–8 students and tell them that they are a committee who have to give awards for achievement to people and places they consider important. On the board, write a list of possible awards tailored to your students' interests, e.g. *Best national sportsman/woman, Best music video, Most attractive actor/actress, Best place to go out in this town.* Students discuss in their groups who or what deserves the awards, and then report back to the other groups, e.g. *Emma Watson deserves to be awarded ...*

HOMEWORK

Students write a paragraph giving their opinion either about students copying from the Internet to do their homework, or about the possible prejudice against women in science.

WEBLINK

Students may like to visit www.nobelprize.org for details of the prize and interactive educational science games.

Revision and Extension p97

Language File p118

Workbook Unit 7 Lesson 2 pp76–77

Photocopiable worksheet p182, notes p160

They couldn't ring up a doctor

Communicative aims	Language	Pronunciation	Vocabulary
Using the phone	Phrasal verbs	Stress and intonation	Mobile phones Telephone language Phrasal verbs

WARMER 1

Game *Broken telephone* See Unit 3, Lesson 1 Warmer for instructions (p59). Use a sentence related to the unit, e.g. *Students shouldn't be allowed to copy from the Internet to do their homework.*

WARMER 2

As a whole class, brainstorm some questions students could ask each other about their mobile phones, e.g. *What brand is your phone? How much do you use it? Who have you got in your address book?* Students then ask a partner about their mobile phone.

Useful information

A recent survey found that 91% of teenagers in Britain own a mobile phone. They use their phones for texting and calling, but tend not to use services such as voicemail that are more expensive. Most said that they felt that mobiles were essential for social networking and for some privacy from their parents.

1 OPENER

- The aim is to set the scene for the text in exercise 2.
- Students look at the words and phrases in the box and predict which they will find in the text. Explain that a *bus conductor* checks tickets, but doesn't drive the bus. Ask students for their ideas, but don't confirm answers at this stage.

2 READING

- Ask students to read and listen to the text, looking out for the words from exercise 1. Encourage them to guess unfamiliar words from context and focus on the overall meaning of the text. Be prepared to translate *entrepreneur*. Ask students what they found most surprising in the article.

⊙ 3.07 Recording
See text on page 92 of the Student's Book.

Answers to exercise 1
bus conductor, business, contact, ladder, landline, signal, subscribers

3 AFTER READING

- Students re-read the text and decide if the statements are true, false or if no information is given. Encourage students to underline or write down the parts of the text which help them identify the answers.
- Check the answers together, before students write the correct information for the false statements.

Answers
1 *No information*
2 *True*
3 *False. Nearly all the population had mobiles.*
4 *False. The French spend more time talking on their mobiles than the Japanese.*
5 *No information*
6 *True*
7 *False. Ordinary Africans buy mobiles.*
8 *True*

Your response

Ask students to work in pairs to discuss their own mobile phone use. Ask pairs to report back to the class. You could try to find out as a class who uses their phone the most and the least.

4 VOCABULARY

- Students work individually or in pairs to rewrite the sentences, replacing the words in italics with the correct form of the phrasal verbs in the box. Encourage students to look back at these verbs in the text in exercise 2 to help them work out meaning. With weaker classes, ask students to find and underline the phrasal verbs first, then look at the sentences.

Answers
1 *ring up*
2 *put up*
3 *cut off*
4 *went on*
5 *pick up*
6 *coming down*
7 *found out; kicks off*
8 *gone up*

Optional activity

Give students three minutes to work in pairs and brainstorm as many other phrasal verbs as they can. They can look through previous units to help them. Tell them to write each phrasal verb and an example sentence. When time is up, ask pairs in turn to read out their verbs and examples.

LANGUAGE WORKOUT OPTION

If you want to pre-teach the language students will use in the following activities, you may like to go to the Language Workout box now.

Extension Students work individually or in pairs to write the sentences.

5 LISTENING

- Set the context of the phone conversation and ask students to look at sentences 1–8 and predict whether they are said by the caller (C) or the receptionist (R).
- Play the recording for students to check their predictions. Confirm the answers with the whole class.
- Play the recording again and ask students to write down the message as they listen. Check the answer together, writing the message on the board.

3.08 Recording

RECEPTIONIST	Good morning, Network Agency, can I help you?
CALLER	Can I speak to Carol Evans, please?
RECEPTIONIST	Hold on, I'll put you through. ... Oh, sorry, the line's engaged. Can I take a message?
CALLER	Yes, please. Could you ask her to call me back?
RECEPTIONIST	Certainly. Can I take your name and number?
CALLER	My name is Simon Gardiner.
RECEPTIONIST	How do you spell your surname?
CALLER	Gardiner – G-A-R-D-I-N-E-R.
RECEPTIONIST	Right ...
CALLER	And my phone number is 01793 954 228.
RECEPTIONIST	01793 954 288?
CALLER	No, 228.
RECEPTIONIST	OK, I've written it down. I'll pass your message on as soon as possible.
CALLER	Thanks very much. Goodbye.

Answers

1 R   2 C   3 R   4 R   5 R   6 C   7 R   8 R
Message: Please call Simon Gardiner back on
01793 954 228.

Optional activity

Ask students to recall or listen again for the phrasal verbs used in the dialogue (*put you through, call me back, written it down, pass your message on*). Check the meanings by asking for an explanation, translation or example sentence.

6 PRONUNCIATION

- Play the recording of the sentences from exercise 5. Pause between sentences for students to repeat each one. Encourage them to use the correct stress and intonation, and to sound friendly.

3.09 Recording

RECEPTIONIST	Good morning, can I help you?
CALLER	Can I speak to Carol Evans, please?
RECEPTIONIST	Hold on, I'll put you through.
RECEPTIONIST	Oh, sorry, the line's engaged.
RECEPTIONIST	Can I take a message?
CALLER	Could you ask her to call me back?
RECEPTIONIST	Can I take your name and number?
RECEPTIONIST	I'll pass your message on as soon as possible.

Optional activity

With a partner, students repeat the conversation, taking a role each. Less confident students can repeat the dialogue exactly, while more confident students can improvise, working with books closed and changing some details, e.g. the caller's name/message.

LANGUAGE WORKOUT OPTION

If you want to pre-teach the language students will use in the following activities, you may like to go to the Language Workout box now.

7 ROLE PLAY

- Set the context of British students visiting your school, with callers from the UK trying to contact the visiting students. Ask students if they have been on a school trip abroad to stay with foreign hosts.
- Divide students into As (who answer the school phone) and Bs (who are calling to give the messages). Give students a few moments to read the role play guidelines and plan what to say. Student Bs can use ideas from the box. Students work in A/B pairs to do the role play. They should repeat with further calls leaving other messages.
- Ask one or two pairs to perform their dialogue for the other students, who listen and note down the message.
- Students then change roles and practise again.

Optional activity

Students could also perform the dialogue of the message-taker passing on the message to the intended recipient.

8 WRITING

- Students write out three of the messages from the phone conversations in exercise 7. Remind them that messages tend to be written in a short, clear style, like the example.

- Monitor, help with use of phrasal verbs and note down errors or examples of good language. With fast-finishers, highlight where they have made mistakes and encourage them to self-correct.
- Students check their own work for spelling, grammar and punctuation, before exchanging writing with a partner to read and check each other's work.
- Go through a few examples of good language or errors with the whole class, writing corrections on the board for students to copy down.

LANGUAGE WORKOUT

- Ask students to look at the Language Workout box and complete the sentences. Confident students can complete first and then check, while others can look back at exercises 2 and 3 and then complete.
- Students turn to pages 118–119 of the Language File to check their answers.

  Answers

  up on up up up up up

- Highlight that:
  - phrasal verbs are very common, particularly in spoken English.
  - not all phrasal verbs take an object. For those not taking an object (1st group in the box), the particle comes directly after the verb and is an adverb.
  - phrasal verbs which take an object can be separable (2nd group in the box) or inseparable (3rd group in the box). A good learner dictionary will indicate which phrasal verbs are which.
  - when using a pronoun object with a separable phrasal verb, this must go between the verb and the adverb particle. A noun object, however, can go before or after the adverb.
  - with inseparable phrasal verbs, the noun and pronoun objects both go at the end of the phrase.
  - the particles tend to be stressed as adverbs and unstressed as prepositions.
- Drill the examples for pronunciation practice, highlighting stress placement.

Optional activity

Ask students to look back at the text in exercise 2 and find more examples of phrasal verbs, noting whether or not there is an object and where it goes.

PRACTICE

- Students do Practice exercise 23 on page 119 of the Language File. They rewrite the sentences, replacing the words in italics with pronouns. Remind students that they may have to change the word order.
- Check the answers together as a whole class.

  Answers

  1 She looked it up.
  2 He wrote it down.
  3 I want to talk to her.
  4 Please switch them off.
  5 We're looking for it.
  6 Don't forget to ring them up.
  7 It took an hour to climb up it.
  8 Can you work it out?

Follow-up activities

- ◆ **Game** *Noughts and crosses* See Review Units 1–2 (p56) for instructions. Put a phrasal verb in each square and have students make up a sentence using the verb.
- ◆ Students look through the unit and use their previous knowledge to make a mind-map of vocabulary and phrases related to telephoning.

HOMEWORK

Ask students to try making a real phone conversation in English to one of their classmates. The receiver could pretend to be unavailable and accept a message, or the caller could leave a message on the answerphone. Students should come to the next lesson and report on who they called, what message they left and how easy or difficult they found having the conversation.

WEBLINK

Students may like to visit www.bbc.co.uk/news/cbbcnews/hi/chat/your_comments/newsid_1975000/1975265.stm for articles and quizzes for young people about mobile phones.

Revision and Extension p97

Language File pp118–119

Workbook Unit 7 Lesson 3 pp78–79

Photocopiable worksheet p183, notes p160

Integrated Skills Discussing Languages

Skills

Reading Connecting ideas: *Language Death or Language Murder?* article
Listening Completing notes on a debate

Speaking Debate
Writing Arguments for and against

Learner independence

Thinking skills
Word creation: verb prefix *re-*

Vocabulary

Languages
Useful expressions

WARMER 1

Game *Languages quiz*   Divide the class into teams of four students, with one 'writer' per group. Read out a list of ten countries, e.g. *Uruguay, Egypt, Korea, Holland.* Ask teams to quietly discuss and write down the main language spoken in each. Check the answers as a class. (Uruguay = Spanish, Egypt = Arabic, Korea = Korean, Holland = Dutch) The winning team has the most correct answers.

WARMER 2

Game *Collocation race*   Remind students that it is useful to remember phrases rather than single words. Give students a word which commonly collocates with other words, e.g. *do, take, give.* Students work with a partner to think of five expressions which collocate with the word, e.g. *do – homework, nothing, exercise, sport, housework.* They shout *Stop!* when they have five, and read their list to the rest of the class.

1   OPENER

- The aim is to set the scene for the text in exercise 2.
- Ask students to discuss the two questions about languages with a partner. Ask a few students to share their answers with the class. Encourage discussion of which languages should be taught.

Useful information

In British schools, the most commonly taught foreign language is French, closely followed by Spanish, which has surged in recent years, and German. In a small number of schools it is possible to study languages such as Mandarin, Japanese or Russian. A growing number of children in British schools have another language as their first language, e.g. Bengali, Urdu, Polish. It is compulsory for students to study at least one modern foreign language, but only up to the age of 14. Only a minority of students continue studying a foreign language after the age of 16. The government is, however, encouraging the expansion of foreign language teaching in primary schools.

2   READING

- Give students five minutes to read the text and complete it with phrases a–h. Encourage them to guess unfamiliar words from the context and concentrate on the overall meaning of the text.
- Play the recording for students to check their answers. Ask students to justify their choices with links to the text before and after each gap.

● 3.10   Recording

Language Death or Language Murder?
Linguists tell us that there are about 6,000 languages in the world. Of these, there are 51 languages with just one speaker left, nearly 500 languages with less than 100 speakers and 1,500 languages with less than 1,000 speakers. About half the world's languages are going to die out during the next century: that's 3,000 languages in 1,200 months.
Should we be worried about this? Yes, in the same way that we ought to be concerned when an animal or a plant species is threatened with extinction. When people die, archaeologists can investigate what they have left behind. But when a spoken language dies, it leaves nothing behind it and can't be recreated.
Why are languages dying? Language death may be caused not only by natural disasters like earthquakes, or man-made ones like war, but also by 'language murder'. This term is used to explain what happens when speakers of a minority language stop using it in favour of a 'killer language', a bigger, more powerful language.
English is often called the world's most dangerous killer language, but linguists say there are at least a half a dozen more. These killers are not only European languages, like French, but also Asian ones, like Chinese.
Can anything be done? The answer is yes. Take the case of Romansch, which is spoken in Switzerland. In the 1980s Romansch, whose five very different dialects were used by fewer and fewer people, was facing a difficult situation. The solution was the creation of a written language for all these dialects. Romansch Grishum, as it is now called, has official status in parts of Switzerland and is increasingly used in its spoken form on radio and television.

The Maori language has been kept alive in New Zealand through lessons, where under-five-year-olds are taught the language. And in Japan new government policies brought the Ainu language, which only had eight fluent speakers left, back from the edge of extinction.

Answers

1 h   2 e   3 a   4 g   5 f   6 b   7 c   8 d

3

- The aim is to encourage the students to deduce meaning from context. Ask the students to find words in the text to match to definitions 1–7.

Answers

1 linguists   2 threatened   3 disasters   4 minority
5 dialects   6 official status   7 fluent

Optional activity

Fast-finishers use a dictionary to find the stress and pronunciation of the words. They can then pronounce them for the class when everyone has finished.

4

- Remind students that we often use 'reference words' in texts to refer back to something that has already been made clear and avoid too much repetition. Ask students to look at the phrases from the text in exercise 2 and identify what the words in italics refer to.
- Check the answers together as a class.

Answers

1 the 6,000 languages in the world
2 That a language will die out somewhere in the world every two weeks or so.
3 disasters
4 killer languages
5 a written language for all the Romansch dialects

5

- Ask students to work with a partner to try to identify the other 'killer languages'.

Suggested answers

Arabic, French, Hindi, Mandarin Chinese, Russian, Spanish

6

- Ask the students to find an example of *not only … but also* in the text. Establish that the expression is used to add emphasis to the fact that there are two ideas.
- Drill the example sentences, highlighting the emphatic pronunciation of *not only* and *also*.

Answers

*… **not only** by natural disasters like earthquakes, or man-made ones like war, **but also** …*
*… **not only** European languages, like French, **but also** Asian ones, …*

7

- Explain that non-defining relative clauses begin with *which, who* or *whose*, give us more information about a noun and are separated from it by a comma. Point out the example sentence and elicit that *which* refers back to the previous noun, *Romansch*.
- Ask students to find two more examples in the text. Point out that it is possible to remove the non-defining relative clause and the sentences still make sense.

Answers

*In the 1980s Romansch, **whose five very different dialects were used by fewer and fewer people**, was facing a difficult situation. …*
*new government policy brought the Ainu language, **which only had eight fluent speakers left**, back from the edge of extinction.*

- In non-defining relative clauses, we use *who* to refer to a person, *which* to a thing or idea and *whose* to indicate possession. We can't use *that* instead of *which* in a non-defining relative clause. Non-defining relative clauses can be contrasted with defining relative clauses, which contain necessary, rather than extra, information. An example would be *The four languages **which are spoken in Switzerland** are French, German, Italian and Romansch. Which* can be replaced with *that* in a defining relative clause. No commas are used in defining relative clauses.

Optional activity

Write a few simple sentences on the board and ask students to try to add extra information of their choice to each by inserting a non-defining relative clause where possible, e.g. *David Beckham played for England – David Beckham, who was a great footballer, played for England.*

8   LISTENING

- Tell students that they are going to hear a debate with the motion *The growth of English is killing other languages. Other foreign languages should be studied at school instead.* Ask students if they agree or disagree.
- Play the recording, telling students that they should listen for the result of the vote. Check the answer as a whole class.
- Play the recording a second time for students to complete the speaker's notes.

(○) 3.11   **Recording**

CHAIR   *Hello, my name's Anna and I'm chairing this debate. The motion today is: 'The growth of English is killing other languages. Other foreign languages should be studied at school instead'. Susy is proposing the motion and Peter is opposing it.*

SUSY   *What I'm going to argue is that we need to be able to speak lots of languages. Firstly, because knowing a language helps us **understand** the people who speak it better. Secondly, because the growth of English all around the world makes everywhere seem **the same**. And thirdly, because people like to buy and sell in their own language. Being able to speak someone else's language is good for **business**.*

The first argument for studying languages other than English is international understanding. If you know the language of a country you can communicate with the people of that country better and learn more about them. Languages tell us about a country's history and culture, and there are often expressions which can't be translated. Secondly, the growth of English all around the world makes everywhere seem the same. Sometimes if you travel, it's hard to know which country you're in because English is the language of the international travel business. It's also the language of globalisation, of big business making us buy the same products wherever we live. The third point's also to do with business. Learning languages other than English can be a good plan because people like to buy and sell in their own language. Your customers may speak English, but they'll be pleased if you've made an effort to learn their language. Good business is about good communication and knowing your customer's language is part of that.

What I've argued is this. We need to be able to speak lots of languages. Firstly, I pointed out that learning languages helps international understanding. Secondly, I showed how the growth of English makes everywhere seem the same. And thirdly, I showed how being able to speak your customer's language is good for business.

CHAIR *Thank you Susy. Now Peter to oppose the motion.*

PETER *What I'm going to argue is that we can't stop English – its success is a fact. Firstly, the world has a **global** language already – and that's English. Secondly, it's better to be able to speak one language really **well** than lots of languages badly. And thirdly, who is going to **decide** which languages are taught?*

To start with it's clear that English has won. It's spoken by around one billion people worldwide. Of course that leaves billions who don't speak it but they're catching up fast. English is everywhere – most websites are written in English. We can't change history.

Then we have to look at the effects of learning lots of languages. Susy claims that it helps you understand different societies better – but surely if you know one language really well you can communicate successfully with anyone. Much better than communicating badly with them in their own language.

Finally, who decides what languages are learnt? If people want to learn English, let them. It's the market that decides what languages people want to learn. How can a teacher tell a student that she has to learn a language that will be no use to her? We're not all going to be international salespeople, you know.

What I've argued is this. Firstly, the world has a global language already – and that's English. Secondly, it's better to be able to speak one language really well than lots of languages badly. And thirdly, who's going to decide which languages are taught?

CHAIR *Now you have one sentence each to sum up your argument before we have a vote.*

SUSY *The more languages the better – not just one.*

PETER *We can't survive without English.*

CHAIR *And now raise your hands to vote. Those in favour of the motion? Thank you. And those against? Thank you. The result is **ten** votes for the motion and **ten** votes against.*

Answers

Result: a tie, ten votes each
1 understand   2 the same   3 business   4 global   5 well
6 decide

9 SPEAKING

- With a large class, divide the students into two or three smaller groups, each to have a debate. With a smaller class, keep the students together as one group.
- Give the group(s) a few minutes to try to agree on which of the three topics (or their own topic) they would like to debate.
- Choose three students per group to be the Chair and the two speakers. Give the speakers a few minutes to prepare their speeches. Encourage the other students to help them prepare their arguments. They can look back at the debate exercise 7 on page 55 to help them.
- The group(s) carry out their debates. Ensure the Chair gives each speaker a chance to speak and then summarise what he/she has said.
- The chair organises a final vote among the students in the group. If there is more than one group, students can tell the other group(s) the result of their debate.

10 GUIDED WRITING

- Students write arguments for and against the topic in their debate.
- With weaker classes, choose a topic as a class and brainstorm ideas, writing them on the board under the headings *for* and *against*.
- Revise useful phrases to help with the writing, e.g. phrases for expressing opinions and for contrasting ideas, e.g. *On the one hand, ... On the other hand, ...*
- While students are writing, monitor and help with vocabulary as necessary. With fast-finishers, point out any errors to encourage them to self-correct.
- Students check their own work and then exchange their writing with a partner to read and check each other's.

11 LEARNER INDEPENDENCE

- The aim is to encourage students to think more about their learning and how to revise effectively.
- Elicit some possible revision techniques and ask them to discuss which ones they use or would like to try.
- Ask students to read the instructions for a revision diary. They could make a revision plan during class time and add to their diary at home once they have tried out the techniques.

12 WORD CREATION

- Ask students if they remember the prefix meaning 'again', used with *create* in the text in exercise 2. Write *re-* on the board and elicit other words beginning with this prefix.
- Students add the prefix *re-* to the verbs in the box and use the verbs to complete the sentences, changing the tense if necessary. Check the answers as a class.
- Ask students to copy the words into their vocabulary notebooks.

Answers

1 *rewrote* 2 *rebuild* 3 *replace* 4 *rediscovered*
5 *reappeared* 6 *repaint* 7 *recreate* 8 *replayed*
9 *retold*

Optional activity

Fast-finishers can write example sentences of their own using some of the verbs. They can read their sentences to the class, omitting the verbs. The class can guess the verbs.

EXTRA PRACTICE

If you would like to give your students more practice in forming words which start with *re-*, please see the Vocabulary EXTRA! Worksheets on the Teacher's Resource Site (www.macmillanenglish.com/inspiration)

13 PHRASEBOOK

- Students look through Unit 7 to find the expressions, noting how they are used.
- Play the recording for the students to listen and repeat the expressions. Check with students where in the unit each expression was used.

- Students then identify which expression goes with meanings 1–4.

3.12 Recording and answers

Well done. (Lesson 1, exercise 2)
Keep it up. (Lesson 1, exercise 2)
know the ropes (Lesson 1, exercise 2)
under the weather (Lesson 1, exercise 2)
Hold on. (Lesson 3, exercise 5)
I'll·put you through. (Lesson 3, exercise 5)
Can I take a message? (Lesson 3, exercise 5)
Can anything be done? (Lesson 4, exercise 2)
The more … the better. (Lesson 4, exercise 8)

1 *I'll put you through*
2 *under the weather*
3 *Hold on.*
4 *know the ropes*

Optional activities

- Students think of a situation in which someone might use each expression, e.g. *Well done* (*teacher to a good student*).
- Students can add expressions which they like to their Personal Phrasebook. Be ready to help with translation as necessary.

Follow-up activity

Divide students into small groups to design a ten-question survey on language, which they use to interview other students. Give students a couple of example questions, e.g. *What language would you like to learn? What is a good age for children to start learning a foreign language?* Students conduct their survey and write a report of their results.

HOMEWORK

Ask students to write a list of as many English words as possible which are used in their own language. Give suggested topic areas, e.g. *technology, sport, food* as a starting point. They should bring their list to the next lesson.

WEBLINK

Students may want to visit www.wikipedia.org/wiki/Languages_of_the_United_Kingdom for an article on the languages of the United Kingdom.

Revision and Extension p97

Workbook Unit 7 Lesson 4 pp80–81

Inspiration EXTRA!

LANGUAGE LINKS

- Write *false friend* on the board and elicit or teach the meaning (a word in another language that looks similar to one in your own language, but has a different meaning).
- Students read the text and decide which of the words are false friends in their language.
- Discuss as a class the best translation for each of the words. In multi-lingual classes, students can work individually or in pairs to decide on the best translation.
- Put students into pairs or small groups to think of more examples of false friends. Write them on the board.

GAME   CALL MY BLUFF

- Divide the class into groups of three.
- Students then follow the instructions, choosing a word from the dictionary and writing three possible definitions, only one of which is correct.
- Students then read their word and definitions to the rest of the class, who try to identify the correct definition.

SKETCH   FIND A FRIEND

- The aim is for students to enjoy using their English while also getting valuable stress and intonation practice. Ask the students to look at the cartoon. Ask *Who do you think the people are? What are they saying?*
- With a more confident class, play the recording with books closed. Then play it again with books open. With a less confident class, play the recording once while the students follow in their books, and then once again with books closed.

  (3.13) Recording
  See text on page 96 of the Student's Book

- Check the students understand that Kevin thought the company could help him find his missing girlfriend, but that when he realises it is a dating agency, he asks for help finding a new girlfriend.
- Divide the class into two equal groups and play the recording again, with one group repeating in chorus as *Sarah* and the other as *Kevin*. Encourage students to exaggerate stress and intonation.
- Ask the students to close their books and play the recording again. Then ask the students to work in pairs and perform the sketch aloud. Choose several pairs to act out the sketch in front of the class.

REVISION

Lesson 1

  Answers

  The cooker has been installed. The sink has been replaced. The window has been repaired. The new cupboards are being made. The walls are being repainted. New furniture is being bought. Some shelves will be put up. The lights will be changed and a new blind will be hung.

Language File pp118–119

Lesson 2
Students' own answers.

Lesson 3
Students' own answers.

EXTENSION

Lessons 1–3
Students' own answers.

YOUR CHOICE!

- The aim is to give students more learner independence and help them to identify their preferred way of learning. Encourage students to choose an activity that they feel less comfortable with if they want a challenge or are aware that they need practice in a particular area.
- Monitor and help groups. Check answers if necessary, or provide written answers for groups to check their own work against.

CONSTRUCTION

  Answers

1 is being spoken	*6 were seen*
2 are being taken	*7 was estimated*
3 are being taught	*8 will be needed*
4 was studied	*9 will be produced*
5 were chosen	

REFLECTION

  Answers

  1 f   2 c   3 e   4 d   5 a   6 b

ACTION

- Students work in groups of four. Each group is given an everyday object and thinks of as many uses as possible for it.
- One student from each group takes the object to another group and mimes the possible uses for them to try to guess. Repeat with a different student taking the object to another group.

INTERACTION

- Students work in small groups.
- They first read the instructions and think of the person they have always wanted to be. They then take it in turns to be interviewed in the role of this person. Point out the example questions and encourage students to ask each other follow-up questions.
- Students could report back to the rest of the class on their most interesting interviews.

Workbook Unit 7 Inspiration EXTRA! pp82–83

7 Your culture

1 READING

- Students read the text and answer the questions. Allow students time to compare their answers in pairs before you check with the class.

  ◯ 3.14 **Recording**
  See text on pages 98–99 of the Student's Book.

  Answers
  1 *You should be clear about your aim.*
  2 *They are good because you never know where they might lead.*
  3 *You shouldn't criticize people's ideas.*
  4 *If you can't get started.*
  5 *You should keep your creativity notebook with you, because you never know when inspiration will arrive.*
  6 *Always stop before the end of a paragraph.*
  7 *Show your friends and family.*
  8 *Reflect on what you've done and decide how you will do better next time.*

Optional activity

Ask students to work in pairs and think of one more piece of advice for creating a piece of creative writing. Ask pairs to report back, and discuss as a class whether each piece of advice is good.

2 VOCABULARY

- Ask students to read the text again and then match the words and phrases with their definitions. Students can work individually or in pairs. Check answers.

  Answers
  1 c 2 f 3 e 4 g 5 h 6 a 7 i 8 d 9 b

3 LISTENING

- Write *creative space* on the board and explain that it is a place where you can be creative and have a lot of ideas. Refer students to the list and allow them time to read it.

- Play the recording for students to listen and note down which alternative Andy prefers. Allow students time to compare their answers in pairs then check with the class.

  ◯ 3.15 **Recording**
  I think it was Virginia Woolf who said that the most important thing for a writer was to have a room of one's own and that's certainly true for an artist too. I work upstairs at home in a quite a big room with four windows so there's lots of light – important for me to be able to see what I'm painting! I often have the windows open. I don't mind the sound of the traffic – it doesn't bother me at all. Of course with the windows open it can get rather cold but I just put another pullover on. I like the smell of paint but unless there's lots of fresh air in the room it's hard to concentrate. What I can't stand is having someone else in the room while I'm working. Even if they don't interrupt me, I know that they're there and that bothers me. I said it's a big room but I've got a lot of paintings I'm working on there so it's quite hard to move around – I don't mind that. I can get loads of ideas from looking at pictures. So as you've probably guessed by now the room is a bit of a mess – I keep on meaning to clear it up but never get around to it. As I've already mentioned I need plenty of light to work and it must be daylight, so I can't work in the evening or at night. Although I don't notice the traffic noise I do like to have some music playing when I'm working – usually something classical, not loud but just in the background. Now, if you'll excuse me, I must get back to work – can't spend all day chatting like this, can I?

  Answers
  well lit, noisy, cool, alone, no space to move around, untidy, morning and afternoon, music

- Students make notes individually on where they work best, then compare their ideas in groups of three. Ask each group to report back to the class.

4 MINI-PROJECT   CREATIVE WRITING

- Put students into pairs to follow the steps and create a piece of writing. Monitor while students are working, and be prepared to feed in ideas and vocabulary. If students are stuck for ideas, encourage them to use the ideas in the text to help them get started. If necessary, allow students to brainstorm in groups of four first.
- When students have produced a draft, ask them to swap with another pair and give feedback. Monitor and help students to give constructive and helpful feedback.
- Students continue working in their pairs and revise their draft. Remind them to check their work for mistakes.
- Pin students' work around the classroom for everyone to read. Encourage students to comment on each other's work in a constructive way.

WEBLINK

Students may like to visit www.dailywritingtips.com/creative-writing-101 for tips on creative writing.

Workbook Culture pp84–85

He wasn't able to get a job

Communicative aims		Language	Pronunciation	Vocabulary
Talking about past ability	Expressing purpose	*could(n't), was(n't) able to, managed to in order to, so that*	Syllable stress	Achievements

WARMER 1

Draw the following grid on the board:

```
E   M   S   A
P   I   O   T
R   H   L   U
A   C   E   B
```

In pairs, students write down as many words as possible, using the letters in the square. They can go in any direction, but all the letters must touch. So you can make *blue*, but you can't make *true*. You can only use each letter once in any word. The pair with the most correct words is the winner. Possible answers: *blue, some, as, at, but, belt, to, so, sat, chip, clue, car, pilot, most, me, race, lie, hot, lip, lot, oil, is, mile, mist, pile.*

WARMER 2

Students work in teams of three. They race to write down 10 jobs which may make you famous. Next to each job they write the name of a famous person who does that job, e.g. *tennis player – Roger Federer; actor – Robert Pattinson; singer – Lady Gaga.*

1 OPENER

- The aim is to set the context for exercise 2.
- Ask students to look at the photos and discuss the questions as a whole class. Use the discussion to review/teach key vocabulary: *composer, classical music, physicist, equation, author, rap poet.*

2 READING

- Read the question with the class and ask students to predict the answer. Student read and listen to the text and find the answer.

🔘 3.16 Recording

See text on page 100 of the Student's Book.

Answer

JK Rowling

3 AFTER READING

- Students read the questions and then re-read the text more carefully to find the best answer. Encourage students to work out the meaning of new words from

the context. Be prepared to explain/translate *broke, rumour, behave.* Check the answers as a whole class.

Answers

1 B   2 A   3 C   4 A   5 B   6 A

Optional activities

- ◆ Fast-finishers can note all the words related to music, science, writing and poetry for the Vocabulary box.
- ◆ Students discuss which of the four people they would like to meet/have met and explain why. They can tell each other what questions they would ask/have asked him/her.

Your response

Ask students to work in pairs to discuss the questions. Ask some pairs to report back to the class.

4 VOCABULARY

- Students work individually or in pairs to find the words in the text. Encourage students to use the information on parts of speech to help them, so they know if they are looking for a noun, verb, adjective, etc. Check answers with the class.

Answers

1 totally   2 quantity   3 best-known   4 failure
5 youth   6 fans   7 instant   8 mentally   9 lazy

Optional activity

Fast-finishers can write their own sentences using some of the words. They can read their sentences to the class when everyone has finished.

5 PRONUNCIATION

- Write *behave* on the board. Elicit the number of syllables and where the stress falls. In pairs, students practise saying the words and decide where the stress falls on each one.
- Play the recording for students to listen and check.
- Play the recording again, pausing after each word for students to repeat.

🔘 **3.17** Recording and answers

be*have*   *classical*   *educate*   *examination*   *institute*

phi*lo*sopher   *poetry*   *relativity*   tech*no*logy   uni*ver*sity

---

LANGUAGE WORKOUT OPTION

If you want to pre-teach the language students will use in the following activities, you may like to go to the Language Workout box now.

6 SPEAKING

- Tell students they are going to read and listen to a poem by Benjamin Zephaniah about someone's first week at school. Ask *What do you think happened in that first week?* Write the ideas on the board.
- Students read and listen. Check their predictions.

🔘 **3.18** Recording

See text on page 101 of the Student's Book.

- Organise the students into groups. Check students understand *confession* (when you say that you have done something wrong for example to your parents or to the police). Students discuss the questions. Monitor and help/correct as necessary.
- At the end, ask groups to summarise some of their ideas for the whole class. Ask students if they liked the poem.

Suggested answers

He is confessing by saying how bad his first week at school was. He discovers on the fourth day that he enjoys running, and on the fifth day he ran away from school so he calls himself a runner.
He most enjoyed the fourth day when he discovered sports, ran and earned a star. He least enjoyed his third day because he cried on that day (although other answers possible here).
'Schoolology' means how things work in school – where things are, who people are, how to behave, and so on.
He has put 'off' + 'a' together.

Optional activity

After the discussion, students practise reading a verse at the same time as the recording is played, to help them pick up the rhythm of the poem and use sentence stress and weak forms appropriately.

> **Extension** Put students into pairs to discuss the questions. If students can't remember their first day at school, they can talk about other experiences from their early years at school.

LANGUAGE WORKOUT OPTION

If you want to pre-teach the language students will use in the following activities, you may like to go to the Language Workout box now.

7 WRITING

- Organise students into groups of five if possible. Otherwise, have smaller groups and ask a fast-finisher to write the extra verse, or, ask the group to write the final verse together.
- Students brainstorm ideas for their poem and then work individually on their verses. Monitor and help/correct as necessary. Encourage students to try to follow the pattern of the poem, keeping the invented lines to between five and eight syllables. Finally, groups put the verses together and invent a title.
- Each group reads their poem to the class. The class decides on the best title / the best read poem / funniest poem.

Optional activities

♦ Students copy their verses and the title out neatly and the poems are displayed.
♦ The class votes on the best one, and add it to the class magazine.

LANGUAGE WORKOUT

- Ask students to look at the Language Workout box and complete the sentences about past ability. Confident students can complete first and then check, while others can look back at exercises 2 and 3 and then complete.
- Students turn to page 119 of the Language File to check their answers.

  Answers
  could   couldn't   wasn't able to, was able to wasn't able to

- Highlight that there are three ways to talk about ability in the past.
- Elicit the negative of the three forms: *couldn't, wasn't/weren't able to, didn't manage to.*
- Elicit the question forms: *Could you...?, Were you able to...?, Did you manage to...?*
- Ask students to read the information about the difference between *could* and *was able to/ managed to.* Check comprehension by asking: *Which do we use when we are talking about one situation in the past?* (was able to, managed to) Point out that *could* and *was able to* have similar meanings, but *managed to* suggests doing something difficult, especially after trying hard.
- Drill the examples, paying particular attention to the pronunciation of *could* and *couldn't* and the weak *was* and *to* in *was able to.*

Optional activity

Students find more examples of past ability in the text in exercise 2, e.g. *he managed to produce, she couldn't afford to heat, he couldn't behave, was able to educate himself.*

PRACTICE

- Students do Practice exercise 24 on page 119 of the Language File. They rewrite the sentences using the correct form of the verbs. Do the first one together as an example. Check answers by asking different students to read the sentences aloud.

Answers

1 Steven Spielberg wasn't able to get into film school because his grades weren't good enough.
2 Maria Sharapova managed to win Wimbledon at the age of 17.
3 Pope John Paul II was able to speak eight languages.
4 Olympic triathlete Michelle Dillon couldn't swim until she was 23.
5 At first, Michael Jordan wasn't able to play for his school basketball team because he was too short.
6 Mozart could play the piano at the age of four.
7 Ming Kipa Sherpa, a 15-year-old girl, was able to climb Mount Everest in 2003.
8 Harry Houdini managed to escape from a locked prison cell in two minutes in 1902.

Optional activity

In pairs, one student says the name of the famous person and their partner, with their book closed, recalls what they *could/couldn't, was able to/wasn't able to, managed/didn't manage to* do.

- Refer students back to the Language Workout box and read the notes on expressing purpose as a class. Note the difference in the use of the two phrases. Students then turn to page 119 of the Language File to read more about the phrases.
- Students do exercise 25 on page 119 of the Language File. They try to join the sentences with *in order to*. If this is not possible, they use *so that*. Do the first one together as an example. Check answers by asking different students to read the sentences aloud.

Answers

1 The students read through all their notes in order to pass the exam.
2 My parents gave me a camera so that I could take photos at the party.
3 The police locked the cell so that the thief couldn't escape.
4 They're visiting the UK in order to learn English.
5 We left home early in order to get to the gig on time.
6 He gave me his number so that I could phone if I got lost.
7 Can you buy some eggs so that I can make a cake?
8 She goes to the gym every day in order to keep fit.

Optional activity

Fast-finishers can write sentences using *in order to* and *so that* which are true for themselves. They can read them to the class when everyone has finished.

Follow-up activities

♦ **Game** *True or false?* Students work in teams. Each team writes five sentences about themselves or famous people they know about, talking about past ability, e.g. *I could read when I was three.* Three of the sentences should be true and two false. Each team reads out their sentences and the other teams guess which two are false.

♦ **Game** *A good excuse* Divide students into two teams. Ask questions e.g. *Why were you running down the road in your pyjamas?* Teams give one answer starting with *so that* or *in order to*, e.g. *in order to escape the fire.* The most convincing answer wins a point. Other possible questions include: *Why did you cut all your hair off? Why did you leave home at 5am this morning? Why are you wearing sunglasses? Why did you throw your computer out of the window? Why did you phone the President/Prime Minister?*

HOMEWORK

Students write about their first day at school, or a day they remember from school when they were younger. They should include two examples of ability in the past.

WEBLINK

Students may like to visit www.benjaminzephaniah.com/kidz to learn more about Benjamin Zephaniah.

Revision and Extension p109

Language File p119

Workbook Unit 8 Lesson 1 pp86–87

Photocopiable worksheet p184, notes p161

2 She needn't have worried

Communicative aims	Language	Pronunciation	Vocabulary	Optional aids
Expressing obligation and ability	Modal expressions in the past and future	Intonation	Education	Follow up activity: large piece of paper/card

WARMER

Tell students that the topic of the lesson is *school*. Students race to write as many words related to school as they can in one minute. Ask the student with the most words to read them out. Other students listen and then say any other words they wrote.

1 OPENER

- The aim is to set the scene for the text in exercise 2.
- Ask students what they can see in the pictures and discuss the questions as a whole class. If necessary prompt students with ideas for differences, e.g. *cost, technology, punishment, age pupils left school*.

2 READING

- Read the question with the class and ask students to speculate on the answer. Ask students to read and listen to the article and answer the question.

  ◉ 3.19 Recording
  See text on page 102 of the Student's Book.

  Answer
  1918

3 AFTER READING

- Students match the beginnings and endings individually. Point out that there are two endings which are not needed. Be prepared to explain/translate *fees, bullying*. Students compare answers in pairs. Then check answers as a whole class.

  Answers
  1 k   2 l   3 c   4 b   5 f   6 i   7 d   8 a   9 g   10 j

Optional activity

Fast-finishers can note down three new words in the text. They look up these words in a dictionary and explain them to the class when everyone has finished.

Your response

Ask students to work in pairs to discuss the questions. Ask some pairs to report back to the class.

Optional activity

Ask students to come up with their own ideas for schools in the future. They can work in pairs or small groups, then report back to the class. The class can decide on the best ideas.

4 VOCABULARY

- Ask students to read through the words in the Word Bank. Explain any words that they don't understand. Point out that there is more than one possible answer for some of the compounds.
- Students work individually to make the compound nouns, then compare their answers in pairs. Elicit possible answers from the class, and write them on the board.

  Suggested answers
  1 entrance fees   2 university degree
  3 school/university fees
  4 national curriculum   5 primary school   6 classroom
  7 school/university rules   8 secondary school
  9 school/university subject   10 school/exam timetable
  11 school uniform   12 whiteboard

5 PRONUNCIATION

- Students read the first three statements. Play the recording for students to decide how the sentence is said. Play the recording again, pausing for students to repeat, copying the intonation.

  ◉ 3.20 Recording and answers
  1 Students will have to stay at school until they're 21. (S)
  2 They'll also need to study more subjects. (F)
  3 They'll be able to do all their classwork on computer. (F)

- Students practise saying the sentences in the manner indicated. Play the recording for students to check their ideas. Pause after each sentence for students to repeat.

  ◉ 3.20 Recording
  4 They won't need to go to school every day. (F)
  5 They'll be able to study online at home. (S)
  6 They won't have to take any examinations. (S)

LANGUAGE WORKOUT OPTION

If you want to pre-teach the language students will use in the following activities, you may like to go to the Language Workout box now.

6 LISTENING

- Students look at the photo. Ask *How old do you think Mary is?* Explain to students that they will hear Mary answering a questionnaire. Students read the questionnaire and Mary's answers.
- Play the recording for students to listen and decide if Mary's answers are true or false. If necessary, play the recording again for students to correct the false information.
- Students compare answers. Then check answers as a whole class. Encourage students to say complete sentences, e.g. *Number one is false. She can swim underwater now and she wasn't able to do that a year ago.*

🔘 3.21 Recording

WOMAN	Now Mary, you're first, here we go with the Then and Now Questionnaire.
MARY	OK.
WOMAN	Question 1: tell me about something you can do now which you weren't able to do a year ago.
MARY	Hm … I know – swim underwater. I wasn't able to and then I learnt when we were in Greece on holiday.
WOMAN	Is there something you had to do in the past, but don't have to do now?
MARY	Mm. Something I had to do? Yes, I had to get help with spreadsheets on the computer, but now I can use them on my own.
WOMAN	And is there something you didn't have to do in the past which you have to do now?
MARY	That's easy – I didn't have to work hard in maths classes, but now I really have to.
WOMAN	Question 4: is there something you needn't have worried about?
MARY	That's difficult… I know – making friends. I used to worry a lot about that – silly really!
WOMAN	Mmm. Next question: is there something you need to do now, but hope you won't need to do in the future?
MARY	Yes, I need to get up really early or else I'll miss the bus. But next year I'll be able to catch a later bus.
WOMAN	Question 6: is there something you can't do now, but will be able to do?
MARY	Lots of things – I can't drive a car, but I hope I'll be able to when I'm older.
WOMAN	Is there something you don't have to do now, but will have to do?
MARY	I don't have to do my washing now, but if I move away from home I'll have to.
WOMAN	And the last question. Is there something you can do now, but won't be able to do?
MARY	Yes, beat my brother at tennis. I'm better than him now, but I know I won't be able to beat him forever.

Answers

1 False. Swim underwater.	2 True
3 False. Work hard in maths classes.	4 True
5 False. Get up early.	6 True
7 False. Do my washing.	
8 False. Beat my brother at tennis.	

7

- Now listen to Matt's answers and repeat the steps in exercise 6.

🔘 3.22 Recording

WOMAN	And now your turn, Matt. Are you ready?
MATT	Sure. Are they the same questions?
WOMAN	Yes, they are. Question 1: is there something you can do know which you weren't able to do a year ago?
MATT	Let me think. Yes, a year ago I wasn't able to ride a motorbike, but I can now.
WOMAN	Right. Is there something you had to do in the past, but you don't have to do now?
MATT	Mm – for years I had to collect my brother from his school and take him home. But now he's old enough to walk home by himself.
WOMAN	And the other way round. Is there something you didn't have to do in the past which you have to do now?
MATT	Yeah, work in a clothes shop on Saturdays. My parents give me some money but it's never enough. And I can get really cheap clothes from the shop because I work there.
WOMAN	Question 4: is there something you needn't have worried about?
MATT	No, I never worry about anything!
WOMAN	Is there something you need to do now, but hope you won't need to do in the future?
MATT	Yes, think before I speak in French. I hope my French will get better and I won't need to think first.
WOMAN	OK. Question 6: what can't you do now, but will be able to do in the future?
MATT	Something I can't do now but will be able to in the future. Yes, I know vote. Why can't we vote at 16?
WOMAN	Next question. What don't you have to do now, but will have to do in the future?
MATT	That's easy – cook my own food. My parents do the cooking at home so I never get a chance.
WOMAN	And the last question: is there something you do now, but won't be able to do in the future?
MATT	You mean not because I won't be allowed to, but because I won't be able to?
WOMAN	Yes, that's right Matt.
MATT	Well, quite soon I won't be able to get into these jeans – they're pretty tight already!

Answers

1 *False. Ride a motorbike.*   2 *True*
3 *False. Work in a clothes shop on Saturdays.*
4 *False. I never worry about anything.*
5 *False. Think before I speak in French.*   6 *True*
7 *False. Cook my own food.*
8 *False. Get into these jeans.*

Extension Students work individually or in pairs to write sentences comparing Mary and Matt's answers. Remind students of expressions for linking and contrasting, e.g. *Both Mary and Matt ..., neither Mary nor Matt ..., Mary could ... whereas Matt ...*

LANGUAGE WORKOUT OPTION

If you want to pre-teach the language students will use in the following activities, you may like to go to the Language Workout box now.

8 SPEAKING

- Students work in groups of three and interview each other using the questionnaire in exercise 6. Point out that they should write notes like Mary's and Matt's.
- Students note each other's answers. Encourage confident students to ask further questions, e.g. *Where did you learn to swim underwater? What time do you have to get up?* and provide more information.

9 WRITING

- Elicit example sentences from different students using their own information.
- Give students ten minutes to write their paragraph. Make a note of any errors, particularly with the modal expressions. Write these on the board for students to correct when they have finished.

LANGUAGE WORKOUT

- Ask students to look at the Language Workout box and complete the sentences. Confident students can complete first and then check, while others can look back at exercises 2 and 3 and then complete.
- Students turn to page 119 of the Language File to check their answers.

Answers
*had to   didn't have to   weren't able to
didn't need to   needn't have   won't have to
will be able to   won't need to*

- Highlight that all of the modal expressions are followed by the infinitive except *needn't have*, which is followed by the past participle.
- Check students understand when to use the different verb structures by asking: *Which do you use for: an obligation, often a rule?* (have to), *a situation where there is no obligation?* (not have to), *something that is/isn't necessary?* (need to/ not need to), *ability or possibility?* (be able to/not be able to).
- Check students understand the difference between *didn't need to* and *needn't have* by drawing their attention to the examples. Ask *Did girls go to school?* (No) *Did she worry?* (Yes) Drill the example sentences chorally and individually, paying particular attention to the weak form of *have* in *needn't have*.

PRACTICE

- Students do Practice exercise 26 on page 120 of the Language File. Ask students to read the paragraph first, ignoring the gaps, to find out what schools in the past and in the future have in common. Check the answer as a whole class (*respect for the teacher*).
- Students complete the gaps with the correct form of the verb. Be prepared to explain/translate *sewing, obey, get on with something, get rid of.* Check answers by asking different students to read the sentences aloud.

Answers
1 *didn't need*   2 *didn't have*   3 *had*   4 *were*   5 *had*
6 *will have*   7 *won't be*   8 *won't need*   9 *will be*
10 *will have*   11 *needn't have been*

Follow-up activity

Draw a word map on the board. Write *SCHOOL* in the centre. Elicit different categories from the class and write them on the word map e.g. *classroom, people, subjects.* Divide students into small groups to draw their own word map on a large piece of paper or card. Encourage them to think of their own categories and add as many words as they can.

HOMEWORK

Students interview their parents about their school life and write about how school life has changed.

WEBLINK

Students may like to visit www.guardian.co.uk/education/2011/may/03/school-i-would-like to read more answers for *The School I'd Like.*

Revision and Extension p109

Language File pp119–120

Workbook Unit 8 Lesson 2 pp88–89

Photocopiable worksheet p185, notes p161

3   MAKING THE GRADE

It made me feel great

Communicative aims	Language	Pronunciation	Vocabulary
Talking about obligation, permission and prohibition	*make* and *let* *be allowed to*	Pronunciation of *ng*	Music Family rules

WARMER 1

Write the following sentence heads on the board: *Last weekend I didn't have to …, Last weekend I wasn't able to …, This morning I had to …, This weekend I will need to …* In pairs, students finish the sentences so they are true for themselves. Encourage students to say more about their sentences, e.g. *I didn't have to do any housework because I had to revise for the exams.*

WARMER 2

Write these questions on the board for students to discuss in pairs: *Can you sing or do you play a musical instrument? Would you like to be a professional singer or musician? Why (not)? What are the advantages and disadvantages of being a professional singer or musician?*

1   OPENER

- The aim is to set the scene for the reading and review vocabulary that students will need to complete the tasks.
- In pairs, students decide which words they think will be in the interview. Be prepared to explain/translate *chords* (a combination of two or more musical notes played at the same time), *gigs* and *lyrics*.

2   READING AND LISTENING

- Students look at the photo of Kezza. Ask *What type of music do you think she plays?*
- Students read the questions a–f. Don't explain any new words at this stage.
- Encourage students to read for general understanding and to match the questions and answers. Students then listen and check their answers.
- Check answers as a class.

🔘 3.23   Recording

See text on page 104 of the Student's Book.

> Answers
> *1 b 2 d 3 e 4 f 5 a 6 c*

> Answers to exercise 1
> *Words mentioned: band, chords, gigs, hum, influence, inspired, lyrics, tune*

3   AFTER READING AND LISTENING

- Students re-read the text more carefully. They decide if the sentences are true or false, or if no information is given. Remind students to correct the false information. Allow students time to compare their answers in pairs before you check with the class.

> Answers
> *1 True*
> *2 False. The tune just came into her head.*
> *3 False. She chose it because it inspired her to start writing songs.*
> *4 No information*
> *5 False. Sometimes the tune comes first, sometimes the lyrics.*
> *6 True*
> *7 True*
> *8 False. She thinks they should listen, but they should decide themselves what to do.*
> *9 No information*

Your response

Ask students to work in pairs to discuss the questions. Ask some pairs to report back to the class.

Optional activities

- ◆ Ask *Who are your favourite singers/songwriters? Why? Do you know how they started their careers?* Students can discuss the questions in pairs and then report back to the class.
- ◆ Students work in pairs to write example sentences for three of the music words in exercise 1. Monitor and check while students are working. Students can then take turns to read out one of their sentences to the class, leaving out the music word. The class must guess the missing word.

4   PRONUNCIATION

- Write the words *long* and *longer* on the board and elicit the different pronunciations of *ng*. Students look at the words in the box and write the words in the right column. They then listen to check their answers. Play the recording a second time for students to listen and repeat.

3.24 Recording and answers

/ŋ/ **long** singer song strong thing young wrong

/ŋg/ **longer** finger hungry single strongest younger

5 VOCABULARY

- Students copy the word map into their notebooks. They look back through the lesson and add all the music words they can find to the map.
- Students then compare their answers and work in small groups to add their own ideas to the map. You could set a target for the number of words to add to the map.

Suggested answers

People: songwriter, singer, musician, drummer, guitarist, fan

Styles: classical, country, house, pop, rock, soul

Instruments: guitar, piano, drum, saxophone, violin, electronic keyboard

Songs: lyrics, verse, chorus, chords, karaoke, soundtrack

Optional activity

Fast-finishers mark the stress on words of two or more syllables.

LANGUAGE WORKOUT OPTION

If you want to pre-teach the language students will use in the following activities, you may like to go to the Language Workout box now.

6 LISTENING

- Read the instructions with the class. Students read the list and work in pairs to guess what Luke's parents make him do and let him do. They then listen and check their answers. If necessary, play the recording a second time, pausing for students to confirm or change their answers.
- Check answers as a whole class.

3.25 Recording

INTERVIEWER	*Do your parents stop you doing things you want to do?*
LUKE	*Yes, they stop me doing all kinds of things.*
INTERVIEWER	*What kind of things?*
LUKE	*Well, whenever I play music in my room, they make me turn it down.*
INTERVIEWER	*They think your music is too loud?*
LUKE	*Yeah, they're always complaining about it.*
INTERVIEWER	*Uh huh.*
LUKE	*And another thing – if I want to stay up late to watch something on TV, they don't let me. They don't let me watch too much TV anyway.*
INTERVIEWER	*Do they make you go to bed at a certain time?*
LUKE	*Oh, yeah. On school days, they tell me to go to bed at 10.30 – it's awful.*

INTERVIEWER	*What about weekends?*
LUKE	*I'm allowed to stay up later on Friday and Saturday night – and in the holidays they let me stay up late if I want.*
INTERVIEWER	*What about housework – are you expected to help with the housework?*
LUKE	*Well, I have to lay the table for meals, and they make me tidy my room, and things like that …*
INTERVIEWER	*That doesn't sound too bad.*
LUKE	*No, I suppose not …*
INTERVIEWER	*And how much freedom do you have? Are you allowed to go out on your own at night?*
LUKE	*Yes, I'm allowed to go out, but I have to let them know where I'm going. And I'm not allowed to stay out late. I think that's wrong, I'm 16, for heaven's sake! All my friends have much more freedom, they're allowed to do what they like …*

Answers

turn his music down M

stay up late to watch TV X

watch too much TV X

go to bed at 10.30 on school days M

stay up later at weekends and in the holidays L

lay the table for meals M

tidy his room M

go out on his own at night L

say where he is going when he goes out M

stay out late X

LANGUAGE WORKOUT OPTION

If you want to pre-teach the language students will use in the following activities, you may like to go to the Language Workout box now.

7 SPEAKING

- Elicit a few examples from the whole class and write an example with each structure (*make, let* and *don't let*) on the board. Make sure students understand the meaning of each sentence. Allow students time to prepare their ideas individually before they work in pairs. They exchange ideas about what Luke's parents make him do, let him do and don't let him do.
- Students then interview two other students and note down their answers. Monitor and help/correct as necessary.

Extension Ask students to work in pairs to discuss the questions. Ask some pairs to report back to the class. You could ask for a show of hands to find out how many students think that Luke's parents are too strict.

Optional activity

In groups, students talk about how the rules in their home have changed over the past ten years, e.g. *When I was young, I wasn't allowed to go out alone. Now my parents let me go out but I have to say where I'm going.*

8 WRITING

- Students write two paragraphs using the notes they made in exercise 7. Remind students of useful expressions for comparing and contrasting, e.g. *both ... and ..., neither ... nor ..., while/whereas.*
- When students have finished, ask them to swap with another student and peer correct.

LANGUAGE WORKOUT

- Ask students to look at the Language Workout box and complete the sentences. Confident students can complete first and then check, while others can look back at exercises 2 and 3 and then complete.
- Students turn to page 120 of the Language File to check their answers.

  Answers
  make   let   made   allowed to

- Highlight the difference between the active and passive forms of *make*. Point out that we use *let* in the active and *be allowed to* in the passive.

PRACTICE

- Students do Practice exercise 27 on page 120 of the Language File. They complete the sentences with the correct form. Check answers by asking different students to read a sentence aloud.

  Answers
  *1 make   2 let   3 aren't allowed to   4 make
  5 were made to   6 Are ... allowed to   7 let
  8 are made to*

Follow-up activities

- **Game** *Race to write*   Students work in teams. Say the beginning of a sentence. Teams race to write a sentence with that beginning which includes *make, let* or *be allowed to*. The sentence must be correct in content and grammar. Remind students that the sentence can be passive. Possible beginnings include: *Her mother ..., Our English teacher ..., Her brother/sister ..., the President/Prime Minister, Kezza.*
- **Game** *Noughts and crosses*   See Review Units 1–2 (p56) for instructions. Put a music word from this unit in each square and have students make a sentence using the relevant word.

HOMEWORK

Students write a paragraph about the rules in their own house, using *make, let* and *be allowed to.*

WEBLINK

Students may like to visit www.wikihow.com/Be-a-Singer for tips on how to become a singer.

Revision and Extension p109

Language File p120

Workbook Unit 8 Lesson 3 pp90–91

Photocopiable worksheet p186, notes p161

Integrated Skills Making an application

Skills		Learner independence	Vocabulary	Optional aids
Reading Topics: letter of application *Listening* Telephone interviews: matching information and checking predictions	*Speaking* Role play: telephone interview *Writing* Application form and letter of application	Thinking skills Word creation: noun suffix -*ness*	Volunteering Useful expressions	Exercise 5: Copies of exercise 4 recording script

WARMER

Game *Play or pass*   Organise students into teams. Ask team A to spell a word. Choose words that your students have had difficulty with. Possible words include: *successful, behaviour, queue, professional, scientist, recognition, entrepreneur, ordinary, archaeologist, advertisement.* They can choose to spell it or pass it to the other team. If they spell it correctly, they win a point. If they spell it incorrectly, they get no points. If they pass it to team B, team B must attempt to spell it. If team B spells it correctly, they get a point. If team B spells it incorrectly, team A gets the point. Continue offering words to each team in turn until all the words have been spelt.

1 OPENER

- The aim is to set the scene and generate interest in the text in exercise 2.
- Students look at the photo and read the advertisement for ReefAID. Ask *Are the people working? Are they being paid?* Elicit *to volunteer/do voluntary* work. Discuss the questions together as a whole class. Check that students understand *coral reef.* Ask *Would you like to do this type of work? Why?*

2 READING

- Students read Tiffany's letter and match the topics in the box with sections of the letter. Check answers together as a whole class. Ask *Do you think Tiffany would be a good volunteer? Why (not)?*

Answers
1 Her address
2 Date
3 Address of person she is writing to
4 Starting the letter
5 Why she is writing
6 Personal details
7 Why she would be a successful volunteer
8 Her personal reasons for choosing a particular expedition
9 Money
10 Ending the letter

Optional activity

Highlight the layout of the letter by asking students to compare it to the layout of a formal letter in their language. Ask *Do the addresses and the date go in the same place?* Ask students what to write if you don't know the name of the person you are writing to (start: *Dear Sir or Madam,* end: *Yours faithfully*).

3

- The aim is to give students practice in form-filling in English.
- Ask students *What colour pen do you need to use?* (black) *Do you need to write in capital letters?* (just the address). Monitor and help/correct as necessary.

Answers
Bell
Tiffany
17, female, single
British
53 MILL LANE, LONDON, AW7 8QQ
English (fluent), Spanish (good)
Keeping fit, dancing, politics, conservation
I enjoy working as a volunteer at our local nature reserve.
I get on well with most people and enjoy making new friends.
Honduras
Because I speak (good) Spanish, I have always wanted to go to South America and the chance to learn scuba diving is a great opportunity for me.

4 LISTENING

- Students look at the four photos and read the eight problems. Deal with any vocabulary issues. Ask students to predict which problem each person has. Students then listen to the first four phone calls and match the applicants with the problems. Pause after each phone call for students to compare answers. Stop the recording before the final phone call. Check the answers together as a class.
- In pairs, students discuss who they think will be offered a place and why. They then listen to the final conversation to check their ideas.

3.26 Recording

JANET Many thanks for your application, Ann – I think it's a very strong one, and we hope you'll be able to join us. But there are one or two points I wanted to check with you over the phone. Is that all right?

ANN Yes, of course. Isn't something clear?

JANET You say that you have a scuba diving qualification. Can you tell me what it is please?

ANN Sure – it's an advanced scuba diving qualification.

JANET Thank you, that's fine. And there was one more thing. On your form it says that you're 16 – when's your birthday?

ANN Oh, in November.

JANET So you'll be 17 then.

ANN Well, actually no – I'll be 16.

JANET Oh dear, Ann. I'm so sorry. I'm afraid that you have to be 16 to join and the expedition's in July. We hope very much that you'll apply again next year.

ANN Yes, I will. Thank you. Bye!

JAKE 'Lo.

JANET Hello – is that Jake?

JAKE Yes. Who's that then?

JANET It's Janet Rawlings from ReefAid. I can hardly hear you.

JAKE Sorry – I'm on a train. I'll go to the end of the carriage... Is that better?

JANET Yes, it's a little better. I'm calling about your application to join one of our expeditions.

JAKE Oh, right.

JANET You didn't complete the section headed 'Give two reasons why we should select you as a volunteer.'

JAKE No, I didn't – because I wasn't sure what to say.

JANET I see. So can you tell me why you want to go?

JAKE Er, it's because of my girlfriend.

JANET You want to get away from her? That's not a good …

JAKE No, because she's going on a ReefAid expedition.

JANET What's her name?

JAKE Tiffany Bell.

JANET Just a moment. Yes, I've got her on the screen now. Very good application. We accepted her and she's going to Honduras.

JAKE I know. Yeah, well, I want to go in order to keep an eye on her. To be with her, you know?

JANET Jake, I'm afraid that's not really a good reason for us to select you. Are there any other…

CAROL Hello?

JANET Hi, is that Carol?

CAROL Yes, it is.

JANET I'm ringing from ReefAid about your application.

CAROL Is it good news? Am I going on the expedition?

JANET I'm afraid we can't say yet. You see, you haven't completed the back of the form which asks for medical details.

CAROL Oh, no! I'm terribly sorry. Silly me – I never thought to look on the back. Does this mean that I'm too late?

JANET No, but our doctors need to check your medical details to see if it's OK for you to dive. And we can't offer you a place until they say yes.

CAROL So it's not 'no' then?

JANET No, Carol, but it isn't 'yes' yet either! Let us have the medical details as soon as you can and we'll get back to you quickly.

CAROL Thank you ever so much. I'll do it today.

JANET Hello. Is that Steve? I'm ringing from ReefAid about your application to join one of our expeditions.

STEVE Right.

JANET I just need to check a couple of things with you. You say that you've been on a similar expedition before.

STEVE That's right I went with a group from school to Australia, and we dived off the Great Barrier Reef.

JANET So you're an experienced diver …

STEVE That's right.

JANET And the other thing – you said on the form that you weren't free until July 20th. You do realise that the expedition you want to go on leaves on July 12th, don't you?

STEVE Oh no! School doesn't finish until the 17th.

JANET Well Steve, I'm afraid that means we can't offer you a place. I'm sorry because you were an excellent applicant and we …

JANET ReefAid, good afternoon. How can I help you?

STEVE Hello, my name's Steve. I'd like to talk to Janet – she rang me earlier.

JANET Speaking.

STEVE Sorry, Janet, I didn't recognise your voice. You remember me, don't you? I'm the one whose school didn't finish until after the expedition had left.

JANET Yes, Steve, I remember you and I'm just getting your details up on the screen. Right, got them. The expedition you want leaves on July 12th, doesn't it?

STEVE Yes, and I've spoken to my teachers and they say that I can miss the last week of school. They think a ReefAid expedition is a great opportunity. So I can leave on July 12th. But the point is – are there any places left?

JANET Yes, there are two – and your name's on one of them now. Congratulations! You'd better get on with your fund-raising!

Answers

Ann 8
Jake 2
Carol 7
Steve 3

Steve is offered a place on the expedition. He talked to his teachers and they have allowed him to miss the last week of school.

5 SPEAKING

- Ask students to copy the ReefAid form into their books. Students complete the form for themselves or an imaginary person.
- Students work in pairs, one as the applicant and one as a worker at ReefAid. Play the recording from exercise 4 again. Before students do the role play, give them a copy of the tapescript of the five telephone conversations in exercise 5. Students find and note useful expressions for the role play, e.g. *It's … from ReefAid, There are one or two points I wanted to check, I'm afraid that means …*, The applicant gives their application form to the ReefAid interviewer, who decides on the questions he/she is going to ask. Students then act out the telephone conversation. Monitor and help/correct as necessary.
- Ask some pairs to role play their telephone conversation for the class.

6 GUIDED WRITING

- This writing task could be set for homework. Students look at the three adverts. In pairs, students discuss which one they would most like to apply for and why.
- With weaker classes, choose one of the organisations as a class and brainstorm ideas and useful phrases students can use.
- Students write a letter of application using the model in exercise 2. Tell students to organise their letter using the same sections. Make a note of good language use and errors. Write these on the board. When students finish, ask them to note the good language and correct the errors.

Optional activity

Students search on the Internet and find their own volunteer project to apply to.

7 LEARNER INDEPENDENCE

- The aim is to introduce students to a technique for improving confidence and possibly performance.
- Tell students the name of the technique is *Visualising exam success*. Students predict what this involves.
- Students read the description and check. Ask *Have you ever heard of this technique before? Have you ever tried it? Would you consider trying it now? What techniques do you use to help you in exams?*

8 WORD CREATION

- The aim is for students to learn one way in which nouns can be formed from adjectives and to extend their vocabulary.
- Students complete the sentences individually and compare their answers in pairs. Check answers by

asking different students to read the sentences aloud. Point out that the spelling of one of word changes when it becomes a noun (*happiness*).

Answers

1 *politeness*   2 *sadness*   3 *Weightlessness*
4 *carelessness*   5 *illness*   6 *thoughtfulness*   7 *fitness*
8 *cleverness*   9 *usefulness*   10 *Happiness*

EXTRA PRACTICE

If you would like to give your students more practice in forming words ending in -*ness*, please see the Vocabulary EXTRA! Worksheets on the Teacher's Resource Site (www.macmillanenglish.com/inspiration).

9 PHRASEBOOK

- Ask students to look through the unit to find the expressions and look at how they are used. Be ready to help with translation as necessary.
- Play the recording, pausing after each expression for students to repeat.

🔵 **3.27** Recording
Lesson 2, Exercise 2
She needn't have worried.
Lesson 3, Exercise 2
round the clock
Practice makes perfect
It drove me mad
It's up to you
That's all that matters.
as far as I'm concerned

- Students find the five expressions which match the definitions.
- Students can add expressions they like to their Personal Phrasebooks.

Answers

1 *That's all that matters.*
2 *It's up to you.*
3 *as far as I'm concerned*
4 *round the clock*
5 *It drove me mad.*

Follow-up activity

Game *Password*   See Unit 3, Lesson 3 Follow-up activities (p67) for instructions. Use words from the Vocabulary box.

HOMEWORK

Students imagine they are on a volunteer project and write a postcard home saying how they spend their time.

WEBLINK

Students may like to visit www.workingabroad.com to find out about volunteer projects around the world.

Revision and Extension p109   **Workbook Unit 8 Lesson 4 pp92–93**

8 MAKING THE GRADE

Inspiration EXTRA!

PROJECT   IDEAL SCHOOL

1 • Explain to students that the aim of the project is to write about their ideal school. Put students into groups and ask them to look back at Lesson 2 and re-read the paragraph in exercise 2 in which the students' ideas for future schools are described. Give students a few minutes to discuss their ideas for an ideal school.

2 • Students do research into different schools around the world. You might like to set this for homework, then get students to continue the project in the next lesson.

3 • Appoint a 'secretary' for each group. The 'secretary' is responsible for taking notes.
  • Students look at the questions and make notes about their ideal school. Monitor and help as necessary. Students can find or draw pictures to go with their ideas.

4 • Ask students to read through the model text to give them ideas for useful vocabulary and phrases. Students then use their ideas to write about their ideal school.
  • When students have finished writing, encourage them to read their work carefully and correct any mistakes. Help as necessary. They copy their texts out neatly and illustrate their work with photos or drawings.
  • Students show their *Ideal School* to other groups. The class can vote on the best one. Display the work in the classroom if possible.

GAME   PUZZLE WORDS

• Students work in pairs to solve the three puzzles. They then create their own puzzle words. Remind students that consecutive letters must touch each other. Point out that they can use the Word List to help. Students exchange their puzzle words and solve each other's.

Answers
interview, education, voluntary

REVISION

Lessons 1–3
Students' own answers.

EXTENSION

Lessons 1–3
Students' own answers.

Language File pp119–120

Song – photocopiable worksheet p190, notes p162

YOUR CHOICE!

• The aim is to give students more learner independence and help them to identify their preferred way of learning. Encourage students to choose an activity that they feel less comfortable with if they want a challenge or are aware that they need practice in a particular area.
• Monitor and help groups. Check answers if necessary, or provide written answers for groups to check their own work against.

CONSTRUCTION

Answers
1 *Thank you! But you needn't have bought me a present.*
2 *He got up early because he had to finish his homework.*
3 *Does your school let you wear what you like?/Do they let you wear what you like at school?*
4 *We are made to do/The teacher makes us do a maths test every week.*
5 *It's OK – you won't need to pay for your ticket.*
6 *I couldn't work out the answer.*
7 *Will you be able to attend an interview next week?*
8 *We are not allowed to wear jewellery at school.*

REFLECTION

Answers
1 e, h   2 a   3 f, g   4 d   5 c   6 b

ACTION

• Organise students into small groups. Students read the instructions in the box and choose their roles. Encourage them to think for a minute about why their character should stay in the balloon.
• Students take it in turns to speak and then finally vote. Ask students to report back on who had to jump out of the balloon and why.

INTERACTION

• Students work in pairs to add adjectives to the list. Individually they then select an adjective for another student and one for themselves.
• Students write a note and give it to the other student. Ask students to report back on the words they got.

You may now like students to do the song *True Colours*. See p162 for the notes and p190 for the worksheet.

Workbook Unit 8 Inspiration EXTRA! pp94–95

1 Ask students to look at the picture and the title and predict what the text will be about. Give students one minute to read the article and check their predictions. Students read the article again and choose the appropriate answer for each space. Do the first one together as an example. This can be done in pairs or individually as a short test.

> **Answers**
>
> 1 B   2 B   3 C   4 A   5 C   6 B   7 A   8 B   9 A
> 10 C   11 B   12 A   13 B   14 C   15 C

Optional activity

Confident students can attempt the task before looking at the options.

2 Ask students to read the paragraph and find out why Mr Gough is often arrested (*he goes walking naked*). Students complete the gaps with the appropriate form of the verb.

> **Answers**
>
> 1 has been sent
> 2 has been arrested
> 3 were called
> 4 was found
> 5 was taken
> 6 is permitted
> 7 is being treated/is treated
> 8 has been asked
> 9 is being held
> 10 will be released

Optional activity

Write the answers on the board. Students use them as prompts to recall the story.

3 Students complete the sentences with the passive infinitive of the verbs.

> **Answers**
>
> 1 to be paid   2 be heard   3 be allowed   4 to be told
> 5 to be given   6 be encouraged   7 to be treated
> 8 be seen

4 Students complete the sentences with the phrasal verbs. Focus on the example with the class and point out that students should use pronouns in their answers. Remind students that the pronoun goes between the verb and the adverb of phrasal verbs. With weaker classes, you could ask students to complete the sentences with the correct phrasal verbs first, then rewrite the sentences using pronouns instead of nouns.

> **Answers**
>
> 1 turn it up   2 fill it in   3 work them out
> 4 switch them off   5 cut it all off   6 put them up
> 7 take it in   8 pass it on

5 Students complete the paragraph.

> **Answers**
>
> 1 couldn't   2 wasn't able   3 managed to   4 could
> 5 was able   6 managed to   7 was able

Optional activity

Ask students to recall the four successful people they read about in Unit 8, Lesson 1 (Beethoven, Benjamin Zephaniah, JK Rowling, Einstein). Students recall what they could(n't) do, were(n't) able to do and managed to do.

6 Students complete the sentences. If necessary, review the difference in meaning between the two structures before students start.

> **Answers**
>
> 1 didn't need to hurry   2 needn't have cooked
> 3 needn't have worried   4 didn't need to   5 didn't need to
> 6 needn't have been

7 Students rewrite the sentences.

> **Answers**
>
> 1 You aren't allowed to park your car here during the day.
> 2 The thief made me give him my mobile.
> 3 Did your teacher let you go home early?
> 4 The hot sun made the ice melt.
> 5 I won't let you talk like that.
> 6 We were made to work 12 hours a day.
> 7 You aren't allowed to carry weapons on planes.
> 8 I know a joke which will make everyone laugh.

VOCABULARY

8 Students complete the sentences with words from the box.

> **Answers**
>
> 1 platform   2 dialect   3 fan   4 cash   5 prejudice
> 6 fees   7 submarine   8 volunteer   9 cupboard
> 10 earthquake

9 Students match the words with their definitions. Confident students can attempt the task without looking at the words in the box, and then look to check.

> **Answers**
>
> 1 lyrics   2 decade   3 solar   4 colleague   5 nautical
> 6 emphasis   7 entrepreneur   8 admire   9 chord

Optional activity

Students write definitions of other words from Units 7 and 8. They exchange definitions and try to guess each other's words.

10 Students match the verbs and phrases first. Check the answers. Students then write eight sentences of their own using the expressions.

> **Answers**
>
> *1 award a prize   2 book a table   3 change your mind*
> *4 climb up a ladder   5 fail an examination*
> *6 install a cooker   7 repaint the walls   8 solve a problem*

Optional activity

In pairs, one student says a word or phrase from list B and their partner recalls the verb.

LEARNER INDEPENDENCE SELF ASSESSMENT

- Explain to students that the aim of the self-assessment is to encourage them to check their own progress and take any necessary action to improve. Point out that the list 1–7 covers areas of functional language from Units 7 and 8. Students tick the 'Fine' box for functional language that they feel confident using, but put a question mark in the 'Not sure' box for functional language that they have difficulties with or still cannot use confidently.
- Encourage students to look at the Language File and re-do exercises from the Workbook in areas where they have problems. They may also like to re-do exercises from the lessons and from the Revision and Extension sections in Units 7 and 8.
- Students write an example sentence for each language area in the list. You may like to elicit grammar students need for each example before students write their sentences, e.g. *Describing changes and experiences: Passive tenses.* Students can refer back to the lessons and the Language File.
- Ask students to compare their sentences with a partner and discuss and correct any mistakes.
- Check students' sentences and note down any language areas for further practice.

Follow-up activities

- ◆ **Game** *Alphabet Categories*   Students work in small groups. On the board, write 4–5 vocabulary categories, e.g. *work, education, music*. Ask students to think of one item in each category beginning with a letter of your choice, e.g. A: *astronaut, art, album*, etc. The first team to find one for each shouts *Stop!* and wins 10 points (but loses 10 points if any of their words are wrong). Teams then read out their words in each category. They score 10 points for a unique suggestion, five if another team has the same word.
- ◆ **Game** *Grammar Auction*   Write 10–15 sentences on the board, some correct and some incorrect. Include grammar areas from throughout the Student's Book. Organise the students into teams. Each team has a total of £100. They can use this money to buy correct sentences. Tell them not to buy sentences that are incorrect. One team offers £5 for a sentence and if another team wants the sentence they must offer over £5 and so on, until no team wants to increase the money and the sentence is sold to the team with the highest offer. The winning team is the one that buys the most correct sentences as cheaply as possible. Students then correct the incorrect sentences.

HOMEWORK

Ask students to write about the things they enjoyed most or remember most in *New Inspiration 4*. They should mention stories that interested them and the characters/people they remember, and give reasons for their preferences.

WEBLINK

Students may like to visit www.lyrics.com for more song lyrics or www.songfacts.com for trivia about many well-known songs.

Language File pp118–120   **Workbook Review Units 7–8 pp96–97**

1.1 Food search

Activity	Wordsearch and questionnaire
Language focus	Verbs not usually used in continuous forms; talking about food
Preparation	Photocopy the worksheet for each pair of students. Cut it in half along the dotted lines.
Procedure	**1** Divide the class in two groups, A and B. Give each student in Group A Wordsearch A and each student in Group B Wordsearch B.
	2 Explain that each wordsearch contains six 'stative' verbs. Remind students that 'stative' verbs are not usually used in continuous forms and describe states or senses.
	3 Tell students to work with a partner from the same group to circle the six verbs. Explain that the verbs can be found in any direction – across, down, diagonally and backwards.
	4 Ask them to complete the questions using the 'stative' verbs but remind them to use the correct form of the verb. Quickly confirm the answers for the gaps with each group.
	5 Ask them to find a partner from the other group. Tell them to ask and answer each other's questions explaining their opinions and giving as many examples as possible.

Key

A
1 consist
2 disagree
3 contains
4 want
5 disliked
6 feel

B
1 include
2 remember, taste
3 think
4 lack
5 matter

1.2 Gadget crossword

Activity	Communicative crossword
Language focus	*for* + gerund to describe a function; gadget vocabulary
Preparation	Photocopy the worksheet for each pair of students. Cut it in half along the dotted lines.
Procedure	**1** Give a definition of an MP3 player, e.g. *It's a gadget for storing and listening to music files.* Ask the students to guess which gadget it is.
	2 Tell the students that they are going to write some definitions of other gadgets to make crossword clues.
	3 Divide the class into two groups, A and B. Give each student in Group A Crossword A and each student in Group B Crossword B. Explain that Group A has the clues going across and Group B has those going down.
	4 Tell them to work with a partner from the same group to write a definition for each word on their crossword using *It's a gadget for ...-ing.*
	5 When students have finished, ask them to find a partner from the other group. Tell them to take turns to ask for and give each other the definitions. They mustn't show their crosswords to each other.
	6 When they have finished, ask them to check their answers with their partner's crossword.

1.3 Relationship problems

Activity	Matching and completing cards
Language focus	Verb + gerund or infinitive; talking about problems and giving advice
Preparation	Photocopy the worksheet for each pair of students. Cut it along the dotted lines.
Procedure	**1** Ask students if they have read problem pages in magazines or on the Internet. Elicit typical problems they have read.
	2 Give the six problem cards to each pair of students. Ask the students to read them and discuss the advice they might give each person.
	3 Now give each pair the six advice cards. Ask them to read and identify which advice goes with which problem.
	4 Do some open class feedback on which advice goes with each problem. If pairs disagree, ask them why they think their answer is correct.
	5 When the matching pairs have been confirmed, tell the students to decide whether the infinitive or gerund should be used in each sentence in the advice and circle the correct answer.
	6 Check the correct answers with the whole class.
Key	1 C 2 E 3 A 4 D 5 F 6 B A comparing, being B going, to contact C losing, to find D to meet, going E joining, to meet F to be, to be

2.1 A winter wonderland

Activity	Matching and completing cards
Language focus	Verb + gerund or infinitive; talking about problems and giving advice
Preparation	Photocopy the worksheet for each pair of students. Cut it along the dotted lines.
Procedure	

1 Write *Harbin ice lantern festival* on the board. Put the students into small groups and ask them to write three or four questions about the festival, e.g. *Where does it take place? When? How long has it been taking place? What can people do there?* Elicit questions from the class.

2 Explain that Student A and B will have the same piece of writing about the festival but that different pieces of information are missing. Their partner has the missing information.

3 Divide students into two groups, A and B. Give Students A, Text A and Students B, Text B.

4 Tell them to work together with a person from the same group to prepare the questions they need to ask to find out their missing information. Monitor to offer help and to check the correct formation of questions.

5 When students have finished, ask them to find a partner from the other group. Tell them to take turns to ask and answer questions and complete their texts.

6 When they have finished, ask them to check their answers with their partner's text.

7 Ask students to turn over their papers and tell you what they can remember about the festival.

2.2 Runner and writer race

Activity	Running dictation gap-fill
Language focus	Present perfect simple and continuous
Preparation	Photocopy the worksheet. Cut it into ten strips along the dotted lines. Stick the ten strips around the classroom.
Procedure	

1 Write on the board *1 I _____ forward to learning to drive.* (look) and dictate it, e.g. 'One I - space - forward to learning to drive - full stop - look in brackets'.

2 Explain that the activity is a race. Students will work in pairs to dictate ten sentences with one student as the runner and one as the writer.

3 Demonstrate by running to a strip, reading it, running back to a student and dictating it to them. Tell students that they must dictate exactly what appears on each strip including the number. The runner must not write and the writer must not move from their seats.

4 Put students into pairs and start the race. After a couple of minutes, ask students to swap roles in their pairs; the runner is now the writer and vice versa.

5 After five minutes, stop the race and declare a winning pair.

6 Ask them to complete the sentences with the present perfect simple or continuous form of the verbs. Check the correct answers with the whole class.

7 Ask them to discuss in their pairs whether the sentences are true or false for them and give feedback to the class.

Key	

1 I have been learning English for five years.

2 I have always wanted to be a film star.

3 I have visited more than three different countries in my life.

4 I have been living in my town since I was born.

5 I have been doing my hobby for over five years.

6 I have eaten spicy food many times.

7 I have been playing volleyball since I was a child.

8 I have read more than two books this year.

9 I have been supporting my favourite football team for more than two years.

10 I have been to the cinema once this month.

2.3 Verb families

Activity	Card game
Language focus	Review of verb forms
Preparation	Photocopy the worksheet for each group of four students. Cut it along the dotted lines.
Procedure	

1 Write the verb *see* on the board and elicit the forms *saw*, *seen* and *seeing*. Write them on the board.

2 Put students into groups of four and explain the rules:

• All cards are dealt so that each student has eight cards.

• Students have to collect verb families, which consist of the four verb forms on the board (infinitive, past simple, past participle, present participle).

• Students take turns to ask each other for cards. Elicit an example question from students and write it on the board, e.g. *Carlos, have you got 'seeing'?* (*Yes, I have. / No, I haven't.*).

• Students can only ask for members of a verb family if they already have one member of that family.

• If the student asked has got the card, they must give that card to the other student. The student who won the card can now have another go. If the student asked hasn't got the card, the other student loses their go. Play now passes to the next student on the right.

• Play continues until all the families have been collected. The winner is the student with the most sets.

3.1 Compare the planets

Activity	Text completion
Language focus	Comparison of adverbs; adverbs of degree
Preparation	Photocopy the worksheet for each pair of students. Cut it in half along the dotted lines.
New vocabulary	*atmosphere, barren, crater, to orbit, probe* (n), *rocky, to spin*
Procedure	**1** Bring a picture of a space rocket to class or draw an outline of one on the board and elicit related vocabulary, e.g. the names of planets, *orbit*. Write the words that the students suggest within the outline.
	2 Write on the board *Neptune is far from the Sun. As a result, it takes Neptune 165 years to complete one orbit.* (*incredibly, approximately*). Ask the students to decide where the adverbs of degree should go in the sentences (*Neptune is incredibly far from the Sun … approximately 165 years to complete one orbit*).
	3 Divide the class into two groups, A and B. Tell Group A that they are going to read about Mercury and Group B that they are going to read about Saturn, but that a number of words have been taken out of the texts.
	4 Tell them to work with a partner from the same group to read their text and add the adverbs in the correct place.
	5 When students have finished, ask them to find a partner from the other group. Ask them to tell their new partner about their planet. Students work in their pairs to write five sentences comparing the two planets.

Key

… Mercury is *incredibly* small.	It is *approximately* 1,425 kilometres from the Sun …
Mercury is *approximately* 58 million kilometres …	… its rings which are *largely* made up of dust …
… it is *incredibly* close if you compare it …	It is *completely* made up of gases, …
This *partly* explains why Mercury is so hot.	… to hold it, Saturn would *actually* float.
Temperatures on Mercury can vary *greatly* …	… it moves at *approximately* 9.64 kilometres …
The surface of Mercury is *incredibly* barren and …	… because it is *incredibly* far from the Sun …
Mercury spins at an *incredibly* slow speed …	… this is *far* more than most of the other planets.
it was discovered that nothing could ever *possibly* live there …	

3.2 It's such an exciting game!

Activity	Guessing game
Language focus	*What (a/an) …! so/such (a/an) …*
Preparation	Photocopy the worksheet for each group of four or five students. Cut it along the dotted lines.
New vocabulary	*atmosphere, barren, crater, to orbit, probe* (n), *rocky, to spin*
Procedure	**1** Divide the students into groups of four or five and give them a set of cards. Tell them to place the cards face down on the desk in front of them. Explain the rules of the game:

- Players take turns to draw one card from the pile.
- They then have two minutes to try and make their group members say the exact phrase that is on the card by inventing a situation in which the phrase would be said.
- If they can do it within the time limit, they score one point and the player who guessed the phrase also scores a point. If nobody can guess the phrase, the card is put aside.
- Students can only use one of the words on the card that they draw from the pile. If they use more, they do not score any points.
- Play then passes to the player on the left.
- The player with the most points at the end of the game is the winner.

2 After **ten minutes** stop the game and get feedback from the groups by asking students to explain the stories they invented for some of the phrases on the cards.

3.3 Holidays in space

Activity	Group discussion
Language focus	Future forms; agreeing and disagreeing
Preparation	Photocopy the worksheet for each group of four students. Cut it along the dotted lines.
New vocabulary	*asteroid belt, faint-hearted, to float, gravity, lunar, luxurious, permanently, turbulent*
Procedure	**1** Ask the students whether they would like to go into space and why or why not. Elicit as many reasons as possible.
	2 Tell the students that the year is 50 years from now. Explain that space travel is now common and quite cheap, and they have won a half-price holiday. However, there is only one for each group, so they all need to agree on where to go.
	3 Divide students into four groups, A, B, C and D, and give the corresponding text to each group. Ask students to read about their holiday and discuss what they like about it e.g. transport, the cost, the length, activities, etc.
	4 Put students into new groups, with one student from each Group A, B, C and D. Ask them to take turns to tell the group about their holiday, and decide as a group which one they want to go on. Remind them that they need to persuade the others in the group that their holiday is the best and to note down reasons for their decision.
	5 Get feedback by asking one member from each group to report where the group is going and why.

4.1 Future inventions

Activity	Jigsaw reading
Language focus	Future continuous; future perfect
Preparation	Photocopy the worksheet for each group of three students. Cut it along the dotted lines.
Procedure	

1 Write on the board *We will be working longer in 2020. We won't have got rid of cars completely.* Ask students to underline the verb that is in future perfect and the one that is in future continuous. Elicit the use and form of each tense.

2 Put the students into pairs and ask them to think of two or three future inventions. Get feedback from each pair.

3 Write the following questions on the board:

In the year 2020:

1 What will people be doing?   3 Who will have invented it?

2 What will have been invented?   4 What will the invention do?

4 Give one reading to each pair. Tell them that they are going to read about a future invention and that they should answer the questions on the board. Monitor to help with any difficult vocabulary.

5 Divide the class into groups of three, making sure that the students in each group read about different inventions. Tell them to describe the different future inventions to each other and decide which one is the best.

6 Do some open class feedback to see which future invention is the most popular in class.

4.2 The airport debate

Activity	Role play
Language focus	Future possibility; first conditional; future time clauses
Preparation	Photocopy the worksheet for each group of four students. Cut it along the dotted lines.
Procedure	

1 Tell students that they all live in a town called Morkham and that the local council has plans to expand the local airport by creating two new runways. There is a meeting today to decide if these plans will go ahead or not.

2 Write the four roles on the board *local resident*, *local councillor*, *environmentalist*, *budget traveller*, and explain that the local councillor is the one who makes the final decision. Tell students that they will be given one of the four roles for the meeting. Divide students into four groups, A, B, C and D.

3 Explain that before the meeting they are going to work with a partner who has the same role so that they can exchange their views. Put students into pairs and give out the role cards. Ask students to read their cards and discuss with their partner what they will say at the meeting. Monitor and help as necessary.

4 When students have finished, put them into groups of four with one student from each group, A, B, C and D.

5 Tell the students to begin their meeting. Monitor and help as necessary.

6 When the groups have finished their meeting and the councillor has made a decision, do some open class feedback on what each group decided and why.

4.3 If I were a bird …

Activity	Board game
Language focus	Second conditional with *wish/if only* + past simple
Preparation	Photocopy one board for each group of four or five students. You will need counters for the students and a dice for each group.
Procedure	

1 Write on the board: *If …, I would …; If only …; I wish ….* Draw a picture of a bird on the board and elicit second conditional sentences from the class, e.g. *If I were a bird, I would fly to Australia. If only birds were bigger we could fly on them. I wish I had a pet bird.*

2 Tell the students that they are going to play a game to practise making sentences like these using picture prompts.

3 Divide students into groups of four or five. Give each group a copy of the board game and a dice, and give a counter to each student.

4 Explain the rules of the game:

- Each student puts their counters on the *Start* square.
- The youngest player throws the dice first and moves their counter around the board to the correct square.
- Once on the square, the player must say a sentence using *If …, I would…, If only …,* or *I wish ….*
- The other students must listen and check to see if the sentence is correct. If not that player must go back to their previous square.
- Play continues with the next player on the left.
- The winner is the first player to reach *Finish*.

5 Students play the game. Monitor and help when necessary, noting down any errors for feedback.

6 When the students have finished, write on the board any errors you noticed and ask students to correct them.

5.1 Guy Fawkes

Activity	Role play
Language focus	Third conditional *wish/if only* + past perfect; second conditional
Preparation	Photocopy the worksheet for each group of three students. Cut it along the dotted lines.
Procedure	**1** Ask students to retell the story of Guy Fawkes. Ask individual students in turn to contribute a sentence to the story.
	2 Tell students they are going to do a role play in which they play the parts of Guy Fawkes and two of his friends. They are in prison trying to understand why their plot failed.
	3 Write *If only* + *catch* and *I wish* + *catch* on the board and elicit what Guy Fawkes would say *If only they hadn't caught me. I wish they hadn't caught me.*
	4 Divide the class into three groups, A, B and C. Student A is Guy Fawkes, B is Jim Boldwell and C is Jess Silverton. Give students their role cards and tell them to work together with a person from the same group to prepare their role. Monitor to offer help
	5 Put students into A, B, C pairs to do the role play. Tell students that Guy Fawkes should start the role play, Jim Boldwell should respond, then Jess Silverton should respond, using the ideas on the cards. Demonstrate using one group.
	6 Students practise their role plays. Monitor and help as necessary.
	7 Ask some groups to perform their role play for the class.

5.2 The best applicant

Activity	Group discussion
Language focus	*must(n't)*, *have to* and *need to*; *don't have to*, *don't need to* and *needn't*
Preparation	Photocopy the worksheet for each group of four students. Cut it along the dotted lines.
New vocabulary	*clown, amateur dramatics, applicant, first aid*
Procedure	**1** Brainstorm with the whole class what qualifications and qualities a clown needs and doesn't need. Write them on the board.
	2 Explain that a company called *Clowns Are Us* is looking for new employees to work as international clowns, travelling around the world, entertaining children in different countries.
	3 Divide the class into groups of four. Explain that they are going to read the advertisement that the company has produced. Hand out the advertisement and ask the groups to read it. Ask them if any of the qualifications and qualities from the brainstorming are mentioned.
	4 Tell students they are now going to read information about an applicant for the job. Hand out one applicant to each person in a group and tell them to think about why their applicant should be given the job.
	5 When the students have finished reading, tell them to discuss and agree who should be given the job. Explain that each student must try to convince the other members of their group that their candidate is the best one for the job. Give the students time to discuss this.
	6 Get feedback from the groups to find out which applicant each group decided on.

5.3 He can't have done that

Activity	Spot the untrue sentences
Language focus	*must have* and *can't have*; *could/may/might have*
Preparation	Photocopy the worksheet for each pair of students. Cut it in half along the dotted lines.
Procedure	**1** Say one untrue and one true sentence about yourself, e.g. *Last year I saw Brad Pitt in New York* and *Last week I bought a new pair of shoes.* Ask students to discuss which they think is true and which they think is false and why.
	2 Review the language of speculating about the past and elicit sentences using the verbs *must have, can't have, could, may* and *might have.* (*Brad Pitt could have been in New York last year. Our teacher might have been there.*)
	3 Tell the students that they are going to write ten sentences about themselves but that six must be true and four must be false. Explain that the false sentences should not be obviously false.
	4 Divide the class into two groups, A and B. Give each student in Group A Worksheet A and each student in Group B Worksheet B. Tell them to work together with a person from the same group to complete the sentences about themselves. They can write sentences about either student.
	5 Put students into groups of four with a pair of Students A and a pair of Students B. Explain the rules:

- Each group draws a noughts and crosses grid on a piece of paper.
- Students in Group A read their first sentence. Group B say whether or not they think the sentence is true using modal verbs of speculation.
- If they are right, they can put a nought in the grid, if they are wrong they can't.
- Students in Group B then read their first sentence and Group A discuss whether or not they think it is true.
- If they are right, they can put a cross in the grid, if they are wrong they can't.
- Play continues until either one of the teams has won a row on the grid or there are no more sentences left.

6.1 Is that right?

Activity	Identifying and correcting mistakes
Language focus	Reported speech
Preparation	Photocopy the worksheet for each pair of students.
Procedure	**1** Explain that students are going to see eight pairs of sentences each containing reported speech. In each pair both, one or neither of the sentences may contain a mistake. Explain that the mistakes are *only* in the reported speech structure.
	2 Put students into pairs and give each a worksheet. Students look at the sentences and decide if they are correct or not.
	3 Put pairs together into groups of four and ask them to compare their results. When they have agreed, they should correct the incorrect sentences.
	4 Check answers with the class.
Key	1 A ✔ B ✘ He refused, so she asked *to see* the manager. 2 A ✔ B ✔
	3 A ✔ B ✘ I explained *that he could walk* or take a bus.
	4 A ✘ The doctor suggested *that I take/took* more … B ✘ … he suggested *eating/that I ate* less.
	5 A ✔ B ✘ … and she told him *not to be* so stupid!
	6 A ✘ My father's in a bad mood. My brother *hopes (that) he cheers* up. B ✔ 7 A ✔ B ✔
	8 A ✘ Anna replied *that she would do* it at the weekend. B ✘ And she said ~~him~~ that she would do last week's too!

6.2 What was she wearing?

Activity	Pronunciation game
Language focus	Pronunciation; reported questions
Preparation	Photocopy the worksheet for each student. Cut it in half along the dotted lines.
Procedure	**1** Give each student Section 1 of the worksheet. Explain that they have seen a woman escaping after a robbery. You (the teacher) are the police officer and you are asking some questions, but not listening very carefully to the answers.
	2 Read the first question from Section 2 of the worksheet and ask students to look at the underlined (stressed) words on the answer sentence. Read the next question and elicit the stressed words for that answer (*long, blue*).
	3 Explain that you are going to read eight more questions, and students should underline the stressed words for each answer on their answer sheet. Read the questions, pausing for the students to underline the stressed words.
	4 Read the questions again, this time asking individual students to respond with the correct stress pattern.
	5 Put the students in pairs and hand out Section 2 of the worksheet. Ask students to change each question into reported speech, using various reporting verbs, e.g. … *wanted to know/asked/wondered what she was wearing*.
	6 Monitor and help as necessary.
Key	1 long blue dress 2 long blue 3 blue 4 She 5 long 6 dress 7 long 8 was 9 wearing 10 She was wearing a long blue dress.
	1 The police officer asked what she had been wearing. 2 He asked if/whether we could describe her dress again. 3 He asked if/whether she had been in her long yellow dress. 4 He asked if/whether we said the man was wearing a long blue dress. 5 He asked if/whether her sister had been wearing a short blue dress. 6 He asked if/whether she had been wearing jeans. 7 He asked if/whether it had been a mini skirt. 8 He asked if/whether she had been wearing a long blue dress. 9 He asked if/whether she had been buying that long blue dress. 10 He asked if/whether we could speak up.

6.3 We must have it done!

Activity	Sentence completion
Language focus	*get/have something done*
Preparation	Photocopy the worksheet for each pair of students. Cut it in half along the dotted lines.
New vocabulary	*mend, repair, tidy up, put back up, cut, fix, reconnect, take away, rebuild*
Procedure	**1** Explain that Bill and Sally have bought a new house. Students are going to look at two pictures – before and after the house has been repaired.
	2 Put students into pairs and hand out Picture 1 to each pair. Tell them to circle all the items that need to be repaired. Deal with any vocabulary issues.
	3 Point to one feature that needs to be repaired and ask *What does Sally say?* Elicit the answer, e.g. *We must have the door repainted*. Students work in their pairs and write similar sentences for the rest of the items (ten in total).
	4 Hand out Picture 2. Tell the students to write ten sentences, e.g. *We've had the door repainted*. Monitor and help as necessary.
	5 Check the answers with the whole class.
Key	Suggested sentences:
	We must have/get the windows fixed/mended/repaired.
	We must have/get the garden tidied up.
	We must have/get the TV aerial put back up.
	We must have/get the grass cut.
	We must have/get the roof fixed/mended/repaired.
	We must have/get the drain pipe fixed/mended/repaired.
	We must have/get the telephone line reconnected.
	We must have/get the rubbish taken away.
	We must have/get the garage rebuilt.

7.1 Off by heart

Activity	Pelmanism
Language focus	Idioms
Preparation	Photocopy the worksheet for each pair of students. Cut it into strips along the dotted lines.
Procedure	**1** Write *off by* _____ on the board and elicit the end of the idiom (*heart*). Elicit that *to know something off by heart* means to remember all the words without help.
	2 Put students into pairs and hand out the idiom strips. Explain that there are 12 idioms on the worksheet and they need to match the strips to complete the idioms. Monitor to offer help because three of the idioms are new.
	3 When the students have finished, elicit the new idioms and write them on the board. Elicit or teach the meaning: *cut to the chase* = get to the point, *let the cat out of the bag* = give away a secret, *have a fit* = get very angry
	4 Put students into small groups and ask them to keep one full set of strips. Tell them they are going to play a game:
	• All the strips are placed face down on the table in a square.
	• Students take turns to choose two strips.
	• If the strips make an idiom, they keep the idiom and have another turn. If the strips don't make an idiom, they put them back in exactly the same place and the student on their left has a turn.
	• The idea is to remember where the matching halves are.
	• The student with the most idioms at the end of the game is the winner.
	5 Students play the game. Monitor to check the game is being played correctly. Find out who won the most idioms.

7.2 Mendel's discovery

Activity	Information gap
Language focus	Passive structures
Preparation	Photocopy the worksheet for each pair of students. Cut it in half along the dotted lines.
New vocabulary	*characteristic*, *generation*, *descendent*, *dominant* and *recessive*
Procedure	**1** Explain that students are going to read a text about Gregor Mendel, the father of modern genetics, and ask questions to complete some missing information.
	2 Write *The experiments were done by* _____ on the board and elicit the question *Who were the experiments done by?*
	3 Divide the students into two groups, A and B. Give each student in Group A Card A and each student in Group B Card B. Tell students to work with a partner from the same group to write the questions they need to ask.
	4 Ask them to find a partner from the other group. Tell them to take turns to ask and answer their questions, and complete the text.
	5 When students have finished, they can compare their texts to make sure they are the same.
	6 Ask students to turn their sheet over and work in pairs to say as much information as they can remember about Mendel.

7.3 Act out!

Activity	Miming
Language focus	Phrasal verbs
Preparation	Photocopy the worksheet. Cut it into 24 strips along the dotted lines.
Procedure	**1** Tell students that they are going to play a game where they have to mime a phrasal verb. The rest of the class has to guess the correct verb.
	2 Demonstrate *take off* by pretending to take off your shoes and coat. Ask students to guess the phrasal verb. If you think your students may not know all the phrasal verbs, teach any that you think they will be unfamiliar with.
	3 Ask the first student to come to the front of the class, take a strip of paper, and act out their phrasal verb. When the correct phrasal verb has been given, ask the next student to come to the front and act out the next phrasal verb. Continue until all the students have had a go at acting out a phrasal verb or all the strips have been used up.
	4 Put students in pairs. Give each pair two or three phrasal verbs and tell them to write a sentence using each one. Give them a couple of minutes to do this.
	5 When they have finished, ask some pairs to read out their sentences. Ask other students to say whether the sentences are correct or not and whether the direct object (if relevant) is in the correct place.

Variations

1 In large classes or with shy students, this activity can be done in small groups. In this case, photocopy one worksheet for each group.

2 This activity could be made competitive by awarding students a point for each phrasal verb they guess correctly.

8.1 School subjects

Activity	Identifying stress; definitions
Language focus	Vocabulary; stressed syllables
Preparation	Photocopy the worksheet for each pair of students.
Procedure	**1** Put students into pairs and hand out the worksheets.
	2 Go through the subject names. Make sure the students understand them all.
	3 Say *history* and write it on the board. Ask the students to identify which is the stressed syllable. Elicit *history* and underline the stressed syllable on the board.
	4 Give pairs 10 minutes to underline the stressed syllables on the words. Encourage them to say the words out loud to help them decide which syllable is stressed. Monitor and help as necessary.
	5 Put pairs together into groups of four and ask students to compare and check their answers. If they have any differences, encourage them to say the words and decide on the correct pronunciation.
	6 Check answers with the class, and model and drill pronunciation of some words if necessary.
	7 Ask students to work individually and complete the definitions. They should then compare their definitions in pairs.
	8 Ask some students to read out their definitions to the class.
Key	**hi**story tech**no**logy soci**o**logy en**vi**ronment **po**etry **lit**erature **Ger**man **dra**ma eco**no**mics a**rith**metic **Eng**lish **cook**ery **phys**ics ge**og**raphy mathe**mat**ics re**li**gion **chem**istry bi**o**logy phi**lo**sophy **mus**ic com**pu**ting **sci**ence **pol**itics ac**coun**ting
	1 history 2 biology 3 geography 4 philosophy 5 mathematics, arithmetic 6 poetry, literature

8.2 How do you compare?

Activity	General knowledge quiz
Language focus	Vocabulary
Preparation	Photocopy the worksheet for each group of four to six students.
Procedure	**1** Divide the class into teams of four to six students.
	2 Explain that this quiz is a competition between the teams. Explain that a team of experts devised a series of questions that they considered the 'average' British 16/18-year-old (6th Form) should be able to answer. The quiz is a selection of the questions that were asked. Point out that the percentage (%) in brackets after each question is the number of British students who answered correctly. Tell students they are going to try to do better than the British students.
	3 Hand out the worksheets and give students a few minutes to read through the questions. Monitor and help with understanding.
	4 Set a time limit of about 15 minutes, then tell the teams to start. They should work quietly so that the other teams don't hear what they are discussing. Tell them to write down the group's answer for each question.
	5 After 15 minutes, stop the activity. Go through the quiz, eliciting the answers for each question from each team. Give teams two points for each correct answer. If they have got most of the answer correct, you could give one point. Check that the students have used the correct English versions of countries, names, etc.
	6 Tell the teams to add up their scores. Find out which team won, and whether they did better than the British students.
Key	1 Neil Armstrong 2 Dmitri Medvedev 3 10 cm 4 Pluto 5 Greece 6 The French Revolution 7 nine 8 USA/Canada 9 The Revelation (or The Apocalypse in students' own language) 10 Homer 11 Christianity, Islam, Buddhism 12 18, 34 13 France, Brazil, Russia, Pakistan, India 14 German 15 Uruguay, Paraguay, Bolivia, Chile, Brazil 16 300 million mps 17 Guernica 18 1948 19 New York 20 5

8.3 School rules

Activity	Information transfer
Language focus	*let* and *make*
Preparation	Photocopy the worksheet for each student. Cut it in half along the dotted lines.
Procedure	**1** Elicit or teach the word *boarding school* (a school where students live during school terms).
	2 Hand out the school rules and ask students to read them. Ask *What kind of school is it? Old-fashioned/modern? Strict? Do you think children will be happy here?* Elicit a range of ideas.
	3 Put students into pairs and hand out the letter. Explain that John Worthington is in his first term at the school. Tell students to read the letter he has written to his parents and notice that it has been edited by the Headmaster. Ask *Do you think John is happy at the school?*
	4 Students work in their pairs to use the information in the rules to complete the letter using *make* or *let*. You might want to review the difference in meaning between *make* and *let* before students do this.
	5 When the students have finished, ask different pairs to read sentences from the letter. Check the correct answers.
Key	1 let 2 make 3 make 4 let 5 let 6 make 7 let 8 make 9 let 10 let

Spooky

Activity	Song
Language focus	Review of language and vocabulary from Units 1–2
Preparation	Photocopy one sheet for each student. Get the recording ready. 3.28
Procedure	**1** Read the question with the class. Elicit or explain the meaning of *spooky* (scary). Play the song and ask students to listen and read the words. Elicit reactions (whether they like the song or not) and ask them to explain why.
	2 Ask students to work in pairs to choose the correct answer. Check answers and ask students to read out lines that support their answer.
	3 Ask students to work in pairs to find the words. Check answers and explain that *a-* is added before *winking* to help the word fit the rhythm of the song.
	4 Ask students to work in pairs to find the verbs. Check answers with the whole class.
	5 Look at the line with the class and elicit or explain that *think* is used here with a different meaning. Explain that *think* with the meaning 'opinion' is not used in the continuous form, but *think* with the meaning 'actively have thoughts' is used in the continuous form because it is an activity.
Key	2 b 3 a) groovy b) guessing c) winking d) ghost 4 a) keep me guessing b) know, seem

Every Breath You Take

Activity	Song
Language focus	Revision of language and vocabulary from Units 3–4
Preparation	Photocopy one sheet for each student. Get the recording ready. 3.29
Procedure	**1** Play the song and ask students to listen and read the words. Elicit their reactions and any information that the students have understood about the singer and who the song is for.
	2 Ask students to work in pairs to choose the correct answer. Check answers and ask students to read out words or lines that support their answer, e.g. *my poor heart, I feel so cold*, etc.
	3 Ask students to work individually to find the words and compare their answer with a partner. Check the answers.
	4 Students work in pairs to find a verb in the future continuous.
Key	2 a 3 a) bond, vow b) aches c) fake d) embrace 4 I'll be watching you.

Hanging on the Telephone

Activity	Song
Language focus	Revision of language and vocabulary from Units 5–6
Preparation	Photocopy one sheet for each student. Get the recording ready. 3.30
Procedure	**1** Read the question with the class. Elicit or explain that *hanging* means 'waiting'. Play the song and ask students to listen and read the words. Elicit their reactions and ask them whether they have ever felt the way the singer feels.
	2 Ask students to work in pairs to choose the correct answers. Check answers and ask students to read out the lines in the song that support their answers.
	3 Ask students to work individually to find the words and compare their answers with a partner. Check the answers.
	4 Ask students to work in pairs to find a reporting verb + object + infinitive. Check answers, then ask students what other verbs can fit this pattern (*advise, ask, invite, promise, warn*).
Key	2 a) making b) is in love with c) see 3 a) ignore b) sensation c) affection d) hang up 4 I told you to ignore.

True Colours

Activity	Song
Language focus	Revision of language and vocabulary from Units 7–8
Preparation	Photocopy one sheet for each student. Get the recording ready. 3.31
Procedure	**1** Play the song and ask students to listen and read the words. Elicit their reactions. Discuss the question with the class and elicit or explain that someone's true colours are their true feelings or character.
	2 Ask students to work in pairs to choose the correct summary. Check answers and ask students to read out the lines in the song that support their answers.
	3 Ask students to work individually to match the words with the definitions and then compare their answers with a partner. Check answer with the whole class.
	4 Ask students to work in pairs to find examples of *make* and *let*. Check their answers.
Key	2 c 3 1 b 2 d 3 a 4 c 4 make you feel small, don't be afraid to let them show

1 Food search

Student A

T	G	U	P	O	S	T	K	J	U
T	H	E	D	H	N	W	R	Z	C
M	S	Z	U	V	I	F	A	C	A
F	G	I	U	H	A	E	S	N	X
N	Z	W	S	C	T	E	V	V	T
B	A	W	O	N	N	L	U	M	A
C	O	O	D	L	O	E	K	A	T
T	K	B	P	U	C	C	N	D	X
E	E	R	G	A	S	I	D	U	C
D	I	S	L	I	K	E	C	X	R

1 What does your favourite meal _____ of?

2 Do you agree or _____ with people who say we shouldn't eat animals?

3 Do you read food labels to see what the food _____ before buying it?

4 Are there any foods which you _____ to try, but haven't yet tried?

5 Are there any foods which you _____ in the past, but now love?

6 When you _____ sad or depressed, is there a food you eat to improve your mood?

Student B

Z	E	O	F	K	M	I	R	P	K
G	O	T	C	K	N	E	E	U	N
G	O	A	S	C	J	N	M	K	I
E	L	H	L	A	S	C	E	A	H
A	M	U	B	H	T	Z	M	K	T
T	D	I	T	H	Q	I	B	E	X
E	R	E	T	T	A	M	E	G	D
U	I	R	R	K	V	S	R	Z	E
T	A	K	E	U	Q	J	I	S	O
B	X	W	N	E	N	S	I	R	L

1 If you had your own restaurant, which dishes would you _____ on the menu?

2 Can you _____ the first time you ate a new or special food? How did it _____?

3 Do you _____ all food served in schools should be healthy or should there be junk food too?

4 Does your diet _____ vitamins and minerals or do you eat healthily?

5 Does it _____ to you if food is produced in the local area or transported from far away?

New Inspiration 4 **PHOTOCOPIABLE**

2 Gadget crossword

Student A

Clues

3 _____

4 _____

9 _____

11 _____

12 _____

14 _____

15 _____

16 _____

17 _____

³SNOOZEBUTTON

⁴ALARMCLOCK

⁹KEYRING

¹¹TELEPHONE

¹²PEDOMETER

¹⁴COFFEEMAKER

¹⁵KETTLE ¹⁶BREADKNIFE

¹⁷TOASTER

Student B

Clues

1 _____

2 _____

5 _____

6 _____

7 _____

8 _____

9 _____

10 _____

13 _____

¹B
²CHEESEGRATER
³
⁴BOTTLEOPENER
⁵PHONECHARGER
⁶CORKSCREW
⁷DIGITAL
⁸SAUCEPAN
⁹KEY
¹⁰TINOPENER
¹¹T
¹²PAN
¹³B
¹⁴CAMERA
¹⁵ER
¹⁶ERA
¹⁷A

 New Inspiration 4 **PHOTOCOPIABLE**

3 Relationship problems

Problem	Advice
1 Help! I'm in love with my best friend's boyfriend. (Gemma, 15)	**A** You've got to stop *comparing/to compare* yourself to her and just enjoy *being/to be* yourself. (Simon, 14)
2 All my mates have got great girlfriends, and I'm the only single one! What should I do? (Chris, 15)	**B** If you want to keep *going/to go* out with her, promise *contacting/to contact* her at least twice a week. Explain to her that calling and texting is quite expensive! (Joseph, 16)
3 I'm so jealous of my best friend. Why is she so much more popular and confident than me? 😞 (Alice, 14)	**C** Don't risk *losing/to lose* her friendship. You need *finding/to find* yourself a single guy instead. 😐 (Anna, 16)
4 My sister wants me to go to a party with her but I'm not sure. I don't like her friends, and we often argue. (Amy, 16)	**D** If you do decide *going/to go*, avoid *getting/to get* annoyed, and focus on having a good time. (Maria, 17)
5 Jane has been my girlfriend for six months now, but I still often think about my ex-girlfriend. I think I'd like to see her again. (James, 16)	**E** Try *joining/to join* a club to meet new people, but don't expect *meeting/to meet* the girl of your dreams immediately! 😊 (Matt, 16)
6 My girlfriend's always complaining that I don't call her or text her often enough. 😣 (Jack, 15)	**F** Don't pretend *being/to be* happy in your relationship if you're not. Be honest and choose *being/to be* with one or the other, not both. (Vicky, 16)

1 A winter wonderland

A

Harbin is the capital city of Heilongjiang province in the north of China. The winter months are extremely cold in Harbin and often reach temperatures of (1)_____. However, the city has been celebrating its frozen winter climate since 1963 by holding an ice festival. This now takes place every year and visitors have been coming to the annual festival for (3)_____. The festival begins in January and lasts for approximately one month. There are two main sections to the festival which occur on opposite sides of the Songhua River.

The smaller section consists of beautifully carved snow sculptures. Artists from all over the world have been presenting their work in this section since (5)_____. Teams of artists from different countries enter their snow sculptures into a competition to win the title of snow sculpture artists of the year. The competition has been running since 1995 and has been entered by a variety of nations including Finland, Canada and Germany.

The main section of the festival consists of (7)_____ made from blocks of ice. There are trains you can sit on, bridges you can walk over and (9)_____ you can enter and look around. These amazing life sized constructions are lit up by coloured lights which twinkle in the cold dark sky. For over a month, the city is brought to life as it embraces the cold of winter.

B

Harbin is the capital city of Heilongjiang province in the north of China. The winter months are extremely cold in Harbin and often reach temperatures of -30ºC. However, the city has been celebrating its frozen winter climate since (2)_____ by holding an ice festival. This now takes place every year and visitors have been coming to the annual festival for the last 21 years. The festival begins in January and lasts for approximately (4)_____. There are two main sections to the festival which occur on opposite sides of the Songhua River.

The smaller section consists of beautifully carved snow sculptures. Artists from all over the world have been presenting their work in this section since the annual festival began. Teams of artists from different countries enter their snow sculptures into a competition to win the title of snow sculpture artists of the year. The competition has been running since (6)_____ and has been entered by a variety of nations including Finland, Canada and Germany.

The main section of the festival consists of huge structures made from blocks of ice. There are (8)_____ you can sit on, bridges you can walk over and castles you can enter and look around. These amazing life sized constructions are lit up by (10)_____ which twinkle in the cold dark sky. For over a month, the city is brought to life as it embraces the cold of winter.

 New Inspiration 4 **PHOTOCOPIABLE**

2 Runner and writer race

2

1) I _____ English for five years. (learn)

2) I _____ always _____ to be a film star. (want)

3) I _____ more than three different countries in my life. (visit)

4) I _____ in my town since I was born. (live)

5) I _____ my hobby for over five years. (do)

6) I _____ spicy food many times. (eat)

7) I _____ volleyball since I was a child. (play)

8) I _____ more than two books this year. (read)

9) I _____ my favourite football team for more than two years. (support)

10) I _____ to the cinema once this month. (be)

New Inspiration 4 **PHOTOCOPIABLE**

2

3 Verb families

make	made	made	making
show	showed	shown	showing
draw	drew	drawn	drawing
write	wrote	written	writing
eat	ate	eaten	eating
take	took	taken	taking
forget	forgot	forgotten	forgetting
appear	appeared	appeared	appearing

 New Inspiration 4 **PHOTOCOPIABLE**

3

1 Compare the planets

Student A

**Mercury
Fact File**

Compared to the other planets in our Solar System, Mercury is small. Its
diameter is 4,878 kilometres, which is 0.06 of the Earth's size.
Mercury is 58 million kilometres from the Sun and while this may sound
like a long distance it is close if you compare it to other distances in space.
This explains why Mercury is so hot. Temperatures on Mercury can vary;
the hottest temperature is 427°C while the lowest temperature is a bitterly
cold -184°C. The surface of Mercury is barren and it is covered with
deep craters, which are so deep that the sunlight never reaches the bottom.
Days on Mercury are very long because Mercury spins at a slow speed. It
travels at 49 kilometres per second and one day is the same as 58.65 days on
Earth. As a result of this, one year on Mercury is 88 Earth days which means
that there are fewer than two days in each year!
The first space probe went to Mercury in 1973. The Mariner probe was sent
by the USA and it was discovered that nothing could ever live there because
there is no water and no atmosphere on the planet. Mercury has no moons
and no rings.

incredibly

approximately
incredibly
partly; greatly

incredibly
extremely
incredibly
approximately

possibly

Student B

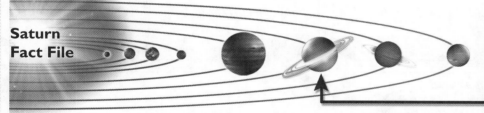

**Saturn
Fact File**

Saturn – also known as the Ringed Planet – is the second largest planet in our
Solar System – only Jupiter is bigger. It is 1,425 kilometres from the Sun and
is best known for its rings which are made up of dust and rocks. Saturn is
120,000 kilometres across which means that it is nine times bigger than the
Earth. It is made up of gases, mainly hydrogen and helium and this means
that it is light. If you could find an ocean big enough to hold it, Saturn would
float. The average temperature on Saturn is an extremely cold -170°C.
One day on Saturn lasts for ten and a half Earth hours; this is because Saturn
rotates at a fast speed – it moves at 9.64 kilometres every second. On the
other hand, because it is far from the Sun it takes Saturn 29½ Earth years
to complete an orbit.
In 1979, the space probe Pioneer 11 travelled to Saturn. It sent photographs of
Saturn back to Earth. Later probes sent information about Saturn's rings and
moons back to Earth. About 46 moons have been recorded around Saturn
and this is more than most of the other planets.

approximately
largely

completely
incredibly
actually

approximately
incredibly

far

New Inspiration 4 **PHOTOCOPIABLE**

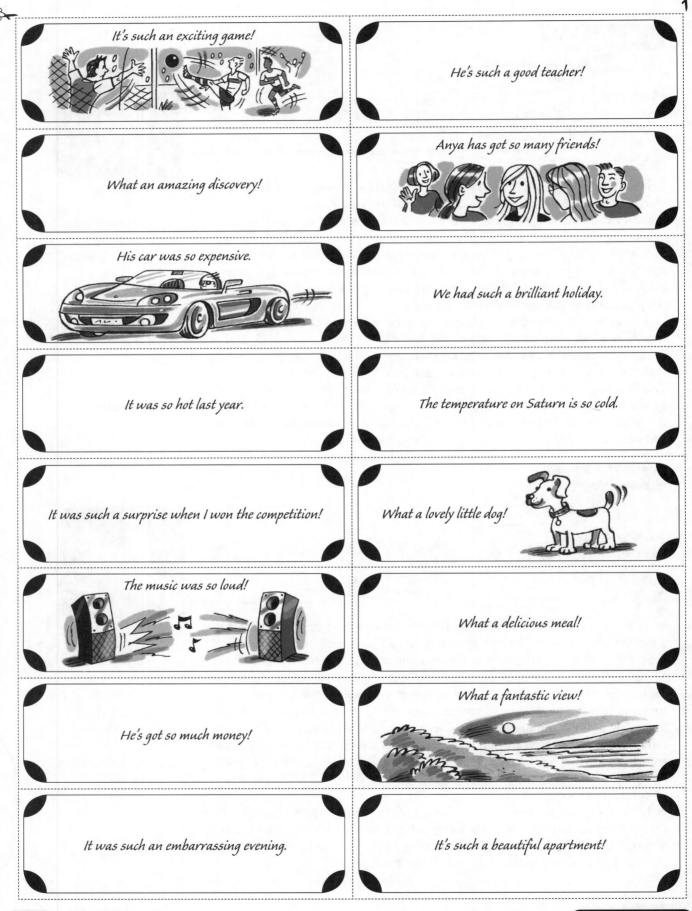

It's such an exciting game!

He's such a good teacher!

What an amazing discovery!

Anya has got so many friends!

His car was so expensive.

We had such a brilliant holiday.

It was so hot last year.

The temperature on Saturn is so cold.

It was such a surprise when I won the competition!

What a lovely little dog!

The music was so loud!

What a delicious meal!

He's got so much money!

What a fantastic view!

It was such an embarrassing evening.

It's such a beautiful apartment!

   New Inspiration 4 **PHOTOCOPIABLE**

A

Venus Viewing Voyager Cost – $10,000

Welcome to the **Venus Viewing Voyager**, the only space station that is permanently in orbit around the most beautiful planet, Venus. This luxurious hotel with 50 en-suite bedrooms floats just two kilometres above Venus and so every room has a view of the planet of love. We offer rooms with and without gravity control and so you can choose whether you want to float in your room or not. Our team of robotic staff are always available to serve you whatever the time of day. To relax on board the Voyager you can try swimming in our outside Space Floatation Tank, or you can play space tennis in one of our unique gravity-free tennis courts on the roof of the Voyager. Alternatively, you could do nothing but watch Venus rotate slowly below you with its orange volcanoes and brown craters. Whatever you want or need we can do it all for you on the **Venus Viewing Voyager**.

Flights leave from Siberia in Russia and it takes three weeks to fly to Venus.

B

Ride the Asteroid Belt! Cost – $10,000

Are you brave enough to experience the most exciting space ride? Our space tours give you the most thrilling experience that you can imagine. Rockets blast off from the Gobi desert in Mongolia and take you to the busiest asteroid belt in our galaxy. If you like a challenge and are not afraid of a bumpy ride then this is the space holiday for you! After take-off we go straight to the Trojan Asteroid Belt, only 100 light years from Jupiter. Our journey only takes one day as our super-fast rockets use the latest technology. We arrive at the asteroid belt and immediately go for a drive through the busiest part of the belt. It is not for the faint hearted as the journey can be turbulent and occasionally the rockets are hit by smaller asteroids. Later this year, we are going to give one lucky passenger the opportunity to fly the rocket through the asteroid belt with the help of one of our pilots.

C

Galactic Tour Cost – $15,000

This wonderful tour gives you the chance to experience three different places in space in two months. Using solar sails our rockets fly at high speeds which allow you to see many different sights. *The Explorer* rocket takes off from the Mojave Desert in the United States and usually goes straight to the Moon. However, on the next tour we are going to orbit the Earth before flying to the moon, giving you the opportunity to view the whole planet. When we arrive on the moon you will have three hours to experience the feeling of being weightless whilst exploring some of the craters! After the Moon, we continue on to Mars. We do not land on Mars, but we land on one of its moons, Phobos. From there you will be able to see the beauty of Mars, the red planet. From Phobos we fly back out to space and we orbit Saturn, the ringed planet, before returning to Earth.

D

Space Elevator Cost – $5,000

Do you want a different holiday? Are you looking for something different to sun and sand? Why not take the Space Elevator to the first hotel on the Moon? You can find the Space Elevator in the middle of the Australian Outback. By taking the Space Elevator you can travel to the Moon in just under six hours without flying at all. When you arrive on the Moon you will be met by one of our astronauts who will drive you in a lunar buggy to the Lunar Lodge, the only hotel there. In the hotel you will live like the first astronauts did, sleeping in shared quarters. Many of our guests like to relax by going on long moonwalks and moon-golf is also very popular with our guests. We also offer guided tours of the Sea of Tranquillity, crater diving and tours of the spot where Neil Armstrong first landed on the Moon!

Creating the Perfect Body

In 2020, people will be designing their perfect face and body in the comfort of their own living room. Cosmetic companies will have designed a system which allows each customer to choose exactly how they will look. The system will use a laser scanner to create a picture of the whole body and will then change and improve that picture to produce a perfect face and form. Customers will be able to choose what they want and see just how it will look. Once the customer has decided on a face and body, they will transfer the information into robots that carry out the surgery. The companies will have made tiny instruments that are put into the patient's body and moved around by the robots using magnetic fields. This system will remove the mistakes that sometimes happen in cosmetic surgery today.

The Briefcase Brain Scanner

In 2020, psychologists will be using brain scanners to treat patients with mental illnesses. Medical companies will have produced a brain scanner that fits neatly into a briefcase and can be transported from one place to another. These brain scanners will be used to activate or calm areas of the brain that are not working properly. In depressed patients the part of the brain that controls joy is switched off, but patients will be trained to use a scanner to turn it on. The scanners will have an effect on brain chemicals called neuropeptides. The companies will have designed the scanners to use these brain chemicals to change emotions. Shy people will be living different lives because they will be able to use the scanners to boost the areas of the brain responsible for confidence.

On a Faster Plane

In 2020, people will be flying from London to New York in just 50 minutes. NASA and Boeing will have jointly created this space-age plane which will fly at 60,000 feet and at an incredible five times the speed of sound. Because the plane will be flying at such speeds the nose and wings will be protected by heat-resistant titanium. This also means that the plane can't have front facing windows so they will have designed a system where the pilot uses TV images to navigate the plane. The pilots will be trained to use this new system by the designers. Tickets to fly on such a plane will be very expensive initially but if the plane becomes mass produced, the fare will be much cheaper. This means that this super plane may even become an option for the budget traveller in the long distant future.

 New Inspiration 4 **PHOTOCOPIABLE**

4

2 The airport debate

Student A –
The Local Resident

You have been a resident of Morkham for over 20 years and many of your family members have also settled here. You are undecided about whether the airport expansion should go ahead or not because you can see both a clear advantage and a clear disadvantage.

Advantage – employment opportunities for the community

Disadvantage – overhead noise from the aircraft using the new runways

Decide exactly what you want to say before the meeting begins.

Student B –
The Local Councillor

You are a member of the Morkham local council and you have been given the authority to give the airport expansion plans the go ahead or not. You need to listen to the views of everyone at the meeting and ask them questions so that you can make the right decision.

Decide exactly what you want to say and what questions you need to ask before the meeting begins.

Student C –
The Environmentalist

You have been working for an environmental charity for the last ten years and are completely against the plans to expand the airport. You have conducted a lot of research on the damaging effects of carbon emissions from planes on the environment. You are also extremely worried about the countryside and natural habitats that will be destroyed for the runways to be built.

Decide exactly what you want to say before the meeting begins.

Student D –
The Budget Traveller

You have travelled extensively throughout your life and are in favour of the airport expansion. Your belief is that because it allows people to experience other cultures, it helps maintain peace and understanding across the world. This is very important in a world where so much conflict takes place between different nations. Expanding the airport will increase the number of flights and reduce the prices, so it will allow more people to travel.

Decide exactly what you want to say before the meeting begins.

New Inspiration 4 **PHOTOCOPIABLE**

4

3 If I were a bird ...

 New Inspiration 4 **PHOTOCOPIABLE**

A GUY FAWKES

Why you failed
- too much noise
- too many people
- someone in the group was not reliable

Life if you hadn't been caught
- different life
- become Prime Minister
- have a family (wife and children)

What's next?
- try to escape
- be friends with the guards
- pretend to be ill
- get explosives from visitors and bomb part of the jail

B JIM BOLDWELL

Why you failed
- too much noise: not true, really careful (explain)
- too many people: needed a lot of people to carry the barrels containing explosives
- someone in the group was not reliable: who? (think of different people)

Life if you hadn't been caught
- different life: would live on the coast, not in London (explain why)
- become Prime Minister: discuss why Guy wouldn't have been a good one
- have a family: no one would have you (explain why)

What's next?
- try to escape: agree with this
- be friends with the guards: imagine how
- pretend to be ill: agree to do this
- get explosives from visitors and bomb part of the jail: what about us?

C JESS SILVERSTON

Why you failed
- too much noise: remember noises you made
- too many people: agree with Jim about the number of people (add an argument)
- someone in the group was not reliable: mention names of people who could have betrayed you and say why

Life if you hadn't been caught
- different life: go to the coast with Jim (explain why)
- become Prime Minister: disagree with Jim
- have a family: you would not get married (explain why)

What's next?
- try to escape: also agree to escape (imagine how)
- be friends with the guards: prefer to kill the guards (explain how)
- pretend to be ill: agree (explain what illness you could fake)
- get explosives from visitors and bomb part of the jail: agree with Jim, it would kill you

2 The best applicant

Clown wanted for international parties!

Do you love life? Do you like to travel? Do you love having fun? If the answer to all of these questions is **yes**, then *Clowns Are Us* wants to hear from you. We are looking for a clown to join our growing company which sends clowns to children's parties anywhere in the world. We provide entertainment for children of the rich and famous at different locations around the world.

You need to have experience of working with children and you must be physically fit. You need to have a degree so that you can get a visa for international travel. You also have to be prepared to travel as the position requires at least one trip abroad a week. A driving licence would also be an advantage so that you can drive to the parties from the airport. You will also need to have safety training before you take the position.

Send your CV and covering letter to:

The Managing Director, Clowns Are Us, Circus Lane, North London.

Start date: as soon as possible

Candidate A: Alexander Boon

Alexander is a former businessman. He used to be an accountant for a multi-national company and so is very good with numbers and money. He made a lot of money and so was able to retire at the age of 45. He is now 50 and is bored, especially because he has no family. He speaks three foreign languages: Japanese, Spanish and French, and has a lot of experience of travelling to other countries. He has a few health problems and had a minor heart attack last year but has made a full recovery now.

Candidate B: Jo Deasley

Jo is aged 32 and is a busy mother with three children. She loves her children and has a very good relationship with them. As a result of this she doesn't want to travel too much. She is happily married and her husband can look after the children while she is away. She loves singing and dancing and can play the guitar very well. She speaks basic Spanish and also has a driving licence.

Candidate C: Chris Murray

Chris is aged 25 and works in a primary school, helping children as a learning assistant. He loves his job because he really loves working with children. He is very good at his current job and has very good references. He has completed a first-aid course and is very confident in this. He doesn't have a degree. He is able to drive and he loves all sports. His favourite sport is football and he plays every day. Chris also really enjoys scuba diving and when he learnt how to do this he did a safety training course.

Candidate D: Doctor Donna Murray

Donna is 21 years old and has just finished a PhD in Spanish Literature at the University of Foreign Languages in London. She speaks French, Spanish, Chinese and Russian. She has never worked with children before and isn't sure how she would cope with lots of screaming children. She has a very positive outlook on life and in her spare time she is a member of an amateur dramatics group. She has experience of living abroad as she spent time in France and Spain as part of her degree. She is going to go travelling in South America for six weeks but is very interested in the job.

   New Inspiration 4 **PHOTOCOPIABLE**

3 He can't have done that

Group A

1 _____ has never _____ .

2 When _____ was younger he/she always used to _____ .

3 _____ best holiday was _____ .

4 At the moment _____ is reading _____ .

5 Last year _____ saw _____ .

6 The worst film _____ has ever seen _____ .

7 _____ parents were really angry when _____ .

8 The last film _____ saw was _____ .

9 The last time _____ did something really exciting was _____ .

10 Last weekend _____ .

Group B

1 _____ was really angry when _____ .

2 When _____ was younger he/she never used to _____ .

3 _____ worst holiday was _____ .

4 The best book that _____ has ever read is _____ .

5 Last week _____ bought _____ .

6 The best film _____ has ever seen _____ .

7 _____ parents were really pleased when he/she _____ .

8 The last CD _____ bought or downloaded was _____ .

9 Last year _____ went to _____ .

10 Yesterday _____ .

New Inspiration 4 **PHOTOCOPIABLE**

Sentence	Correct ✓	Incorrect ✗
1 **A** She asked the waiter to turn the music down. **B** He refused, so she asked that she see the manager.		
2 **A** When he left he promised that he would email me when he arrived home … **B** … and he promised that he would phone me every week.		
3 **A** I explained to the visitor that there was a good restaurant in the town centre. **B** I explained him to walk or take a bus.		
4 **A** The doctor suggested me to take more exercise … **B** … and he suggested me eating less.		
5 **A** The boy asked the girl to go to the cinema with him … **B** … and she told him that he not be so stupid!		
6 **A** My father's in a bad mood. My brother hopes he cheer up. **B** He suggested that we take him out at the weekend.		
7 **A** Anna's teacher reminded her to do her homework. **B** And he reminded her that she hadn't done last week's yet.		
8 **A** Anna replied to do it at the weekend. **B** And she said him that she would do last week's too!		

 New Inspiration 4 **PHOTOCOPIABLE**

2 What was she wearing?

Section 1

1 She was wearing a <u>long</u> <u>blue</u> <u>dress</u>.

2 She was wearing a long blue dress.

3 She was wearing a long blue dress.

4 She was wearing a long blue dress.

5 She was wearing a long blue dress.

6 She was wearing a long blue dress.

7 She was wearing a long blue dress.

8 She was wearing a long blue dress.

9 She was wearing a long blue dress.

10 She was wearing a long blue dress.

Section 2

1 What was she wearing?

2 Can you describe her dress again?

3 Was she in her long yellow dress?

4 You say the man was wearing a long blue dress?

5 Was her sister wearing a short blue dress?

6 So was she wearing jeans?

7 Was it a mini skirt?

8 So she wasn't wearing a long blue dress?

9 So was she buying this long blue dress?

10 Sorry, I'm a bit deaf today. Can you speak up?

Picture 1

telephone line
TV aerial
roof
drain pipe
garage
grass
rubbish
garden

Picture 2

New Inspiration 4 **PHOTOCOPIABLE**

be under	the weather
keep	it up
be a	guinea pig
touch	wood
know	the ropes
be in	the red
have	a fit
give someone	the sack
let the cat	out of the bag
pull someone's	leg
cut to	the chase
be down	to earth

A

Our understanding of genetic inheritance was established through experiments with pea plants. The experiments were done by an Austrian monk called Gregor Mendel in (1)_____. It is because of this work that he is thought to be the father of modern genetics. Mendel spent many years of his life as a teacher and was known to want (3)_____ but was unable to pass the exam.

It was during the middle of his life that Mendel began his groundbreaking research. He studied seven basic characteristics (5)_____ and by following these characteristics through a number of generations discovered three basic laws of inheritance, which are:

1 The inheritance of each characteristic is determined by units (now known to be genes) that are passed on to (7)_____ in an identical form.

2 An individual inherits one of these units from each parent for each characteristic. One unit is dominant and one is recessive.

3 A characteristic may not be shown in an individual because it is recessive but can still be passed on to the next generation.

These findings were published in (9)_____ but were sadly ignored until after Mendel's death. It was not until 1900 that he was discovered to have revealed the secrets of heredity.

B

Our understanding of genetic inheritance was established through experiments with pea plants. The experiments were done by an Austrian monk called Gregor Mendel in the 19th century. It is because of this work that he is thought to be (2)_____. Mendel spent many years of his life as a teacher and was known to want a teaching qualification but was unable to pass the exam.

It was during the middle of his life that Mendel began (4)_____. He studied seven basic characteristics of the pea plant and by following these characteristics through a number of generations discovered three basic laws of inheritance, which are:

1 The inheritance of each characteristic is determined by (6)_____ (now known to be genes) that are passed on to descendents in an identical form.

2 An individual inherits one of these units from each parent for each characteristic. One unit is dominant and one is recessive.

3 A characteristic may not be shown in an individual because it is recessive but can still be passed on to (8)_____.

These findings were published in 1886 but were sadly ignored until after Mendel's death. It was not until 1900 that he was discovered to have (10)_____.

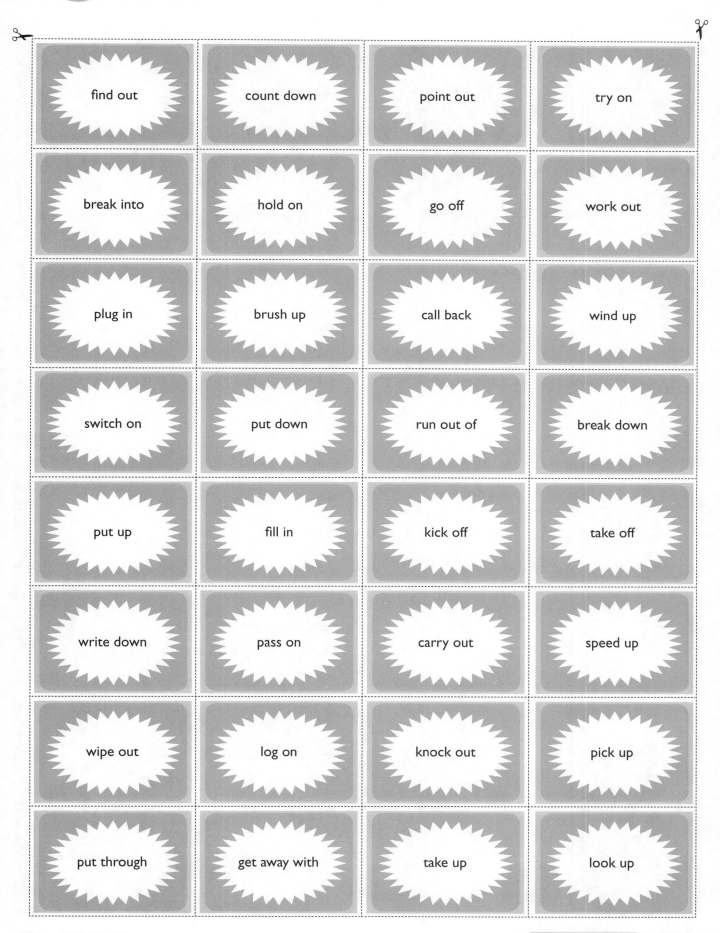

find out	count down	point out	try on
break into	hold on	go off	work out
plug in	brush up	call back	wind up
switch on	put down	run out of	break down
put up	fill in	kick off	take off
write down	pass on	carry out	speed up
wipe out	log on	knock out	pick up
put through	get away with	take up	look up

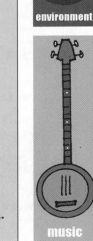

SYLLABLE STRESS

<u>hi</u>story	technology	sociology	environment
poetry	literature	German	drama
economics	arithmetic	English	cookery
physics	geography	mathematics	religion
chemistry	biology	philosophy	music
computing	science	politics	accounting

DEFINITIONS

1 _____ is the study of things in the past.

2 _____ is the study of living things.

3 _____ is the study of the world, countries and continents.

4 _____ is the study of ideas.

5 _____ and _____ are the study of numbers.

6 _____ and _____ are the study of the written word.

New Inspiration 4 **PHOTOCOPIABLE**

1 Who was the first man to set foot on the Moon? (100%)

2 Who is the President of Russia? (89%)

3 The two shorter sides of a right-angle triangle are 8cm and 6cm respectively. Calculate the length of the third side. (99%)

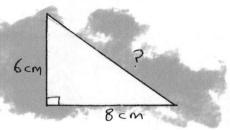

4 What was discovered in 1930: Pluto, Venus or Mars? (80%)

5 In which country were the modern Olympic Games first held? (70%)

6 1989 was the 200th anniversary of which major European event? (25%)

7 How many symphonies did Beethoven write? (31%)

8 Which two countries share the longest border in the world? (23%)

9 What is the last book of the New Testament? (44%)

10 Who wrote 'The Odyssey'? (30%)

11 What are the three most practised religions in the world? (14%)

12 What are the two missing numbers in this sequence: 3, 4, 6, 10, ___, ___, 66? (76%)

13 In what countries are these rivers mainly found? Seine, Amazon, Ob, Indus, Ganges (0%)

14 What nationality is the present Pope? (89%)

15 Name three countries that border Argentina. (35%)

16 What is the approximate speed of light in metres per second? (32%)

17 Which of his paintings did Pablo Picasso **not** allow to be returned to Spain while President Franco's government was in power? (6%)

18 When was the state of Israel founded? (5%)

19 Where is Harlem? (63%)

20 How many athletic events are there in a pentathlon? (82%)

School Rules

1   You will get up when the bell rings at 6 o'clock.

2   All boys will have a cold shower before breakfast.

3   Lessons are from 8.00 to 5.00 every day, except from 1.30 to 3.30 when you may choose to play rugby or football.

4   There is a break for lunch from 12.30 to 1.00.

5   There are lessons all day on Saturday. There are no sports in the afternoon.

6   You may have a free day on Sunday, but you must do your week's homework.

7   You may write one letter a week to your parents. This will be checked by the Headmaster.

8   You will be in bed by 8.00. The lights will then go out. There will be no talking.

    If you disobey any of these rules you will be punished.

Dear Mum and Dad,

I have been here a week now. I'm sorry I haven't written before, but they only

(1)_____ us write one letter a week.

It's really ~~awful~~ *wonderful* here. They (2)_____ us get up at 6 in the morning and have a cold

shower before breakfast. They (3)_____ us study all day except in the afternoon

when they (4)_____ us choose between playing rugby and football. I ~~hate~~ *love* both

those games! Although they (5)_____ us have a free day on Sunday they still

(6)_____ us do all our homework.

They ~~only~~ (7)_____ us have half an hour for lunch, which ~~is not nearly long enough~~ *more than enough*.
And the food is really ~~horrible~~ *super*.

Then they (8)_____ us go to bed at 8, and they won't (9)_____ us talk after

lights out.

Please, ~~don't make~~ (10)_____ me stay here. I can't think of a ~~worse~~ *better* place to be.

Your loving son

John

Dear Mr and Mrs Worthington.
John is settling in nicely and seems to be very happy.
The Headmaster

     New Inspiration 4 **PHOTOCOPIABLE**

Song: Spooky

1 Look at the title of the song. What does *Spooky* mean?
Listen to the song and read the words.

SPOOKY

In the cool of the evening
When everything is getting kind of groovy
You call me up and ask me
Would I like to go with you and see a movie?
First I say no, I've got some plans for tonight
And then I stop and say all right
Love is kind of crazy with a spooky little boy like you

You always keep me guessing
I never seem to know what you are thinking
And if a girl looks at you
It's for sure your little eye will be a-winking
I get confused, I never know where I stand
And then you smile and hold my hand
Love is kind of crazy with a spooky little boy like you
Spooky

If you decide some day
To stop this little game that you are playing
I'm gonna tell you all the things
My heart's been a-dying to be saying
Just like a ghost you've been haunting my dreams
But know I know you're not what you seem
Love is kind of crazy with a spooky little boy like you
Spooky

Oh oh oh spooky
Mmm spooky
Oh oh oh spooky

2 Read the song again and choose the best summary.
Tick ✓ the correct box.

a) The songwriter doesn't really like the boy. ☐

b) The songwriter likes the boy but doesn't
understand him. ☐

c) The songwriter is angry with the boy. ☐

3 Find words in the song with the following meanings.

a) exciting (old-fashioned) _____

b) trying to find out the answer _____

c) closing one eye _____

d) a spirit of a dead person _____

4 Find in the song the following:

a) a verb + gerund _____

b) Two verbs that are not used in the continuous form.

_____

5 Look at the line: *I never seem to know what you are thinking.*

Why is *think* used in the continuous form here?

_____

_____

_____

Song: Every Breath You Take

1 Listen to the song and read the words.

EVERY BREATH YOU TAKE

Every breath you take
Every move you make
Every bond you break, every step you take
I'll be watching you

Every single day
And every word you say
Every game you play, every night you stay
I'll be watching you

Oh, can't you see
You belong to me
How my poor heart aches
With every step you take
Every move you make
And every vow you break
Every smile you fake, every claim you stake
I'll be watching you

Since you've been gone I've been lost without a trace
I dream at night, I can only see your face
I look around but it's you I can't replace
I feel so cold and I long for your embrace
I keep crying, baby, baby, please

Oh, can't you see
You belong to me
How my poor heart aches
With every step you take
Every move you make
And every vow you break
Every smile you fake, every claim you stake
I'll be watching you
Every move you make, every step you take
I'll be watching you
I'll be watching you
I'll be watching you
I'll be watching you
I'll be watching you

2 How would you describe the feeling of the song? Tick ✓ the correct box.

a) sad because a relationship is over ☐

b) happy because a new relationship is beginning ☐

c) angry because someone has left ☐

3 Find words in the song with the following meanings.

a) a promise (2 words) _____ , _____

b) when something is painful _____

c) pretend to do something _____

d) the act of holding someone in your arms _____

4 Find a verb in the song in the future continuous.

_____

 New Inspiration 4 **PHOTOCOPIABLE**

Song: Hanging on the Telephone

1 Read the title of the song. What does *hanging* mean?
Listen to the song and read the words.

HANGING ON THE TELEPHONE

I'm in the phone booth, it's the one across the hall
If you don't answer, I'll just ring it off the wall
I know he's there, but I just had to call
Don't leave me hanging on the telephone
Don't leave me hanging on the telephone

I heard your mother, now she's going out the door
Did she go to work or just go to the store?
All those things she said, I told you to ignore
Oh, why can't we talk again?
Oh, why can't we talk again?
Oh, why can't we talk again?
Don't leave me hanging on the telephone
Don't leave me hanging on the telephone

It's good to hear your voice, you know it's been so long
If I don't get your calls then everything goes wrong
I want to tell you something you've known all along
Don't leave me hanging on the telephone
Don't leave me hanging on the telephone

I had to interrupt and stop this conversation
Your voice across the line gives me a strange sensation
I'd like to talk when I can show you my affection
Oh, I can't control myself
Oh, I can't control myself
Oh, I can't control myself
Don't leave me hanging on the telephone

Hang up and run to me! Oh!
Hang up and run to me! Oh!

2 Circle the correct answers.

a) The songwriter is *making / receiving* a phone call.
b) The songwriter is *in love with / is angry with* the other person.
c) The songwriter wants to *see / forget* the person.

3 Find words in the song with the following meanings.

a) not listen to   _____
b) a feeling   _____
c) feelings of love   _____
d) end a telephone conversation   _____

4 Find an example of a reporting verb + object + infinitive.

_____

Song: True Colours

1 Listen to the song and read the words. What do you think someone's 'true colours' are?

TRUE COLOURS

You with the sad eyes
Don't be discouraged
Oh, I realise
It's hard to take courage
In a world full of people
You can lose sight of it all
And the darkness inside you
Can make you feel so small

Chorus 1
But I see your true colours
Shining through
I see your true colours
And that's why I love you
So don't be afraid to let them show
Your true colours
True colours are beautiful,
Like a rainbow

Show me a smile then
And don't be unhappy, can't remember when
I last saw you laughing
If this world makes you crazy
And you've taken all you can bear
You call me up
Because you know I'll be there

Chorus 2
And I see your true colours
Shining through
I see your true colours
And that's why I love you
So don't be afraid to let them show
Your true colours
True colours are beautiful,
Like a rainbow

Oh, I can't remember
When I last saw you laugh
If this world makes you crazy
And you've taken all you can bear
You call me up
Because you know I'll be there

Repeat Chorus 2

2 What is the main message of the song? Tick ✓ the correct box.

a) to express the songwriter's own sad feelings ☐
b) to explain why someone else is sad ☐
c) to offer love and support to someone ☐

3 Match the words from the song in column A with their definitions in column B.

A
1 discouraged
2 take courage
3 shining through
4 bear

B
a) easy to see
b) sad and disappointed
c) cope with or deal with
d) feel strong

4 Find examples of *make* and *let* + object + infinitive.

_____
_____

  New Inspiration 4 **PHOTOCOPIABLE**

WORKBOOK
Answers

UNIT 1 LESSON 1

1

1 lower   2 contain   3 reduce   4 depends
5 have   6 need   7 believe   8 prove   9 healthy
10 cereal   11 ate   12 skip

2

1 am really enjoying; agree
2 Do ... feel; don't know, depends
3 is laughing; doesn't matter; know
4 is/are playing; like; think, sounds
5 are ... looking; don't understand, mean
6 is walking; don't believe

3

1 were watching, rang, sounded
2 tasted, smelled, liked
3 saw, didn't recognise
4 phoned, didn't realise, were having
5 promised, was travelling

4

1 nightmare   2 protein   3 diet   4 exaggerate
5 digest   6 junk food   7 Scientific   8 portion

5

1 balanced diet   2 dried fruit   3 food label
4 fruit juice   5 tap water   6 tooth decay

6

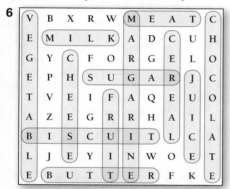

7

1 O   2 S   3 O   4 S   5 G   6 S

8

acidic 3   advertising 4   balanced 2   emphasise
3   exaggerate 4   margarine 3   mineral 3
scientific 4   unhealthy 3   vitamin 3

9

1 ✗   2 ✗   3 ✓   4 ✓   5 ✗   6 ✓   7 ✗

UNIT 1 LESSON 2

1

1 b   2 f   3 d   4 a   5 c   6 e

2

1 Making Spaghetti Carbonara isn't difficult.
2 Boiling an egg takes about four minutes.
3 Getting up in the morning is sometimes hard.
4 Sleeping under the stars is fun.
5 Winning the football match felt great.
6 Getting tickets for the gig wasn't easy.
7 Meeting the band was exciting.
8 Being at home alone seemed strange.

3

1 by wearing a 'sleep inducer'.
2 by following a recipe.
3 by setting your alarm clock.
4 by pressing this button
5 by using a dictionary.
6 by dialling 999.

4

1 It's for locking the door.
2 It's for listening to music.
3 It's for opening bottles.
4 It's for telling the time.
5 It's for doing calculations.
6 It's for ironing clothes.
7 It's for carrying water.
8 It's for serving soup.

5

1 after passing
2 before putting
3 before going
4 after eating
5 after washing
6 after finishing

6

1 chop   2 drain   3 beat   4 stir   5 boil   6 fry

7

1 cheese grater   2 coffee maker   3 corkscrew
4 frying pan   5 tin opener

8

1 e   2 a   3 f   4 c   5 b   6 d

UNIT 1 LESSON 3

1

1 using   2 driving   3 travelling   4 flying
5 climbing   6 getting   7 looking   8 screaming
9 working   10 swimming   11 seeing
12 panicking   13 living   14 being

2

1 to help   2 to hurt   3 to take   4 to be, to go
5 to study   6 to get   7 to try   8 to stop

3

1 feeling
2 flying, to take
3 to go, to relax
4 to get, reading
5 to take, to keep taking
6 seeing
7 to put, to take

4

1 for   2 with   3 of   4 about   5 for   6 of   7 to

5

¹H	O	S	P	I	T	A	L
²A	S	P	I	R	I	N	
³N	E	E	D	L	E	S	
⁴S	U	R	G	E	O	N	
⁵B	R	A	I	N			
⁶P	A	T	I	E	N	T	
⁷P	A	I	N				
	⁸D	O	C	T	O	R	
⁹I	L	L	N	E	S	S	

6

1 alternative medicine   2 general anaesthetic
3 headache   4 open-heart surgery
5 natural remedy

7

1 at best   2 harmless   3 remember   4 illness
5 calm   6 natural   7 positive   8 real

8

sound: amount, count, doubt, round, thousand
touch: country, cousin, enough, trouble, young

9

acupuncture 4   alternative 4   anaesthetic 4
experiment 4   individual 5   operation 4
placebo 3   popularity 5   reaction 3   remedy 3
surgeon 2   synthetic 3

UNIT 1 LESSON 4

1

A 4   B 2   C 1   D 5

2

1 myth   2 although   3 sensible   4 fact
5 regularly   6 appears   7 power   8 larger
9 stopped   10 normal   11 common   12 prove
13 treatment   14 remedy   15 illnesses
16 However   17 avoid   18 cause   19 trial
20 bowls

3

¹K	E	²T	T	³L	E			⁴A	D	⁵D	
N		A		O		⁶H				I	
⁷I	M	P	R	O	V	E		⁸A		S	
F		E		K		A				H	
⁹E	A	¹⁰T		¹¹S	I	L	L	Y			
		R		T		T			¹²S		
¹³C	R	E	A	¹⁴M		H		¹⁵H	E	A	T
H		A		E		Y				O	
O		T		A				¹⁶U		P	
¹⁷P	O	S	I	T	I	V	E	S			

UNIT 1
Inspiration EXTRA!
Revision

Lesson 1

1 contain   2 are you eating   3 includes
4 consists   5 smells, are you cooking   6 need
7 don't want, am trying   8 is having

Lesson 2

1 It's for keeping food cold.
2 It's for waking you up.
3 They're for cutting things.
4 It's for washing clothes.
5 It's for listening to music.
6 It's for watching films.
7 It's for carrying things.
8 It's for taking pictures.

Lesson 3

1 eating   2 to have   3 to phone   4 seeing
5 to stop talking   6 to be   7 to learn to drive
8 doing

Lesson 4
1 e   2 b   3 a   4 d   5 c   6 f

Spelling
1 although   2 biscuit   3 design   4 doubt
5 iron   6 lightning   7 muscle   8 nightmare   9
scientific   10 spaghetti   11 surgeon   12 wrist

Brainteaser
nothing

Extension
Lessons 1 - 4
Students' own answers

Spelling
1 break   2 dye   3 grater   4 genes   5 plane   6
roll   7 source   8 whether

Brainteaser
The surgeon was the boy's mother.

CULTURE
Happiness and success
1
1 Said   2 Jess   3 Meleike   4 Linda
5 Tina and Meleike   6 Pablo   7 Jess   8 Shinko
9 Jess   10 Linda   11 Said   12 Markos

2
1 j   2 f   3 h   4 c   5 i   6 g   7 b   8 e   9 a   10 d

3
1 rule   2 aggressive   3 trust   4 base
5 appearance   6 brand   7 salary   8 behaviour

4
Students' own answers

UNIT 2   LESSON 1
1
1 T   2 F   3 F   4 F   5 T

2
1 How long have the band been playing? They've been playing for 45 minutes.
2 How long has Jake been painting? He's been painting since 11 am.
3 How long has Sally been learning to drive? She's been learning to drive for two months.
4 How long has Robbie been watching TV? He's been watching TV since 9.10.
5 How long have the team been training? They've been training for six weeks.
6 How long has Libby been talking to Jim? She's been talking to him since 9.45.
7 How long has Paul been making films? He's been making films for X years. [answer depends on the year now]
8 How long have the actors been rehearsing? They've been rehearsing since Monday.

3
1 metal   2 plaster   3 stone   4 rubber
5 concrete   6 iron   7 sand   8 gold
9 polystyrene

4
1 S   2 G   3 S   4 O   5 O   6 G   7 O   8 S
9 G   10 G   11 S   12 G

5
concrete 2   cupboard 2   domestic 3   heritage 3
material 4   polystyrene 4   reappear 3
represent 3   sculpture 2   staircase 2   tribute
2   unique 2

6
1 Statue   2 domestic   3 displayed   4 striking
5 tribute   6 murder   7 symbol   8 unique

7
1 cable car   2 waste of money
3 free of charge   4 striking example
5 stand still   6 terraced house

8
use: human, reduce, statue, student, tribute, unique, usually
us: culture, cupboard, public, rubber, sculpture, structure, study

UNIT 2   LESSON 2
1
1 She's been going out with Tom.
2 She hasn't been going out with Andy.
3 She hasn't been having music lessons.
4 She's been having driving lessons.
5 She hasn't been doing aerobics..
6 She's been doing yoga.
7 She hasn't been playing basketball.
8 She's been playing tennis.
9 She's been going to the cinema.
10 She hasn't been going to the theatre.

2
1 How often has she been out with Tom? Seven times.
2 How many driving lessons has she had? Five.
3 How many films has she seen? Four.
4 How often has she played tennis? Two times/ Twice.
5 How often has she done yoga? Three times.

3
1 haven't been
2 have been
3 have been trying
4 haven't had
5 have made
6 have written
7 have been learning
8 haven't passed
9 have been looking
10 haven't found
11 have been staying
12 have just called
13 have offered
14 have always wanted
15 haven't had
16 have been enjoying

4
1 of   2 in   3 on   4 about   5 for   6 on   7 of
8 as   9 of   10 in   11 for   12 for

5
1 extraordinary, necessary, temporary
2 autograph, paragraph, photograph
3 instruction, location, reaction
4 commercial, material, special
5 careful, helpful, successful
6 particular, regular, similar

6
Students' own answers

7
1 C   2 B   3 E   4 A   5 D

UNIT 2   LESSON 3
1
1 had gone
2 had been snowing

3 had just stopped
4 had caught
5 had seen
6 had looked
7 had been
8 had imagined
9 had been watching
10 hadn't seen
11 had seen
12 had been standing

2
1 After the pilot had completed the pre-flight checks, he prepared for take-off.
2 After the ship had reached the Bahamas, it sailed to Cuba.
3 After the climbers had taken photos, they started coming down the mountain.
4 After the explorers had caught some fish, they cooked them over a camp fire.
5 After we had collected some wood, we built a shelter.
6 After I had walked through the forest for three hours, I found my way out.
7 After she had seen the film Twilight, she decided to read the book.
8 After he had travelled round China, he wrote a book about the experience.
9 After the coast guard had rescued the children, they were taken to hospital.
10 After the police had arrested the thieves, they took them to the police station.

3
1 Because she'd been dancing all night.
2 Because he'd been working on his car.
3 Because she'd been stealing from shops.
4 Because she'd been watching a horror film.
5 Because they'd been lying on the beach.
6 Because he'd been listening to very loud music.
7 Because they had been fighting.
8 Because they'd been revising for a long time.

4
1 childhood   2 entertain   3 construct
4 monster   5 teenager   6 extraordinary
7 produce   8 interact

5
1 giant   2 completed   3 life   4 inside   5 ugly
6 artificial   7 previous

6
1 young   2 new   3 long   4 tall   5 easy   6 soft
7 wrong   8 left   9 noisy   10 loud

7
1 best-selling   2 crash land   3 fighter pilot
4 horror story   5 human being   6 science fiction
7 volcanic eruption

8
1 ✗   2 ✓   3 ✓   4 ✗   5 ✓   6 ✓   7 ✗   8 ✗

UNIT 2   LESSON 4
1
A 2   B 5   C 4   D 1   E 6   F 3
1 d   2 c   3 g   4 f   5 h   6 b   7 i   8 a   9 e

2
1 Because it was a mixture of all the darkest colours he had ever grown.
2 Because he was only interested in the beauty of the flower.
3 Because he didn't want anyone to steal the bulb.
4 Because he wanted to win the prize.
5 Because she thought it was an onion.
6 If they had seen a tulip bulb.

7 Because he had eaten the tulip bulb.
8 When the tulip the thief left in its place flowered.
9 Probably very disappointed.
10 Students' own answers.

3

Crossword:
- 1 INNOCENT / IMAGINE
- NO / O / N
- 6 ADVENTURES / SENSE
- GE / CN / EE
- 7 ILL / 8 RESULT
- NE / NU
- 10 ABOUT / 11 IVE / 12 E
- RY / EE / QUSE
- 13 USE
- 14 TRIBUTE

UNIT 2
Inspiration EXTRA!

Revision

Lesson 1
1 How long has Jamie been playing the guitar? For a month. Since [name of last month].
2 How long has Susie been painting her room? For two days. Since [name of day two days ago].
3 How long has Rob been cooking a meal? For half an hour. Since [time half an hour ago].
4 How long has Dave been learning German? For six months. Since [name of month six months ago].
5 How long have Holly and Ben been travelling round the world? For four weeks. Since [date four weeks ago].

Lesson 2
1 Sarah has been taking photos for 30 minutes. She's taken 60 photos.
2 Rick has been writing emails for 15 minutes. He's written three emails.
3 Kate has been applying for jobs for six months. She's applied for nine jobs.
4 Maria and Paul have been driving for five hours. They've driven 450 kilometres.
5 Pete and Helen have been recording songs for two weeks. They've recorded 20 songs.

Lesson 3
1 Alex had been cooking supper.
2 Dan had been watching TV.
3 Alice had been playing computer games.
4 Mike had been listening to music.
5 Tammy had been drying her hair.
6 Sam had been downloading songs.

Lesson 4
1 Where did the ferryman live?
2 How much did he make from the ferry?
3 How did he learn a lot about life?
4 What was the professor wearing?
5 Why hadn't the ferryman studied any history, geography or science?
6 Why did the professor drown?

Spelling
1 building   2 cupboard   3 folk   5 knowledge
6 lighting   7 might   8 scene   9 unique

Brainteaser
'incorrectly'

Extension

Lesson 1
Students' own answers.

Lesson 2
1 John has been looking for work for six months.
2 Den has had two jobs this year.
3 How long have you been reading Frankenstein?
4 How many text messages have you sent today?
5 They've been watching TV since six o'clock.
6 I've seen six movies this month.
7 How much TV have you watched recently?
8 How long have you known your best friend?

Lesson 3
Students' own answers.

Lesson 4
Students' own answers.

Spelling
1 ambulance   2 appearance   3 balance
4 difference   5 distance 6 evidence
7 importance   8 independence   9 performance
10 science   11 sequence   12 silence

Brainteaser
They had been on a snowman before the snow melted (coal for eyes and buttons, a carrot for the nose).

REVIEW UNITS 1–2

1
1 C   2 D   3 B   4 C   5 C   6 A   7 D   8 A
9 D   10 C   11 B   12 B   13 A   14 C   15 D

2
1 childhood   2 amazement   3 creation
4 mixture   5 sensible   6 operation
7 unhealthy   8 knowledge

3
1 Before reading the book she saw the film.
2 You can use this gadget for opening bottles.
3 You start the machine by pressing a button.
4 Creating a website isn't hard.
5 Do you remember meeting him last year?
6 Don't forget to lock the door when you leave the house.
7 When he had done his homework, he went out.
8 It has been raining for a few minutes.

4
1 stir   2 beat   3 metal   4 healthy   5 myth   6 collar   7 walk   8 improve   9 exactly

Learner independence

2
1 That's a different matter
2 It's not a good idea to …
3 on the other hand
4 The sensible thing is to …
5 It's a complete waste of money.
6 there's no excuse for
7 Believe it or not ….
8 You might as well …

UNIT 3   LESSON 1

1
1 usually   2 accurately   3 slowly   4 Extremely
5 further   6 far   7 better   8 approximately

2
1 further   2 the quickest   3 quicker
4 slower   5 further   6 the quickest 7 quicker
8 the slowest   9 the furthest   10 slower

3
1 best   2 worse, worst   3 harder
4 the furthest, further   5 better, worse
6 faster, slower   7 more often

4
1 in space for 747 days
2 in a spacecraft longest
3 quickly in the 1960s
4 on the Moon in July 1969
5 strangely on the Moon
6 in space in 1965
7 successfully on the Moon in 1969

5
1 breathe oxygen
2 disagree about something
3 expand in size
4 measure distance
5 weigh a tonne

6
1 furthest   2 created   3 expand
4 approximately, about   5 amazing, astonishing
6 rapidly, fast, quickly

7
1 four and a half billion
2 two trillion
3 three million, five hundred and seventy-five thousand
4 six trillion, four hundred billion
5 six hundred and twenty-five thousand

8
accurately 4   approximately 5   astonishing 4
equator 3   expand 2   organism 3   oxygen 3
percentage 3   rotate 2   universe 3

UNIT 3   LESSON 2

1
1 Because it is very dark there.
2 It is difficult to find food because it's hard to see anything.
3 It has its own light on a rod above its head, which attracts other fish.
4 They swim over to see what the light is.
5 It has a very big mouth.

2
1 What an   2 so   3 What a   4 What a
5 such a   6 What an

3
1 The water was so cold that no one went swimming.
2 Amy was such a good guitar player that they didn't want her to stop.
3 The fish was so delicious that Paul asked for some more.
4 It was such a beautiful rainbow that Sam took a picture of it.
5 It was such a huge crab that Sue screamed.
6 It was such a great party that no one wanted to leave.

4
opinion: clever, delicious, pretty, unexpected
size: big, large, short, tall
age: adult, ancient, modern, teenage
colour: colourless, multi-coloured, pink, yellow
origin: British, international, Polish, Swiss

5
1 fantastic, new, American
2 comfortable, old, long, blue

3 *fantastic, big, brightly-coloured*
4 *lovely, new, short, Italian*
5 *delicious, large, fresh, pink*
6 *frightening, giant, round, green*

6
1 O   2 G   3 S   4 G   5 S   6 O   7 S   8 G
9 O   10 S

7
chimney 2   *descend* 2   *disturb* 2   *evaporate* 4
observer 3   *rainbow* 2   *spacious* 2
submersible 4   *underwater* 4   *unexpected* 4
volcano 3

8
1 ✗   2 ✓   3 ✓   4 ✓   5 ✓   6 ✗   7 ✗   8 ✓

UNIT 3   LESSON 3

1
1 tourism   2 hotel   3 flights   4 afford   5 risk
6 spaceships   7 human   8 robots   9 colony
10 won't   11 temperature   12 believe   13 will
14 air   15 dream   16 species

2
1 *are (you) going*
2 *am spending*
3 *will be*
4 *Are (you) travelling*
5 *am going*
6 *is taking*
7 *does (your flight) depart*
8 *arrives*
9 *will have*
10 *am going to do*
11 *Won't (you) be*
12 *will be*
13 *are (you) doing*
14 *am taking*
15 *will be*

3
1 *are you going to sing*
2 *am not going to sing*
3 *am going to have*
3 *will bring*
4 *Will you get*
5 *is going to rescue*
6 *won't reach*
7 *won't swim*
8 *will buy*

4
1 hang   2 look   3 put   4 come   5 take   6 count

5
1 luxurious   2 rumour   3 honeymoon   4 orbit
5 alien   6 elevator

6
1 *factory, history, memory*
2 *elevator, simulator, calculator*
3 *weightlessness, business, illness*
4 *expensive, alternative, positive*
5 *luxurious, spacious, delicious*
6 *prediction, population production*

7
spaceship, space tourism, space tourist,
spaceport, space flight, space center, space
movie, spaceflight simulator, space station,
space elevator, space factory

8
astronaut 3   *elevator* 4   *experience* 4

---

grandchildren 3   *honeymoon* 3   *initially* 4
luxurious 4   *production* 3   *rumour* 2
simulator 4

UNIT 3   LESSON 4

1
1 Picture C   2 Picture D   3 Picture B
4 Picture A

1 g *for stopping a lift in an emergency*
2 d *to reach higher floors*
3 j *that the Earth orbited the Sun*
4 a *about our universe*
5 i *which was later developed into a*
   commercial freezer
6 e *in shops and supermarkets*
7 h *it was the first man-made orbiting satellite*
8 b *until many years after his death*

2
1 *stopped a lift in an emergency*
2 *people no longer had to climb hundreds of stairs*
3 *hearing about the invention of the telescope*
4 *Galileo's discoveries*
5 *is safe and keeps its taste and appearance*
6 *started modern global communications*

3

¹U	²N	D	³E	R	⁴W	A	T	E	⁵R	
N	E		E		R				I	
⁶I	M	P	A	C	T				A	D
V	A		E		⁷O	N	C	E		
E	R		N		S					
⁸R	O	T	A	T	E		⁹	¹⁰	¹¹M	¹²P
S			G		Q			I		A
¹³E	¹⁴G		¹⁵E	Q	U	A	T	O	R	
	E				A					T
¹⁶S	T	A	R		¹⁷L	A	N	D	S	

UNIT 3
Inspiration EXTRA!
Revision

Lesson 1
more accurately, most accurately
worse, worst
earlier, earliest
further, furthest
faster, fastest
longer, longest
more quickly, most quickly
more slowly, most slowly
straighter, straightest
better, best

Lesson 2
1 What an   2 such a   3 so   4 such a   5 What
6 so   7 such   8 such a

Lesson 3
1 is seeing   2 will be   3 is moving   4 will be   5
is leaving   6 won't be able   7 is going   8 will be

Lesson 4
1 *did Pasteur discover?*
2 *has protected millions of people from disease?*
3 *did Silent Spring cause?*
4 *did Marconi make the first ever transatlantic*
   radio transmission?
5 *was the signal picked up?*

Spelling
1 accurate   2 approximate   3 bottom
4 impossible   5 massive   6 passenger
7 process   8 successfully   9 suddenly
10 trillion   11 transmission   12 vaccination
13 village   14 weightlessness

Brainteaser
the future

Extension

Lesson 1
Students' own answers.

Lesson 2
1 so   2 such   3 such   4 so   5 such   6 so
7 so   8 such
(sentence endings: students' own answers)

Lesson 3
Students' own answers.

Lesson 4
Students' own answers.

Spelling
1 beautiful   2 chemical   3 colourful
4 comfortable   5 controversial   6 environmental
7 incredible   8 medical   9 possible   10
submersible   11 natural   12 signal

Brainteaser
the Moon

CULTURE
Teenagers who make a difference

1
1 Wacky and James   2 James
3 Wacky and James   4 Stacey   5 Wacky
6 Stacey   7 Wacky   8 James   9 Stacey

2
1 f   2 e   3 d   4 a   5 h   6 c   7 b   8 g

3
1 fashion-conscious   2 fortunate   3 well off
4 improve   5 funding   6 tough   7 bullying
8 launched   9 street crime   10 promote

4
1 G   2 O   3 G   4 S   5 O   6 S   7 O

5
Students' own answers.

UNIT 4   LESSON 1

1
Zak won't be sleeping at seven o'clock tomorrow,
   he'll be getting up.
Zak won't be arriving at school at nine o'clock
   tomorrow, he'll be starting work.
Zak won't be having an English lesson at two
   o'clock tomorrow, he'll be having lunch.
Zak won't be playing football at four o'clock
   tomorrow, he'll be walking around the town
   centre dressed as a chicken.
Zak won't be doing his homework at six o'clock
   tomorrow, he'll be working as a waiter in the
   restaurant.
Zak won't be watching TV at eight o'clock
   tomorrow, he'll be sleeping.

2
1 *He won't have gone to school but he will have*
   dressed as a chicken.
2 *He will have had chicken for lunch but he*
   won't have had an English lesson.

3 He won't have played football but he will have walked around the town centre.
4 He will have worked as a waiter but he won't have done his homework.
5 He won't have watched TV but he will have dreamed about chicken.
6 He will have earned some money but he won't have had a quiet day.

3
1 How many hours will he have slept, Forty.
2 How many chicken burgers will he have eaten, Twenty.
3 How many times will he have washed his chicken costume, Seven.
4 How much money will he have earned, £120.
5 How many burgers will it have sold, Two thousand, one hundred.
6 How much TV will he have watched, None.

4
1 will have discovered
2 will be enjoying
3 will be doing
4 will have stopped
5 will be arguing
6 will be living
7 will have fallen
8 will have used
9 will be rising
10 will be discussing

5
1 pointed *2* carried *3* work *4* missed *5* wipe

6
1 household *2* life expectancy
3 microchip *4* nuclear energy *5* pulse rate
6 health problems *7* wristwatch

7
advance 2 combine 2 executive 4
indication 4 expectancy 4 microchip 3
obtainable 4 researcher 3 retirement 3
vaccine 2 wireless 2

UNIT 4 LESSON 2

1
1 solution *2* atmosphere *3* greenhouse
4 emissions *5* won't *6* unless *7* take *8* will
9 Whenever *10* travel

2
1 If you promise to listen carefully, I'll explain about carbon emissions.
2 Unless you explain clearly, I won't understand what you mean.
3 If you fly, you'll damage the environment.
4 Unless I fly, I won't have much time with my friends.
5 Will it matter if you don't go at all?
6 My friends will be disappointed if I don't visit them.
7 Your friends will understand if you explain why you can't come.
8 If you go by train, I'll come with you.

3
1 will continue, unless, becomes
2 If, want, will have to
3 will be, if, rises
4 Unless, do, will be
5 will make, if, don't fly
6 If, have, won't need
7 Unless, decreases, will continue
8 will have to, if, travel

4
1 will go, finishes
2 won't decide, listens
3 will be, know
4 will laugh, hears
5 pass, won't be allowed
6 will ring, hear

5
1 as soon as *2* when *3* until *4* When
5 as soon as *6* until

6
1 fund a project *2* plant trees
3 reduce the impact *4* solve a problem
5 take action *6* work together

7
1 global warming *2* carbon dioxide *3* flood
4 drought *5* energy crisis

8
atmosphere 3 balance 2 crisis 2 emission 3
energy 3 fertiliser 4 offset 2 organisation 5
unless 2 whenever 3

UNIT 4 LESSON 3

1
1 were E *2* ate B *3* met D *4* decided A
5 stole F *6* lost C

2
1 would you speak, wanted, I'd speak to my sister
2 would you say, gave
3 would you do, found
4 could, would it be
5 could, would it be
6 would you ask, needed
7 would you miss, had
Students' own answers to the questions.

3
1 If you listened, we wouldn't argue all the time.
2 If we had a map, we would know where to go.
3 If she didn't complain all the time, people wouldn't ignore her.
4 If I didn't cycle to school, I would spend money on bus fares.
5 If he didn't chat with everyone, he would finish his work.
6 If we didn't like the singer, we wouldn't buy tickets for all her concerts.

4
1 were *2* grew *3* had *4* could *5* didn't feel
6 knew *7* didn't like *8* shone

5
1 magical *2* log on *3* trekking *4* chat
5 traditional *6* pace *7* in theory

6
1 ✗ *2* ✓ *3* ✗ *4* ✓ *5* ✓ *6* ✓ *7* ✗ *8* ✗

UNIT 4 LESSON 4

1
1 freedom *2* overland *3* transport *4* able
5 animals *6* wars *7* example *8* damage
9 guesthouse *10* agree *11* danger *12* only
13 difference *14* flights *15* result *16* Thirdly
17 stealing *18* partly *19* arguing *20* strongly

2
Students' own answers.

3
Students' own answers.

4
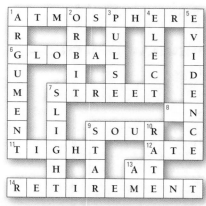

Learner independence
1 A *2* A *3* C *4* C *5* A *6* C *7* C *8* A
9 C *10* A

UNIT 4
Inspiration EXTRA!
Revision

Lesson 1
1 have drunk   *5* will have learnt
2 will be waiting   *6* will be spending
3 will be doing   *7* will (you) be using
4 will have finished *8* will have eaten

Lesson 2
1 If they don't run, they'll miss the bus. Unless they run, they'll miss the bus.
2 If she saves enough money, she'll be able to afford a new coat. Unless she saves enough money, she won't be able to afford a new coat.
3 If he asks me, I'll tell him the answer to the puzzle. Unless he asks me, I won't tell him the answer to the puzzle.
4 If you don't hurry, you'll be late for school. Unless you hurry, you'll be late for school.
5 If we join the queue, we'll get tickets for the gig. Unless we join the queue, we won't get tickets for the gig.

Lesson 3
1 If I knew what to do, I wouldn't ask for help.
2 If she had enough time, she'd learn the local language.
3 If only my father understood why I came home late.
4 If only I could remember her phone number.
5 If you could choose, where would you like to live?

Lesson 4
1 d *2* b *3* f *4* g *5* e *6* c *7* a

Spelling
1 advance *2* decision *3* decrease *4* case
5 certain *6* crisis *7* democracy *8* evidence
9 expectancy *10* offset *11* pace *12* produce
13 publicity *14* race *15* slight *16* violence

Brainteaser
Hello, hello, hello!

Extension
Lessons 1–4
Students' own answers.

Spelling
1 action *2* addition *3* clash *4* crucial
5 emission *6* expression *7* issue *8* motion
9 organisation *10* racial *11* relationship
12 politician *13* wish

Brainteaser
White – the man was at the North Pole.

REVIEW UNITS 3–4

1
1 B   2 B   3 D   4 D   5 C   6 A   7 D   8 B
9 C   10 A   11 C   12 B   13 D   14 C   15 D

2
1 expectancy   2 obtainable   3 retirement
4 organisation   5 representative   6 opponents
7 demonstration   8 magical

3
1 Light travels faster than lightning.
2 Neil Armstrong and Buzz Aldrin were the two astronauts who first walked on the Moon.
3 They didn't expect to see any fish because the dive was so deep.
4 Each passenger will pay $200,000 for the two-hour flight.
5 By 2050 we will have killed the last whale.
6 Unless we do something about carbon emissions soon, it will be too late.
7 If you don't answer my questions, I'll tell your parents.
8 If I had enough money, I'd spend all my holidays in Nepal.

4
1 reduce   2 crisis   3 debate   4 lovely
5 segregation   6 destroy   7 weight   8 trek

Learner independence

2
1 What a fantastic sight!
2 What has this got to do with …
3 The most incredible thing is …
4 The whole point is …
5 If only people were like that …
6 It takes ages.
7 Only time will tell.
8 It sounds silly.

UNIT 5   LESSON 1

1
1 wouldn't   2 known   3 can   4 world
5 estimated   6 bigger   7 extraordinary
8 mobiles   9 check   10 dictionaries   11 users
12 heard

2
1 Sue would have caught the bus if she hadn't been late.
2 Sue would have got wet if she hadn't opened her umbrella.
3 The car would have hit Sue if she had crossed the road a moment earlier.
4 The piano would have fallen on Sue if she hadn't run for the bus.
5 Sue would have fallen into the hole if Sam hadn't shouted.
6 Sam would have called an ambulance if Sue had been hurt.

3
1 Sue would have said thank you to Sam if she hadn't been late.
2 She would have got a taxi if she had seen one.
3 She wouldn't have been late for work if she had got a taxi.
4 Sue's boss wouldn't have shouted at her if she had been on time.
5 Sue wouldn't have shouted back at her boss if she had thought about the consequences.

6 She wouldn't have lost her job if she hadn't shouted at her boss.

4
1 I wish I hadn't missed the programme.
2 If only he had remembered to post the packet.
3 I wish you hadn't said that.
4 If only she had phoned and apologised.
5 I wish I hadn't broken your camera.
6 If only I knew the right thing to say.
7 She wishes she had read the instruction book first.
8 If only they had been at the party.

5
1 conspirator   2 noble   3 bishop   4 gang
5 hero   6 MP

6
1 O   2 S   3 S   4 G   5 O   6 G   7 G   8 O

7
conspirator 4   destruction 3   execute 3
explosive 3   farmhouse 2   gunpowder 3
Parliament 3   persecute 3   petrol 2

UNIT 5   LESSON 2

1
1 doesn't need to   2 must   3 have to
4 don't need to   5 (do) need to   6 have to
7 must   8 don't have to   9 don't have to
10 must   11 have to

2
1 have to   2 mustn't   3 have to   4 needn't
5 mustn't   6 needn't   7 have to   8 mustn't   9 needn't   10 have to/needn't (answer is subjective)

3
1 didn't need to   2 had to   3 didn't have to
4 needed to   5 needed to   6 had to   7 have to
8 didn't need to

4
1 need   2 need to   3 need   4 needn't
5 need to   6 needn't   7 need to   8 need

5
1 earn a living   2 get accustomed   3 get to know
4 see clearly   5 stay calm

6
1 driving licence   2 farmyard   3 fish market
4 flight attendant   5 guidelines   6 hairstyle
7 tourist attraction   8 university degree

7
1 G   2 G   3 S   4 S   5 O   6 S   7 O   8 O   9 S

8
1 ✓   2 ✓   3 ✓   4 ✗   5 ✗   6 ✓   7 ✗   8 ✓   9 ✗

UNIT 5   LESSON 3

1
1 lights   2 have   3 solo   4 sailing   5 later
6 crew   7 although   8 may   9 disappearance
10 pulled   11 flew   12 However   13 sent
14 take-off   15 mid-air   16 part   17 crashed
18 wrecks

2
1 have happened
2 have made
3 have got
4 have hit, have run
5 have abducted
6 have disappeared
7 have been, have returned

8 have attacked
9 have drowned
10 have run, crashed
11 have attempted
12 have lost

3
1 must have happened, can't have disappeared
2 can't have been
3 must have failed
4 must have been
5 can't have got
6 must have landed
7 must have been

4
1 must have been
2 might have been
3 must have made
4 could have happened
5 must have taken
6 may be
7 might have been
8 could have been

5
1 ended   2 blow   3 grow   4 give   5 take   6 sum

6
1 air traffic   2 emergency landing
3 radar screen   4 radio equipment
5 search operation   6 snowstorm

7
1 a record   2 up in a place   3 a trip
4 out of fuel   5 a message   6 down a plane

8
abduct 2   attempt 2   disappearance 4
navigator 4   pioneer 3   snowstorm 2
speculation 4   transatlantic 4

UNIT 5   LESSON 4

1
1 e   2 h   3 a   4 c   5 b   6 f   7 d

2
Sample answers
1 she was a child.
2 they have been treated badly by their owners; they have been injured by mines; they come from towns where there is not enough food and water for them.
3 hadn't rescued them.
4 that year he was 86; he was the oldest runner in the race.
5 charity; St Francis Hospice.
6 his goal is to get to the finishing lines in less than six hours.

3

	E	M	E	R	G	E	N	C	Y		
	X			E				H		R	
P	A	I	D			W	H	A	L	E	
	L			S	H	E		O		G	
	O			A	N		P	A	I	R	
	S	T	A	N	D			C		E	
	I			D		A		T		T	
	V				E	A	S	I	E	S	T
	E				D		A	R		E	
S	P	Y				R	A	I	S	E	D

UNIT 5
Inspiration EXTRA
Revision

Lesson 1
1 If you had asked me, I would have helped you.
2 If we had known what would happen, we wouldn't have opened the door.
3 If she had had her phone, she would have rung him.
4 If he hadn't known that the water was deep, he wouldn't have dived in.
5 If they had realised you were waiting, they wouldn't have been late.

Lesson 2
1 don't have to, need to
2 have to
3 needn't, have to
4 needn't, have to
5 have to, needn't

Lesson 3
1 She must have forgotten.
2 She can't have got the text.
3 It can't have been easy.
4 You must have been happy to hear from her.
5 You must have forgiven her!

Lesson 4
1 How many goals has Maribel scored in international matches?
2 How old was she when she started to play football?
3 How old was she when she joined the Mexican national team?
4 When did she play in the Athens Olympics? / When did the Mexican women's team reach the Olympic quarter-finals?
5 When did Maribel join Celaya?
6 How much per month did Maribel earn in Mexico?

Spelling
1 barrel   2 cellar   3 flatten   4 lottery
5 cannonball   6 degree   7 attendant   8 pattern
9 accustomed   10 traffic   11 disappearance
12 pioneer   13 announce   14 confess
15 professional

Brainteaser
Are you asleep?

Extension

Lesson 1
Students' own answers.

Lesson 2
Students' own answers.

Lesson 3
Sample answers
1 It can't have been me.
2 It must have been someone else.
3 It could have been my friend Sally's.
4 It might have been me, but I can't remember.
5 It could have been me, but I don't know.
6 It may have been from my best friend.

Lesson 4
Students' own answers.

Spelling
1 burglar   2 career   3 cellar   4 character
5 conspirator   6 diver   7 dollar   8 gunpowder
9 hairdryer   10 junior   11 major
12 navigator   13 neither   14 passenger
15 pioneer   16 radar   17 quarter   18 shower

Brainteaser
the letter 'e'

CULTURE
Saying the right thing

1
1 A: I'd like to return these, please. They're the wrong size.
   B: Have you got the receipt with you?
2 A: Can I see your driving licence, please?
   B: I'm sorry. I haven't got it with me.
3 A: Did you pack this bag yourself? Are you carrying anything for someone else?
   B: Yes, I did. And no, I'm not.
4 A: Are there any tickets left for the concert tonight?
   B: No, I'm afraid it sold out weeks ago.
5 A: Could I have the bill, please?
   B: Yes, of course. It was two coffees, wasn't it?
6 A: That's £5.10. I don't suppose you've got the 10p?
   B: No, I'm sorry, I haven't.

2
Hello – do you want any help?
No thank you, we're just looking.
Oh – look, Andy, these dresses are nice.
How much are they?
Only £25! That's quite cheap.
Which one do you like?
The blue one.
Great – so do I.
Excuse me, could I try this on, please?
Yes, of course. The fitting rooms are over there.
I don't think it fits properly.
No, it's a bit too big.
Do you have it in a smaller size?
I don't think we have a smaller one in blue. What about this one?
Red doesn't really suit me. It isn't my colour.
I think I'd better leave it.

3
1 Would you mind driving me to the station?
2 Do you mind if I make a phone call?
3 Would you mind turning the music down?
4 Do you mind if I borrow your bike this afternoon?
5 Would you mind laying the table?
6 Do you mind if I invite some friends round this evening?

4
1 change   2 passport   3 money   4 receipt
5 evening   6 nights   7 reservation   8 afraid   9 double   10 possible   11 shower   12 form

5
Sample answers
Can I have a ticket to Bristol, please?
Single or return?
Single, please.
That'll be £10.80 – thank you. Here's your change.
When does the next train leave?
In three minutes.
Which platform?
Platform 2
Do I have to change?
No, it's a direct train.
Thank you.

UNIT 6   LESSON 1

1
1 Sara told Jake to pour liquids into plastic bottles. She told him not to pack glass bottles.
2 Dan explained that it was best to drink lots of water during the flight so that he would feel less tired when he landed.
3 Ken advised him to eat lots of garlic if he ran out of insect spray because it would help to keep mosquitoes away.
4 Holly suggested that he should cover his guidebook so he didn't look like a tourist.
5 Max reminded him to leave his room key at hotel reception so that he couldn't lose it.
6 Jenny warned him not to drink tap water or have ice in his drinks unless he was sure it was safe.
7 Kate said that she always took a book called Point It with photos of things like food and drink. She said if he didn't know the word for something, he could point at its picture.

2
Sample answers
1 TOM: Would you like to have lunch in a restaurant?
2 SALLY: I'd love to.
3 WAITER: You can sit where you like.
4 SALLY: Let's sit by the window.
5 TOM: I'll have the prawn salad.
6 SALLY: But you don't like seafood.
7 TOM: I've changed my mind.
8 TOM: The prawns are too spicy.
9 WAITER: I'm sorry, sir. I'll bring you something else.
10 SALLY: Why don't you drink some water?

3
1 James asked to have a room with a sea view.
2 The tour guide advised everyone to visit the old castle.
3 Anna reminded Peter to change some money.
4 Mike invited Janet to go to the pool.
5 Kathy warned the children not to spend too long on the beach.
6 The children promised to put on lots of sun cream.

4
1 James complained that there weren't any towels in his room.
2 Anna hoped that it would stop raining soon.
3 Kathy suggested that they go on a boat trip.
4 The children agreed that a boat trip would be fun.
5 Janet explained that she was feeling too tired to go swimming.
6 The tour guide said that no one should swim in the sea when the red flag was up.

5
1 book a plane ticket
2 carry luggage
3 come round this evening
4 complain that something's wrong
5 invite someone for supper
6 travel halfway round the world

6
1 aisle seat   2 grandparents   3 insect spray
4 malaria tablet   5 best friend   6 snowboard
7 toothache   8 newspaper

7
1 loud, crowd   2 aisle, mile   3 bowl, whole
4 seat, sheet   5 burnt, learnt   6 ache, wake
7 change, strange   8 warn, born

UNIT 6   LESSON 2

1
1 check-in   2 full   3 accent   4 pardon
5 hesitated   6 questions   7 uncomfortably
8 sweetly   9 hard

2
1 The man asked how big the room was.
2 He wanted to know what 'quite big' meant.
3 The receptionist wondered if he would like to see the room.
4 The man asked where the Rock was.
5 He wanted to know how long it took to get there.
6 He asked if there was a restaurant in the hotel.
7 He wanted to know what time dinner was served.
8 He asked if you could see the Rock from the dining room.
9 The woman asked if there was a hairdresser's.
10 She wanted to know how late it opened.
11 She asked where she could send postcards.
12 She asked where the gift shop was.
13 She wanted to know if the gift shop took US dollars.
14 Bill wondered if they had a room.

3
1 13   2 11   3 10   4 2   5 6   6 14   7 8   8 5
9 9   10 3   11 12   12 1   13 7   14 4

4
1 He asked if I enjoyed travelling.
2 He wondered where I would like to go next.
3 He wanted to know what my favourite country was.
4 He asked how many languages I could speak.
5 He wanted to know if I took a laptop with me.
6 He asked which book I had enjoyed writing most.
7 He wondered if I had ever felt in danger.
8 He asked what every traveller should take with them.
9 He wanted to know when my new book would come out.
10 He asked me if I could give some advice to a new writer.

5
1 bread roll   2 cash register   3 paper napkin   4 salad dressing   5 iced water

6
1 dressing   2 gravy   3 waitress   4 napkin
5 cash register   6 cutlery   7 tray

7
1 damp   2 wipe   3 starring   4 push off
5 wrap   6 mainly

8
cutlery 3   hesitate 3   homeland 2
ketchup 2   napkin 2   rediscover 4   remark 2
uncomfortably 5   waitress 2

UNIT 6   LESSON 3

1
1 sense   2 having   3 luxury   4 plan   5 chosen
6 have   7 served   8 washed   9 taken   10 expects   11 planned   12 myself

2
1 Has she had her holiday photos printed yet? No, but she's going to have them printed.
2 Has she had her suitcase mended yet? No, but she's going to have it mended.
3 Has she had new keys cut yet? No, but she's going to have them cut.
4 Has she had new software installed yet? No, but she's going to have it installed.
5 Has she had a new tyre put on her bicycle yet? No, but she's going to have one put on.

6 Has she had her jacket dry-cleaned yet? No, but she's going to have it dry-cleaned.
7 Has she had her car serviced yet? No, but she's going to have it serviced.
8 Has she had her hair cut yet? No, but she's going to have it cut.

3
Students' own answers to the questions.
1 When did you last have a tooth filled?
2 When did you last have your hair cut?
3 When did you last have your eyes tested?
4 When did you last have some clothes dry-cleaned?
5 When did you last have a passport photo taken?

4
1 It's time (that) he got it washed.
2 It's time (that) they got it painted.
3 It's time (that) she got them checked.
4 It's time (that) we got it repaired.
5 It's time (that) he got it dry-cleaned.
6 It's time (that) I got them turned up.
7 It's time (that) she got it mended.

5
1 behave responsibly   2 do your hair
3 dry-clean clothes   4 install software
5 pick flowers   6 tip a waiter

6
1 O   2 S   3 O   4 G   5 S   6 O   7 O   8 O

7
1 behaviour   2 best-behaved   3 behave
4 worst-behaved   5 well-behaved
6 badly behaved

8
1 ✘   2 ✘   3 ✓   4 ✓   5 ✘   6 ✓   7 ✓   8 ✓

UNIT 6   LESSON 4

1
1 f   2 h   3 e   4 d   5 l   6 g   7 i   8 c   9 k   10 b

2
1 theatre   2 shell   3 cramped   4 lizard   5 mood   6 deck

3

UNIT 6
Inspiration EXTRA!
Revision

Lesson 1
1 He asked me to help him.
2 I agreed to help him.
3 He told me to listen carefully.
4 I offered to take notes.
5 He warned me not to tell anyone about it.
6 I promised not to tell anyone.

Lesson 2
1 He wanted to know how many people lived in the town.
2 He asked where the nearest cinema was.
3 He wondered if there was somewhere he could play basketball.
4 He wanted to know if you needed ID to get into the clubs.
5 He asked when the last bus in the evening was.
6 He wanted to know which was the best football team to support.
7 He wondered if there were lots of things to do in the evening.
8 He asked if it took a long time to walk to school.

Lesson 3
1 She's had the walls painted in bright colours.
2 She's had the rowing machines repaired.
3 She's had laptops bought for every student.
4 She's had a swimming pool built.
5 She's had lots of trees planted.
6 She's had the library turned into a resource centre.

Lesson 4
Sample answers
1 How long did it take to fly from London to Buenos Aires?
2 What did Isabel learn how to make?
3 What language do Isabel's relatives speak? / What language is Isabel trying to learn?
4 Where do her father's family live?
5 Why did they all go to Mar del Plata?

Spelling
1 brilliant   2 feedback   3 freezer   4 install
5 politeness   6 roll   7 spill   8 tipping
9 shopping   10 snorkelling

Brainteaser
'Smiles' – there's mile between the first s and the last s.

Extension

Lesson 1
1 Laura reminded Nisha to come to dinner tonight.
2 Nisha complained that Laura kept telling her not to forget things.
3 Laura said she was sorry and promised not to do it again.
4 Nisha explained that she was upset because her father was cross with her.
5 Laura suggested she should talk to her father about the problem.
6 Nisha agreed that that was a good idea.

Lesson 2
1 Greg asked when he had to check in.
2 He wanted to know if that was enough time to go through security.
3 He wondered if he could choose his seat.
4 He wanted to know if he could use his mobile phone on the plane.
5 He wondered if he could take pictures on the plane.
6 He asked if he could have a vegetarian meal.

Lesson 3
Students' own answers.

Lesson 4
Students' own answers.

Spelling
1 aisle   2 laze   3 wrap   4 seen   5 tyre   6 warn

Brainteaser
Your temper.

REVIEW UNITS 5–6

1

1 A 2 B 3 B 4 D 5 D 6 C 7 D
8 C 9 C 10 B 11 B 12 A 13 C
14 D 15 B

2

1 destruction 2 measurements
3 disappearance 4 luxurious 5 injection
6 rediscover 7 best-behaved 8 well known

3

1 If he had had enough money, he would have bought the laptop.
2 She wishes that she had asked for some advice.
3 You mustn't dive on your own.
4 They must have left the party before I arrived.
5 My mother suggested (that) I invite them.
6 Laura promised to phone every day.
7 Nisha asked Laura what she felt like doing tonight/that night.
8 I had my hair cut.

4

1 release 2 parliament 3 flower 4 pioneer
5 change 6 tablet 7 hand-carved 8 reappear

Learner independence

1

Students' own answers.

2

1 I don't know why.
2 In other words …
3 I just wanted to be given the chance.
4 What could have happened?
5 I've changed my mind
6 It's time that people realised …
7 It's out of the question.
8 In fact, it was the opposite.

UNIT 7 LESSON 1

1

1 suggested 2 explain 3 written 4 described
5 been 6 origin 7 expression 8 have 9 will
10 experiments 11 used 12 tested

2

1 are being invented 2 is used
3 is constantly changing 4 is meant
5 are being created

3

1 His hair has been cut and washed.
2 His shoes have been cleaned.
3 His nails have been cut.
4 New clothes have been bought for him.
5 Everything has been paid for by the TV company.

4

1 is being used
2 have been created
3 were sent
4 are expected
5 has been caused
6 is transmitted
7 is affected
8 will be solved
9 are not expected
10 is sent
11 are being replaced
12 will be forbidden

5

1 twist an ankle
2 hang a blind
3 install computer software
4 keep up in the air
5 repaint a wall
6 send a chain email

6

1 O 2 S 3 G 4 G 5 S 6 O 7 G 8 S

7

1 be under the weather
2 jumbo
3 know the ropes
4 be given the sack
5 wicked
6 keep it up

8

constantly 3 demonstration 4 employer 3
encourage 3 experience 4 expression 3
idiomatic 5 nautical 3 repaint 2 unusually 5

UNIT 7 LESSON 2

1

1 be allowed
2 protected
3 provided
4 be given
5 be offered
6 be made
7 be taught

2

1 be awarded
2 be given
3 to be honoured
4 be understood
5 to be remembered
6 be pointed out
7 to be acknowledged
8 be recognised
9 be called
10 to be given

3

1 to be done
2 be obeyed
3 be allowed
4 be given
5 be shown

4

1 either, or
2 both, and
3 Both, and
4 either, or
5 either, or
6 Both, and

5

Crossword:
1 DNA
2 STARS
3 COMET
4 XRAY
5 FISSION
6 CANCER
7 ATOM
8 CHEMISTRY
9 SCIENTIST
10 AWARD

6

1 award a prize
2 change your mind
3 be put in one's place
4 benefit from something
5 solve a mystery

7

astronomer 4 brilliant 3 chemistry 3
comet 2 deserve 2 forbid 2 ironically 4
nuclear 2 persuade 2 prejudice 3

UNIT 7 LESSON 3

1

1 F 2 T 3 F 4 T 5 F

2

1 She wrote it down.
2 He looked it up in his address book.
3 He held it up.
4 She wanted to speak to them.
5 I put it down when I had finished.
6 He remembered to switch it on.
7 She climbed up them.
8 She chatted to them for an hour.

3

1 call back
2 has turned into
3 speed up
4 hold on
5 found out
6 fill in
7 pass on
8 go on
9 put me through

4

Crossword:
1 CONDUCTOR
2 SUBSCRIBER
3 DECADE
4 VENDOR
5 MAST
6 PLATFORM
7 ORAL
8 USER
9 EMPHASIS

5

1 Good afternoon, can I help you?
2 I'd like to speak to the manager, please.
3 I'm afraid she's busy at the moment. Would you like to speak to her assistant?
4 Yes, that would be fine.
5 Oh dear, I'm afraid his line's engaged too.
6 I see. Can I leave a message then?
7 Yes, of course. What's the message?
8 Please ring Helen on 983586.
9 OK, I'll pass it on when she comes off the phone.
10 Thank you very much. Goodbye.

6

1 off a call 2 a deal 3 on a message
4 up someone 5 on a phone 6 a bus

7

1 bus conductor 2 email address 3 host family
4 landline subscriber 5 storytelling
6 street vendor

8

decade 2   conductor 3   emphasis 3   engaged 2
entrepreneur 4   landline 2   network 2
platform 2   revolution 4   sociologist 5
subscriber 3   transform 2

UNIT 7   LESSON 4

1

1 benefit   2 invented   3 official   4 published
5 based   6 simple   7 tenses   8 produce
9 pronounced   10 estimated   11 speakers
12 magazines   13 regularly   14 broadcast   15 communication

2

which was invented by Ludwig Lazarus Zamenhof who was a Polish eye doctor
which brought together nearly 700 people from 20 countries
whose alphabet has five vowels and 20 consonants which end in -a
which people from different countries could learn easily and use to communicate

3

1 The Cambodian alphabet, which has 74 letters, is the world's largest alphabet.
2 The world's shortest alphabet, which is used in the Solomon Islands, has only 11 letters.
3 The Berbers, who live in North Africa, hardly ever write in their language.
4 Basque, which is spoken in north-west Spain and south-west France, is not apparently related to any other language.
5 The Japanese, whose language is difficult to learn, have four writing systems: kanji (adapted from Chinese), hiragana, katakana and romaji.

4

	S	H	E	L	V	E	S			U		P
W		M		I		A				R		
I	M	P	O	S	S	I	B	L	E			
T		L		A		L			S			
C	O	O	L			T	O	O	L	S		
H		Y			N	O	R		E			
		B	E	L	O	W		A	G	O		
J		R	E	T	E	L	L		R			
E			S		R		S		A			
T	W	I	S	T			G	O	A	L		

UNIT 7
Inspiration EXTRA!

Revision

Lesson 1

1 was repainted
2 is being cleaned
3 will be installed
4 is being repaired
5 was prepared
6 will be expected
7 is being cooked
8 will be replaced

Lesson 2

1 be persuaded
2 to be thanked
3 to be forbidden

4 to be acknowledged/to have been acknowledged
5 be told
6 to be recognised
7 be given
8 be changed

Lesson 3

1 Remember to ring her up when you arrive.
2 He said it was coming down.
3 My mobile couldn't pick one up in the kitchen.
4 Can you work it out for me, please?
5 Are they allowed to put them up near schools?

Lesson 4

1 f   2 a   3 b   4 e   5 d   6 c

Spelling

1 acknowledge   2 archaeologist   3 chemistry   4 colleague   5 Ghana   6 honour   7 ironically   8 mystery   9 rebuild   10 taught

Brainteaser

A man on a horse holding a chicken.

Extension

Lessons 1–4

Students' own answers.

Spelling

1 creation   2 extinction   3 fission   4 official
5 recognition   6 revolution   7 shuttlecock
8 social   9 telecommunications   10 traditional
11 transmission

Brainteaser

8

CULTURE
Tips for creative writing

1

1 everywhere   2 inspiration   3 shops
4 conversations   5 unusual   6 empty   7 easier
8 short   9 longer   10 enjoy   11 different
12 creative   13 draft   14 revise   15 brainstorm
16 friends   17 criticism   18 better

2

1 d   2 g   3 a   4 f   5 b   6 h   7 e   8 c

3

Sample answers
1 By listening to other people talking in the street, in cafés and in shops.
2 Because it is easier to do something else instead.
3 You will write better if you are fresh and enthusiastic and enjoy what you are doing.
4 So you can find out when is the most creative time for you.
5 You can brainstorm ideas, exchange work with other writers and get feedback on your writing.
6 You shouldn't be afraid of it. You should use it to improve your work.

4

		B	A	D	L	Y	
N	O	T	E	B	O	O	K
S	T	U	C	K			
	C	A	R	E			
	R	E	F	L	E	C	T
	A	L	O	U	D		
	T	I	M	E	S		
	I	D	E	A	S		
	V	I	D	E	O		
	E	D	I	T			

5

Students' own answer.

UNIT 8   LESSON 1

1

1 won   2 described   3 inspiration   4 ideas
5 school   6 couldn't   7 managed   8 boring
9 burnt   10 were   11 ability   12 short
13 missed   14 failed
Paragraph 1 – Walt Disney
Paragraph 2 – Pablo Picasso
Paragraph 3 – Akio Morita
Paragraph 4 – Michael Jordan

2

1 Daniel Tammett became a savant at the age of three and was able to see numbers as shapes and colours.
2 As a child he could do mathematical calculations amazingly quickly.
3 But his eight younger brothers and sisters were able to do things like kicking a ball and swimming better than him.
4 By the time he was 26, he had managed to learn six foreign languages.
5 Last year Tammett met Kim Peek, another savant who could read two books as the same time, one with each eye.
6 Recently Tammett was able to create his own language.

3

1 in order to   2 so that   3 in order to   4 so that
5 In order to   6 in order to   7 in order to   8 so that

4

1 earn a star   2 dragged   3 twin   4 grumble
5 stuck in red tape

5

1 G   2 G   3 O   4 S   5 O

6

1 approved school   2 classical composer
3 entrance examination   4 rap poet   5 problem student

7

1 ✗   2 ✗   3 ✓   4 ✓   5 ✓

UNIT 8   LESSON 2

1

1 uniform   2 compulsory   3 respected   4 strict
5 didn't   6 had   7 weren't   8 behaviour   9 to
10 have   11 won't   12 able

2

1 weren't able
2 had to
3 didn't need to
4 wasn't able to
5 were able to
6 didn't need to
7 wasn't able to

3

1 won't be able to
2 will need to
3 will be able to
4 won't have to
5 will you be able to
6 will need to
7 won't be able to
8 will need to

4

1 needn't have phoned
2 didn't need to get up
3 didn't need to show
4 needn't have ordered
5 needn't have bothered
6 needn't have brought

5

6

1 bookshop   2 classwork   3 national curriculum
4 online   5 solar system   6 spreadsheet
7 whiteboard

7

1 get married   2 pay fees   3 respect each other
4 show respect   5 study a subject   6 take action

8

classwork 2   comfort 2   curriculum 4
interactive 4   pressure 2   spreadsheet 2
submarine 3   waterproof 3   whiteboard 2

UNIT 8   LESSON 3

1

1 star   2 made   3 tool   4 let   5 musical
6 inspired   7 admire   8 succeed   9 online   10
progressed   11 dream   12 amazing

2

1 makes   2 lets   3 'm not allowed to   4 makes
5 was made   6 Are you allowed to   7 let
8 don't let

3

1 We aren't allowed to use mobiles in class.
2 They were made to train hard before the match.
3 I let my brother borrow my calculator.
4 Did they make him return the money?
5 At my last school we weren't allowed to wear jeans.
6 My parents used to let me stay up late on Saturday nights.
7 Global warming is making the sea rise.
8 Why won't you let me have a second chance?

4

1 came   2 take   3 save   4 note   5 turn
6 stay

5

1 gig   2 lyrics   3 hum   4 round the clock
5 chord   6 finger picking

6

1 S   2 S   3 O   4 S   5 G   6 S

7

1 be true to yourself
2 fit words to a tune
3 play a chord

4 take shape
5 work hard at

8

advice 2   concerned 2   hummed 1
influence 3   instrument 3   lyrics 2
perform 2   personal 3   songwriting 3

UNIT 8   LESSON 4

1

1 projects   2 education   3 opportunity
4 contribution   5 volunteer   6 fundraise
7 host   8 accommodation   9 fare   10 pocket
11 injections   12 skills   13 experience
14 application   15 successful   16 advance

2

Students' own answer.

3

```
¹U      ²E X ³P L ⁴O R E D ⁵D
 N       Q   R   P         E
⁶E D U C A T E D             V
 X       A   C   R   ⁷B E
⁸P U T   ⁹T R A V E L
 E       I   I   S   ¹⁰D O
¹¹C ¹²H O O S E   ¹³F     P
¹⁴T I N   E   ¹⁵S O   I
 E           ¹⁶    ¹⁷R A N G
 D       ¹⁸D R E A M
```

UNIT 8
Inspiration EXTRA!
Revision

Lesson 1

1 managed to   2 was able   3 couldn't   4 wasn't
able   5 managed to   6 could   7 wasn't able   8
could

Lesson 2

1 didn't need to
2 won't be able to
3 had to
4 will need to
5 was able to
6 had to
7 will need to
8 didn't need to

Lesson 3

1 let
2 made
3 Am I allowed to
4 were made
5 will not be allowed to
6 let

Lesson 4

1 f   2 c   3 h   4 b   5 a   6 g   7 e   8 d

Spelling

1 application   2 chill-out   3 confession
4 curriculum   5 embarrassed   6 hopeless
7 mentally   8 married   9 opportunity
10 pressure   11 prize-winner   12 spreadsheet
13 reef   14 totally   15 volunteer

Brainteaser

The man's horse was called Friday.

Extension

Lesson 1

Students' own answers.

Lesson 2

Students' own answers.

Lesson 3

Sample answers

1 Who are her strongest musical influences?
2 What was her first song called?
3 What was she doing when the tune of Inspired! came into her head?
4 When did she get her first guitar?
5 How did she get her first guitar?
6 Which comes first, the music or the lyrics?

Lesson 4

Students' own answer.

Spelling

1 classical   2 comfortable   3 coral
4 crumble   5 global   6 level   7 local
8 mental   9 national   10 personal   11 single
12 successful   13 thoughtful   14 total

Brainteaser

The paragraph contains every letter of the alphabet except E.

REVIEW
UNITS 7–8

1

1 C   2 B   3 A   4 B   5 A   6 C   7 A   8 A   9
C   10 A

2

1 increasingly   2 recognition   3 unusually
4 endangered   5 applicant   6 confession

3

1 The injured boy was taken to hospital by ambulance.
2 Someone has stolen my bicycle!
3 We weren't able to understand what the man said.
4 He managed to get a place at university.
5 You needn't have bought so much food.
6 The police made the driver stop the car.

4

1 platform   2 scientist   3 alarm   4 tablet
5 period   6 accommodation   7 jet   8 linguist

Learner independence

2

1 I'll put you through.
2 Keep it up.
3 Can anything be done?
4 Can I take a message?
5 As far as I'm concerned …
6 She needn't have worried.
7 It drove me mad.
8 It's up to you.

Bear Creek

Bear Creek encourages students to read for pleasure, while consolidating language covered in Inspiration 4. Chapters 1-8 of the story correspond to Units 1-8, and Chapter 9 revises language from the whole book. Each chapter begins with a question to focus students on the story and ends with a prediction question. The story is followed by a series of exercises testing comprehension. These stories can be read in class, or set as homework. Teachers may also find that students read ahead because they are keen to know the end of the story!

1 Monday 7.00am

1

1 *Their film is being shown at a film festival.*
2 *It's a documentary.*
3 *Their film is missing.*
4 *A man who was on their plane.*
5 *To ask her to send a copy of the film.*
6 *Someone had broken into the house and stolen Tony's laptop.*

2

1 *break into a house*
2 *come true*
3 *cut down trees*
4 *shoot a film*
5 *spend a long time*
6 *turn on a phone*

3

1 *pretend*   2 *documentary*   3 *struggle*   4 *survive*

Optional activity

Students make a list of the characters featured so far in the story and note down key information about each one. They can add to their list as new characters appear in the other chapters.

2 Monday 9.30am

1

1 *Tony's mother and father*
2 *Tony's sister Kelly*
3 *Tony's mother*
4 *Mike and Tony*
5 *Mike's mother*
6 *the 'detective'*
7 *the policeman*
8 *Mike and Tony*

2

1 *than*   2 *since*   3 *from*   4 *with*   5 *on, for*   6 *beside*   7 *down*

3

Students' own answers.

Optional activity

In pairs, students roleplay the phone conversation between Mike and his mother. Students then reverse roles and act out the phone conversation between Tony and his mother from Chapter 1. Confident students can do this with books closed.

3 Monday 10.00am

1

1 *E*   2 *H*   3 *G*   4 *C*   5 *A*   6 *I*   7 *B*   8 *F*   9 *D*

2

Sample answers
1 *So the man in black wouldn't recognise them.*
2 *Kelly rang to tell him she was in New York and had a DVD with their film on it.*
3 *Because someone was probably watching the hotel.*
4 *Yes, he did.*
5 *Yes, they did.*
6 *Yes, he did.*

3

1 *fast*   2 *behind*   3 *stupid*   4 *dirty*   5 *top*   6 *well*   7 *leaves*

4 Monday 11.30am

1

1 *left the queue*
2 *Mike, Tony and Kelly*
3 *Macy's*
4 *the Internet café*
5 *the film*
6 *Tony's*
7 *Mr Cross*
8 *the men who broke into Tony's house*

2

1 *carry out orders*
2 *join a queue*
3 *drive someone crazy*
4 *communicate with people*
5 *order something to eat*
6 *record music*

3

1 *ages*   2 *entrance*   3 *full of people*   4 *starving*   5 *wipe out*   6 *horrible*

Optional activity

In pairs, students retell the story so far.

5 Monday 12.30pm

1

1 *d*   2 *f*   3 *a*   4 *c*   5 *b*   6 *e*

2

1 *A*   2 *B*   3 *B*   4 *A*   5 *A*   6 *B*

3

Students' own answers.

Optional activity

In pairs, students discuss what they would do if they found extra money in their own bank account. *Would they spend it or tell the bank or the police? Would the amount of money make a difference?*

6 Monday 1.30pm

1

1 Kelly 2 Mike 3 Kelly 4 Tony 5 Kelly 6 Tony 7 Mike 8 Teresa

2

1 apply for permission
2 do something wrong
3 make sense
4 ring a number
5 run a film forward
6 sound shocked

3

1 remote
2 now and again
3 said after a while
4 obvious
5 investigate
6 out of the question

Optional activity

Ask students to find examples of direct speech in the chapter and transform them into indirect speech (and vice versa), eg *"I'll try and make it clearer"* → *Kelly said she'd try and make it clearer.*

7 Monday 2.30pm

1

1 D 2 G 3 A 4 H 5 C 6 F 7 B 8 E

2

1 the apartment
2 the New Yorkers Mike could see in the street
3 the fact that Peter didn't ask any questions
4 the news broadcast
5 the police visiting Bear Creek
6 Mike and Tony
7 the money
8 the shot of a man getting out of a car

3

1 going about their business   2 connection   3 overlooking   4 urgently   5 know the ropes   6 studied

Optional activity

Students recreate one of the emails between Ed and Mr J on the subject of what to do about the boys and their film.

8 Monday 6.00pm

1

1 Because they had filmed him and he was trying to hide his identity.
2 They had seen him on the plane and in the hotel and then he had followed them through the streets and into the park.
3 Because they thought it would keep Cross's men away.
4 He realised that one of Cross's men had been very close and could have shot them.
5 They didn't know what he looked like and they had no evidence against him.
6 By staying in remote places, using private planes and not staying long in one place.
7 They didn't have enough money to send someone there for months at a time.
8 He was going to email the picture of Mr Cross to his office.

2

1 A 2 A 3 B 4 B 5 B 6 B

Optional activity

Books closed, students answer questions about the story so far from memory.

9 Monday 7.00pm

1

1 c 2 f 3 i 4 b 5 h 6 e 7 a 8 g 9 d

2

1 climb the stairs
2 discuss an idea
3 give someone a few minutes
4 make a copy
5 sit in the audience
6 stop a taxi
7 switch on the light

3

1 at once   2 half a dozen   3 rushed   4 brave   5 astonished   6 nightmare

Optional activities

• *Who says this?* Read sentences from different chapters of the book. Students identify the speaker. Students could continue in pairs.
• Books closed. Summarise the story, but make some mistakes. Students listen. When they hear a mistake, they shout *Stop!* and correct the mistake. Alternatively, this could be a reading/writing activity.

After reading activities

Write the activities below on the board. Students choose the activities they are most interested in. The written work can be displayed in the classroom. The first activity could be videoed.

1 Choose one chapter of the story and act it out with another student/in a group.
2 Choose one chapter. Write as many questions as you can about this chapter of the story. Then give your questions to another student to answer.
3 Summarise each chapter in just one sentence.
4 Draw a timeline for the story from 7am-7pm. Write important events in the story at the correct times.
5 Write a new ending for the story.
6 Write a study of one of the characters in the story. Include information about their personality, their importance in the story and why you chose this character.
7 Choose 3 pictures from the story. Ask a partner to describe what's happening in the picture, what had happened before and what's going to happen next.
8 In groups of three, take the roles of Mike, Tony and the film producer and have the discussion about making a film of their experiences. Choose the actors who will star in the film and the music for the soundtrack.

Units 1–2 CLIL TEACHING NOTES
Media studies

Cinematography

Aims	To learn about cinematography.
Activities	Guessing vocabulary from pictures and from context; reading for gist and specific information; completing a table; doing a cinematography quiz; creating a film storyboard.
Language	Present simple; present perfect simple and continuous; present simple passive; film-making; story-telling.
To use	After Unit 2, either in class, as self-study or as homework.
Procedure	• This CLIL lesson can be given as homework or be done in pairs in class. For each activity, students can either check answers in pairs and then with the whole class, or use a monolingual dictionary to help with vocabulary if they are working at home.

- Ask students to look at the pictures of the film shots and camera angles and to match them with the words. Students can check answers first in pairs then skim read the text quickly to see if they were correct.

- Next, ask students to scan read the text in exercise 2 carefully and complete the missing information in the table.

- Ask students to do the quiz about cinematography individually. They can refer back to the two texts to check their answers.

- The project stage can be set as homework or done in class. Draw the template of the storyboard below on the board and ask students to copy this onto a piece of paper.

- Talk the students through the various stages of the storyboard. Invite them to think of a well-known story they know such as *Romeo and Juliet* and try to think of how they can change the perspective on a scene in that story cinematographically. Encourage them to think of the use of different camera shots (angles) and camera movements in such a way that the characters of the story are viewed differently. Remind students that they need a title for their short films, maybe one reflecting the new perspective and that each square of the storyboard should contain a rough sketch and detailed information about the camera shots and movement techniques. Encourage students to have fun with this activity and experiment with the cinematographic knowledge they have gained. Allow them to work in small groups of two or three if they prefer.

- If there is filming equipment available, students can produce short films from their storyboards as a follow-up to the project.

Key

Exercise 1
1 e 2 f 3 d 4 b 5 c 6 a 7 g

Exercise 2

Technique	Camera movements	Examples of use	Atmosphere or effect created
tracking	camera moves from left to right	following the movement of an escaping hero	emotion
tilting	vertically up and down	to show the side of a building as our hero climbs out of a window and escapes	suspense
dollying	the movement of the camera closer or further from a scene	moving from a close-up of two people arguing inside a car to the long shot of the car in a deserted road	context
zooming	camera lens zooms in and out	moving from close-ups to long shots	attention or reveal hidden details

Exercise 3
1 B 2 A 3 C 4 A 5 A 6 B 7 C 8 B 9 B 10 C

Units 3–4 CLIL TEACHING NOTES
Social science

Social and political campaigning

Aims	To learn about modern social and political campaigning
Activities	Matching famous campaigners with their causes and their campaign strategies; reading for gist and specific information; guessing vocabulary from context and completing sentences with vocabulary; categorizing different forms of communication; researching; planning and organising a campaign.
Language	Past simple; *if only* + past simple; infinitive of purpose; linking words; politics; campaigning.
To use	After Unit 4, either in class, as self-study or as homework.
Procedure	• This CLIL lesson can be given as homework or be done in pairs in class. For each activity, students can either check answers in pairs and then with the whole class, or use a monolingual dictionary to help with vocabulary if they are working at home.
	• Ask students if they have ever campaigned to change something or what they think they might campaign for in the future. Then ask them to look at the pictures of famous campaigners and match them with the cause they think they campaigned for and how they did it.
	• Then ask them to read the text about *Campaigning for change: famous campaigners* and check their answers.
	• Ask students to look at the different campaign techniques and categorise them as visual, written or oral. Students can read the second text *Campaigning for change: How do you do it?* to check their answers.
	• Next, ask students to complete the sentences with the vocabulary. Students can refer back to the text to check the meaning of vocabulary in context.
	• The project stage can be set as homework or done in class if you feel students have access to appropriate reference books, Internet etc. Tell the students they are going to research, design and organise a campaign in small groups of three or four people. First, ask them to choose a campaign issue and give examples of global, national and local issues that they might campaign about. Suggest they visit the listed websites as part of their research. Tell them that it is important that they feel strongly about the issue if they are going to persuade other people to support them. Next, invite them to research other successful campaigns referring to the suggested list of websites or search for campaigns on issues similar to the one they have chosen. Then invite students to plan their campaign including information about: the issues, the communication strategy, the aim of their campaign, what they will do to raise awareness and get people involved.
	• As an extra activity in the following lesson, students can present their campaigns to the class who then vote for the best planned campaigns. If possible students can actually carry out the most popular campaigns in the subsequent weeks.

Key

Exercise 1

Who	What	How
Emmeline Pankhurst	the vote for women	chained herself to railings of 10, Downing St
Bob Geldof	to raise money and awareness about poverty in Africa	organised a big pop concert
Rosa Parks	equal rights for black people	refused to give up her seat on a bus to a white passenger
Lord Shaftesbury	better working conditions for children	lobbied parliament

Exercise 2

Visual	Written	Oral
logo	letter	street campaigning
banner	blog	debate
body painting	email	making a speech
dressing up	leaflet	telephoning
film	petition	vox pop
flash mob	postcard	
human chain	press release	
photo	social networking	
slide show	text messaging	
poster		
symbol		

Exercise 3

1 flash mob   2 debate   3 banners   4 press release   5 petition   6 vox pops   7 leaflets   8 blog

Units 5-6 CLIL TEACHING NOTES
Science

Genetically Modified Organisms (GMOs)

Aims	To learn about GMOs
Activities	Matching titles with paragraphs; reading for gist and specific information; guessing vocabulary from context and matching words with definitions; labelling a diagram; completing a table and reporting information about GMOs; researching, preparing and undertaking a debate about GMOs.
Language	Present simple passive; past simple passive; reported speech; *will* for future; science; agriculture; GMOs.
To use	After Unit 6, either in class, as self-study or as homework.
Procedure	• This CLIL lesson can be given as homework or be done in pairs in class. For each activity, students can either check answers in pairs and then with the class, or use a monolingual dictionary to help if they are working at home.
	• Ask students the questions about GMOs. Then ask them to skim read the text and match the questions with the paragraphs.
	• Next, ask students to match the vocabulary with the definitions, referring back to the text to check meaning in context.
	• Ask students to complete the missing information by labelling the diagram, completing the tables and reporting the information from the text.
	• The project stage can be set as homework or done in class if you feel students have access to appropriate reference books, Internet etc. Tell the students they are going to have a class debate about GMOs. Tell half the class they are for GMOs and the other half that they are against them. Ask them to research their positions and prepare a short presentation for / against GMOs. Remind students to include information about facts, figure and examples; to report what different organisations have said about GMOs; and to try to be as convincing as possible in their argument.

Key

Exercise 1

1 c   2 a   3 f   4 e   5 d   6 b

Exercise 2

1 vaccine   2 nutrients   3 cloning   4 genetic disorder
5 crop   6 fertiliser   7 DNA   8 herbicide

Exercise 3

a 1 cell   2 nucleus   3 chromosomes   4 genes   5 DNA
b GM processes

Process	Examples
Combining the DNA of one organism with the DNA of another	• Bell pepper with the DNA of a fish to survive in cold weather • Dairy cows are modified to increase milk production.
Cloning	• Dolly the sheep • Pigs, horses and dogs.

GMO uses

Area of use	Purpose
Agriculture	• To resist herbicides • To produce a poison which kills predators • To withstand extreme weather • To provide extra nutrients
Environment	• Biodegradable plastics • To help protect endangered species
Medicine	• To develop drugs such as insulin • To stop the spread of malaria • To treat diseases or genetic disorders

c

For	Against
Organisations in favour of GMOs thought they could solve the problem of world hunger as they will lead to increased production of cheaper food which is healthier and doesn't damage the environment.	Leading environmental organisations claimed GMOs would not solve the problem of world hunger as most of the world's agriculture was not GM.
Researchers predicted salmon would be cheaper to buy and would help reduce heart disease.	They argued that GM crops used artificial fertilizers and poisonous chemicals so they polluted the atmosphere, and were dangerous to humans and animals. They also believed that GMOs led to loss of biodiversity and climate change.
Pro-GM groups argued that GMOs were vital to medical and technological research as well as improving economies.	They thought that the only people to benefit economically would be the multinational biotechnology companies, not the developing countries and not the farmers.
The WHO and FAO said that all the GM products currently on the market were safe for humans.	The WHO and FAO warned that GMOs should be tested for allergies and not produced to resist antibiotics.

d

1 GM crops will be <u>more common, more resistant to disease and extreme weather and have additional nutrients in them.</u>
2 GM animals will be <u>larger to provide more food.</u>
3 GM plants and animals will help <u>produce vaccines for human diseases.</u>

Units 7–8 CLIL TEACHING NOTES
Music

Rock 'n' roll

Aims	To learn about the origins and style of rock and roll music.
Activities	Reordering and guessing paragraph headings from context; matching vocabulary and pictures; matching vocabulary and definitions; reading for gist and specific information; completing a table with missing information from the text; doing a rock and roll quiz; researching and writing an article about a musical genre, a group and their music.
Language	Past simple; music; films; youth culture.
To use	After Unit 8, either in class, as self-study or as homework.
Procedure	• This CLIL lesson can be given as homework or be done in pairs in class. For each activity, students can either check answers in pairs and then with the whole class, or use a monolingual dictionary to help with vocabulary if they are working at home.
	• Ask students what they know about rock and roll music. Then ask them to reorder the words to form questions and to match the questions to paragraphs 1–5 of the text.
	• Next, ask students to match the pictures with the words and phrases, referring back to the text in exercise 1 to help with understanding.
	• Then ask them to match the words with the definitions, referring back to the text in exercise 1 to help with understanding.
	• Ask students to read the text in exercise 1 again and complete the missing information in the table.
	• Next, ask students to read the text again and do the quiz individually.
	• The project stage can be set as homework or done in class if you feel students have access to appropriate reference books, Internet etc. Tell the students that they are music journalists and that they have been asked to write an article for a music magazine about a particular genre, group and single/album of their choice. Remind them to include: information about the origins of the music style; a description of the characteristics of that musical style; brief biographical information about the group (when and where they formed; group members, important moments etc.); a short discography (list of important singles and albums); an analysis of a particular single/album by the band; their own positive or negative opinion of the group with reasons why they like or dislike them. Suggest they visit the listed websites as part of their research.
	• As an extra activity in the following lesson, students can read or listen to each others' articles and maybe listen to the bands chosen and give feedback to each other.

Key

Exercise 1
a Where did rock and roll originate?
b What were the characteristics of rock and roll?
c What caused the end of rock and roll?
d Who were the big names in rock and roll?
e How did rock and roll influence youth culture?

1 a   2 d   3 e   4 b   5 c

Exercise 2
1 DJ   2 album   3 recording studio   4 concert   5 electric guitar

Exercise 3
1 backbeat   2 soundtrack   3 rhythm   4 cover version

Exercise 5
1 A   2 A   3 A   4 B   5 B   6 B   7 B   8 A

Exercise 4

Actor	Dance	Film	Song	Musical artist	Musical genre
James Dean	Jitterbug	Blackboard Jungle	Rock Around the Clock	Bill Haley and His Comets	Blues
Marlon Brando	Sock hop	Rebel Without a Cause		Buddy Holly	Country and western
	Twist	The Wild One		Chuck Berry	Gospel
				Elvis Presley	Rock
				Fats Domino	Rock and roll
				J.P. Robinson (Big Bopper)	
				Jerry Lee Lewis	
				Little Richard	
				Richie Valens	

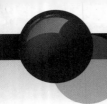

AUDIO CDs

Audio Track List

CD 1

1.01	**Preview, Units 1 and 2**	Exercise 3
1.02	**Unit 1** Lesson 1	Exercise 2
1.03		Exercise 4
1.04	Lesson 2	Exercise 2
1.05		Exercise 4
1.06		Exercise 5
1.07		Exercise 6
1.08	Lesson 3	Exercise 2
1.09		Exercise 4
1.10	Lesson 4	Exercise 2
1.11		Exercises 4 and 5
1.12		Exercise 10
1.13	**Inspiration EXTRA!** Sketch	
1.14	**Culture**	Exercise 1, Happiness and success
1.15	**Unit 2** Lesson 1	Exercise 2
1.16		Exercise 4
1.17		Exercise 5
1.18	Lesson 2	Exercise 2
1.19		Exercise 5
1.20	Lesson 3	Exercise 2
1.21		Exercise 4
1.22		Exercise 6
1.23	Lesson 4	Exercise 2
1.24		Exercise 6
1.25		Exercise 11
1.26	**Preview, Units 3 and 4**	Exercise 3
1.27	**Unit 3** Lesson 1	Exercise 3
1.28		Exercise 4
1.29		Exercise 5
1.30	Lesson 2	Exercise 2
1.31		Exercise 5
1.32	Lesson 3	Exercise 2
1.33		Exercise 4
1.34		Exercise 5
1.35	Lesson 4	Exercise 2
1.36		Exercise 5
1.37		Exercise 10
1.38	**Inspiration EXTRA!** Sketch	
1.39	**Culture**	Exercise 1, Young scientists

CD 2

2.01	**Unit 4** Lesson 1	Exercise 2
2.02		Exercise 5
2.03	Lesson 2	Exercise 2
2.04		Exercise 3
2.05		Exercise 5
2.06	Lesson 3	Exercise 2
2.07		Exercise 4
2.08		Exercise 6
2.09	Lesson 4	Exercise 2
2.10		Exercise 6
2.11		Exercise 11
2.12	**Preview, Units 5 and 6**	Exercise 3
2.13	**Unit 5** Lesson 1	Exercise 2
2.14		Exercise 5
2.15		Exercise 7
2.16	Lesson 2	Exercise 2
2.17		Exercise 4
2.18		Exercise 5
2.19	Lesson 3	Exercise 2
2.20		Exercise 5
2.21	Lesson 4	Exercise 2
2.22		Exercise 5
2.23		Exercise 10
2.24	**Inspiration EXTRA!** Sketch	
2.25	**Culture**	Exercise 1, Saying the right thing
2.26	**Culture**	Exercise 4, Saying the right thing cont.
2.27	**Unit 6** Lesson 1	Exercise 2
2.28		Exercise 3
2.29		Exercise 4
2.30	Lesson 2	Exercise 2
2.31		Exercise 5
2.32		Exercise 6
2.33	Lesson 3	Exercise 3
2.34		Exercise 5
2.35	Lesson 4	Exercise 2
2.36		Exercise 5
2.37		Exercise 10

CD 3

3.01	**Preview, Units 7 and 8**	Exercise 3
3.02	**Unit 7** Lesson 1	Exercise 2
3.03		Exercise 4
3.04		Exercise 5
3.05	Lesson 2	Exercise 2
3.06		Exercise 5
3.07	Lesson 3	Exercise 2
3.08		Exercise 5
3.09		Exercise 6
3.10	Lesson 4	Exercise 2
3.11		Exercise 8
3.12		Exercise 13
3.13	**Inspiration EXTRA!** Sketch	
3.14	**Culture**	Exercise 2, Your Culture
3.15	**Culture**	Exercise 3, Your Culture cont.
3.16	**Unit 8** Lesson 1	Exercise 2
3.17		Exercise 5
3.18		Exercise 6
3.19	Lesson 2	Exercise 2
3.20		Exercise 5
3.21		Exercise 6
3.22		Exercise 7
3.23	Lesson 3	Exercise 2
3.24		Exercise 4
3.25		Exercise 6
3.26	Lesson 4	Exercise 4
3.27		Exercise 9
3.28	**Song**	*Spooky*
3.29	**Song**	*Every Breath You Take*
3.30	**Song**	*Hanging on the Telephone*
3.31	**Song**	*True Colours*